Mood and Human Performance: Conceptual, Measurement and Applied Issues

Mood and Human Performance: Conceptual, Measurement and Applied Issues

Andrew M. Lane
Editor

Nova Science Publishers, Inc.
New York

NOTICE TO THE READER

The Publisher has taken reasonable care in the preparation of this book, but makes no expressed or implied warranty of any kind and assumes no responsibility for any errors or omissions. No liability is assumed for incidental or consequential damages in connection with or arising out of information contained in this book. The Publisher shall not be liable for any special, consequential, or exemplary damages resulting, in whole or in part, from the readers' use of, or reliance upon, this material.

This publication is designed to provide accurate and authoritative information with regard to the subject matter covered herein. It is sold with the clear understanding that the Publisher is not engaged in rendering legal or any other professional services. If legal or any other expert assistance is required, the services of a competent person should be sought. FROM A DECLARATION OF PARTICIPANTS JOINTLY ADOPTED BY A COMMITTEE OF THE AMERICAN BAR ASSOCIATION AND A COMMITTEE OF PUBLISHERS.

LIBRARY OF CONGRESS CATALOGING-IN-PUBLICATION DATA
Available upon request.

BF481
.M66
2007

ISBN 13 978-1-60021-269-7
ISBN 10 1-60021-269-7

0124082671

Published by Nova Science Publishers, Inc. ✦ *New York*

CONTENTS

INTRODUCTION

Andrew M. Lane

School of Sport, Performing Arts and Leisure,
University of Wolverhampton, UK

Cus D'Amato, the former trainer of World Heavyweight Champions Floyd Patterson and Mike Tyson proposed that: *"Fights are won and lost in the head"* (cited in Terry, 1989, p. 147). The heavyweight boxing title is arguably the most prestigious prize in sport, and if we accept that intense mood states will be prevalent before, during and after important competition, we acknowledge D'Amato could have been describing mood. What mood states or emotional states do athletes experience before, during and after competition? The answer to this question is dependent on many factors. Emotional states are triggered every time an athlete thinks about an impending contest; Olympic athletes can spend four years dreaming of success and pondering over how they will be able to control their emotions on the day of competition. The pre-competition period is riddled with attempts to control the build-up of emotions; and people experience a range of different emotions. Some successful athletes feel excited and nervous; other athletes feel the same emotions but feel angry also. Unsuccessful athletes can also feel nervous, but these athletes tend also to feel saddened by anticipated expectations of failure. Most athletes have ways to control emotions; some athletes engage in positive self-talk, some try to sleep, others listen to music, some become talkative, while others become reclusive. In most cases, people learn to cope through experience; through trial and error, by observing experienced performers cope successfully, and in some cases, with the help of a professional consultant, which has been the focus of a great deal of my consultancy work. Returning to the main issue, what should be clear is that situations that are perceived to be personally important typically evoke intense mood states and emotions; individuals will try to control mood states and emotions, and mood and emotions influence our thoughts and behaviours.

Consider a different example to further illustrate this point. A candidate is sitting in the waiting room before an important interview for job that she/he desperately wants. When he/she thinks about the interview, she/he becomes nervous and starts to feel hot and begins to sweat, which in turn, makes him/her feel more nervous. If we ask the same question we posed in the sport example, when do people start to become emotional before the interview? The answer is likely to share many characteristics as those described in the sport example. Emotions are likely to start to be experienced when the individual learns the date of the interview. When we compare emotions experienced before an interview with those described before sport, we see that a similar pattern of emotions and coping strategies, and this is a phenomenon we have observed in our research (Lane, Whyte, Nevill, and Terry, 2005). What should be clear is that mood states are intense before all tasks that are perceived to be of personal importance. The perception of the importance of the task is crucial to understanding why people respond differently; some candidates at a job interview might not be extremely keen on getting the job, maybe they already have a good job and so feel relaxed; maybe having a good job is not an important personal goal; the values that people attach to performance will vary from person to person, but predicting the intensity of emotion that stem from these thoughts is influenced by how important the task is perceived. Sometimes we go into potentially important tasks experiencing very mild emotions. However, for most people, situations such as an interview, an examination, a competition, a public performance, and other aspects of daily life are fuelled with factors that can illicit intense emotions.

Given the intense emotions and mood states experienced in preparation and performance in important situations, it should not be surprising that consultants devote a great deal of time to enable performers to cope better. Whilst a wealth of anecdotal evidence exists on the proposed influence of moods and emotions on performance, arguably the most fruitful way to develop better intervention strategies is through the availability of a sound knowledge base founded on theory and research. Providing the sound knowledge base is a driving factor behind a great deal of the ensuing research and forms the content of many of the chapters of this book.

The focus of the first four chapters is on conceptual issues. I provide a review of the conceptual model of mood developed for use in sport (Lane and Terry, 2000). This model was developed using factors measured in the Profile of Mood States (McNair, Lorr, and Droppleman, 1971). Despite an intuitive link between mood states and performance, the early researchers were guilty of following a largely atheoretical design, and spurious results emerged from these studies. Some studies pointed to mood having a powerful effect on performance and other studies pointed to a weak mood-performance link. In this chapter I allude to differences between mood states and emotions, something the discerning researcher could be getting irritated by my failure to accurately distinguish between the two concepts thus far. The conceptual model developed by Lane and Terry (2000) provided theory-led hypotheses for researchers to test. The chapter begins by examining many of the methodological shortcomings that preceded the model (Lane, Beedie, and Stevens, 2005), goes on to review work that has tested the model before proposing a new model and suggests some studies for future research. Exploring the link between mood states and emotional intelligence, integrating aspects of the revised conceptual model and looking at applied and intervention based work represents the future directions in this area.

In chapter 2, Gendolla, Brinkmann, and Richter offer a theoretical framework that relates mood, motivation and performance. Their contribution to examining the mechanisms that underlie mood-performance relationships is substantial, and offers theory-driven hypotheses that I hope my students and colleagues test in a sporting context. When I present at conferences on mood-performance relationships, one question that I am frequently asked is; do you have any experimental evidence to substantiate these claims? Gendolla and colleagues, through a series of controlled experiments demonstrate significant mood-performance relationships, and importantly, propose the mechanisms that underlie such relationships.

In chapter 3, Chris Beedie looks at philosophical distinctions between mood and emotion. Dr Beedie's work has focused on exploring these distinctions and his article '*Distinguishing mood from emotion*' (Beedie, Terry, and Lane, 2005) represents a significant study in mood research as it explores differences and similarities between the two constructs used interchangeably in the literature. In this chapter, he offers some of the philosophical issues on the nature of mood and emotion.

In chapter 4, Matt Stevens presents a transactional framework for assessing changes in mood states over time. He looks at relationships with variables such as personality and cognition. Dr Stevens provides a convincing case on why tightly delineated distinctions between mood and emotions when used in applied situations are difficult to apply. A transactional is proposed that could be used to identify such changes.

Chapter 5 focuses on measurement issues. Although measurement issues arguably transcend through all chapters, and the relationship between theory-testing and construct measurement means that researchers are indebted to pay close attention to validation issues; indeed science relies on the availability of valid and reliable measures. I argue that researchers cannot pay enough attention to methodological issues in their quest to conduct meaningful research. We often find that non-significant results are helpful as they delimit future research, which in time means that researchers invest time in exploring the variables that matter. However, if we find out that the validity of the measure is in question, we cannot trust results of studies that used that measure. I have been involved in numerous studies that have focused specifically on validity and reliability. We have developed measures (Greenlees, Lane, Thelwell, Holder, and Hobson, 2005; Jones, Lane, Bray, Uphill, and Catlin, 2005; Karageorghis, Terry, and Lane, 1999) and tested the validity of an existing measure (Fazackerley, Lane, and Mahoney, 2003; Lane, Harwood, and Nevill, 2005; Lane, Harwood, Terry, and Karageorghis, 2004; Lane, Lane, and Matheson, 2004; Lane, Sewell, Terry, Bartram, and Nesti, 1999; Terry, Lane, and Fogarty, 2003). We have used qualitative techniques to propose a theoretical framework (Lane, Hall, and Lane, 2002), investigated the utility of normative mood data for use with athletes (Terry and Lane, 2000) and have also investigated the influence of response timeframe on the nature of mood state responses (Terry, Stevens, and Lane, 2005). Our recent work has focused on the stability of self-report measures (Lane, Nevill, Bowes, and Fox, 2005; Nevill, Lane, Kilgour, Bowes, and Whyte, 2001). This chapter extends the validity of the Brunel Mood Scale (BRUMS: Terry et al., 1999; 2003) to Italian and Hungarian athletes via collaboration with Istvan Soos, Eva Leibinger, Istvan Karsai, and Pal Hamar. It goes on to develop and validate a 21-item and 32-item version of the BRUMS, which adds calmness and happiness to the measure.

Chapter 6 looks at the nature of emotional intelligence. As I indicate in my suggestions for future research, links between emotional intelligence and mood states represent a fruitful way forwards. Barbara Meyer and Sam Zizzi provide an overview of conceptual, methodological and applied issues related to the study of emotional intelligence. Chapter 7 looks at the relationships between mood and personality. Dr Matt Stevens outlines conceptual models on mood-personality relationships. In Chapter 8 Tracey Devonport provides an example of theory-led intervention work with netball players. A model of research that I believe could, and should, be applied to other domains of human performance.

Chapter 9 focuses on issues related to diet and mood, a topic that is intuitively interesting but one that is difficult to study. Helen Lane looks at the issue of attitudes toward diet and emotional responses among exercisers, and by doing so, highlights the point that certain groups require methodologies around their specific characteristics. Helen Lane develops a model and provides a measure for examining emotions and diet among exercisers which should be the focus of future research. The link between diet, coping and emotional intelligence is pioneering work which should forward both theory and practice. In Chapter 10 Attila Szabo examines the effects of two strategies designed to enhance mood states. Sport and exercise psychologists often emphasise possibly over-emphasise the positive psychological effects of exercise through evidence of improved mood states. Dr Szabo offers evidence that shows humour also has a potent effect on mood states.

The focus of the final seven chapters is on applied issues. In Chapter 11, Lloyd, Pedlar, Lane, and Whyte describe a case study of mood state changes during an expedition to the South Pole of a female explorer. Their paper shows the nature of mood states in extreme conditions and how an individual learned to cope with unpleasant conditions, and in this case, unpleasant mood states. In Chapter 12, Jürimäe and Jürimäe outline the methodological issues and describe and validate a scale design to assess perceived recovery-stress state. Mood states vary considerably in response to changes in training and their paper details the changes among a sample of highly trained rowers. Consistent with the theme of mood states and stress, in Chapter 13, Benoît Bolmont examines the relationship between mood states and performances, and how studies that investigate mood-performance relationships at altitude can cast light on the nature of mood and research conducted at sea level.

In Chapter 14, Lane, Whyte, George, Shave, Stevens and Barney describe a study designed to look at mood state changes during running a marathon. The project is exploratory and seeks to look at relationships between mood states and dispositional factors. An aim is to describe and evaluate mood profiles of those runners who cope successfully. In Chapter 15, the theme of running is maintained where Mark Uphill and Marc Jones outline an intervention with a runner, outlining how they employed intervention strategies to reduce anxiety, or more accurately, change perceptions of anxiety from debilitative to facilitative. On the theme of evidence-based intervention, in Chapter 16, Richie Fazackerley, Andy Lane, and Craig Mahoney describe three studies in which measurement issues are considered, relationships between mood and performance are investigated, and an intervention is conducted and evaluated. Chapter 17, Martin, Lane, Nevill, Dowen, and Homer look at the utility of a massage as an intervention to enhance mood among office workers; sometimes being a participant in research is not so bad. Each author provides future directions for research and reiterating these points, especially my own, seems unnecessary. I hope you enjoy this book.

REFERENCES

Beedie, C. J., Terry, P. C., and Lane, A. M. (2005). Distinguishing mood from emotion. *Cognition and Emotion, 19,* 847-878.

Fazackerley, R., Lane, A. M., and Mahoney, C. (2003). Confirmatory factor analysis of the Brunel Mood Scale for use in water-skiing. *Perceptual and Motor Skills, 97,* 657-661.

Greenlees, I., Lane, A. M., Thelwell, R., Holder, T., and Hobson, G. (2005). Team referent attributions among sports team players. *Research Quarterly for Exercise and Sport, 76,* 477-487.

Jones, M. V., Lane, A. M., Bray, S. R., Uphill, M., and Catlin, J. (2005). Development of the Sport Emotions Questionnaire. *Journal of Sport and Exercise Psychology, 27,* 407-431.

Karageorghis, C. I., Terry, P. C., and Lane, A. M. (1999). Development and initial validation of an instrument to assess the motivational qualities of music in exercise and sport: The Brunel Music Rating Inventory. *Journal of Sports Sciences, 17,* 713-724.

Karageorghis, C. I., Terry, P. C., and Lane, A. M. (1999). Revised Brunel Music Rating Inventory. *Journal of Sports Sciences.*

Lane, A. M. (2004). Measures of emotions and coping in sport. *In Coping and Emotion in Sport.* Pp255-271. Editors Lavallee, D., Thatcher, J., and Jones, M. Nova Science, NY.

Lane, A. M., Hall, R., and Lane, J. (2002). Development of a measure of self-efficacy specific to statistic courses in sport. *Journal of Hospitality, Leisure, Sport and Tourism Education, 1,* 47-56.

Lane, A. M., Harwood, C., and Nevill, A. M. (2005). Confirmatory factor analysis of the thoughts of occurrence questionnaire among adolescent athletes. *Stress Anxiety and Coping, 18,* 245-254.

Lane, A. M., Harwood, C., Terry, P. C., and Karageorghis, C. I. (2004). Confirmatory factor analysis of the Test of Performance Strategies (TOPS) among adolescent athletes. *Journal of Sports Sciences, 22,* 803-812.

Lane, A. M., Nevill, A. M., Bowes, N., and Fox, K. R. (2005). Investigating indices of stability using the task and ego orientation questionnaire. *Research Quarterly for Exercise and Sport, 76,* 339-346.

Lane, A. M., Sewell, D. F., Terry, P. C., Bartram, D., and Nesti, M. S. (1999). Confirmatory factor analysis of the Competitive State Anxiety Inventory-2. *Journal of Sports Sciences, 17,* 505-512.

Lane, A. M., Whyte, G. P., Terry, P. C., and Nevill, A. M (2005). Mood and examination performance. *Personality and Individual Differences, 39,* 143-153.

Lane, H. J., Lane, A. M., and Matheson, H. (2004). Validity of the eating attitude test among exercisers. *Journal of Sports Science and Medicine, 3,* 244-253.

Nevill, A., Lane, A. M., Kilgour, L., Bowes, N., and Whyte, G. (2001). Stability of psychometric questionnaires. *Journal of Sports Sciences, 19,* 273-278.

Terry, P. C., and Lane, A. M. (2000). Normative values for the Profile of Mood States for use with athletic samples. *Journal of Applied Sport Psychology, 12,* 93-109.

Terry, P. C., Lane, A. M., and Fogarty, G. (2003). Construct validity of the Profile of Mood States-A for use with adults. *Psychology of Sport and Exercise, 4,* 125-139.

Terry, P. C., Lane, A. M., Lane, H. J., and Keohane, L. (1999). Development and validation of a mood measure for adolescents: POMS-A. *Journal of Sports Sciences, 17,* 861-872.

Terry, P. C., Stevens, M. J., and Lane, A. M. (2005). Influence of response time frame on mood assessment. *Stress Anxiety and Coping, 18,* 279-285.

In: Mood and Human Performance: Conceptual, Measurement...   ISBN 1-60021-269-7
Editor: Andrew M. Lane, pp. 1-33   © 2006 Nova Science Publishers, Inc.

Chapter 1

THE RISE AND FALL OF THE ICEBERG: DEVELOPMENT OF A CONCEPTUAL MODEL OF MOOD-PERFORMANCE RELATIONSHIPS

Andrew M. Lane[*]

School of Sport, Performing Arts and Leisure,
University of Wolverhampton, UK

ABSTRACT

This chapter reviews mood-performance research in sport psychology, offering the work of Terry (1995) as an important contribution to the development of a theoretical model by Lane and Terry (2000). Lane and Terry's model provides a theoretical framework for testing the mood states identified in the Profile of Mood States (McNair, Lorr, and Droppleman, 1971). Studies that have tested Lane and Terry's model are reviewed, leading to a revised theoretical model that includes a greater number of positive mood states, namely calmness and happiness. Suggestions for future research are offered, particularly examining relationships between emotional intelligence, mood states and performance.

INTRODUCTION

The notion that emotions and mood states influence behaviour has considerable intuitive appeal. The term mood is used to describe how we feel and is proposed to influence how we think and what we do. For example, '*I was really nervous*' typically describes how we feel before performing in public, or before being interviewed for an important job. We tend to feel intense emotions when successful performance is perceived to be of personal importance. However, people rarely experience a single emotion but rather tend to experience a range of emotions simultaneously. In sport, where a great deal of research has been conducted, we

---

[*] A.M.Lane2@wlv.ac.uk

know that many athletes report feeling both excited and nervous shortly before competition. In some athletes, feeling excited and nervous could be recognition of the importance of the competition. In such circumstances, athletes can try to use these emotions to motivate themselves to try harder to attain performance goals. By contrast, when some athletes feel nervous, they can also feel saddened. In this case, depressed mood in combination with anxiety, may reflect an athletes anticipated failure. Expecting defeat on a task of great personal importance leads to sadness. A phrase such as "*I am not in the mood today*" is often cited as a reason for a lacklustre performance. The phrase '*not in the mood today*' could mean many of different combinations of emotions; it could describe feeling saddened, confused, and fatigued, or it could describe feeling angry, anxious and miserable. What should be clear is that in real-life situations, people experience combinations of mood states, and it is the interaction among these mood states that influences how we act, and therefore, ultimately, how mood states influence performance. It is the study of emotions as they are experienced in real time in the real world where the most fruitful research will occur.

Relationships between mood and human performance have been examined in various domains. Findings have consistently pointed to significant mood effects on performance in many diverse areas of endeavour, including work (Lee and Allen, 2002; Eisenberger, Armeli, Rexwinkel, Lynch, and Rhoades, 2001), creativity (Grawitch, Munz, and Kramer, 2003) and sport (Beedie, Terry, and Lane, 2000; Totterdell and Leach, 2001). Pleasant moods tend to be linked with good performance. Unpleasant moods tend to be linked with poor performance, although some studies have shown unpleasant moods facilitate performance (Beedie et al., 2000; Hanin, 1997; Schwarz and Bless, 1991). Others have shown pleasant moods are unhelpful towards performance (Hanin, 2000). Lane and colleagues developed and tested a conceptual model of mood and performance relationships in sport and academic settings (Lane and Terry, 2000; Lane, Beedie, and Stevens, 2005). Although in contemporary research it is common for researchers to define and test theoretical models of mood-performance relationships, this has not always been the case. The aims of this chapter are threefold. The first aim is to review methodological and theoretical limitations of mood literature preceding the theoretical framework developed by Lane and Terry (2000). The second aim is to describe and evaluate studies that have tested Lane and Terry's model. The third aim is to consider future directions for mood research in sport and other performance-related domains. It is important to note that the work completed by Lane and colleagues begins in sport, but has been expanded to academic and vocational settings.

MOOD STATES AND SPORT PSYCHOLOGY: 'THE RISE AND FALL OF THE ICEBERG'

The intuitive link between mood states and performance provided a catalyst for psychologists seeking empirically to evaluate this assumption. Within sport psychology, this line of investigation gathered momentum during the 1970s. The relative infancy of sport psychology as a discipline contributed to researchers utilising tools validated and used in general psychology. Most research assessed mood using the Profile of Mood States (POMS: McNair, Lorr, and Droppleman, 1971), a 65-item self-report questionnaire that describes six mood states: Anger, confusion, depression, fatigue, tension, and vigour. The POMS was developed for use in clinical settings, and was later used on student populations. To complete the POMS, the participant rates the extent to which he/she feels each mood descriptor on a 5-point Likert scale from 0 = "*not at all*" to 4 = "*extremely*" using either "*during the past week including today*" or "*right now*" response sets. Raw scores for each of the six states are then converted to standard T score format ($M = 50$, $SD = \pm 10$) using normative data derived from students. For example, a respondent with a raw score of 11 on the Confusion scale (a sum of responses to the items: Confused, Unable to concentrate, Muddled, Bewildered, Efficient, Forgetful, Uncertain about things) is at the 50th percentile for American students. When exploring the link between mood states and performance, performance was operationalised in a number of different ways. These include qualification, selection, goal achievement, win/loss, ranking, and level of performance. Researchers hoped to establish the extent to which mood and performance was related.

Studies of mood-performance relationships led Morgan (1980) to argue that the POMS was the test of champions. He proposed that successful sport performance was associated with the "iceberg" profile (see Figure 1), the name being derived from the shape of the graph. Average mood scores, established using normative data derived from students, are represented by the water line. Successful sport performance was related to above average vigour with below average anger, confusion, depression, fatigue, and tension. For example, Morgan (1979) found that POMS scores were able to correctly classify 70% of athletes who were selected or not selected for an Olympic squad. Examination of the iceberg profile became the main line of investigation from which much of the later work has evolved.

In testing the iceberg profile, researchers focused on identifying differences between the mood states of elite athletes and non-elite athletes or between athletes and non-athletes. It often followed a procedure whereby the POMS was posted to athletes. The athlete was asked to complete the POMS using a '*past month*' response timeframe, that is, think back over the previous month and provide a single score that summarises these feelings. However, no consideration of situational factors was undertaken. The athlete completed the POMS, indicated his/her level of athletic ability and posted this information back to the researcher. Consider the following example to illustrate the problem. Athlete A receives the POMS in the post on a day when he also received an enormous gas bill. Athlete B receives the POMS in the post on a day when he received a huge tax rebate. If both complete the POMS when they receive it, and we do not know this has happened in research, but will assume it to be true for the purpose of this example, it is likely that athlete A will report a negative mood and athlete B a positive mood.

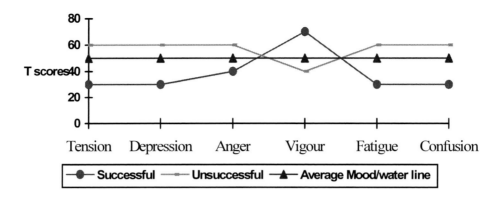

Figure 1. The mood profiles of successful and unsuccessful athletes as proposed by Morgan (1980)

If Athlete A is a club athlete and athlete B is an elite athlete, the POMS scores posted back to the researcher will show that mood correlates with performance. However, it should be obvious that mood is influenced by the different situations in which the questionnaire was completed and a mood-performance link occurred by chance.

The major limitation with the research design described is that the nature of mood is not considered. By not adequately accounting for situational factors, mood is treated as a stable construct, which it clearly is not. Elite athletes neither have a monopoly of good mood states, nor are mood states stable. It is illogical to assume that either supposition is true. We know that elite athletes experience intense unpleasant emotions before important competition (see Terry, 1995). Notwithstanding problems linked with posting the POMS to athletes and assuming mood is stable, normative data of student's mood responses is also an issue. We do not know the situational conditions in which students completed the POMS when the normative data set was collected (McNair et al., 1971). We would assume that if mood states were assessed in the examination period, where anxiety and unpleasant mood states might prevail, normative values would be different to mood states at the start of term, where happiness and hope might prevail. It could be argued that if normative data for sport were available, an iceberg profile would not have emerged. This is of course the benefit of hindsight, but there are few credible lines of research that simply compare data against existing norms, and where data are similar (i.e., the emergence of an iceberg profile) to norms, that these are results worth publishing.

We know that a range of factors influence moods and emotions. After accepting that mood states are transitory in nature, one of the most influential limitations, but one that is often overlooked, is the influence of the response timeframe on the nature of mood. In the meta-analysis of Rowley, Etnier, Landers, and Kyllo (1995), many studies did not report the response timeframe, hence it is unclear whether participants completed the POMS using the *'how do you feel right now'* or a *'past week'* response timeframe. The right now response timeframe assesses a different construct than a past week response timeframe, a mood assessment that is influenced by memory, personality and ambient mood states (see Terry, Stevens, and Lane, 2005). Clearly, the methods used should reflect the nature of the construct being investigated, which much of the early research did not.

Given the methods used in mood and performance research, it should not be surprising that subsequent findings have led to extensive discussion regarding the predictive effectiveness of mood. Although Morgan reported impressive figures for performance prediction (see Morgan, 1985 for review), in the 1990s, two review articles (see Renger, 1993; Rowley et al., 1995) downplayed the predictive effectiveness of mood. Meta-analysis results of Rowley et al. (1995) showed that although successful athletes reported a mood profile that resembled more of an iceberg than unsuccessful athletes, POMS could explain only 1% of the variance in performance. They concluded that researchers should abandon mood profiling and look for other variables to predict performance. By contrast, Terry (1995), in a review which predominantly comprised the same studies, proposed that scores on the POMS were an effective predictor of performance when certain conditions are met. Renger and Rowley et al.'s proposal that mood *per se* is a poor predictor of performance is based on studies, which according to Terry (1995) were studies where mood-performance relationships should be weak due to methodological limitations.

Terry (1995) argued that mood states will have a relatively sensitive influence on performance and the design used needs to consider this point. It is unrealistic to expect mood states to predict team performance if we assess an individuals mood (and not the team's) and analyse performance by win/loss. For example, a soccer goalkeeper performing in a negative mood may perform badly but not concede any goals due to good performances from the surrounding defenders, or may concede three goals but his team scores four. It is also unrealistic to expect mood states to predict objective measures of performance in cross-sectional research where participants are heterogeneous in terms of skill and ability. Consider the following example to illustrate this point. There are two track athletes competing in a 100 metres race. Athlete A, an elite sprinter with a personal best time of 10.00 seconds, reports a negative mood before the present race. Athlete B, a club sprinter with a personal best time of 11.00 seconds, reports a positive mood before the same race. If both athletes run 10.5 seconds and no consideration is given to the relative quality of their performances, then results would indicate no relationship between mood and performance. Contrastingly, if the same elite athlete is compared to another elite athlete, with the same personal best, who reports a positive mood before the present race and runs 10.00 seconds, the result would suggest that mood and performance are related. To be able to accept or reject the effect of mood states on performance, cross-sectional research designs should control for homogeneity in skill and fitness levels. It is therefore important to develop a self-referenced measure of performance to detect the relatively subtle influence of mood on performance (Hall and Terry, 1995; Terry, 1993). Using the example of the elite and club sprinters cited above, a self-referenced measure of performance, e.g., comparing current performance against previous performance, would show that the elite athlete under-performed and the novice athlete performed above expectation, and this is reflected by variations in mood. It is suggested that the greater the heterogeneity of the participants in terms of skill and fitness, the greater the need to assess performance using a self-referenced method. Therefore, it is argued that the review of Terry (1995) makes an important contribution to the mood literature as it starts to address the link between theoretical issues regarding the nature of mood and methods used by researchers to assess this relationship.

POMS Research: The Baby and the Bathwater

In 1995, any would-be mood researcher could be forgiven for thinking that using the POMS was more trouble than it is worth. Conceptual ambiguity surrounding mood research was huge. For example, in the commonly used sport psychology textbook *Foundations of Sport and Exercise Psychology,* Weinberg and Gould (1995) used the term *"negative traits"* (p. 50) to describe POMS mood dimensions, with the reference to mood scores as assessed by the POMS being traits as the key point to observe. Mood states are clearly not personality traits due to their transient nature. A further limitation of the POMS is the unpleasant orientation. Only vigour out of the six mood states is pleasant. This limitation is exacerbated by the fact that the POMS was developed for use with clinical samples, and therefore might not be valid for use in sport. Early researchers were more interested in addressing questions such as 'do POMS scores predict performance?' than a question such as 'is the POMS a valid scale for use with athletes?' The later question requires a large sample of responses and the use of complex statistics to provide an answer. Researchers opted to look at the first question, and in doing so, assumed that the validity of the POMS transferred from clinical outpatients to athletes. It is of course possible that it did not, and poor validity of the POMS could be an additional factor in weak mood-performance relationships identified by Rowley et al. (1995). Therefore, with inconsistent mood-performance relationships and a measure of unsubstantiated validity, researchers could make the decision to abandon the POMS and start a new line of research from theoretical principles related to the nature of mood. However, it is argued that this is akin to *throwing the baby out with the bathwater.* Terry and co-workers demonstrated the POMS could predict performance under certain conditions. Further, Terry's work was applied in nature and used elite competitors. Indeed, many of his publications are evaluations of consultancy work rather than pre-planned studies. I argue that this is a positive aspect of the research. Athletes would not complete the POMS (and Terry used the POMS repeatedly in his work) if they had little respect for the process of mood profiling. Indeed, Terry reports some impressive figures. He found that 100% of performers were correctly classified as either successful or unsuccessful in rowing (Hall and Terry, 1995), 92% of performers were correctly classified in karate (Terry and Slade, 1995), and 71% of performers correctly classified in bobsleigh (Terry, 1993).

In an attempt to provide some sense to the mood literature in sport, Beedie et al. (2000) conducted two meta-analyses. The first meta-analysis summarised findings from studies that sought to link mood and athletic achievement by comparing the mood responses of elite and non-elite athletes, a research question for which the rationale is questionable (i.e., we would not expect the mood of an elite athlete and a club athlete to differ in any predictable way). The overall effect size (ES) was very small (Weighted Mean *ES* = 0.10, *SD* = 0.07), a finding consistent with the previous meta-analysis by Rowley et al. (1995). The second meta-analysis completed by Beedie et al. included studies that examined the relationship between pre-competition mood and subsequent performance, arguably a more productive line of enquiry (i.e., we would expect an athlete's mood to influence her/his performance). The overall effect was moderate (Weighted Mean *ES* = 0.31, *SD* = 0.12), with stronger relationships evident when self-referenced performance measures were used. In terms of the effect size for each mood state, effects were moderate for confusion, depression and vigour, small for anger and tension, and very small for fatigue. Although all mean effects were in the direction associated with an iceberg profile (Morgan, 1980, 1985), the direction of mood-performance relationships for anger and tension varied across studies. High scores for anger and tension were associated with poor performance in some studies and with good performance in other studies. Beedie et al. showed that pre-competition mood, that is where the athlete completes the mood measure using a *'how do you feel right now'* response timeframe, predicts performance when certain conditions are met. In terms of mood-performance relationships for each scale they showed that:

- Vigour is associated with facilitated performance, while confusion, fatigue, and depression are associated with debilitated performance;
- Anger and tension were associated with facilitated performance in some studies and debilitated performance in others;
- Effects were very small for the debilitative effects of fatigue.

At this point, we decided to develop a theoretical framework and appropriate methodology for investigating mood performance-relationships using the POMS model of mood. Theory-testing and construct measurement are inextricably interlinked and therefore developing the two went hand-in-hand.

THE NATURE OF MOOD: DEVELOPMENT OF A THEORETICAL MODEL WITH A FOCUS ON DEPRESSION

Terry (1995) alluded to the transient nature of mood in his paper when arguing the importance of temporal factors. Lane and Terry (2000) offered a definition of mood as *"a set of feelings, ephemeral in nature, varying in intensity and duration, and usually involving more than one emotion"* (p.16). Lane, Beedie et al. (2005) recently acknowledged a limitation of this definition in that emotion and mood are defined by each other. Lane et al. accepted that measurement issues drove their early definition of mood. Lane et al. used definitions of mood and emotion from the general psychology literature and both of these propose that mood and emotion are transitory. Lazarus (2000) offered the following definition of emotion as *"an organized psycho-physiological reaction to ongoing relationships with the environment...what mediates emotions psychologically is an evaluation, referred to as an appraisal, of the personal significance for the well-being that a person attributes to this relationship (...relational meaning), and the process" (p. 230)*. Parkinson, Totterdell, Briner, and Reynolds (1996) proposed that *"mood reflects changing non-specific psychological dispositions to evaluate, interpret, and act on past, current, or future concerns in certain patterned ways"* (p.216). Beedie, Terry, and Lane (2005) discuss issues related to mood and emotion distinctions, these discussions are extensive and the interested reader is referred to this work. A key part of the definition forwarded by Lane and Terry (2000), for the purpose of this chapter, is the statement that mood states are ephemeral in nature. Mood should be assessed using a right now response timeframe and as close to competition as possible.

Once methodological limitations are adequately considered, a more pressing question is not 'can mood states predict performance?' but 'why do mood states predict performance'? Several theorists have proposed that mood influences performance by serving an informational function, whereby moods signal the likely outcome of events and helps identify potential problems; particularly in the case of important tasks where the outcome is uncertain (Bless, 2001; Brehm, 1999; Gendolla and Krusken, 2002; Schwarz, 1990). For example, positive moods provide information about the task (*this is enjoyable*), about the self (*I am good at the task*), or about a strategy (*I am doing this right*). Therefore, positive moods indicate that a situation carries little threat whereas unpleasant moods signal that a situation is potentially problematic (Clore, Wyer, Dienes, Gasper, Gohm, and Isbell, 2001).

Martin (2001) emphasized how context influences this process. For example, an individual is likely to accept feeling sad at a funeral but would be less likely to accept feeling sad at a birthday party, and would tend to engage in efforts to adjust such feelings. Similarly, before performing a task of critical importance (e.g., a pilot flying a plane, a surgeon performing an operation) or a task of personal importance (e.g., an athlete trying to win an Olympic medal, a manager giving a presentation to a board of directors), an individual could expect to feel a wide range of positive and negative feelings. Given that individuals seek to repair negative moods perceived as a threat to performance (Bower, Gilligan, and Monterio, 1981; Erber and Erber, 2001), conscious recognition of the likely functional impact of mood states is very important. Indeed, it has been shown that individuals who report positive moods before performing important and uncertain tasks tend to have previously regulated moods perceived as unpleasant and dysfunctional (Totterdell and Leach, 2001).

Negative moods are proposed to derive from discrepancies between personal standards and perceived current status (Carver and Scheier, 1990; Martin and Tesser, 1996; Wicklund, 1979). People in a negative mood who feel that their performance will be further from the standard of performance set as a goal, may analyse the situation carefully, attending to specific details in order to reduce this discrepancy (Cervone, Kopp, Schaumann, and Scott, 1994). When people perform objectively difficult tasks, perceived goal attainability influences the functional impact of negative mood on effort. Those in a negative mood either mobilize little effort because they perceive task demands to be too high, or increase effort because negative mood acts as a warning signal that attainment of achievable goals is threatened (Cervone et al., 1994; Gendolla and Krusken, 2002).

Lane and Terry (2000) developed a conceptual model to try and explain these effects (see Figure 2). A key part of Lane and Terry's model is the assumption that different dimensions of mood interact to influence performance. Central to the model is the pivotal position of depression. Theoretically, depressed mood, characterised by themes such as misery, downheartedness and unhappiness should be associated with low confidence to perform due to an inability to mobilise personal resources. Bandura (1990) argued that individuals could become depressed by their perceived inability to achieve valued goals. The likelihood of depression increases when goal attainment is needed to maintain a sense of self-worth. Lane and Terry suggested that depressive cognitive generalisations have a pervasive effect across all mood dimensions, and that at the pre-competition phase such feelings will result in anticipated failure.

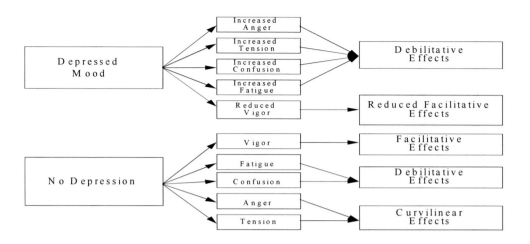

Figure 2. Lane and Terry's (2000) conceptual model of mood and performance with a focus on depression

Research has shown depression to be associated with a tendency to focus on negative previous experiences, which may in turn, reduce perceptions of ability and coping (see Rokke, 1993). Further, it has been proposed that depressed mood requires more regulation than other elements of mood and therefore uses up more of a limited resource, reducing capacity for other types of regulation such as physical performance (see Muraven, Tice, and Baumeister, 1998).

An additional reason for focusing on depressed mood stemmed from the way in which athletes respond to self-report scales that assess depressed mood. A question that might be asked is why single out depression as the key mood state? Could tension have a similar effect on other mood states? To test whether depression or tension was the most influential mood state, mood responses from 1,317 athletes were analysed, and importantly, the effect of depression on other mood states was tested, as was the effect of tension on other mood states (Lane and Terry, 1999b). Results showed that 48% reported tension in the absence of depressed mood symptoms, 35% reported symptoms of both depressed mood and tension, 13% reported no tension or depressed mood symptoms, but only 4% reported depressed mood symptoms and no tension. It was concluded that, among athletes, tension is experienced both in the presence and in absence of depressed mood, but by contrast depressed mood symptoms are rarely experienced in the absence of tension.

Possibly the most influential aspect of Lane and Terry's model is the notion that depressed mood influences performance through its interaction with anger and tension. They hypothesized that anger and tension can be either facilitative or debilitative of performance, depending on interactions with depressed mood. Lane and Terry proposed that individuals in a depressed mood tend to direct feelings of anger internally, leading to suppression, self-blame and, ultimately, performance decrements (Spielberger, 1991). Similarly, such individuals tend to transfer tension into feelings of threat and worry, also leading to performance decrements. Conversely, in the absence of depressed mood, it is easier for the arousal component of anger and tension to serve a functional role by signalling the need for positive action (Bless, 2001; Schwarz, 2001). Specifically, anger is likely to be expressed outwardly at the source of the original frustration (or displaced toward another object or person) and may be channelled productively into determination to succeed; and symptoms of tension are more likely to be interpreted as indicating a readiness to perform and be seen as facilitative of performance.

Lane and Terry (2000) proposed four main hypotheses. The first hypothesis is that anger, confusion, fatigue and tension will be higher and vigour will be lower among athletes experiencing depressed mood. The second hypothesis is that interrelationships among anger, confusion, fatigue, tension and vigour will be stronger for athletes experiencing depressed mood. The third hypothesis is that vigour will facilitate performance and confusion and fatigue will debilitate performance regardless of the presence or absence of depressed mood. The fourth hypothesis is that anger and tension will be associated with debilitated performance among individuals reporting symptoms of depression, whereas anger and tension will show a curvilinear relationship with performance among individuals reporting no symptoms of depression.

TESTING LANE AND TERRY'S MODEL

The relationship between theory testing and construct measurement is illustrated clearly by the following quote. Chelladurai and Selah (1980) proposed that: *"The elaboration of any theory entails an obligation to measure its constructs or specify behavioural manifestations which can adequately be measured. Otherwise, theoretical formulations only yield a proliferation in terminology, instead of fulfilling a promise of empirical advance"* (cited in Horn, 1992, p. 35). Four issues are relevant; a) the validity of the mood measure, b) temporal factors, c) operationalising depressed mood groups, d) measures of performance.

a) The Validity of the Mood Measure

Lane and Terry (2000) used the POMS model of mood. However, at this time, sport psychology research suggested that the psychometric properties of the POMS had a number of limitations. First, the factor structure of the POMS had not been tested on athletes. Second, Terry (1995) suggested that there was also a need for the POMS to be validated on participants under the age of 18 years as the original validation used adults only. Third, the 65-item POMS has been criticised for taking too long to complete (Curren, Andrykowski, and Studts, 1995; Grove and Prapavessis, 1992; Shacham, 1983). This point is particularly relevant when the POMS is used to assess mood close to competition where brevity is important. Fourth, the POMS items have been criticised for having an excessive North American orientation, particularly items such as "grovely" and "blue" (Grove and Prapavessis, 1992). Terry, Keohane and Lane (1996) stressed a need to develop a version of POMS validated for use with a British population. Fifth, Terry and Lane (2000) suggested that there was a need to validate the factor structure of the POMS using the *"how do you feel right now"* response set. McNair et al. (1971) used the *"how have been feeling over the past week including today"* response set in all their validation studies.

To address these issues, Terry and colleagues (Terry, Lane, Lane, and Keohane, 1999; Terry, Lane, and Fogarty, 2003) conducted a great deal of work to develop and validate a 24-item measure of mood that assesses the POMS, named the Brunel Mood Scale (BRUMS). It is named the BRUMS in recognition of Brunel University where most of the work was completed. Arguably, the BRUMS is the most comprehensively validated measure of mood available in the sport psychology literature. The scale has demonstrated face validity with adolescents, factor validity with adolescents and adults, and used a sample size of over 2000 participants. It has shown predictive validity (Lane and Lane, 2002) and concurrent validity (Terry et al., 1999, 2003). As validation was initiated with adolescents, comprehensibility is less of an issue, and this characteristic should speed up completion time. Therefore, the BRUMS represents a valid measure for assessing mood in sport.

b) Temporal Factors

For studies that assess mood states in real time, rather than retrospectively, a 'how do you feel right now' response set should be used as this reflects the ephemeral nature of the mood construct (Lane and Terry, 2000). Mood-performance research seeks to assess feelings before competition. From a research perspective, the ideal design would be to assess mood states during performance. This approach would not be popular with participants who usually oblige researchers by completing self-report measures, but it is important to recognise that the research is less important to the athlete than preparing for competition. Therefore, a compromise between the interests of the athlete and the interests of the researcher has to be reached. Research exploring anxiety and performance relationships uses a standardized time of one hour before competition for administering the measure (Martens, Vealey, and Burton, 1990). Although some researchers have applied the same approach to mood research (see LeUnes and Burger, 1998; LeUnes, 2000), this has not been universally done. It is suggested that a standardized procedure for assessing mood is adopted, which in practical terms is probably best conducted by gathering data approximately one hour before competition.

c) Operationalising Depressed Mood Groups

The term depression, used differentially by the clinician and the layperson, warrants some clarification. Lane and Terry (2000) advocated using the BRUMS, which assesses depressed mood by asking respondents how they feel in relation to four items, "depressed", "downhearted", "unhappy", and "miserable". Low scores on these items may indicate a slightly depressed, although sub-clinical, mood state that is part of the normal human reaction to daily events (see Kendall and Hammen, 1995). Extremely high scores reported over a number of repeated administrations may, but do not necessarily, indicate a clinical mood disorder. Even maximum scores on the four depression items may represent extreme, but not clinically significant, dissatisfaction or distress in relation to a particular event or situation. To diagnose mood disorder would require far more information. Clinical depression scales, on their own are not sufficient for diagnosing clinical depression, typically address factors such as sleep disturbance, anhedonia, loss of appetite and libido, and social withdrawal. To avoid confusion with clinical depression, Lane and Terry (2000) used the term depressed mood to refer to elevated scores on the depression subscale.

To test the model, Lane and Terry (2000) suggested that participants should be grouped into depressed mood and no-depression groups on the basis of responses to the four depression items on the BRUMS. Participants reporting zero for all items form the no-depression group, whereas those scoring one or more form the depressed mood group. Given the zero to 16-point range of this scale, the latter group would potentially be quite heterogeneous in reporting symptoms of depressed mood.

d) Measure of Performance

Performance measures need to be sufficiently sensitive if studies are to capture the relatively subtle influence of mood on performance. There are different ways to assess performance using self-referenced techniques. For example, the relative success of a performance can be judged by comparing an objective measure of performance outcome, such as finish time or finish position, with a pre-performance goal (e.g., Hall and Terry, 1995; Lane and Karageorghis, 1997; Terry, 1993). Alternatively, it can be judged by comparing an objective performance measure with a personal best or previous performance for that event (e.g., Martin and Gill, 1991, 1995). However, either method has limitations. For example, an athlete who sets a goal of 20 minutes to complete a 5 km race and runs 22 minutes may be said to have under-performed by two minutes. However, if the athlete's personal best time for 5 km was 23 minutes, and personal best was used to assess performance, then the athlete may be said to have over-performed by one minute. A performance measure that simply compares objective outcome with a pre-performance goal, and does not adequately account for the relative difficulty of the goal, is unlikely to be a useful measure. Using the above example, it is not possible to determine whether failure to achieve the performance goal was a consequence of setting a standard of performance that was beyond current abilities, or due to some other factor such as lack of effort. Hence, the relative difficulty of the pre-competition goal is very important when assessing performance.

Research has also acknowledged the importance of considering previous experiences when assessing the relative goal difficulty. For example, Martin and Gill (1991, 1995) found that track and field athletes were able to predict their finish position in races. They ascribed this to the comparative information gained during previous races against the same opponents, which provided a basis for predictions. They proposed that the combined knowledge of the characteristics of the course, the outcome of previous races and the degree of effort they were prepared to expend facilitated accurate predictions of finish time. Therefore, it is suggested that a true self-referenced measure of performance should involve a comparison of an objective performance outcome with both a pre-performance goal and, as an indicator of goal difficulty, the result of previous performance (s).

As studies of mood and performance tend to be conducted in real-world setting, each study requires consideration of how best to develop an ecologically valid self-referenced measure of performance. Most measures of performance account for the goal set by each individual, and, through comparison with previous performance, the difficulty of the goal for that individual. For example, Lane, Terry, Beedie, Curry, and Clark (2001) investigated running performance in two schools. In School 1, where the objective performance measure was distance, self-referenced performance was calculated using the formula: (Distance Covered – Previous Performance) + (Distance Covered – Race Goal). In School 2, where the objective performance measure was time, the calculation was: (Previous Performance – Finish Time) + (Race Goal – Finish Time). All performance data were standardised using T-score transformations and were then merged into a single sample.

Performance has been measured in other studies using a self-reported perception of the quality of the performance by the individual. For example, Lane, Lane and Firth (2002) assessed running performance through two items: "How do you feel about your time in the last race?" and "To what extent did your finish time relate to your pre-race expectations?' Items were rated on a nine-point scale anchored by 'extremely dissatisfied' (1) and 'extremely pleased' (9). The two-items correlated significantly ($r = .73$, $p < .01$), thus lending support to the decision to sum these items to produce a single score for performance satisfaction.

REVIEW OF STUDIES THAT HAVE TESTED LANE AND TERRY'S MODEL

A difficulty and advantage of summarising your own work is that you have access to all of the published studies. Ongoing work remains an issue and the decision as to whether to include these studies in the present chapter is difficult. Seventeen studies were reviewed (see Table 1). In terms of the first hypothesis in which Lane and Terry hypothesised that participants in the depressed mood group would simultaneously report higher scores for anger, confusion, fatigue, and tension but lower vigour scores. All 17 studies provided evidence to support this hypothesis. The mean effect sizes (Cohen's d) for these mood dimensions were in the moderate to large categories – Anger: $M = .85$, $SD = .25$; Confusion: $M = .93$, $SD = .25$; Fatigue: $M = .79$, $SD = .37$; Tension: $M = .61$, $SD = .27$, and Vigour: $M = .51$, $SD = .34$.

Hypotheses 3 and 4, which are the central proposition of the Lane and Terry model were tested. Data from studies that tested these assumptions using structural equation modelling (i.e., Lane and Terry, 1998, 1999a; Lane et al., 2001, 2004) were subjected to further analysis. Structural equation modelling requires large samples and so these studies reflected the major tests of the model. In addition, the results of structural equation modelling are provided in standardized coefficients, thereby making results directly comparable. Overall, a summary analysis showed that when comparing results for depressed mood and no-depression groups, mood-performance relationships essentially remained constant for confusion, fatigue, and vigour, whereas the direction of the relationship switched for anger and tension (see Table 2). Average standardised coefficients showed that anger and tension were positively related to performance in the no-depression group, and negatively related to performance in the depressed mood group. The switching effect was significant for both anger and tension but was clearly greater for anger. Vigour showed a moderate positive relationship with performance in both groups, whereas confusion and fatigue showed weak negative relationships. These findings support the notion that depressed mood moderates mood-performance relationships for anger and tension but not for confusion, fatigue and vigour, as hypothesized by Lane and Terry (2000).

Table 1. Studies testing Lane and Terry's (2000) conceptual model examined by Lane and Terry (2005)

Study	H1	H2	H3	H4
Lane and Terry, 1998 (running)	Support	Support	Support	Partial Support-no support for curvilinear relationship with performance for anger and tension in the No depression group.
Lane, Terry, Karageorghis, and Lawson, 1999 (kick boxing)	Partial support No support for vigour	Support	Support	Partial support Tension and Anger debilitated performance when associated with depression. Anger showed no association with performance in no-depression group.
Lane and Terry 1999 (a) (running)	Support	Support	Partial Support	Anger associated with successful performance in no depression group and poor performance in the depression group.
Lane and Terry 1999 (b, mixture of sports)	Support	Not Tested	Not Tested	Not Tested
Janover and Terry 2002 (swimming)	Support	Support	Support	Support
Lane, Whyte, Shave, and Wilson (cycling)	Support	Not Tested	Not Tested	Not Tested
Lane, Whyte, George, Shave, Stevens, Barney and Terry 2004 (marathon)	Support	Not Tested	Not Tested	Not Tested
Owen, Lane, and Terry 2000 (tennis)	Support	Support	No Support	No Support
Hall, Lane and Devonport 2001 (running)	Support	Not Tested	Not Tested	Not Tested
Lane, Terry, Beedie. Curry, and Clark 2001 (running)	Support	Support	Partial Support	Anger associated with debilitated performance in depression group.
Lane and Levitt 2002 (soccer)	Support	Not Tested	Not Tested	Not Tested
Lane, Lane and Firth 2002 (running)	Support	Not Tested	Not Tested	Not Tested
Fazackerley, Lane and Mahoney 2004 (wake boarding)	Support	Not Tested	No Support	Tension associated with facilitated performance in the no-depression group.
Lane, Terry, Beedie and Stevens 2004 (Cognitive performance)	Support	Support	Partial Support	Partial Support Anger associated with successful performance in no depression group and poor performance in depression group
Lane, Whyte, Terry and Nevill, 2005. (Academic performance)	Support for differences in anger, confusion, and tension	No tested	Support	Support
Lane 2001 (runners)	Support	Support	Partial Support	Partial Support
Lane and Lovejoy, 2001 (aerobic dance)	Support	Support	Not Tested	Not Tested

Table 2. Standardized Coefficients for Mood-Performance Relationships in No-depression and Depressed Mood Groups

	No-depression		Depressed mood		
	M	SD	M	SD	t
Anger	0.15	0.14	-0.31	0.12	5.62*
Confusion	-0.10	0.24	-0.09	0.30	-.02
Fatigue	-0.01	0.10	-0.07	0.08	1.11
Tension	0.16	0.13	-0.06	0.20	2.12*
Vigour	0.23	0.20	0.27	0.12	-.37

* $p < .05$ (one-tailed)

In terms of some of the specific findings from these studies, Lane and Terry (1999a) found that vigour was only significant in the no-depression group. Lane, Terry, et al. (2001) found no support for the notion that confusion and fatigue would debilitate performance. Lane, Terry, Beedie and Stevens (2004) found that fatigue and tension had no effect on performance. Of these studies, Lane, Terry, et al. (2004) found that anger was related to good performance in the no-depressed group and poor performance in the depressed group. Fazackerley et al. (2004) found that anger was related to poor performance in the depressed mood group. Fazackerley et al. (2004) found that tension was associated with facilitated performance in the no-depressed group. Lane, Terry, et al. (2001) found that anger was associated with poor performance in the depressed group. For the tension-performance relationship results were not significant. There was also no support for the proposed curvilinear relationship. Lane and Terry (1999a) found that anger was associated with good performance with the absence of depression and poor performance in the depression group. Tension was unrelated to performance in the no-depression group and related to poor performance in the depression group.

Lane (1998) provided possibly the most robust test of the model in a single study, and therefore the methods used warrant some description. He investigated the invariance of hypothesised relationships in two studies of running performance (see Lane and Terry, 1998; Lane and Terry, 1999a). Multisample structural equation modelling was used to test the invariance of hypothesised relationships in the two no-depression groups and the two depression groups. Participants were 250 male adult runners. Sample A comprised 91 runners (Age: M = 32.3 yr.; SD = 9.8 yr.) recruited from 10 km races in the South of England. Participants were relatively heterogeneous in terms of ability (10 km PB Time M = 39 min., 35 s; SD = 5 min. 36 s). All runners set a time goal for the race (Goal time: M = 42 min., 03 s; SD = 8 min., 9 s). Only 20 runners set a position goal. Sample B comprised 167 male runners (Age: M = 35.7 yr., SD = 11.4 yr.). The sample comprised experienced runners (M = 10.2 yr., SD = 7.2 yr.) although participants were relatively heterogeneous in terms of ability (10 Km PB: M = 40.18 min, SD = 7.67 min.). All runners set a time goal (Time goal: M = 41.77 min., SD = 7.00 min.) for the race. Only 23 runners also set a position goal.

Multisample strutural equation modelling analysis to examine mood and performance relationships, and intercorrelation coefficients among mood dimensions in depressed mood and no-depression groups are contained in Table 3. Results regarding the invariance of hypothesised relationships in the two no-depression groups indicated a poor fit (Comparative Fit Index (CFI) = .47). Contrastingly, multisample strutural equation modelling results to test the stability of relationships in the depression groups indicated a good model fit (CFI = .91).

Further, the multisample LMT to compare differences in equality constraints placed on hypothesised relationships between the two depression groups indicated no significant differences ($p > .01$).

Table 3. Multisample Structural Equation Modelling to Examine Mood and Performance Relationships and Interrelationships among Mood Dimensions in the Two Samples of Depression Groups and the Two Samples of No-depression Groups

	Depression group	No Depression group
X^2: df ratio	1.99	2.85
Bentler Bonett Normed Fit Index	.84	.45
Bentler Bonett Nonnormed Fit Index	.84	.12
Comparative Fit Index	.91	.47

The LMT results to indicate the strength of equality constraints placed on hypothesised relationships in the two no-depression groups are contained in Tables 4 and Table 5. As Table 4 indicates, relationships between fatigue and confusion ($X^2 = 15.75$, $p < .01$), and fatigue and vigour ($X^2 = 5.00$, $p < .01$) were significantly different between the no-depression group from Sample A, and the no-depression group from Sample B. In Sample B, the relationship between confusion and fatigue was significantly stronger (Sample A: $r = .10$; Sample B: $r = .39$). The vigour and fatigue relationship was significantly stronger in the no-depression from Sample B (Sample A: $r = -.06$; Sample B: $r = -.24$). As Table 5 indicates, mood and performance relationships remained invariant across the two samples of no-depression groups.

Table 4. Multisample Lagrange Multiplier Test Scores to Examine Differences in Hypothesised Relationships between the Two Depression Groups: Univariate Test Results

Constrained relationship	Univariate X^2 Value
1. Confusion – Anger	0.18
2. Fatigue – Anger	2.33
3. Fatigue – Confusion	2.50
4. Tension – Anger	.00
5. Tension – Confusion	2.57
6. Tension – Fatigue	0.32
7. Vigour – Fatigue	2.65
8. Performance – Anger	2.03
9. Performance - Confusion	.36
10. Performance – Fatigue	2.90
11. Performance – Tension	.12
12. Performance – Vigour	.13

Table 5. Multisample Lagrange Multiplier Test Scores to Examine Differences in Hypothesised Relationships between the Two samples of No-depression Groups: Univariate Test Results

Constrained relationship	Univariate X^2 Value
1. Confusion – Anger	.43
2. Fatigue – Anger	.09
3. Fatigue – Confusion	15.75*
4. Tension – Anger	1.88
5. Tension – Confusion	3.11
6. Tension – Fatigue	.50
7. Vigour – Fatigue	4.95*
8. Performance – Anger	2.14
9. Performance - Confusion	0.68
10. Performance – Fatigue	0.24
11. Performance – Tension	0.44
12. Performance – Vigour	2.70

* $p < .01$

Table 6. Multivariate multisample Lagrange Multiplier Test Scores to Examine Differences in Hypothesised Relationships between the Two Samples of No-depression Groups: Significant X^2 Values Only (p < .05)

Constrained relationship	Univariate X^2 Value	Multivariate X^2 Value
1. Fatigue - Confusion	15.75	15.75
2. Vigour - Fatigue	4.95	20.71

Multisample structural equation modelling analysis is proposed to provide a robust test of theory (Bentler, 1995) as it tests the extent to which findings from one sample can be generalised to a second sample. Therefore, theoretical propositions are tested more rigorously through multisample analysis than with one-sample analysis as it is possible to generalise findings with greater confidence. Results support the notion that anger, confusion, and tension are associated with debilitated performance, and vigour is associated with facilitated performance among depressed athletes. Findings for fatigue indicated that it was not significantly associated with debilitated performance among depressed athletes.

Findings indicated that mood and performance relationships remained invariant in the two no-depression groups. Vigour significantly predicted performance in both samples lending support to the notion that it is associated with facilitated performance. Results for confusion were less clear. Confusion was significantly associated with debilitated performance in Sample B only. Fatigue was not significantly associated with performance. In addition, results indicated that intercorrelation coefficients among mood dimensions for fatigue, confusion and vigour differed significantly between the two samples.

The most recent study that has tested Lane and Terry's model sought to address the issue of assessing mood states in laboratory based research (Lane, 2005). Studies that have tested Lane and Terry's (2000) model have tended to be conducted in ecologically valid settings. Controlling extraneous variables that could influence performance can be difficult when conducting research in real world settings. Lane and Terry (2000) have tested their model in running events in terms of 10k running (Lane and Terry, 1998, 1999a) and cross-country running (Lane, Terry, et al., 2001). Course and weather conditions will vary from course to course, and therefore, it is possible that the performance used as the dependent measure in these studies contained factors that are beyond the control of the researchers, which in turn dilutes mood-performance relationships. The aim of the study by Lane (2005) was to investigate Lane and Terry's model in a research context where potential confounding variables could be controlled. The Multi Stage Fitness Test (Ramsbottom, Brewer, and Williams, 1988) was used as the performance task.

Lane (2005) used a sample of 85 Sport Studies students (Age $M = 19.41$, $SD = 2.31$; Males: $n = 66$ and Females: $n = 19$) that reported exercising for an average of training 1.5 hours per week ($SD = 4.21$ hours). Participants completed the BRUMS simultaneously approximately 2 minutes before participating in the Multi Stage Fitness Test (Ramsbottom et al., 1988). As participants were heterogeneous in terms of training status, a self-referenced measure of performance was used. Participants completed the self-report scale immediately after finishing the bleep test. Performance Satisfaction was assessed using a two-item measure. Items included: "How do you feel about your performance in the bleep test?" and "To what extent did your performance relate to your test expectations?" Items were rated on a nine-point scale anchored by 'Extremely dissatisfied' (1) and 'Extremely pleased' (9). A provisional check indicated that objective performance did not correlate with subjective performance ($r = .19$, $p > .05$). This result was expected given the heterogeneous nature of participants in terms of skill and fitness.

Multivariate analysis of variance to investigate mood scores between depressed mood groups is contained in Table 7. As Table 7 indicates, participants reporting symptoms of depressed mood indicated significantly high anger, confusion, fatigue and tension with lower vigour. Effect sizes were moderate to large.

Structural equation modelling techniques were used to investigate the proposed moderating effects of depressed mood on mood-performance relationships. Equality constraints were placed on hypothesized mood-performance relationships. Structural equation modelling results indicated adequate fit for the Comparative Fit Index = .96, although a Root Mean Square Error of Approximation of .11 suggested poor model fit. Lagrange Multiplier test results indicated that the relationship between fatigue and performance was significantly stronger in the depressed mood group ($X^2 = 5.86$, $P < .05$).

Table 7. Mood scores between depressed mood and no-depression groups

	No-depression (N = 49)		Depressed Mood (N = 36)			
	M	SD	M	SD	F	Effect size
Anger	0.27	0.67	2.06	2.70	19.95*	.98
Confusion	1.29	2.35	2.74	3.05	6.10**	.54
Tension	3.71	3.03	5.66	3.80	6.80**	.58
Fatigue	5.08	3.78	9.49	3.88	27.14*	1.15
Vigour	7.02	3.34	4.11	2.29	19.79*	.99
	Hotelling's Trace = 0.55, $F_{5,78} = 8.51$, $P < .001$, $Eta^2 = .35$					

Path coefficients are contained in Figure 3. As Figure 3 indicates, mood states accounted for 39% and 22% of performance variance in the no-depression and depression groups respectively, with vigour and fatigue significantly relating to performance in both groups.

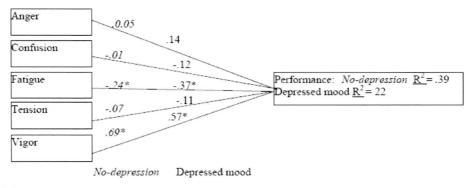

* p < .05

Figure 3 Structural Equation Model to Predict Performance in the No-Depression (N =49) and Depressed Mood (N = 36) Group

Lane (2005) found that mood states significantly predicted performance satisfaction on the multistage shuttle run test. In contrast to theoretical propositions forwarded by Lane and Terry (2000), depressed mood did not moderate performance relationships for anger and tension. By contrast, results indicate that fatigue hindered performance. It is argued that the nature of the task could explain these results. Vigour and fatigue reflect psychological states related to the perceived capacity to produce work, characteristics arguably that are required for success for an endurance based fitness test. It should be noted that scores for tension and anger were lower than those reported in previous research assessing psychological states before endurance tasks for adult samples (Lane and Terry, 1998, 1999a). However, Lane and Terry (1998, 1999a) assessed mood states in ecologically valid settings. Tension should be higher before tasks in which performance has a greater personal meaning. An acknowledged limitation of the study by Lane (2005) is that the relative importance of participating in the study was not investigated. Therefore, whilst the present study showed increased internal validity, it is arguable that the loss of ecological validity is possibly a more important factor when conducting mood-performance research.

In conclusion, Lane (2005) found support for the notion that depressed mood is associated with a negative mood profile characterized by high anger, confusion, fatigue, and tension and low vigour. Further, results show that mood states influenced performance, but the proposed moderating effect of depression on anger and tension was not evidenced.

EXTENSION STUDIES TO THE LANE AND TERRY MODEL

Several studies have extended the Lane and Terry (2000) model by including additional variables. The notion that depressed mood has a pervasive effect should mean that differences should be detected in variables such as self-efficacy and perceptions of environmental and situational factors. Lane (2001) investigated the relationships between mood states, self-confidence and course suitability. He found that vigour was closely associated with self-confidence in the no-depression group, but with course suitability in the depressed mood group. Lane (2001) argued that depressed mood influences memory processes, and that individuals experiencing feelings of depression and vigour simultaneously will attribute the positive feelings externally to the ease of the task in an attempt to maintain a negative view of self (Bandura, 1990; Bower, 1981; Rokke, 1993). A depressed individual will find it difficult to justify to himself/herself that he/she is experiencing feelings that might be beneficial to performance. Thus to minimize the potentially beneficial effects of these positive feelings, the depressed individual will attribute the cause of these feelings externally, and consequently, this information might serve to reduce perceptions of vigour. In addition, anger showed a positive relationship with self-confidence in the no-depression group, and an inverse relationship in the depressed mood group.

Lane and Levitt (2002) found that depressed mood was associated with low scores of group cohesion as evidenced by low scores on the Group Environment Questionnaire (Carron, Brawley, and Widmeyer, 1985). Hall, Lane, and Devonport (2002) investigated relationships between mood and Competitive State Anxiety Inventory-2 (Martens et al., 1990) with the directional scale among a sample of runners. They found that depressed mood was associated with perceiving cognitive anxiety and somatic anxiety as harmful for performance. They also found depression to be inversely related to self-confidence direction, and self-confidence intensity, a finding that prompted authors to suggest that low-self-confidence and depressed mood are closely associated.

Lane, Whyte, Shave, and Wilson (2003) investigated the interaction between changes in depression and other mood dimensions during intense endurance exercise among a sample of 10 highly trained cyclists who completed a 4 hour cycling task at a high intensity. Participants completed the BRUMS before performance, at hourly intervals and immediately post performance. Results indicated that a sharp increase in fatigue could lead to depressed mood. It is suggested that individual's feel depressed because of a perceived inability to cope with the demands of the task. Once depressed mood is activated, it is associated with a negative mood profile as suggested by Lane and Terry (2000).

LANE AND TERRY (2000) - CONCLUSIONS AND DEVELOPMENT OF A REVISED MODEL

When viewed collectively, studies testing Lane and Terry's model offer reasonable support for the central hypotheses. Thus, the model may represent a plausible theoretical explanation for the apparently contradictory findings highlighted in previous reviews of the mood-performance research. Secondly, the model provides testable hypotheses relevant to the POMS, a measure that despite much controversy is still widely used by researchers and applied sport psychologists.

Although the conceptual model has arguably advanced POMS-based research, Lane, Beedie et al. (2005) highlighted that the POMS assesses a limited range of mood states. The revised model is contained in Figure 4, which shows that two additional pleasant mood states (calmness and happiness) have been included with confusion being removed. The decision to revise the number of mood states was based on a number of reasons. Confusion was removed because it is more of a cognitive state than a mood. Indeed, the POMS is the only model of mood to include it as a mood state. Beedie (2005) argued that confusion was a manifestation of a mood disorder, rather than a mood state itself. Second, it is possible that a model based on the experience of athletes could resolve the narrow conceptualisation of mood offered by the POMS. Whilst part of our work has focused on reconciliation of the POMS research, a research project that ran alongside this work explored the nature of emotion using a grounded approach. This has led to the development of the Sport Emotion Questionnaire (SEQ), a psychometrically robust measure designed to assess pre-competition emotional states (see Jones, Lane, Bray, Uphill, and Catlin, 2005).

Jones et al. (2005) developed a sport-specific measure of pre-competitive emotion to assess anger, anxiety, dejection, excitement, and happiness. It is proposed that dejection shares many of the characteristics of depression but does not have clinical connotations. A recurring issue with reviews of Lane and Terry's model has been the question of whether depressed mood referred to a clinical condition. Even though the original paper and all model tests have indicated that it is a transient mood state rather than a clinical condition, conceptual confusion remains. Therefore, to avoid such superfluous commentary, Jones et al. used the less contentious term dejection. Their explanation of the nature of the concept largely mirrors descriptions of depressed mood forwarded by Lane and Terry (2000).

Jones et al. (2005) used sufficiently rigorous validation methods in the development of the SEQ and are comparable with those used by Terry et al. (1999, 2003). In stage one, 264 athletes completed an open-ended questionnaire to identify the emotions athletes experience in sport. In stage two, 148 athletes verified the item pool leading to the third stage in which confirmatory factor analysis of data from 518 athletes before competition indicated that a 22-item and five-factor structure provided acceptable model fit. It should be noted that cross-validation of the SEQ is desirable.

An interesting feature of the validation process is the relationship with BRUMS scores that were assessed concurrently. Results indicated high correlations for the two anger scales ($r = .94$, $p < .01$), anxiety and tension ($r = .93$, $p < .01$), dejection and depression ($r = .87$, $p < .01$), and excitement and vigour ($r = .85$, $p < .01$). Interestingly, correlations indicated a moderate relationship between happiness and vigour ($r = .69$, $p < .01$), suggesting that the two scales assess a slightly different aspect of pleasant mood, also indicating that happiness is a concept worth including on a mood measure. When the results are viewed collectively, it is argued that BRUMS and SEQ assess a great deal of common ground. The SEQ could replace the BRUMS, and given the starting point in terms of developing face validity among athletes, such a decision might be justifiable. However, in our research, we have modified the BRUMS to include a greater number of positive mood states, namely, happiness and calmness.

Thirdly, the decision to include a greater number of positive mood states stems from applied work in which mood state responses were followed among biathletes training at altitude (Lane, Whyte, Godfrey, and Pedlar, 2002, 2005). Given the proposed influence of depressed mood, special attention was given to its detection. Data for happiness and depression were extremely useful in detecting maladaptive training responses. What tended to occur is that athletes reported high scores on the happiness scale and simultaneously reported zero on the depressed mood scale. Although inversely related, symptoms of depression usually followed a period of scoring progressively lower on the happiness scale. It appeared that happiness offered an early indicator to depression symptoms.

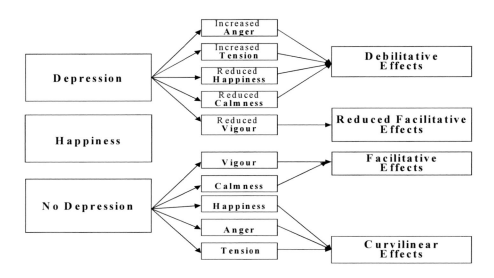

Figure 4. Revised conceptual model of mood-performance relationships

Calmness was included not only to increase the range of positive mood states but also as it could offer insight into the nature of tension and anger when experienced in the absence of depressed mood. It is argued that if athletes are using anger and tension to motivate behaviour, and are in control of these states, athletes should report feeling calm, angry and tense. Studies that have used happiness and calmness have used the UWIST (Matthews, Jones, and Chamberlain, 1990) and included them in the BRUMS. Lane and Jarrett (2004) reported acceptable internal consistency coefficients for the 4-item scales of Calmness (alpha = .84) and Happiness (alpha = .89).

The revised model focuses on the influence and interaction between pleasant mood states, unpleasant mood states and performance (see Figure 4). Happiness is proposed to show a curvilinear relationship with performance. It is argued that happiness is associated with the superficial processing of information, which can have negative performance effects (Sinclair and Mark, 1992). Happiness is also proposed to increase the accessibility of positive material in the memory and, according to Hirt, Melton, McDonald, and Harackiewics (1996), often leads to the recall of sufficient information to fill cognitive capacity, thereby debilitating performance through attentional overload. By contrast, happiness could be linked with high self-efficacy and therefore associated with enhanced performance through similar mechanisms. Therefore, it is argued that two additional hypotheses be included. The first is that happiness will show a curvilinear relationship with performance; the second is that calmness will show facilitative performance effects.

IDEA 2: EMOTIONAL INTELLIGENCE, MOOD STATES AND PERFORMANCE

The aim of the present study is to investigate relationships between emotional intelligence and mood states associated with successful performance in sport. The research will use quantitative techniques in which participant's complete emotional intelligence questionnaires and mood states to assess how they felt before competition and relate measures with performance. This study extends work by initiated Lane, Soos et al. (2005) and Lane, Thelwell et al. (2005). It is proposed that mood is assessed in real-time and that multiple measures of mood are taken from each individual in order to obtain individual mood-performance relationships.

IDEA 3: EMOTIONAL INTELLIGENCE, MOOD STATES AND TRAINING ADAPTATION

The quest to understand the reciprocal relationship between training and physiological and psychological responses to training is a key line of research in sport sciences. It is generally accepted that intervention strategies to bring about improved performance should be theory-driven and that athletic achievement is underpinned by training. Training should be progressive so that individual performance improves over time. The aim of this study would be to investigate the relationship with psychological and physiological variables and performance.

The POMS has been recommended as the instrument of choice to monitor psychological responses to training (Morgan, Brown, Raglin, O'Connor, and Ellickson, 1987). Research has shown that mood changes as a consequence of training intensity, whereby it is suggested that mood is a potential indicator of overtraining (Cox, Costill, Thomas, and Bate, 1994; Raglin, Morgan, and O'Connor, 1991; Raglin and Morgan, 2001). There has been an absence of theory to explain why mood should reflect changes in training load. Specifically, research has not investigated why each POMS dimension should change as a consequence of training intensity. The aim of this proposed study is to investigate relationships between emotional intelligence and mood states responses to repeated bouts of intense exercise.

CONCLUSIONS

In conclusion, mood and performance remains an intuitively interesting line of research, and it has been the subject of a plethora of studies. Theory-driven research that considers the nature of mood is likely to produce the most fruitful results. Emotional intelligence is a popular construct, and establishing links between mood states and emotional intelligence will be the focus of future research efforts.

REFERENCES

Bandura, A. (1990). Perceived self-efficacy in the exercise of personal agency. *Journal of Applied Sport Psychology, 2,* 128-163.

Beedie, C. J. (2005). If the POMS measures it, then it's a mood, isn't it...? Paper presented at the International Society of Sport Psychology conference, Sydney Australia, August 14-19, 2005.

Beedie, C. J., Terry, P. C., and Lane, A. M. (2000). The Profile of Mood States and athletic performance: Two meta-analyses. *Journal of Applied Sport Psychology, 12,* 49-68.

Beedie, C. J., Terry, P. C., and Lane, A. M. (2005). Distinguishing mood from emotion. *Cognition and Emotion, 19,* 847-878.

Bentler, P. M. (1995). *EQS Structural equation program manual.* Los Angeles; CA: BMDP Statistical software.

Bless, H. (2001). Mood and the use of general knowledge structures. In Martin, L. L., and Clore, G. L. (Eds.), *Theories of mood and cognition,* (pp 9-26). Mahwah, NJ: Lawrence Elbaum.

Bower, G. (1981). Mood and memory. *American Psychologist, 36,* 129-148.

Bower, G. H., Gilligan, S. J., and Monteiro, K. P. (1981). Selectivity of learning caused by affective states. *Journal of Experimental Psychology: General, 110,* 451-473.

Brehm, J. W. (1999). The intensity of emotion. *Personality and Social Psychology Review, 3,* 2-22.

Calmels, C., Berthoumieux, C., and d'Arripe-Longueville, F. (2004). Effects of an imagery training program on selective attention of national softball players. *The Sport Psychologist, 18,* 272-296.

Carron, A. V. Brawley, L. R., and Widmeyer, W. N. (1985). The development of an instrument to measure cohesion in sport teams: The Group Environment Questionnaire. *Journal of Sport Psychology, 7,* 244-266.

Carver, C. S., and Scheier, M. F. (1990). Origins and functions of positive and negative affect: A control process view. *Psychological Review, 97,* 19-35.

Chelladurai, P., and Selah, S. (1980). Dimensions of leader behaviour in sports: Development of a leadership scale. *Journal of Sport Psychology, 2,* 34-45.

Clore, G. L., Wyer, R. S., Dienes, B., Gasper, K., Gohm, C., and Isbell, L. (2001). In Martin, L. L., and Clore, G. L. (Eds.), *Theories of mood and cognition,* (pp 27-62). Mahwah, NJ: Lawrence Erlbaum.

Curren, S. L., Andrykowski, M. A., and Studts, J. L. (1995). Short form of the Profile of Mood States (POMS-SF): Psychometric information. *Psychological Assessment, 7,* 80-83.

Eisenberger, R.; Armeli, S., Rexwinkel, B., Lynch, P. D., and Rhoades, L. (2001). Reciprocation of perceived organizational support. *Journal of Applied Psychology, 86,* 2001, 42-51.

Erber, R., and Erber, W. M. (2001). Mood and processing: A view from a self-regulation perspective. In Martin, L. L., and Clore, G. L. (Eds.), *Theories of mood and cognition,* (pp 63-84). Mahwah, NJ: Lawrence Erlbaum.

Fazackerley, R., Lane, A.M., and Mahoney, C. (2004). Mood and performance relationships in wakeboarding. *Journal of Sport Behavior, 27,* 18-30.

Gendolla, G. H. E., and Krusken, J. (2002). The joint effect of informational mood impact and performance-contingent consequences on effort-related cardiovascular response. *Journal of Personality and Social Psychology, 83*, 271-283.

Grawitch, M. J., Munz, D. C., and Kramer, T. J. (2003). Effects of member mood states on creative performance in temporary workgroups. *Group Dynamics: Theory, Research, and Practice, 7*, 41-54.

Grove, J. R., and Prapavessis, H. (1992). Preliminary evidence for the reliability and validity of an abbreviated Profile of Mood States. *International Journal of Sport Psychology, 23*, 93-109.

Hall, A., and Terry, P.C. (1995). Predictive capability of pre-performance mood profiling at the 1993 World Rowing Championships, Roundnice, the Czech Republic [abstract]. *Journal of Sports Sciences, 13*, 56-57.

Hall, R., Lane, A.M., and Devonport, T.J. (2002). Relationships between mood and anxiety among runners: test of two conceptual models. *Journal of Sports Sciences, 20*, 63-64.

Hanin, Y. (2000). Successful and poor performance and emotions. In Y. Hanin (Ed.), *Emotions in sport* (pp. 157-189). Champaign, IL: Human Kinetics.

Hanin, Y. L. (1997). Emotions and athletic performance: Individual zones of optimal functioning model. *European yearbook of sport psychology, 1*, 29-72.

Hirt, E. R., Melton, R. J., McDonald, H. E., and Harackiewics, J. M. (1996). Processing goals, task interest, and the mood-performance relationship: A mediational analysis. *Journal of Personality and Social Psychology, 71*, 245-261.

Horn, T. S. (1992). *Advances in sport psychology*. (1st edition). Human Kinetics, Champaign, IL.

Hrycaiko, D.W., and Martin, G.L. (1996). Applied research studies with single subject designs: Why so few? *Journal of Applied Sport Psychology, 8*, 183-199.

Janover, M. A., and Terry, P. C. (2002). Relationships between pre-competition mood and swimming performance: Test of a conceptual model with an emphasis on depressed mood. *Australian Journal of Psychology, 54*, S46-47.

Johnson, J. J. M., Hrycaiko, D. W., Johnson, G. V., and Halas, J. M. (2004). Self-talk and female youth soccer performance. *The Sport Psychologist, 18*, 44-59.

Jones, M. V., Lane, A. M., Bray, S. R., Uphill, M., and Catlin, J. (2005). Development of the Sport Emotions Questionnaire. *Journal of Sport and Exercise Psychology, 27*, 407-431.

Kendall, P. C., and Hammen, C. (1995). *Abnormal psychology*. Boston, MA: Houghton Mifflin.

Lane, A. M. (1998). Mood and sport: conceptual, measurement and performance issues. A thesis submitted for a doctoral degree, Brunel University.

Lane, A. M. (2001). Relationships between perceptions of performance expectations and mood among distance runners; the moderating effect of depressed mood. *Journal of Science and Medicine in Sport, 4*, 235-249.

Lane, A. M. (2005). Mood and multi-stage shuttle run performance relationships. Paper presented at the International Society of Sport Psychology (ISSP) 11th World Congress of Sport Psychology, 15-19 August 2005, Sydney Convention and Exhibition Centre, Sydney, Australia.

Lane, A. M., and Karageorghis, C. I. (1997). Discriminant effectiveness of goal confidence and goal difficulty in predicting goal attainment in junior high school cross-country runners. *Perceptual and Motor Skills, 84*, 747-752.

Lane, A. M., and Levitt, P. (2002). The influence of depressed mood on other mood states and cohesion. *Journal of Sports Sciences, 20*, 67.

Lane, A. M., and Lovejoy, D. J. (2001). The effects of exercise on mood changes: The moderating effect of depressed mood. *Journal of Sports Medicine and Physical Fitness, 41*, 539-545.

Lane, A. M., and Lowther, J. P. (2005). Relationships between emotional intelligence and psychological skills among athletes. *Journal of Sports Sciences, 23*, 1253-1254.

Lane, A. M., and Terry, P. C. (1998). Prediction of athletic performance from mood: Test of a conceptual model. *The Psychologist*, p.109.

Lane, A. M., and Terry, P. C. (1999a). Mood states as predictors of performance: A test of a conceptual model. *Journal of Sports Sciences, 17*, 606.

Lane, A. M., and Terry, P. C. (1999b). The conceptual independence of tension and depression. *Journal of Sports Sciences, 17*, 605-606.

Lane, A. M., and Terry, P. C. (2000). The nature of mood: Development of a conceptual model with a focus on depression. *Journal of Applied Sport Psychology, 12*, 16-33.

Lane, A. M., and Terry, P. C. (2005). Test of a conceptual model of mood-performance relationships with a focus on depression: A review and synthesis five years on. Paper presented at the International Society of Sport Psychology (ISSP) 11th World Congress of Sport Psychology, 15-19 August 2005, Sydney Convention and Exhibition Centre, Sydney, Australia.

Lane, A. M., Beedie, C. J., and Stevens, M. J. (2005). Mood matters: A response to Mellalieu. *Journal of Applied Sport Psychology, 17*, 319-325.

Lane, A. M., Lane, H. J., and Firth, S. (2002). Relationships between performance satisfaction and post-competition mood among runners. *Perceptual and Motor Skills, 94*, 805-813.

Lane, A. M., Soos, I., Leibinger, E., Karsai, I., and Hamar, P. (2005). Emotional intelligence, mood states and successful and unsuccessful performance. *Journal of Sports Sciences, 23*, 1254.

Lane, A. M., Terry, P. C., Beedie, C. J., and Stevens, M. (2004). Mood and concentration grid performance: The moderating effect of depressed mood. *International Journal of Sport and Exercise Psychology, 2*, 133-145.

Lane, A. M., Terry, P. C., Beedie, C. J., Curry, D. A., and Clark, N. (2001). Mood and performance: Test of a conceptual model with a focus on depressed mood. *Psychology of Sport and Exercise, 2*, 157-172.

Lane, A. M., Terry, P. C., Karageorghis, C. I., and Lawson, J. (1999). Mood states as predictors of kickboxing performance: A test of a conceptual model [abstract]. *Journal of Sports Sciences, 17*, 61-62.

Lane, A. M., Thelwell, R., Weston, N., and Devonport, T. (2005). Emotional intelligence, mood states and performance. *Journal of Sports Sciences, 23*, 1254-1255.

Lane, A. M., Whyte, G. P., George, K., Shave, R., Barney, S., and Terry, P.C. (2004). Marathon: A fun run? An investigation of mood state changes among runners at the London Marathon. Paper presented at the annual conference for the British Psychological Society, Imperial College, London, April 15th-17th, 2004.

Lane, A. M., Whyte, G. P., Shave, R., and Wilson, M. (2003). Mood state responses during intense cycling. *Journal of Sports Sciences*, *21*, 352-353.

Lane, A. M., Whyte, G. P., Terry, P.C., and Nevill, A.M. (2005). Mood and examination performance. *Personality and Individual Differences, 39*, 143-153.

Lane, A. M., Whyte, G. P., Godfrey, R., and Pedlar, C. (2005). Relationships between mood and perceived exertion among elite biathletes at altitude. Paper presented at the International Society of Sport Psychology (ISSP) 11th World Congress of Sport Psychology, 15-19 August 2005, Sydney Convention and Exhibition Centre, Sydney, Australia.

Lane, A. M., Whyte, G. P., Godfrey, R., and Pedlar, C. (2003). Adaptations of psychological state variables to altitude among the Great Britain biathlon team preparing for the 2002 Olympic Games. *Journal of Sports Sciences, 21*, 281-282.

Lazarus, R.S. (2000). How emotions influence performance in competitive sports. *The Sport Psychologist, 14,* 229-252.

Lee, K., and Allen, N. J. (2002). Organizational citizenship behavior and workplace deviance: The role of affect and cognitions. *Journal of Applied Psychology, 87*, 131-142.

LeUnes, A. (2000). Updated bibliography on the Profile of Mood States in sport and exercise psychology research. *Journal of Applied Sport Psychology, 12,* 110-113.

LeUnes, A., and Burger, J. (1998). Bibliography on the Profile of Mood States in sport and exercise, 1971-1995. *Journal of Sport Behavior, 21,* 53-70.

Martens, R. S. Vealey, and D. Burton (Eds.), *Competitive anxiety in sport.* (pp. 117-178). Champaign, IL: Human Kinetics.

Martin, G., and Pear, J. (2003). *Behavior modification: What it is and how to do it (7th ed.).* Englewood Cliffs, NJ: Prentice-Hall.

Martin, J. J., and Gill, D. L. (1991). The relationships among competitive sport orientation, sport-confidence, self-efficacy, anxiety, and performance. *Journal of Sport and Exercise Psychology, 13*, 149-159.

Martin, J. J., and Gill, D. L. (1995). The relationships among competitive orientations and self-efficacy to goal importance, thoughts, and performance in high school distance runners. *Journal of Applied Sport Psychology, 7,* 50-62.

Martin, L. L. (2001). Mood as input: A configural view of mood effects. In Martin, L. L., and Clore, G. L. (Eds.), *Theories of mood and cognition*, (pp 135-158). Mahwah, NJ: Lawrence Erlbaum.

Martin, L. L., and Tesser, A. (1996). Some ruminative thoughts. In R.S. Wyer (Ed.), *The handbook of social cognition* (Vol. 9, pp. 1-48). Mahwah, NJ: Lawrence Erlbaum.

Matthews, G., Jones, D. M., and Chamberlain, A. G. (1990). Refining the measurement of mood: The UWIST Mood Adjective Checklist. *British Journal of Psychology, 81,* 17-42.

Mayer, J. D. and Salovey, P. (1997). What is emotional intelligence? In P. Salovey and D. Sluyter (Eds). *Emotional Development and Emotional Intelligence: Implications for Educators* (pp. 3-31). New York: Basic Books. Retrieved July 29, 2005, from *http://www.unh.edu/emotional_intelligence/EIreprints1.htm*

McNair, D. M., Lorr, M., and Droppelman, L. F. (1971). *Manual for the Profile of Mood States.* San Diego, CA: Educational and Industrial Testing Services.

McNair, D. M., Lorr, M., and Droppelman, L. F. (1992). *Revised Manual for the Profile of Mood States.* San Diego, CA: Educational and Industrial Testing Services.

Meyer, B. B., and Zizzi, S. (2007). Emotional intelligence in sport: Conceptual, methodological, and applied issues. In A. M. Lane (ed.), *Mood and human performance: Conceptual, measurement, and applied issues* (pp. 131-154). Hauppauge, NY: Nova Science.

Morgan, W. P. (1980). Test of champions: The iceberg profile. *Psychology Today, 14*, 92-108.

Morgan, W. P., and Johnson, R. W. (1978). Personality characteristics of successful and unsuccessful oarsmen. *International Journal of Sport Psychology, 9,* 119-133.

Muraven, M., Tice, D. M., and Baumeister, R. F. (1998). Self-control as a limited resource: Regulatory depletion patterns. *Journal of Personality and Social Psychology, 74*, 774-789.

Owens, A.J.N., Lane, A.M., and Terry, P.C. (2000). Mood states as predictors of tennis performance: A test of a conceptual model. *Journal of Sports Sciences, 18,* 55-56.

Parkinson, B., Totterdell, P., Briner, R. B., and Reynolds, S. (1996). *Changing moods: The psychology of mood and mood regulation.* London: Longman.

Ramsbottom, R., Brewer, B., and Williams, C. (1988). A progressive shuttle run test to estimate maximal oxygen uptake. *British Journal of Sports Medicine,* 22: 141-144.

Renger, R. (1993). A review of the Profile of Mood States (POMS). in the prediction of athletic success. *Journal of Applied Sport Psychology, 5,* 78-84.

Rokke, P. D. (1993). Social context and perceived task difficulty as mediators of depressive self-evaluation. *Emotion and Motivation, 17,* 23-40.

Rowley, A. J., Landers, D. M., Kyllo, L. B., and Etnier, J. L. (1995). Does the iceberg profile discriminate between successful and less successful athletes? A meta-analysis. *Journal of Sport and Exercise Psychology, 16,* 185-199.

Russell, J. A. (1980). A circumplex model of affect. *Journal of Personality and Social Psychology, 39,* 1161-1178.

Russell, J. A., and Feldman Barrett, L. (1999). Core affect, prototypical emotional episodes, and other things called emotion: Dissecting the elephant. *Journal of Personality and Social Psychology, 76,* 805-819.

Schwarz, N. (1990). Feelings as information: Informational and motivational functions of affective states. In Sorrentino, R. M., and Higgins, E. T. (Eds.), *Handbook of motivation and cognition: Foundations of social behavior* (Vol. 2, pp. 527-561). New York: Guildford.

Schwarz, N. (2001). Feelings as information: Implications for affective influences on information processing. In Martin, L. L., and Clore, G. L. (Eds.), *Theories of mood and cognition,* (pp 159-176). Mahwah, NJ: Lawrence Erlbaum.

Schwarz, N., and Bless, H. (1991). Happy and mindless, but sad and smart? The impact of affective states on analytic reasoning. In Forgas, P. (Ed.), *Emotion and social judgement* (pp. 55-71). Oxford: Pergamon.

Schwarz, N., and Bless, H. (1991). Happy and mindless, but sad and smart? The impact of affective states on analytic reasoning. In P. Forgas (Ed.), *Emotion and social judgement* (pp. 55-71). Oxford: Pergamon.

Shacham, S. (1983). A shortened version of the Profile of Mood States. *Journal of Personality Assessment, 47,* 305-306.

Sinclair, R. C., and Mark, M. M. (1992). The influence of mood state on judgement and action: Effects on persuasion, categorisation, social justice, person perception, and judgmental accuracy. In L. L. Martin and A. Tesser (Eds.), *The construction of social judgement,* (pp. 165-193). Hillsdale, NJ: Erlbaum.

Spielberger, C. D. (1991). *Manual for the State-Trait Anger Expression Inventory.* Odessa, FL: Psychological Assessment Resources.

Stevens, M. J. (2007). A Transactional Model of Mood. In A. M. Lane (ed.), *Mood and human performance: Conceptual, measurement, and applied issues* (pp. 89-118). Hauppauge, NY: Nova Science.

Terry, P. C. (1993). Mood state profile as indicators of performance among Olympic and World Championship athletes. In S. Serpa, J. Alves, V. Ferreira, and A. Paulo-Brito (Eds.). *Proceedings of the VIIIth ISSP World Congress of Sport Psychology* (pp. 963-967). Lisbon: ISSP.

Terry, P. C. (1995). The efficacy of mood state profiling with elite performers. A review and synthesis. *The Sport Psychologist, 9,* 309-324.

Terry, P. C., and Slade, A. (1995). Discriminant capability of psychological state measures in predicting performance outcome in karate competition. *Perceptual and Motor Skills, 81,* 275-286.

Terry, P. C., Keohane, L., and Lane, H. J. (1996). Development and validation of a shortened version of the profile of mood states suitable for use with young athletes. *Journal of Sports Sciences, 14,* 49.

Terry, P. C., Lane, A. M., and Beedie, C. J. (2005). The Iceberg has melted: Theoretical, measurement and applied developments in the area of mood and physical activity. International Society of Sport Psychology (ISSP). 11th World Congress of Sport Psychology, 15-19 August 2005, Sydney Convention and Exhibition Centre, Sydney, Australia.

Terry, P. C., Lane, A. M., and Fogarty, G. (2003). Construct validity of the Profile of Mood States-A for use with adults. *Psychology of Sport and Exercise, 4,* 82-96.

Terry, P. C., Lane, A. M., Lane, H. J., and Keohane, L. (1999). Development and validation of a mood measure for adolescents. *Journal of Sports Sciences, 17,* 861-872.

Terry, P. C., Stevens, M. J., and Lane, A. M. (2005). Influence of response time frame on mood assessment. *Stress Anxiety and Coping, 18,* 279-285.

Thelwell, R.C., and Maynard, I.W. (2003). The effects of a mental skills package on 'repeatable good performance' in cricketers. *Psychology of Sport and Exercise, 4,* 377-396.

Totterdell, P., and Leach, D. (2001). Negative mood regulation expectancies and sports performance: An investigation involving professional cricketers. *Psychology of Sport and Exercise, 2,* 249-265.

Watson, D., and Clark, L. A. (1997). Measurement and mismeasurement of mood: Recurrent and emergent issues. *Journal of Personality Assessment, 68,* 267-296.

Watson, D., and Tellegen, A. (1985). Toward a conceptual structure of mood. *Psychological Bulletin, 98,* 219-235.

Weinberg, R. S., and Gould, D. (1995). *Foundations of sport and exercise psychology (1st edition)*. Champaign, IL: Human Kinetics.

Wicklund, R. A. (1979). The influence of self-awareness on human behavior. *American Scientist, 67,* 187-193.

Zeidner, M., Matthews, G., and Roberts, R. D (2004). Emotional intelligence in the workplace: A critical review. *Applied Psychology: An International Review, 53,* 371–399.

Zigmund, A.S., and Snaith, R.P. (1983). The Hospital and Depression Scale. *Acta Psychiatrica Scandinavia, 67,* 361-370.

In: Mood and Human Performance: Conceptual, Measurement...   ISBN 1-60021-269-7
Editor: Andrew M. Lane, pp. 35-61   © 2006 Nova Science Publishers, Inc.

Chapter 2

MOOD, MOTIVATION, AND PERFORMANCE: AN INTEGRATIVE THEORY, RESEARCH, AND APPLICATIONS

Guido H. E. Gendolla, Kerstin Brinkmann and Michael Richter*
University of Geneva, Switzerland

ABSTRACT

An integrative theory about mood and motivation—the mood-behavior-model (MBM) (Gendolla, 2000)—is presented and the results of related studies on mood and motivational intensity are discussed. A series of experiments with implications for motivation in organizational and educational settings assessed motivational intensity as cardiovascular reactivity in the context of task performance. The results support the theoretical predictions and demonstrate that (1) moods do not per se have an effort mobilizing function, (2) moods are pragmatically used as information for demand appraisals, (3) mood congruent demand appraisals determine effort-related cardiovascular response, (4) performance-contingent incentive determines the level of maximally justified effort, (5) effort is linked to achievement. The findings specify and extend other approaches to the role of affect in motivation and have direct implications for clinical psychology, work psychology, and health psychology.

Key Words: Mood, Motivation, Task Engagement, Cardiovascular Reactivity.

Individuals' affective experiences are a central variable in the person system mediating between external stimuli and people's behavioral reactions (Mischel and Shoda, 1995). This applies, of course, also to organizational and educational settings: On the one hand, work settings directly influence the moods and emotions people experience (Kelly and Barsade,

---
*Mailing Address: Guido H.E. Gendolla, University of Geneva, Department of Psychology, 40, Bd. du Pont d'Arve CH-1211 Geneva 4, Switzerland, Email: guido.gendolla@pse.unige.ch. This research was supported by the German (DFG Ge 987/1-1, Ge 987/7-1) and the Swiss National Science Foundations (SNF 100011-108144/1).

2001). On the other hand, moods and emotions have multiple effects on performance and organizational behavior (see Baron, 1993; Forgas and George, 2001; George and Brief, 1992; Isen and Baron, 1991 for reviews). Furthermore, moods' motivational effects can play significant roles in psychological problems and the development of physical disease (Gendolla and Brinkmann, 2005; Gendolla and Richter, 2005-a).

In the last decade, an abundance of research has identified manifold influences of affective states on motivation and task performance. Although most of this research was not conducted in applied settings, there are numerous insights of direct relevance for work motivation. In an attempt to contribute to this understanding, the present chapter focuses on one special type of affective experience—*mood states*—and on one special aspect of motivation—*motivational intensity*, which corresponds to *effort* mobilization or task *engagement*. After presenting an integrative theoretical framework about mood and motivation, we will discuss research on mood and motivational intensity. Finally, we will outline implications for applied issues, such as work motivation, clinical psychology, and health psychology.

AFFECT AND MOTIVATION

Emotions have the motivational function to guide behavior. Specific emotions, such as anger, fear, or interest control goal priorities and involve action tendencies, such as anger-aggression, fear-flight, or interest-exploration. Thus, emotions facilitate a fast and effective adaptation of the organism to the environment (see Frijda, 1986; Scherer, 2001; Smith and Lazarus, 1990). Emotions' motivational function becomes, for instance, visible in their effects on autonomic nervous system activity (see Cacioppo, Berntson, Larsen, Poehlmann, and Ito, 2000 for a review). Autonomic adjustments as a component of specific emotions reflect the fast and short-lived mobilization of body resources to prepare the organism for action.

The motivational implications of moods are less clear than those of emotions. Moods are defined as relatively long lasting affective states that are experienced without concurrent awareness of their elicitors. That is, moods are "feeling states themselves" (Clore, Schwarz, and Conway, 1994; Frijda, 1993; Wyer, Clore, and Isbell, 1999). While individuals typically know the incidents and stimuli that elicit specific and short-lived emotions (e.g., happy or sad about...) they are usually not aware of the origins of their moods (e.g., feeling good, or bad) (e.g., Wilson, Laser, and Stone, 1982). Given that moods have been conceptualized as always-present frames of mind (Morris, 1989), it appears likely that they should also influence motivation and performance. A recent integrative theory about the role of mood in the motivation process aims to explain how this takes place.

THE MOOD-BEHAVIOR-MODEL (MBM)

According to the *mood-behavior-model* (MBM) (Gendolla, 2000), transient mood states can have highly context dependent, though predictable, effects on behavior (Richter, Gendolla, and Krüsken, 2006). Unlike specific emotions, moods per se do neither have stable effects on *goal priorities* nor on the *intensity* or *persistence* of behavior—the three aspects of behavior that are determined in the motivation process (Geen, 1995). Moods can, however, influence motivation and behavior through two processes—*directive* and *informational* mood impacts. The strength of each process depends on variables that refer to the context in which moods are experienced, as summarized in five basic postulates presented in Figure 1.

The *Mood-Behavior-Model* (MBM)

(1) *Moods have—in contrast to emotions—no stable or specific motivational implications or function.* Moods are experienced without simultaneous awareness of their causes. Consequently, moods do not urge the organism to act in a specific way toward objects or incidents that elicited the moods.

(2) *Moods influence behavior by their informational and directive impacts.* The informational impact refers to congruency effects on behavior-related judgments and appraisals. The directive mood impact refers to the pursuit of a hedonic motive, and thus behavioral preferences are affected.

(3) *The informational and directive mood impacts can influence behavior independently.* Either of these impacts is sufficient to mediate mood states to behavior, but both can occur simultaneously as well. In addition, both mood impacts can be so weak that neither has a significant influence.

(4) *The strength of the informational mood impact is a function of the effective informational weight of mood and the extent of mood-primed associations.* Mood is particularly diagnostic for evaluative judgments, and mood-primed associations are especially likely to be activated in specific mood states, when moods are residuals of specific emotions.

(5) *The strength of the directive mood impact is jointly determined by the strength of the hedonic motive and the magnitude of behaviors' instrumentality for motive satisfaction.* The strength of the hedonic motive is, in turn, determined by mood intensity, mood salience, and situational context. The magnitude of behaviors' instrumentality for motive satisfaction is determined by the hedonic tone of behavior itself, the hedonic tone of behavioral outcomes, and mood valence.

Figure 1. The five basic postulates of the mood-behavior-model (MBM) (Gendolla, 2000)

Directive Mood Impact

The *directive mood impact* influences the *direction* of behavior in compliance with a *hedonic motive* and turns out in preferences for affect regulative behaviors. However, if and how strongly the directive mood impact works depends on context variables: The MBM predicts that the strength of a person's *hedonic motive*—i.e., the need to feel good—increases with both *mood intensity* and *mood salience* and that it decreases with *situational circumstances* that prohibit pleasant feelings (like visiting a funeral). Only if the hedonic motive is strong, a person will prefer behaviors that are *instrumental* for hedonic affect regulation in that they promise positive feelings as a result of pleasant associations of a behavior itself (i.e., intrinsic pleasure) or pleasant consequences of behaviors in terms of hedonic reward (i.e., extrinsic pleasure).

The directive mood impact on behavior is particularly visible in decision-making—a major aspect of human behavior and organizational work. Besides having an influence on judgments of expectancy and value in the decision process (Isen, 2000), moods can also influence behavioral decisions because these are often oriented to their hedonic consequences (e.g., Damasio, 1994; Loewenstein, 1996). Referring to the role of mood valence (i.e., feeling good or bad) in the latter process, the actual state of research is not conclusive. On the one hand, there is evidence for the assumption that negative mood is particularly powerful in instigating affect regulative behaviors in terms of mood repair (e.g., Schaller and Cialdini, 1990). On the other hand, positive mood is a major trigger of affect regulation in terms of mood maintenance (e.g., Wegener and Petty, 1994). This equivocal evidence suggests that mood valence cannot be the critical variable that strengthens a person's hedonic motive. Rather, the MBM postulates that mood intensity is the crucial variable that triggers the interest in mood repair or mood maintenance. Thus, both intense negative and positive moods lead to preferences for behaviors that promise positive affective experiences (e.g., Handley and Lassiter, 2002). Consequently, the MBM predicts that especially people in an *intense* mood—either negative *or* positive—who are *aware* of their current feeling state (e.g., McFarland and Buehler, 1998), are highly interested in hedonic affect regulation in terms of mood repair and mood maintenance when the experience of well-being is not forbidden in the person's actual *context*.

An example for the directive mood impact on behavior may be a manager who needs to make some investment decisions at the stock market. If this person is in an intense negative or positive mood, the MBM suggests that he or she will experience a strong hedonic motive and thus prefer stock options that promise fast and high gains and thus positive affective experiences. In a less intense mood, the manager should experience a weaker hedonic motive. Thus, he or she should be less interested in stock market operations that seem to promise fast and high gain and consequently positive affect. Likewise, a personnel manager in an intense good or bad mood who has to choose among applicants for opened positions may orient his decisions on applicants' charm and the pleasantness of their physical appearance rather than on their mere qualification. However, the MBM also predicts that the strength of this manager's hedonic motive would be significantly lower if it is clearly inappropriate to feel good in the organizational setting. Under this condition, decisions should be less influenced by concerns of hedonic affect regulation (see Parrott, 1993).

Informational Mood Impact

The *informational mood impact* influences behavior-related judgments and appraisals and takes effect on the *persistence* and the *intensity* of behavior. Informational mood impact refers to the answers people find when they ask themselves implicit questions once they are confronted with a demand. Examples are "Can I cope with this demand?", "Have I already achieved enough?", "How much effort do I have to mobilize?", or "How difficult is the task?". The MBM posits that moods can influence these appraisals in terms of mood congruency effects (e.g., Erez and Isen, 2002; Kavanagh and Bower, 1985; Lane, Whyte, Terry, and Nevill, 2005; Wright and Mischel, 1982). The result is that people are more optimistic in a positive mood than in negative mood (e.g., Efklides and Petkaki, 2005).

Imagine a person who comes to work in a bad mood. Imagine further this person has a desk full of work, which he or she needs to complete as soon as possible. According to the MBM, the person's mood will not have much visible impact on behavioral *decisions*, like preferences for pleasant activities. Sufficient commitment provided, there are actually not many choice options regarding what to do today. Consequently, the directive mood impact is rather weak. But the MBM posits that the employee's mood state will have a systematic influence on his or her *performance*. At least, the mood state will influence work persistence in that it can determine the point in the work process at which the employee will believe that enough is done. According to studies by Martin, Ward, Achee, and Wyer (1993), this point is reached later in a bad mood than in a good mood, because negative mood can signal a lack of approach to the working goal. And the mood state will influence how vigorously the work is done—as will be shown in more detail below. The MBM suggests that these mood effects on *persistence* and *engagement* occur because people will use their momentary mood state as information for evaluating if enough has been accomplished or how much engagement is necessary to complete the work.

In more detailed terms, the MBM posits that informational mood impact on persistence and effort mobilization occurs because people use their mood as a piece of information and integrate it with all other available information into an evaluative judgment (e.g., Abele and Gendolla, 1999; Abele and Petzold, 1994). In the present context evaluative *behavior-related* judgments are critical. The result is that people who face a challenge judge task difficulty, subjective ability, required effort, and the likelihood of success lower in a negative mood than in a positive mood, resulting in lower subjective demand in a positive mood than in a negative mood (e.g., Gendolla, Abele and Krüsken, 2001). The MBM also considers that moods may activate associations, like remembering pleasant events in a good mood and unpleasant events in a bad mood. These associations can also contribute to mood congruency effects, because people are expected to use all available information for making judgments. However, such "mood as priming" effects are only predicted for mood states that are residuals of specific emotions (Niedenthal, Halberstadt, and Setterlund, 1997). But concerning evaluative judgments, like demand appraisals, the effective weight of mood as a piece of diagnostic information is higher than that of remembered events. We agree with Clore et al. (1994) in that mood congruency effects on *evaluative judgments* are the most reliable and best replicated finding in affect-cognition research, because the valence of an experienced mood provides direct information for answering an evaluative question.[1]

It is of note that the MBM differs from other accounts of mood-cognition linkages, like, for example, the affect-infusion-model (AIM) (Forgas, 1995). The AIM posits that mood is either used as diagnostic information (heuristic processing) *or* makes memory associations accessible (substantial processing). By contrast, the MBM does not make processing style assumptions and predicts that mood is always more or less informative for evaluative judgments and that it can activate knowledge when mood is the residual of a specific emotion. As we have shown in the studies to be discussed below, the extent of engagement in information processing (processing style, respectively) is an *effect* rather than a *determinant* of informational mood impact. Other differences between the MBM and leading approaches

---

[1] It is of course also possible that moods activate memories for emotional events that in turn elicit mood states. But even in this case, the resulting mood state rather than the memory itself is used as a piece of information for an evaluative judgment.

concerning the role of mood in information processing and behavior are discussed elsewhere (Gendolla, 2000).

MOOD AND MOTIVATIONAL INTENSITY

According to the MBM, moods can influence motivational intensity through the following process: Moods provide information for demand appraisals. Consequently, the extent of subjective demand is higher in a negative mood than in a positive mood when people are confronted with a challenge. Moods can then systematically influence effort intensity, because subjective demand directly determines engagement as long as it is possible and worthwhile to perform a task (Brehm and Self, 1989). However, given that moods themselves are not conceptualized as motivational states, it is of note that these mood effects should *not* occur before moods are experienced in a context that directly calls for effort. Thus, moods should only influence the mobilization of effort when people are confronted with a challenge and make the necessary appraisals of its extent of demand. In this context, people can use their moods as information for demand appraisals, which in turn determine the level of engagement. Furthermore, the MBM predicts that moods are only one piece of information people use for appraising task demand. When more information about the extent of demand is provided—e.g., in terms of a given performance standard—people use and integrate it simultaneously into the final judgment.

The deeper reason for this "pragmatic" use of all available diagnostic information to evaluate the level of subjective demand is the effort conservation principle (Ach, 1935; Hull, 1943; Tolman, 1932). That is, people try to avoid wasting resources. Therefore, they try to mobilize only as much effort as necessary for goal attainment (Brehm and Self, 1989) and try to use all available diagnostic information for demand appraisals.

Measuring Engagement

The psychological literature is full of attempts to measure motivational intensity or effort mobilization. Examples are self-reports, persistence, or achievement. Unfortunately, each of these measures is ambiguous and thus problematic as motivational intensity index (see Gendolla, 2004, for a discussion). A pioneering research program of psychophysiologist Paul Obrist has offered an alternative way to assess motivational intensity in terms of *cardiovascular reactivity* in the performance context (e.g., Obrist, 1981). Accordingly, the changes in the activity of the heart and the vasculature in the performance context can reliably reflect task engagement. It is of note that these cardiovascular changes are independent of metabolic demand and thus apply to both physical and cognitive tasks. Among the possible indices of cardiovascular arousal one index—systolic blood pressure (SBP), i.e., the pressure in the vasculature on the peak of a pulse wave—is especially responsive to the extent of task demand (see Gendolla, 2004; Gendolla and Wright, 2005; Obrist, 1981; Wright, 1996; Wright and Franklin, 2004; Wright and Kirby, 2001, for overviews). Other indices, like diastolic blood pressure (DBP) (e.g., Storey, Wright, and Williams, 1996) and heart rate (HR) (e.g., Gellatly and Meyer, 1992) are less sensitive.[2]

EMPIRICAL EVIDENCE

A number of experimental studies in our laboratory have investigated the impact of mood states on motivational intensity quantified as cardiovascular response. Specifically, these studies examined engagement under three performance conditions that are of direct relevance for work motivation: These are performance settings without clear performance standards, performance settings with a clear performance standard, and settings in which reward is contingent vs. non-contingent upon performance.

Typically, an experiment in this program of research consisted of three parts: (1) A habituation period to assess participants' cardiovascular baseline values, (2) a mood manipulation in which positive vs. negative moods were induced, and (3) a task performance period with one of the three performance settings mentioned above. In the performance period, participants worked on a cognitive task. That is, performance was mentally, rather than metabolically demanding, and thus reflected the mobilization of mental effort (see Hockey, 1997). Cardiovascular indices were assessed during habituation, the mood inductions, and task performance. According to the psychophysiological understanding about the determination of cardiovascular reactivity during task performance, our primary effort-related measure has been SBP reactivity relative to the baseline values assessed during habituation (see Obrist, 1981; Wright, 1996).

Tasks without Performance Standard

The MBM posits for tasks that are performed without a clear performance standard that people will use their moods as task-relevant information to evaluate the extent of demand and that the magnitude of subjective demand will in turn determine engagement, because the demand-effort relationship is proportional (Ach, 1935, Brehm and Self, 1989). Given that moods usually produce congruency effects when people use them as diagnostic information for evaluative judgments, like demand appraisals, the predicted result is higher engagement in a negative mood than in a positive mood—as long as the diagnostic value of mood is not called into question.

---

[2] SBP is the pressure in the vasculature on the peak of a pulse wave. It depends on the contractility of the heart muscle, which is systematically related to β-adrenergic sympathetic discharge to the heart and the flow resistance in the vasculature (Brownley, Hurwitz, and Schneiderman, 2000). DBP describes the pressure between two pulse waves. It depends on vascular resistance, which is unsystematically related by sympathetic arousal—sympathetic arousal leads to dilatation of vascular beds and to vasoconstrictions in others. HR is independently affected by both sympathetic and parasympathetic arousal and should only respond to effort mobilization when the actual sympathetic impact is stronger (Berntson, Cacioppo, and Quigley, 1993; Obrist, 1981). Consequently, SBP is the most reliable measure of effort mobilization among these cardiovascular indices. SBP, DBP, and HR can, however, also respond simultaneously during task performance (e.g., Bongard and Hodapp, 1997; Gendolla and Richter, 2005-b; Lovallo et al., 1985; Smith, Allred, Morrison, and Carlson, 1989).

Gendolla and Krüsken (2002-a) tested these predictions in an experiment. After habituation and assessment of cardiovascular baseline values, participants watched depressing vs. elating video excerpts to induce positive vs. negative moods. After completion of filler questions and a mood manipulation check, participants received instructions for a learning task. The task was to correctly memorize in five minutes as many items of a list of 20 letter series (e.g., Q P T Z) as they could and to write them down afterwards ("do-your-best"). In addition to mood, the diagnostic value of mood as task-relevant information was manipulated. Therefore, half the participants read a short note under the task instructions that provided a cue for the mood manipulation: In the "cue" conditions participants read that previous research would suggest that the video excerpts they had seen may have long lasting effects on people's feeling states. This hint to the possibility that the moods may have been manipulated was expected to reduce the diagnostic weight participants assigned to their feelings as task-relevant information. Consequently, no significant mood effect on task engagement was anticipated in the cue condition. The other half of the participants performed in a "no-cue" condition. Here, nothing was mentioned with regard to the previously presented video excerpts. Thus, participants in this condition were expected to use their moods as diagnostic information for their demand appraisals and to mobilize more effort in a negative mood than in a positive mood.

The results were as expected. Mood had no effects on the cardiovascular responses assessed during the mood inductions, although the mood inductions were highly effective according to the manipulation check. However, in all experimental conditions the cardiovascular values remained on the baseline levels during the film presentations, supporting the MBM notion that moods do not per se mobilize effort. But the reactivity of SBP during performance on the learning task—i.e., when mood was experienced in a setting that directly called for effort mobilization—exactly described the predicted pattern. As depicted in Figure 2, SBP increased significantly higher in a negative mood than in a positive mood when no cue for the mood manipulation was provided. In further support of the predictions, this mood effect diminished in the cue-condition.

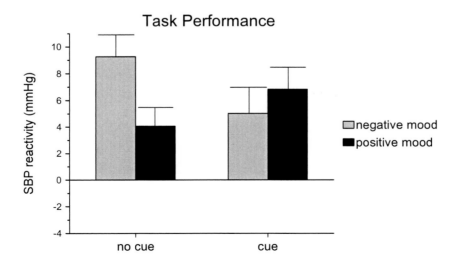

Figure 2. Systolic blood pressure (SBP) reactivity in the experiment by Gendolla and Krüsken (2002-a). Copyright: American Psychological Association

Achievement effects corresponded to those of systolic reactivity during task performance. As presented in Table 1, participants in the no-cue condition memorized significantly more items in a negative mood than in a positive mood. By contrast, no reliable mood effect emerged in the cue condition. Thus, achievement effects resembled those of effort intensity and the relatively high engagement in the negative-mood/no-cue condition had the merit of better performance. This association between effort and achievement was also visible in a significant, positive correlation between SBP reactivity during task performance and the total number of remembered letter series.

Table 1. Mean number of recalled letter series in Study 1 by Gendolla and Krüsken (2002-a)

	Negative Mood	Positive Mood
No-cue	8.65	6.71
Cue	6.65	8.12

Note: $n = 17$ in each cell.

A follow-up experiment administered a letter cancellation task for the performance period and replicated the effort-related findings of the first study. Additionally, the follow-up study involved a second mood manipulation check after task performance and found that the cue manipulation had no effect on mood intensity—mood remained stable in all experimental conditions. This is an important finding, because it makes an alternative explanation implausible, according to which the mood zero-effect in the cue-condition emerged because the cue manipulation neutralized participants' moods. Furthermore, the follow-up experiment found a mood congruency effect on ratings of subjective task difficulty in the no-cue condition, but not in the cue condition. This finding further demonstrates that mood influenced task engagement because it had a congruency effect on demand appraisals.

In summary, the studies by Gendolla and Krüsken (2002-a) have demonstrated that moods per se have no effects on effort mobilization, but that they lead to higher engagement in a negative mood than in a positive mood when people use their moods as diagnostic information for demand appraisals. The results of further studies on the effects of mood under performance conditions without performance standards even allow generalizing these findings. Experiments that used different mood induction techniques (music, autobiographical recollection, video excerpts) and different types of mental demand revealed identical results: In line with the predictions, effort-related SBP reactivity was stronger in a negative mood than in a positive mood during performance on a letter cancellation task (Gendolla et al., 2001; Gendolla and Krüsken, 2002-b, Study 2) or a verbal creativity task that was additionally manipulated in terms of task valence (Gendolla and Krüsken, 2001-a). Thus, the informational mood impact on task engagement as conceptualized in the MBM is a robust effect.

Tasks with Performance Standards

In order to predict mood effects on motivational intensity when a performance standard is provided it is necessary to note that the MBM posits that people use their moods as task-relevant information in a *pragmatic way*. As outlined earlier, this means that people use all available diagnostic information to evaluate the level of task demand that in turn determines effort intensity due to the conversation of resources principle. Thus, mood is one piece of diagnostic information that is integrated, according to Anderson's (1981) averaging rule, into a judgment together with all other available information (Abele and Gendolla, 1999; Abele et al., 1998; Abele and Petzold, 1994). It follows that people in a positive or negative mood who are confronted with a task and receive information about a performance standard should consider *both* of the available diagnostic pieces of information—their mood state and the performance standard—to appraise the extent of demand. The resulting actual engagement is predictable through an application of the MBM reasoning on informational mood impact to Brehm's motivational intensity theory (e.g., Brehm and Self, 1989), as illustrated in Figure 3.

Panel A of Figure 3 shows the general relationship between task difficulty and effort intensity. Effort is mobilized proportionally to the magnitude of subjective task difficulty up to the level of maximally justified effort. Once this point is accomplished no more effort will be mobilized. The same happens on task difficulty levels that clearly exceed a person's ability, making success impossible. Panel B of Figure 3 shows the informational impact of mood in this process: (1) Individuals in a negative mood will mobilize more effort than individuals in a positive mood when the task is easy. This is because subjective task demand is higher in a negative mood than in a positive mood. (2) If a task is difficult, individuals in a negative mood will mobilize only little effort, because they already perceive task demand as too high for them, resulting in disengagement. Individuals in a positive mood will, by contrast, mobilize high effort, because they perceive task demand as high, but not yet too high. (3) If a task is extremely difficult so that success is obviously impossible, mood will play no significant role and only little effort reflecting disengagement will be mobilized. This is predicted because the diagnostic weight of the information that task difficulty is extreme is so high that the effective weight of mood as a piece of diagnostic information becomes very low, according to the mood-and-information-integration perspective applied to the MBM.

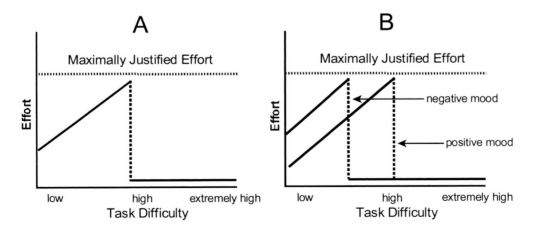

Figure 3. The relationship between subjective task difficulty and effort intensity (Panel A) and the role of mood in this process (Panel B). Figure adapted from Gendolla and Krüsken (2001-a). Copyright: Society for Psychophysiologic Research

An experiment by Gendolla and Krüsken (2001-b) tested these predictions. After habituation and assessment of cardiovascular baseline values, we induced positive vs. negative moods by exposing participants to either elating or depressing music. After a short distraction task and assessment of the mood manipulation check participants received instructions for a letter cancellation task—the so called "d2 task" (Brickenkamp, 1981). The task materials consisted of rows with random sequences of the letters *d, p,* and *q*. Placed above or below each letter were one, two, or no apostrophes. Participants received instructions to mark all *d*s that carried two apostrophes (e.g., d'', d,,). To get an impression of the task, participants performed one practice line of 47 letters. Thereafter, all participants received the feedback that they had needed 25 seconds to complete the line (which was about the actual performance time). For the upcoming five minute performance period half of the participants were then informed that they would have to complete each line within 20 seconds (difficult condition), while the other half was told that they would have 30 seconds per line (easy condition). That is, participants in the difficult condition had to work 20% faster than during practice while those in the easy condition could work 20% slower.

The results showed no mood effects on cardiovascular reactivity during the mood inductions, although the mood manipulation was highly effective according to the manipulation check. However, participants remained on their cardiovascular baseline levels and showed even slight decreases in systolic reactivity, lending further support to the MBM notion that moods do not per se mobilize effort. Effects on SBP and DBP reactivity during task performance are depicted in Figure 4.

As anticipated, cardiovascular reactivity was significantly stronger in a negative mood than in a positive mood when the task was easy. Conversely, reactivity was significantly stronger in a positive mood than in a negative mood when the task was difficult. That is, mood state and performance standard had the anticipated joint effect on effort-related cardiovascular response.

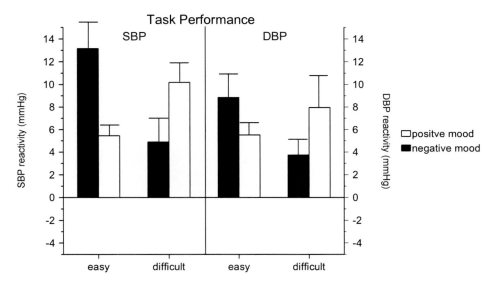

Figure 4. Reactivity of systolic blood pressure (SBP) and diastolic blood pressure (DBP) in the experiment by Gendolla and Krüsken (2001-a). Copyright: Society for Psychophysiologic Research

Achievement was quantified as the number of correctly marked target symbols. As presented in Table 2, mood had no impact on this measure in the easy condition. Presumably, the performance standard was so low that modest engagement was sufficient for success.

Table 2. Mean number of correctly marked target letters in the experiment by Gendolla and Krüsken (2001-b)

	Negative Mood	Positive Mood
Easy	456.43	454.07
Difficult	490.64	529.50

Note: $n = 14$ in each cell.

However, in the difficult condition, where the standard was high and where relatively intense effort was thus necessary for performing well, the achievement pattern corresponded to the pattern of effort-related cardiovascular response: Participants in the positive mood condition, where relatively high effort was mobilized, marked significantly more target letters correctly than participants in the negative mood condition, where only low effort was mobilized.

Participants in another experiment by Gendolla and Krüsken (2002-b, Study 1) were first induced into positive vs. negative moods through autobiographical recollection of happy vs. sad life events and then performed a learning task. A number of letter series had to be memorized in five minutes. Specifically, participants tried to memorize four series in an easy condition, seven series in a difficult condition, and 20 series in an extremely difficult, actually impossible condition. The results exactly showed the pattern of SBP reactivity predicted in Figure 3: Systolic reactivity was stronger in a negative mood than in a positive mood when the task was easy, while it was stronger in a positive mood than in a negative mood when the task was difficult. Most relevant, mood had no significant impact in the extremely difficult condition—SBP reactivity was low in both mood states. This extends the findings of the above-discussed experiment by Gendolla and Krüsken (2001-b), because it demonstrates that mood loses, as predicted, its impact on motivational intensity when a performance standard provides the clear information that success is impossible. Furthermore, achievement was positively correlated with SBP reactivity in this study and systolic reactivity did not differ between the conditions during the effective mood inductions.

Effects of Performance-Contingent Reward

So far, the experimental evidence suggests that people use their moods as task-relevant information to evaluate the extent of subjective demand that determines the intensity of effort and that the use of moods as information follows pragmatic principles in that people consider mood and other diagnostic information, like performance standards, simultaneously. However, it remained open if performance-contingent reward has an impact on this process. This is an important question, because other researchers have claimed that performance-contingent reward directly determines the intensity of motivation (e.g., Eisenberger, 1992; Fowles, 1983). Given that reward has not been manipulated in the studies from our laboratory discussed so far it might be possible that the informational mood impact on effort mobilization only works when reward is relatively unclear or non-contingent upon success, but that reward directly determines engagement when it is clear and performance-contingent. Two recent experiments by Gendolla and Krüsken (2002-c) addressed these questions. Again, predictions were derived from an application of the MBM reasoning on informational mood impact to Brehm's motivational intensity theory (e.g., Brehm and Self, 1989).

Brehm's theory distinguishes the level of maximally justified effort, defined as the level of *potential motivation*, from actual effort, which is *motivational intensity*. The level of potential motivation is determined by the importance of success: Relatively important outcomes justify more engagement than relatively unimportant outcomes. Up to the level of potential motivation, motivational intensity is proportional to the extent of subjective demand in accordance with the difficulty law of motivation (Ach, 1935). That is, following the principle of resource conservation, the organism does not mobilize more effort than necessary and disengages if success necessitates more engagement than justified by performance-contingent reward. Thus, performance-contingent reward for accomplishing a goal (only) indirectly influences motivational intensity by setting the level of maximally justified effort.

What are the predictions for performance conditions where reward is contingent vs. non-contingent upon success? In terms of Brehm's theory these two performance conditions differ only with regard to the level of maximally justified effort: An attractive performance-contingent reward makes success relatively important. Thus, performance-contingent reward justifies more effort than non-contingent reward. However, a person's actual engagement depends, up to the level of potential motivation, on the level of subjective demand, which is systematically influenced by the informational mood impact on demand appraisals. Consequently, effort should not differ between contingent and non-contingent conditions when a task is easy or when a difficult task is performed in a positive mood, because the extent of subjective demand is identical in both contingency conditions. But for succeeding on a difficult task in a negative mood task engagement should be highly increased when success promises valuable consequences. The reason for this effect is that the very high effort that is perceived as necessary in this condition then becomes justified. Consequently, performance-contingent incentive can eliminate the above-presented motivational deficit of people in a negative mood who face a difficult task.

An experiment by Gendolla and Krüsken (2002-c, Study 1) tested these predictions. Cardiovascular assessments were made during habituation, during the mood inductions through exposure to depressing vs. elating video excerpts, and while participants performed an easy or difficult memory task. The task was to memorize either four (easy) or seven (difficult) series of four randomized letters in five minutes. Reward contingency was manipulated as follows: Half the participants (non-contingent reward) were told that a relaxation period with exposure to pleasant music would follow the performance period, irrespective of achievement. The other half (reward contingent) was told that the relaxation period would follow the performance period *only* if they succeeded on the memory task. Results are depicted in Figure 5.

When reward was non-contingent upon success, SBP responses were in a pattern consistent with the view that negative mood participants tried harder than positive mood participants under easy conditions, but withheld effort under difficult conditions.

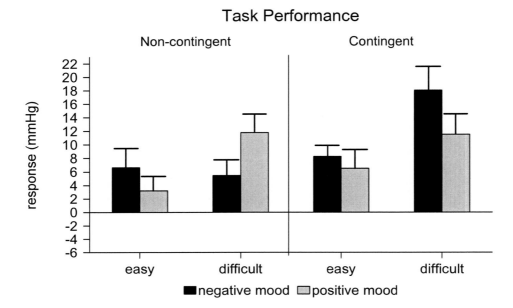

Figure 5. Systolic blood pressure (SBP) reactivity in the experiment by Gendolla and Krüsken (2002-c). Copyright: American Psychological Association

As anticipated, the same pattern occurred in all but one condition when reward was contingent upon performance: The exception was that the motivational deficit of participants in the negative-mood/difficult condition disappeared, as predicted, when reward was contingent upon success. The subjectively necessary very high effort in this condition was only mobilized when it was justified by performance-contingent reward. Furthermore, achievement on the memory task was positively correlated with SBP reactivity during task performance and demand appraisals assessed prior to performance showed that mood and performance standard had the anticipated additive effect on the extent of subjectively experienced demand. A follow-up experiment that promised non-contingent exposure to unpleasant materials vs. performance-contingent exposure to pleasant materials replicated these findings. Given that the performance-contingent incentive in these studies allowed hedonic affect regulation, the findings also support the MBM notion that informational and directive mood impact can occur simultaneously. Effort intensity was determined by the informational mood impact during the attempt to regulate the actual affective state by means of instrumental behavior that lead to hedonically pleasant consequences of success.

CONCLUSIONS AND IMPLICATIONS

After outlining the predictions of the MBM (Gendolla, 2000) for the role of mood in motivation, the here discussed studies have focused on mood effects on motivational intensity. As predicted by the MBM, the empirical evidence demonstrates that moods can influence task engagement and performance through their informational impact. With reference to the question if moods have stable motivational implications—which has been suggested by other researchers (e.g., Morris, 1992; Schwarz, 1990)—it is of note that none of the present studies has found mood effects on cardiovascular reactivity *before* task performance, although the mood states were successfully manipulated according to the manipulation checks and although mood had the predicted effects during task performance. That is, mood had no effects on effort mobilization until it was experienced in a setting that directly called for the mobilization of resources and in which it would be used as task-relevant information.

Basic Findings and Relations to other Approaches

As conceptualized in the MBM as informational impact, participants used their moods as diagnostic information for demand appraisals, which in turn determined task engagement (Ach, 1935; Brehm and Self 1989). When participants performed tasks without performance standards, mood was used as the only source of information for demand appraisals (e.g., Gendolla et al., 2001; Gendolla and Krüsken, 2001-a; 2002-b, Study 2). Consequently, more effort was mobilized in a negative mood than in a positive mood. As predicted, this effect diminished when the diagnostic value of mood as task-relevant information was called into question (Gendolla and Krüsken, 2002-a). It is of note that this latter finding makes it implausible that the reported mood effects occurred because mood influenced mental capacity (e.g., Ellis and Ashbrook, 1988), which could have made cognitive tasks objectively more difficult (low capacity) in a negative mood than in a positive mood (high capacity). Likewise, the present findings are hard to explain with a mood-as-priming process (Bower, 1991; Forgas, 1995) in which mood congruency effects occur because moods activate related concepts in memory. According to both approaches, the present findings are only explicable by a mood decay effect of the cue manipulation—but this effect did not occur.

As further predicted by the MBM, participants pragmatically used two available sources of information—mood and performance standard—to evaluate the extent of demand when they faced tasks with a fixed performance standard. Engagement was then proportional to the magnitude of experienced difficulty, resulting in low effort when an easy task was performed in a positive mood (low subjective difficulty) and when a difficult task was performed in a negative mood (disengagement). Engagement was high when an easy task was performed in a negative mood and when a difficulty task was performed in a positive mood (high subjective difficulty in both cases). When task difficulty was extremely high, so that success was clearly impossible, mood had no significant impact and effort was low in general (disengagement) (Gendolla and Krüsken, 2001-b; 2002-b, Study 1). It is of note, that these findings contradict the view that moods can only be used as information according to an "all-or-nothing" principle as Schwarz and Clore (1988) have proposed. Obviously, our participants considered their moods and other diagnostic information simultaneously.

Most interestingly, the motivational deficit of people facing a difficult task in a negative mood disappeared when reward for successful performance was contingent upon performance (Gendolla and Krüsken, 2002-c). However, rather than determining effort intensity directly, as suggested by some researchers (e.g., Eisenberger, 1992; Fowles, 1983), performance-contingent reward had this effect by increasing only the magnitude of maximally justified effort. These findings fit Brehm's motivational intensity theory (Brehm and Self, 1989) and contribute to the whole body of evidence for its applicability to effort mobilization in various settings (see Gendolla, 2004; Gendolla and Wright, 2005; Wright, 1996, 1998; Wright and Franklin, 2004; Wright and Kirby, 2001, for reviews).

It is noteworthy that also other researchers have considered informational effects of affective states on cardiovascular response. Blascovich and Berry-Mendes (2000) have posited that so called "affective cues" (e.g., sounds, smells, objects etc.) can determine if tasks are appraised as "challenge" or "threat." Challenge is then claimed to coincide with a strong cardiac response, while threat should coincide with a moderate cardiac and a strong vascular response. Beside numerous other problems of this framework and research that has already been discussed elsewhere (see Wright and Kirby, 2003) it is unclear how challenge and threat appraisals affect DBP, SBP, and mean arterial pressure (MAP) since these indices are determined differently (Brownley et al., 2000; Obrist, 1981). Furthermore, Blascovich and Berry-Mendes make no predictions on the impact of manipulated performance standards and thus cannot precisely predict the magnitude of cardiovascular response when people perform tasks of different difficulty levels. Also, neither the role of mood states nor the impact of performance-contingent consequences is considered in their approach. Thus, it is unclear how Blascovich and Berry-Mendes' analysis could refer to the present findings.

Implications for Work Motivation in Organizational Settings

The here discussed studies on mood and effort mobilization investigated university student samples rather than employees and administered standardized cognitive tasks rather than real life work challenges. Nevertheless, the findings have clear and direct implications for work motivation and performance. In work settings people have to cope with demands that are related to memory, attention, and verbal creativity, as had the participants in the present experiments. Likewise, organizational performance conditions either provide clear performance standards or they do not (Locke and Latham, 1990) and reward in work settings is either contingent or non-contingent upon performance. Furthermore, studies by Krüsken (2002) have found that naturally occurring mood states have the same effects on the intensity of motivation as experimentally manipulated mood states. This suggests that the present findings apply to organizational and educational settings, because the basic organizational performance conditions correspond to those of our laboratory research.

The major suggestion of the present research is that organizations should take care about their employees' moods. Moods are not only a key variable for work climate (e.g., George and Brief, 1992) but also for work motivation and performance as the here presented studies suggest (see also Grawitch and Munz, 2005). Likewise, it is necessary to care about work climate and work conditions, because they will have consequences on workers' mood states. Mood states can in turn systematically influence work motivation and thus performance and efficiency. However, it should also be considered that in the present studies the achievement gain through high effort was not very high, although significant. One has to keep in mind that the relationship between effort and achievement is complex and that it depends on several moderator variables such as inter-individual ability differences and the type of task (see Eysenck, 1982). Effort refers to the mobilization of resources in order to carry out instrumental behavior, while achievement (only) describes the outcome of behavior—which depends on more factors than only engagement. Consequently, associations between effort and achievement can, but do not need to occur (Gendolla, 2004; Gendolla and Richter, 2006; Richter and Gendolla, 2006).

However, in the studies discussed above, engagement explained about 4-9% of the variance in achievement. This may be an important share that can decide about success or failure. But in the light of the potential health costs of chronically high work motivation, it might be worth considering that conditions, which elicit moderate effort intensity, could also be sufficient for maintaining adequate performance.

Implications for Ergonomics and Mental Workload

A central variable of interest in ergonomics is "mental workload." Conceptualized as a multidimensional construct it is assumed to reflect an individual's level of attentional and mental engagement in a task (Wickens, 1984). In the last decades a vast bulk of techniques, among them behavioral, subjective, and physiological measures (Baldwin, 2003; O'Donnell and Eggemeier, 1986; Wierwille and Eggemeier, 1993), has been developed and applied for the assessment of mental workload. If one considers only the mental effort component of the mental workload construct, implications of our integrative approach are obvious. So far, most applied research in the area of ergonomics assessing mental effort has been primarily based on the rather simple assumption that mental effort will increase proportionally with the complexity or the difficulty of the task (e.g., Veltman and Gaillard, 1998). Correspondingly, mental effort is often used as indicator of task difficulty.

The presented studies from our laboratory and other empirical evidence based on motivational intensity theory suggest that this view might be oversimplified. First, according to motivational intensity theory (Brehm and Self, 1989) and the supporting empirical evidence (Wright and Kirby, 2001), mental effort is not only determined by task difficulty, but by the importance of success, as well. Correspondingly, success importance determines the maximal level of mental effort one is willing to invest in the task. That is, mental effort indicators of mental workload might be biased by participants' potential motivation to work hard. A measure indicating low mental workload might actually imply an easy task or a task for which the necessary engagement was not justified by the participant's potential motivation. Furthermore, applied research often does not consider the influence of affective states. According to the here discussed MBM, moods can have an influence on mental effort via mood-congruency effects on appraisals of task difficulty. Again, mental effort measures of mental workload can be ambiguous. For instance, a mental effort measure indicating low mental workload might result from an indeed easy task, from a difficult task which was appraised as easy by an individual in a positive mood, or from a moderately difficult task which was appraised as too difficult by an individual in a negative mood.

In summary, the integrative approach developed in this chapter offers some insights in problems involved in the assessment of mental workload by means of mental effort and the use of mental effort as indicator of task complexity and difficulty. Since not only the willing to invest energy in the task has an influence on these measures, but affective states as well, the assessment of mental workload via measures of mental effort should always take the affective and motivational state of the individual into consideration.

Implications for Health Psychology: The Development of Cardiovascular Disease

There is clear and replicated evidence that the extent of cardiovascular reactivity during effortful coping with demands predicts the risk of hypertension and cardiovascular disease (see Blascovich and Katkin, 1993). The stronger the cardiovascular system reacts to a mental demand, the higher is the likeability of developing hypertension and a cardiovascular disease. A longitudinal study by Light, Dolan, Davis, and Sherwood (1992), for example, found that especially the magnitude of SBP reactivity during performance on a mental demand predicted baseline blood pressure and the magnitude of cardiovascular reactivity to stressors 15 years later. The stronger the SBP responses were during earlier effortful coping, the higher was the probability of developing hypertension. Furthermore, there is clear evidence that personality characteristics that are related to negative affective experiences are correlated with the vulnerability to cardiovascular disease (Rugulies, 2002; Steptoe, Cropley, and Joekes, 2000). Examples are hostility (Smith, 1992) and neuroticism (Byrne, 1992). According to an analysis by Gendolla and Richter (2005-a), the here discussed laboratory findings from our laboratory may contribute to an explanation of how this can happen. Accordingly, people who experience negative affect evaluate the extent of subjective demand higher when they face mental challenges. Consequently, they mobilize more effort than people who experience positive affect as long as they believe that it is possible and worthwhile to attain a goal. This is particularly important for work settings in which people are chronically confronted with mental demands. If people who chronically experience negative affect also chronically face such demands, they are especially vulnerable for the development of cardiovascular disease. This suggests that work settings that promote high cardiovascular reactivity over a long work period—like working without a clear performance standard in a negative mood—are harmful and provide a health risk (Gendolla and Richter, 2005-a).

From this perspective, work and educational settings should facilitate the experience of positive rather than negative moods during work. This is relatively easy to be realized by pleasant illumination, pleasant odors, or ergonomically well structured work places (see Gendolla, 2000), and any variables that are known for long as being related to high work satisfaction (see Locke, 1976). Positive mood during work may prevent the development of cardiovascular disease. This is especially relevant because the achievement deficit due to mobilizing only moderate effort for routine tasks seems to be relatively small. Positive mood is, however, not beneficial when people have to attain high performance standards. Consequently, both performance standards and mood have to be considered in order to prevent health risks, qualifying other approaches that have proposed that positive affect has mainly or even only health benefits (e.g., Fredrickson, 2001; Ryff and Singer, 1998; Salovey, Rothman, Detweiler, and Steward, 2000).

Nevertheless, negative mood during work seems to bear multiple risks: The cardiovascular system reacts strongly during performance on easy tasks and tasks without performance standards. When reward is contingent upon performance, which is frequently the case in work settings, very strong reactivity is facilitated. Creating work settings that facilitate effective but non-harmful performance is thus a major challenge for effective leadership, ergonomics, and organizational behavior.

Implications for Clinical Psychology: Mood, Depression, and Motivation

As outlined above, an important aspect for organizations and for the construction of work settings is the mental health of their employees. In this context it is important to note that not only diagnosed clinical pathologies but also minor subsyndromal symptoms may have an impact on employees' work, the working atmosphere, and organizational structures. In this section, we will highlight implications of our integrative approach for depressed mood and depression, respectively. However, there is also evidence for the implications of the MBM with regard to other individual difference variables like e.g., dispositional anxiety or low self-esteem. Research on depression is particularly important because depression is considered by the World Health Organization as the most burdensome disease in the world in terms of total disability-adjusted life years among people in the middle years of life (Kessler, 2002). The prevalence rates for depression are high and still rising, not only for clinically diagnosed depression (e.g., major depressive disorder) but also for subsyndromal depressive symptoms (e.g., minor depression), which means that many students' and employees' working life may be affected at some time and in some way by a depressive period.

An integrative approach of mood and motivation regarding depression and dysphoria lends itself, because a persistent negative mood is considered as one of the two core symptoms of major depressive disorder (DSM-IV, American Psychiatric Association, 1994). Thus, it allows the investigation of the role of naturally occurring negative mood. In addition, research among clinically depressed individuals as well as subclinical populations supports the notion that depression is associated with emotional, cognitive, functional, and motivational deficits (e.g., Heckhausen, 1991). The motivational deficit—defined as an inability to initiate actions, to mobilize efforts, and to persist on these actions—has been demonstrated in research from different perspectives (see for example Abramson, Alloy, and Rosoff, 1981; Henriques and Davidson, 2000; Fowles, 1993; Layne, Merry, Christian, and Ginn, 1982; Tomarken and Keener, 1998). Thus, considering that moods can influence behavior, as for instance action initiation and effort mobilization, our integrative approach may help explaining and investigating depressed individuals' motivational deficit.

Evidence for an *informational impact* of naturally occurring mood stems, for example, from studies by Lyubomirsky, Tucker, Caldwell, and Berg (1999). Dysphoric individuals rated the likelihood of solving a personal problem and implementing their solution significantly lower than nondysphorics. The authors concluded that dysphoric rumination might interfere with efforts to take steps to problem solving. In terms of the MBM this means that dysphoric individuals have a motivational deficit due to their more negative evaluation of the actual situation on the basis of their negative mood. Evidence for the conceptualization of a *directive mood impact* of naturally occurring mood is provided by a body of research showing that depression and other negative affect dispositions coincide with a weak directive mood impact in terms of deficits in self-regulation of affective experiences. As Josephson, Singer, and Salovey (1996) reported, depressed individuals are not able to self-regulate their negative affect by activating positive memories ("mood-incongruent recall"). Moreover, Gilboa and Gotlib (1997) showed that previously dysphoric individuals better remembered negative stimuli and stayed longer in negative affect after a negative mood induction than never-dysphoric individuals. Further evidence for individual differences in self-regulation stems from research showing that depressives are unable to withdraw from a "depressive self-focusing style" (Pyszczynski and Greenberg, 1987): Depressives tended to reflect on themselves after failure but not after success, whereas nondepressives showed the inverse pattern.

Moreover, in the extensive literature about depressives' undervaluation of rewards there is evidence for both *informational* and *directive* mood impact. Costello (1972) suggested that depression decreases the effectiveness of reward insofar as depressed individuals showed a lack of responsiveness to pleasurable stimuli. Henriques and colleagues have explained this with decreased activity in the left anterior cortex, which is considered to produce an underactivation of the reward-based system (e.g., Henriques and Davidson, 2000). Moreover, Tillema, Cervone, and Scott (2001) found that a dysphoric individuals' actual negative mood state elicited the undervaluation of a perceived outcome. These findings regarding the undervaluation of rewards by depressives show on the one hand that a depressed individuals' actual mood state may influence the *evaluation* of a perceived outcome, which is explicable in terms of an informational mood impact on self-regulation. On the other hand, this leads to low perceived *instrumentality* of potential affect-regulative acts and thus reduces the strength of directive mood impact. This interpretation is consistent with the MBM postulate that informational and directive mood impacts can occur simultaneously.

In support of our approach, recent research from our laboratory has investigated and shown the influence of vulnerability for depression on cardiovascular reactivity (Brinkmann and Gendolla, 2005). Students with high depression scores were compared to a control group while being confronted with a cognitive task without fixed performance standard. The results showed that depressed students—who were at the time of the experiment also in a more negative mood—showed stronger SBP reactivity than the control group. Thus, depressed individuals mobilized more mental effort, indicating higher motivational intensity at the time of task performance. Interestingly, the high effort of depressives' was accompanied by poorer performance. That is, depressives' mobilized relatively high effort without the merits of better performance.

Besides this evidence for the relations between depression and motivation and the implications for the MBM, there has been a body of recent research showing that depression is among the risk factors for development and worsening of coronary heart disease (Frasure-Smith and Lespérance, 2005; Rugulies, 2002; Wulsin and Singal, 2003). One of the most prominent explications states that dysregulation of the autonomic nervous system may explain why depressed patients are at increased risk for coronary heart disease. The altered autonomic nervous system activity found in depressed patients is seen as an indicator of increased sympathetic nervous system activity (Carney, Freeland, and Veith, 2005). As outlined above, a stable disposition to stronger cardiovascular reactivity can be considered as a risk factor for cardiovascular disease. Moreover, there is evidence that also other negative psychological states like hopelessness, pessimism, rumination, anxiety, and anger are linked in varying degrees to cardiovascular diseases (Kubzansky, Davidson, and Rozanski, 2005). One may speculate if among other factors, also affective states play an important role in the linkage between depression and coronary heart disease.

REFERENCES

Abele, A. E., and Gendolla, G. H. E. (1999). Satisfaction judgments in positive and negative moods: Effects of concurrent assimilation and contrast producing processes. *Personality and Social Psychology Bulletin, 25,* 893-905.

Abele, A. E., Gendolla, G. H. E., and Petzold, P. (1998). Positive mood and ingroup-outgroup differentiation in a minimal group setting. *Personality and Social Psychological Bulletin, 24,* 1343-1357.

Abele, A. E., and Petzold, P. (1994). How does mood operate in an impression formation task? An information integration approach. *European Journal of Social Psychology, 24,* 173-187.

Abramson, L. Y., Alloy, L. B., and Rosoff, R. (1981). Depression and the generation of complex hypotheses in the judgment of contingency. *Behvioural Research and Therapy, 19,* 35-45.

Ach, N. (1935). Analyse des Willens. [Analysis of will]. In E. Abderhalden (Hg.), Handbuch der biologischen Arbeitsmethoden. [Handbook of biological methods]. Berlin: Urban and Schwarzenberg. American Psychiatric Association. (1994). *Diagnostic and statistical manual of mental disorders* (4th ed.). Washington, DC: American Psychiatric Association.

Anderson, N. H. (1981). *Foundations of information integration theory.* New York: Academic Press.

Baldwin, C. L. (2003). Neuroergonomics of mental workload: new insights from the convergence of brain and behaviour in ergonomics research. *Theoretical Issues in Ergonomics Science, 4,* 132-141.

Baron, R. A. (1993). Affect and organizational behavior: When and why feeling good (or bad) matters. In J. K. Murnighan (Ed.), *Social psychology in organizations: Advances in theory and research* (pp. 63-88). Englewood Cliffs, NJ: Prentice Hall.

Berntson, G. G., Cacioppo, J. T., and Quigley, K. S. (1993). Cardiac psychophysiology and autonomic space in humans: Empirical perspectives and conceptual implications. *Psychological Bulletin, 114,* 296-322.

Blascovich, J., and Berry-Mendes, W. (2000). Challenge and threat appraisals. The role of affective cues. In J. P. Forgas (Ed.), *Feeling and thinking* (pp. 59-82). New York: Cambridge University Press.

Blascovich, J., and Katkin, E. S. (Eds.) (1993). *Cardiovascular reactivity to psychological stress and disease.* Washington, DC: American Psychological Association.

Bongard, S., and Hodapp, V. (1997). Active coping, work-pace, and cardiovascular responses: Evidence from laboratory studies. *Journal of Psychophysiology, 11,* 227-237.

Bower, G. H. (1991). Mood congruity of social judgments. In: Forgas, J. P. (Ed.) *Emotion and social judgments* (pp. 32-54). Oxford: Pergamon Press.

Brehm, J. W., and Self, E. A. (1989). The intensity of motivation. *Annual Review of Psychology, 40,* 109-131.

Brickenkamp, R. (1981). *Test d2 (7th.ed.).* Göttingen, Germany: Hogrefe.

Brinkmann, K., and Gendolla, G. H. E. (2005). Impact of vulnerability for depression on cardiovascular reactivity in active coping. *Psychophysiology, 42,* S39.

Brownley, K. A., Hurwitz, B. E., and Schneiderman, N. (2000). Cardiovascular psychophysiology. In J. T. Cacioppo, L. G. Tassinary, and G. G. Berntson, *Handbook of psychophysiology* (pp. 224-264). New York: Cambridge University Press.

Byrne, D.G. (1992). Anxiety, neuroticissm, depression and hypertension. In E. H. Johnson, W.D., Gentry and S. Julius (Hg.), *Personality, elevated blood pressure, and essential hypertension* (pp. 67 - 85) Washington, DC: Hemisphere.

Cacioppo, J. T., Berntson, G. G., Larsen, J. T., Poehlmann, K. M., and Ito, T. A. (2000). The psychophysiology of emotion. In M. Lewis and J. M. Haviland-Jones (Eds.), *Handbook of emotions (2nd ed.)* (pp. 173-191). New York: Guilford.

Carney, R. M., Freeland, K. E., and Veith, R. C. (2005). Depression, the autonomic nervous system, and coronary heart disease. *Psychosomatic Medicine, 67*, S29-S33.

Clore, G. L., Schwarz, N., and Conway, M. (1994). Affective causes and consequences of social information piocessing. In R. S. Wyer, and T. K. Srull (Eds.), *Handbook of social cognition (2nd edition).* (Vol. 1, pp. 323-417). Hillsdale, NJ: Erlbaum.

Costello, C. G. (1972). Depression: Loss of reinforcers or loss of reinforcer effectiveness. *Behavior Therapy, 3*, 240-247.

Damasio, A. R. (1994). *Descartes' error.* New York: Avon Books.

Eisenberger, R. (1992). Learned industriousness. *Psychological Review*, *99*, 248-267.

Efklides, A., and Petkaki, C. (2005). Effects of mood on students' metacognitive experiences. *Learning and Instruction, 15,* 415-431.

Ellis, H. C., and Ashbrook, P. W. (1988). Resource allocation model of the effects of depressed mood states on memory. In K. Fiedler and J. P. Forgas (Eds.), *Affect, cognition, and social behavior* (pp. 25-43). Göttingen, Germany: Hogrefe.

Erez, A., and Isen, A. M. (2002). The influence of positive affect on the components of expectancy motivation. *Journal of Applied Psychology, 87,* 1055-1067.

Eysenck, M. W. (1982). *Attention and arousal.* New York: Springer.

Forgas, J. P. (1995). Mood and judgment: The affect infusion model (AIM). *Psychological Bulletin, 117,* 36-66.

Forgas, J. P., and George, J. M. (2001). Affective influences on judgments and behavior in organizations: An information processing perspective. *Organizational Behavior and Human Decision Making, 86,* 3-34.

Fowles, D. C. (1983). Motivational effects on heart rate and electrodermal activity: Implications for research on personality and psychopathology. *Journal of Research in Personality, 17,* 48-71.

Fowles, D. C. (1993). Behavioral variables in psychopathology: A psychobiological perspective. In P. B. Sutker and H. E. Adams (Eds.), *Comprehensive handbook of psychopathology* (2nd ed., pp. 57-82). New York: Plenum Press.

Frasure-Smith, N., and Lespérance, F. (2005). Depression and coronary heart disease: Complex synergism of mind, body, and environment. *Current Directions in Psychological Science, 14,* 39-43.

Fredrickson, B. L. (2001). The role of positive emotions in positive psychology. The broaden-and-built theory of positive emotions. *American Psychologist, 56,* 218-226.

Frijda, N. H. (1986). *The emotions.* Cambridge: Cambridge University Press.

Frijda, N. H. (1993). Moods, emotion episodes, and emotions. In M. Lewis, and J. M. Haviland (Eds.), *Handbook of emotions* (pp. 381-404). New York: Guilford.

Geen, R. G. (1995). *Human motivation.* Pacific Grove, CA: Brooks/Cole.

Gellatly, I. R., and Meyer, J. P. (1992). The effects of goal difficulty on physiological arousal, cognition, and task performance. *Journal of Applied Psychology, 77,* 694-704.

Gendolla, G. H. E. (2000). On the impact of mood on behavior: An integrative theory and a review. *Review of General Psychology, 4,* 378-408.

Gendolla, G. H. E. (2004). The intensity of motivation when the self is involved: An application of Brehm's theory of motivation to effort-related cardiovascular response. In R. A. Wright, J. Greenberg, and S. S. Brehm (Eds.), *Motivational analysis of social behavior: Building on Jack Brehm's contributions to psychology* (pp. 205-244). Mahwah, NJ: Erlbaum.

Gendolla, G. H. E., Abele, A. E., and Krüsken, J. (2001). The informational impact of mood on effort mobilization: A study of cardiovascular and electrodermal responses. *Emotion, 1,* 12-24.

Gendolla, G.H.E., and Brinkmann, K. (2005). The role of mood states in self-regulation: Effects on action preferences and resource mobilization. *European Psychologist, 10,* 187-198.

Gendolla, G. H. E., and Krüsken, J. (2001-a). Mood state and cardiovascular response in active coping with an affect-regulative challenge. *International Journal of Psychophysiology, 40,* 169-180.

Gendolla, G. H. E., and Krüsken, J. (2001-b). The joint impact of mood state and task difficulty on cardiovascular and electrodermal reactivity in active coping. *Psychophysiology, 38,* 548-556.

Gendolla, G. H. E., and Krüsken, J. (2002-a). Informational mood impact on effort-related cardiovascular response: The diagnostic value of moods counts. *Emotion, 2,* 251-262.

Gendolla, G. H. E., and Krüsken, J. (2002-b). Mood, task demand, and effort-related cardiovascular response. *Cognition and Emotion, 16,* 577-603.

Gendolla, G. H. E., and Krüsken, J. (2002-c). The joint effect of informational mood impact and performance-contingent incentive on effort-related cardiovascular response. *Journal of Personality and Social Psychology, 83,* 271-285.

Gendolla, G. H. E., and Richter, M. (2005-a). The role of mood states in the development of cardiovascular disease: Implications of a motivational analysis of cardiovascular reactivity in active coping. In P. Shohov (Ed.), *Advances in psychology research* (Vol. 33, pp. 139-157). Hauppauge, NY: Nova Science.

Gendolla, G. H. E., and Richter, M. (2005-b). Ego involvement and effort: Cardiovascular, electrodermal, and performance effects. *Psychophysiology, 42,* 595-603.

Gendolla, G. H. E., and Richter, M. (2006). Ego-involvement and the difficulty law of motivation: Effects on effort-related cardiovascular response. *Personality and Social Psychology Bulletin, 32,1188-1203.*

Gendolla, G.H.E., and Wright, R. A. (2005). Motivation in social settings: studies of effort-related cardiovascular arousal. In J.P. Forgas, K. Williams and W. von Hippel, (Eds.). *Social motivation* (pp. 71-90). New York: Cambridge University Press.

George, J. M., and Brief, A. P. (1992). Feeling good-doing good: A conceptual analysis of the mood at work-organizational spontaneity relationship. *Psychological Bulletin, 112,* 310-329.

Gilboa, E., and Gotlib, I. H. (1997). Cognitive biases and affect persistence in previously dysphoric and never-dysphoric individuals. *Cognition and Emotion, 11,* 517-538.

Grawitch, M. J., and Munz, D. C. (2005). Individual and group affect in problem-solving workgroups. In C. E. J. Härtel, W. J. Zerbe, and N. M. Ashkanasy (Eds.), *Emotions in organizational behavior* (pp. 119-142). Mahwah, NJ: Erlbaum.

Handley, I. M., and Lassiter, G. D. (2002). Mood and information processing: When happy and sad looks the same. *Motivation and Emotion, 26,* 223-255.

Heckhausen, H. (1991). *Motivation and action.* New York: Springer.

Henriques, J. B., and Davidson, R. J. (2000). Decreased responsiveness to reward in depression. *Cognition and Emotion, 14,* 711-724.

Hockey, G. R. J. (1997). Compensatory control in the regulation of human performance under stress and high workload: A cognitive-energetical framework. *Biological Psychology, 45,* 73-93.

Hull, C. L. (1943). *Principles of behavior.* New York: Appleton-Century-Crofts.

Isen, A. M. (2000). Positive affect and decision making. In M. Lewis and J. M. Haviland-Jones (Eds.), *Handbook of emotions (2nd, ed.)* (pp. 417-435). New York: Guilford.

Isen, A. M., and Baron, R. A. (1991). Positive affect as a factor in organizational behavior. In B. M. Staw and L. L. Cummings (Eds.), *Research in organizational behavior* (pp. 1-53). Greenwich, CT: JAI Press.

Josephson, B. R., Singer, J. A., and Salovey, P. (1996). Mood regulation and memory: Repairing sad moods with happy memories. *Cognition and Emotion, 10,* 437-444.

Kavanagh, D. J., Bower, G. H. (1985). Mood and self-efficacy: Impact of joy and sadness on perceived capabilities. *Cognitive Therapy and Research, 9,* 507-525.

Kelly, J. R., and Barsade, S. G. (2001). Mood and emotions in small groups and work teams. *Organizational Behavior and Human Decision Processes, 86,* 99-130.

Kessler, R. C. (2002). Epidemiology of depression. In I. H. Gotlib, and C. L. Hammen (Eds.), *Handbook of depression* (pp.23-42). New York: Guilford Press.

Kubzansky, L. D., Davidson, K. W., and Rozanski, A. (2005). The clinical impact of negative psychological states: Expanding the spectrum of risk for coronary artery disease. *Psychosomatic Medicine, 67,* S10-S14.

Krüsken, J. (2002). *Stimmungseinflüsse auf Anstrengung und Leistung bei der Bearbeitung von Kreativitätsaufgaben. [Mood influences on effort and achievement during performance on creativity tasks].* Berlin, Germany: Mensch and Buch Verlag.

Lane, A. M., Whyte, G. P., Terry, P. C., and Nevill, A. M. (2005). Mood, self-set goals and examination performance: The moderating effect of depressed mood. *Personality and Individual Differences, 39,* 143-153.

Layne, C., Merry, J., Christian, J., and Ginn, P. (1982). Motivational deficit in depression. *Cognitive Therapy and Research, 6,* 259-274.

Light, K. C., Dolan, C. A., Davis, M. R., and Sherwood, A. (1992). Cardiovascular responses to an active coping challenge as predictors of blood pressure patterns 10 to 15 years later. *Psychosomatic Medicine, 54,* 217-230.

Locke, E. A. (1976). The nature and causes of job satisfaction. In M. D. Dunnette (Ed.), *The handbook of industrial and organizational psychology.* Chicago, IL: Rand McNally.

Locke, E. A., and Latham, G. P. (1990). *A theory of goal setting and performance.* Englewood Cliffs, NJ: Prentice Hall.

Loewenstein, G. (1996). Out of control: Visceral influences on behavior. *Organizational Behavior and Human Decision Making, 65,* 272-292.

Lovallo, W. R., Wilson, M. F., Pincomb, G. A., Edwards, G. L., Tompkins, P., and Brackett, D. J. (1985). Activation patterns to aversive stimulation in man: Passive exposure versus effort to control. *Psychophysiology*, *22*, 283-291.

Lyubomirsky, S., Tucker, K. L., Caldwell, N. D., and Berg, K. (1999). Why ruminators are poor problem solvers: Clues from the phenomenology of dysphoric rumination. *Journal of Personality and Social Psychology, 77*, 1041-1060.

McFarland, C., and Buehler, R. (1998). The impact of negative affect on autobiographical memory: The role of self-focused attention to moods. *Journal of Personality and Social Psychology,75,* 1424-1440.

Martin, L. L., Ward, D. W., Achee, J. W., and Wyer, R. S. (1993). Mood as input: People have to interpret the motivational implications of their moods. *Journal of Personality and Social Psychology*, *64*, 317-326.

Mischel, W., and Shoda, Y. (1995). A cognitive-affective system theory of personality: Reconceptualization situations, dispositions, dynamics, and invariance in personality structure. *Psychological Review*, *102*, 246-268.

Morris, W. N. (1989). *Mood. The frame of mind.* New York: Springer.

Morris, W. N. (1992). A functional analysis of the role of mood in affective system. In M. S. Clark (Ed.), *Review of personality and social psychology* (Vol. 13, pp. 256-293). Newsbury Park, CA: Sage.

Niedenthal, P. M., Halberstadt, J. B., and Setterlund, M. B. (1997). Being happy and seeing „happy": Emotional state mediates visual word recognition. *Cognition and Emotion, 11*, 403-432.

Obrist, P. A. (1981). *Cardiovascular psychophysiology.* New York: Plenum Press.

O'Donnell, R., and Eggemeier, F. T. (1986). Workload assessment methodology. In K. Boff, L. Kaufmann, and J. Thomas (Eds), Handbook *of perception and human performance* (Vol. 2, pp. 42.1 – 42.49). New York: Wiley.

Parrott, W. G. (1993). Beyond hedonism: Motives for inhibiting good moods and for maintaining bad moods. In D. M. Wegner and J. W. Pennebaker (Eds.), *Handbook of mental control* (pp. 278-305). Englewood Cliffs, NJ: Prentice Hall.

Pyszczynski, T., and Greenberg, J. (1987). Self-regulatory perseveration and the depressive self-focusing style: A self-awareness theory of reactive depression. *Psychological Bulletin, 102*, 122-138.

Richter, M., and Gendolla, G.H.E. (2006). Incentive effects on cardiovascular reactivity in active coping with unclear difficulty. *International Journal of Psychophysiology, 61*, 216-225.

Richter, M., Gendolla, G. H. E., and Krüsken, J. (2006). Context-dependent mood effects on mental effort mobilization: A view from the mood-behavior-model. In A.V. Clark (Ed.), *The psychology of moods* (pp.57-79). Hauppauge, NY: Nova Science.

Rugulies, R. (2002). Depression as a predictor for coronary heart disease: A review and meta-analysis. *American Journal of Preventive Medicine, 23*, 51-61.

Ryff, C. D., and Singer, B. H: (1998). Contours of positive human health. *Psychological Inquiry, 9,* 1-28.

Salovey, P., Rothman, A. J., Detweiler, J. B., and Steward, W. T. (2000). Emotional states and physical health. *American Psychologist, 55,* 110-121.

Schaller, M., and Cialdini, R. B. (1990). Happiness, sadness, and helping. In E. T. Higgins and R. M.Sorrentino (Eds.), *Handbook of motivation and cognition* (Vol. 2, pp. 265-296). New York: Guilford.

Scherer, K. R. (2001). Appraisal considered as a process of multilevel sequential checking. In K. R. Scherer, A. Schorr and T. Johnstone (Eds.), *Appraisal processes in emotion: Theory, methods, research* (pp. 92-120). New York: Oxford University Press.

Schwarz, N. (1990). Feelings as information: Information and motivational functions of affective states. In E. T. Higgins and R. M. Sorrentino (Eds.), *Handbook of motivation and cognition* (Vol. 2, pp. 527-561). New York: Guilford Press.

Schwarz, N., and Clore, G. L. (1988). How do I feel about it? The informative function of affective states. In K. Fiedler and J. P. Forgas (Eds.), *Affect, cognition and social behaviour* (pp. 44-62). Göttingen, Germany: Hogrefe.

Smith, C. A., and Lazarus, R. S. (1990). Emotion and adaptation. In L. A. Pervin (Ed.), *Handbook of personality* (pp. 609-637). New York: Guilford.

Smith, T. W. (1992). Hostility and health: Current status of a psychosomatic hypothesis. *Health Psychology*, *11*, 139-150.

Smith, T. W., Allred, K. D., Morrison, C. A., and Carlson, S. D. (1989). Cardiovascular reactivity and interpersonal influence: Active coping in a social setting. *Journal of Personality and Social Psychology, 56*, 209-218.

Steptoe, A., Cropley, M., and Joekes, K. (2000). Task demand and the pressures of everyday life: Associations between cardiovascular reactivity and work blood pressure and heart rate. *Health Psychology, 19*, 46-54.

Storey, P. L., Wright, R. A., and Williams, B. J. (1996). Need as a moderator of the difficulty-cardiovascular response relation: The case of fluid deprivation. *Journal of Psychophysiology, 10*, 228-238.

Tillema, J. L., Cervone, D., and Scott, W. D. (2001). Negative mood, perceived self-efficacy, and personal standards in dysphoria : The effects of contextual cues on self-defeating patterns of cognition. *Cognitive Therapy and Research, 25*, 535-549.

Tomarken, A. J., and Keener, A. D. (1998). Frontal brain asymmetry and depression: A self-regulatory perspective. *Cognition and Emotion, 12*, 387-420.

Tolman. E. C. (1932). *Purposive behavior in animals and men.* New York: Appleton-Century.

Veltman, J. A., and Gaillard, A. W. K. (1998). Physiological workload reactions to increasing levels of task difficulty. *Ergonomics, 41*, 656-669.

Wegener, D. T., and Petty, R. E. (1994). Mood management across affective states: The hedonic contingency hypothesis. *Journal of Personality and Social Psychology, 66*, 1034-1048.

Wickens, C. D. (1984). Processing resources in attention. In R. Parasuraman and R. Davies (Eds), *Varieties of attention* (pp. 62-102). Orlando, FL: Academic Press.

Wierwille, W. W., and Eggemeier, F. T. (1993). Recommendations for mental workload measurement in a test and evaluation environment. *Human Factors, 35*, 263-281.

Wilson, T. D., Laser, P. S., and Stone, J. I. (1982). Judging the predictors of one's own mood: Accuracy and the use of shared theories. *Journal of Experimental Social Psychology, 18*, 537-556.

Wright, J., and Mischel, W. (1982). Influence of affect on cognitive learning person variables. *Journal of Personality and Social Psychology, 43*, 901-914.

Wright, R. A. (1996). Brehm's theory of motivation as a model of effort and cardiovascular response. In P. M. Gollwitzer and J. A. Bargh (Eds.), *The psychology of action: Linking cognition and motivation to behavior* (pp. 424-453). New York: Guilford.

Wright, R. A. (1998). Ability perception and cardiovascular response to behavioral challenge. In M. Kofta, G. Weary, and G. Sedek (Eds.), *Personal control in action: Cognitive and motivational mechanisms* (pp. 197-232). New York: Plenum.

Wright, R. A., and Franklin, J. (2004). Ability perception determinants of effort-related cardiovascular response: Mood, optimism, and performance resources. In R. A. Wright, J. Greenberg, and S. S. Brehm (Eds.), *Motivational analysis of social behavior: Building on Jack Brehm's contributions to psychology* (pp. 187-204). Mahwah, NJ: Erlbaum.

Wright, R. A., and Kirby, L. D. (2001). Effort determination of cardiovascular response: An integrative analysis with applications in social psychology. In M. P. Zanna (Ed.), *Advances in experimental social psychology* (Vol. 33, pp. 255-307). New York: Academic Press.

Wright, R. A., and Kirby, L. D. (2003). Cardiovascular correlates of challenge and threat appraisals: A critical examination of the psychobiosocial analysis. *Personality and Social Psychology Review, 7*, 216-233.

Wulsin, L. R., and Singal, B. M. (2003). Do depressive symptoms increase the risk for the onset of coronary disease? A systematic quantitative review. *Psychosomatic Medicine, 65*, 201-210.

Wyer, R. S., Clore, G. L., and Isbell, L. M. (1999). Affect and information processing. In M. P. Zanna (Ed.), *Advances in experimental social psychology* (Vol. 31, pp. 1-77). New York: Academic Press.

In: Mood and Human Performance: Conceptual, Measurement...   ISBN 1-60021-269-7
Editor: Andrew M. Lane, pp. 63-87   © 2006 Nova Science Publishers, Inc.

Chapter 3

TOWARDS EMPIRICAL DISTINCTIONS BETWEEN EMOTION AND MOOD: A SUBJECTIVE CONTEXTUAL MODEL

Christopher J. Beedie

Canterbury Christ Church University, Canterbury, UK

ABSTRACT

Despite the publication of a large number of diverse proposals, the question over which criterion distinguishes emotion from mood has yet to be addressed empirically to any significant degree. Although the question seems at first sight quite academic, moving towards some resolution might have significant implications for the reliable measurement of mood and emotion and for the success of subsequent treatment or intervention. The paper uses previous data and a process of logical deduction to propose a subjective contextual model by which empirical distinction between emotion and mood might be made. The model is tentative but fits available data, is consistent with generally accepted distinguishing criteria, and might explain how one phenomenon, in this case anxiety, can be experienced as either emotion or mood depending on subjective contextual factors. The model differs from the theorising that has characterised the issue to this point in time in that it is testable, that is, it is a relatively simple task to develop self-report items to assess any individual's awareness of the perceived cause and focus of a state of, for example, anxiety or anger.

It is interesting that when asked to define 'mood', the response of most people, including it would appear, academic psychologists, contains the word 'emotion' (see for example Lane and Terry, 2000). The opposite seems not to be the case, that is, emotion is rarely defined in terms of mood. A logical conclusion might then be that moods are, along with constructs such as temperament and sentiment, examples of the category 'emotion', perhaps in the same sense that hockey and swimming are examples of the category 'sport'. As is the case with many psychological phenomena however, things are not so simple. We can easily observe, identify and differentiate between the phenomena of hockey and swimming, and by using any of a number of approaches, for example, the definition of necessary and sufficient criteria, the comparison of 'family resemblances', or the development of a taxonomy for the category 'sport', we can subsequently classify hockey and swimming as members of that category. Furthermore, using the same processes we can distinguish hockey and swimming from, for example, painting or reading, which are not members of the category 'sports'. We cannot however so easily observe and identify emotions and moods, distinguish them from one another, or distinguish between them and other constructs such as motivation and personality. To illustrate the point, consider that a construct such as anxiety can be used to describe an emotion (e.g., test anxiety), a mood (e.g., free floating anxiety), and a personality type (e.g., trait anxiety). Anxiety is arguably also a motivational process, in that it is likely to motivate avoidance behaviour in relation to the cause or focus of that anxiety, it may also be considered a psychopathological condition, and an existential state.

Several authors have suggested that distinctions between emotion and mood are irrelevant (e.g., Strongman, 1996). It is possible that the degree to which any distinction between emotion and mood matters is probably determined by the degree to which any one individual is examining them, or the degree to which they are relevant to the practice of that individual[1]. For a practitioner working with an overly anxious athlete one hour before an Olympic final, any such distinction is probably immaterial: the manifest anxiety will need to be addressed in whatever way the practitioner deems appropriate given their previous experience with this particular athlete in similar situations. In short, the practitioner is unlikely to ask "is the anxiety a mood or an emotion?". However, perhaps this is an oversimplification: the same practitioner's ability to identify, for example, that a *mood*-regulation strategy described in a research paper as 'ineffective' might not be inherently so, but was ineffective in that specific study as the result of being inappropriately applied to an athlete experiencing *emotional* anxiety, might well be a critical factor in the practitioner's subsequent clinical effectiveness.

So, somewhat confusingly, distinctions between emotion and mood may, or may not, matter. There is little point trying to argue for either possibility. The aim of the present chapter is to explore any distinctions between the two from both a philosophical and an empirical perspective (or at least, to argue for a method whereby they may be distinguished empirically, which is arguably a slightly different proposition). The present chapter does not aim to provide a *definitive* distinction between emotion and mood, but to indicate one process by which such a distinction might be found, and to present one possible distinguishing criterion, 'subjective context'. This criterion is derived from qualitative analysis of several classifications of potential distinguishing criteria derived empirically by Beedie, Lane, and Terry (2005a). Recent research (Beedie, Lane, and Terry, 2005b) has lent quantitative empirical support to this subjective contextual model. It is recognised that these data might equally support several competing models, and that on this basis, the model presented should not be seen as conclusive but simply, and hopefully, a step in the right direction.

---

[1] In response to a recent paper summarising the emotion-mood distinctions literature (Beedie et al., 2005a), requests for reprints were received from researchers in psychiatry, artificial intelligence, robotics, perception, and biology from the UK, USA, China, France and Brazil.

DEFINING 'GENERALLY ACCEPTED CRITERIA'
FOR EMOTION-MOOD DISTINCTIONS

In the present chapter it will on occasion be necessary to make generalisations in relation to published distinctions between emotion and mood. Although Ekman and Davidson (1994) noted that most interested researchers insist on distinguishing between the two, the criteria used to achieve such distinctions vary considerably, and these are understandably often based on the researcher's particular area of interest; a psycho-physiologist such as Panksepp may choose to differentiate the two by comparing the respective neural and somatic correlates or mechanisms of each, while a psycho-linguist such as Wierzbicka may choose to emphasize semantic distinctions in everyday language. However, despite the variety of proposed criteria, commonalities are evident (quite possibly because each individual theorist is essentially examining the same distinctions from a different perspective, see Beedie et al., 2005a, for discussion). Specifically, although theorists may not all agree about the distinguishing criterion *per se,* most are in agreement about the polarity of each distinction. That is, although not all theorists cite, for example, *intensity* as a distinction, those that do generally agree that emotions are more intense than mood. Such commonalities permit the defining of what shall in the present chapter be termed 'generally accepted criteria' for distinctions between emotion and mood. These are:

1. emotion is brief and intense, whereas mood is enduring and diffuse;
2. emotions result from, are focused on, and are 'about' specific events of which the individual is aware; moods do not result from, are not focussed on and are not about any one specific event of which the individual is aware;
3. emotions signal to the individual the state of the environment in relation to goal-directed behaviour, whereas moods signal the state of the self in relation to existential, life issues;
4. the consequences of emotions are mostly behavioural, whereas those of moods are mostly cognitive.

A percentage-wise comparison of the criteria by, and degree to which, academic and non-academic populations define distinctions between emotion and mood is presented in Table 1. It can be seen that the criteria of cause and duration were most frequently cited by academics and non-academics alike, and that the criterion of intentionality, which shall be returned to below, was cited by almost half the academics but by only just over ten percent of the non-academics (see Beedie et al., 2005a for discussion).

Table 1. Percentage-wise Comparison of Non-academic and Academic Distinctions between Emotion and Mood

Criterion	Non-academic	Academic
Cause	65%	31%
Duration	40%	62%
Control	25%	-
Experience	15%	-

Criterion	Non-academic	Academic
Consequences	14%	31%
Display	14%	-
Intentionality	12%	41%
Anatomy	11%	-
Intensity	11%	17%
Timing	8%	-
Function	7%	18%
Physiology	7%	8%
Stability	7%	-
Awareness of cause	4%	13%
Clarity	3%	-
Valence	3%	-

PHILOSOPHICAL PROBLEMS IN DISTINGUISHING EMOTION AND MOOD

Although it is evident that academics and non-academics alike tend to agree on the polarity of a variety of distinctions between emotion and mood, there is little agreement about which of these distinctions might be most salient in actually defining any tangible difference between the two. This is not surprising, as to move even tentatively towards a consensual criterion is problematic. A question which must be addressed is that of exactly what type of evidence or data are required to lend empirical support to any one criterion. The data of many scientific phenomena are self-evident and unambiguous, for example the litre of volume or the angle of rotation. The data of psychology are not so unambiguous and not so easily quantified, and in the case of emotion-mood distinctions, are problematic in the extreme. It has been suggested, in a statement attributed to many different authors, that if something exists, it exists in some amount, and if it exists in some amount, that amount can be measured. If emotion and mood are distinct constructs, they are theoretically distinct in terms of some criterion variable, be it biochemical, neurological, psychological, or behavioural. As such, it is a logical proposition that emotion and mood should theoretically be measurable as distinct constructs via measurement of that criterion variable. However, prior to any empirical investigation several philosophical questions need to be addressed, the most salient being whether the words 'emotion' and 'mood' represent two distinct physical or biological realities.

In theory, and based on a common language approach (see below), a person who is 'angry' may be experiencing the emotion of anger, be in an angry mood, be experiencing both simultaneously or sporadically, or may be high on trait anger (i.e., s/he possesses an angry personality). This apparent linguistic ambiguity may suggest that the words 'emotion', and 'mood' are simply different words for the same thing, that they describe a single aspect of human psychological experience in the same way as, for example, the words 'lift' and 'elevator' describe the same means of transporting people between the floors of buildings. Although the example of the words 'lift' and 'elevator' may seem a little obscure, it is used to emphasise that although humans *usually* employ different words to describe different things (e.g., 'chalk' and 'cheese'), we sometimes use different words to describe the same thing (e.g., 'lift' and 'elevator'), different words to describe fine distinctions between two very similar things (e.g., 'maroon' and 'burgundy'), and different words to describe the same thing in two different contexts (e.g., 'game' and 'sport'). We also, on occasion, use the same word to represent many different things, for example the word 'pound' can denote a unit of mass or economic value, a place of detention; and a heavy blow from an object such as a sledgehammer. Thus, in addressing the question of the relationship between emotion and mood, one first has to examine whether the words 'emotion' and 'mood' are used to express a relationship similar to that between 'chalk' and 'cheese', 'burgundy' and 'maroon', 'game' and 'sport', or 'lift' and 'elevator'. Once this is done, a harder question presents itself; if the relationship between the *words* 'emotion' and 'mood' is established, *does this relationship accurately represent the real world?* That is, if, for example, we establish that the words 'emotion' and 'mood' share a similar *semantic* relationship to the words 'chalk' and 'cheese', can we subsequently demonstrate that emotion and mood differ as *real* entities in the same way that we can demonstrate that chalk and cheese differ as real entities? Differentiation might be made via objective criteria, such as structure (what they are made of), function (what they are used for or *do*), subjective experience (how they feel to touch, appear to the eye, taste), and origin (sedimentation in the case of chalk and fermentation in the case of cheese). One in effect has to establish that emotions and moods are like chalk and cheese, and not like lifts and elevators.

Conceptual Frameworks from which to Examine Emotion/-Mood Distinctions

The question of whether emotion and mood are distinct constructs seems a relatively simple and probably closed-ended problem. That is, there appear to be three possible conclusions: (1) that emotion and mood are distinct phenomena and are measurable as such; (2) that emotion and mood are distinct phenomena but not measurable as such, at least with present technology; or (3) that emotion and mood are not distinct phenomena. However, philosophically speaking, not only is the question problematic to answer, it may be considered somewhat problematic to ask! It has been proposed that the act of asking a question implies a shared perspective and a degree of shared knowledge between the questioner and those questioned (Semin, 1995). Whether this perspective is the result of all humans sharing a similar experience of a tangible 'real' World, or is the result of us all being part of the same social group with shared *concepts* of the World, is a matter open to some debate. The two possible relationships between language and reality, one in which language describes a tangible and consensual reality, and one in which language refers to perceptions of reality, represent 'realist' or 'common sense' (Hospers, 1997; Searle, 1999) and 'relativist' (Grayling, 1982) philosophical standpoints. These standpoints are perhaps best represented in the psychology literature by the contrasting tenets of *folk psychology* and *social constructionism* respectively.

The Realist Paradigm: Folk Psychology
Searle (1999) proposed that "there exists a real world that is totally independent of human beings and of what they think or say about it, and statements about the objects and states of affairs in that world are true or false depending on whether things in the world really are the

way we say they are" (p. 13). This proposal infers a 'realist' stance towards the World. In the discipline of psychology, this approach is typified by what is termed 'folk theory' or 'folk psychology'. Folk psychology theories are common-sense explanations of the behaviour of ourselves and others (Bem and Looren de Jong, 1997). They are theories and assumptions we use to understand and predict many aspects of the social world based on our experience of that world. Many emotion researchers believe that folk theories are of scientific value (e.g., Lazarus, 2000; LeDoux, 1998; Levenson, 1994). Lazarus, for example, stated:

> If we believe that emotions result from the way people construe and evaluate events, the most useful theory [of emotion] will be based on those construals and evaluations…if formulated appropriately, folk theory can be evaluated by observation, which is the hallmark of science, just as readily as can any other theory (p. 61).

Implicit in folk theories of emotion and mood, and scientific theories are often 'little more than folk theories, clothed in the scientific jargon of the time' (Averill, 1996, p. 24), is that the words used to describe these phenomena relate to concrete, real events, and that these events are separate entities to any linguistic representation of them. Thus, in relation to distinguishing emotion from mood, adoption of a realist stance would allow us to argue that because people distinguish between the two concepts of emotion and mood, and furthermore these distinctions seem consistent (see Beedie et al, 2005a), emotion and mood exist as separate entities in the real world. We, as individuals and as a species, have simply observed them, experienced them, and labelled them. As has been suggested, "there are phenomena for which the word 'emotion' has been invented, and which phenomena existed prior to the word having been invented" (Frijda, Markam, Sato, and Wiers, 1995, p. 121).

The Relativist Paradigm: Social Constructionism

Social constructionsim disputes the positivist-empiricist conception of science and its reliance on observation, facts and data as indicators of truth (Semin, 1995). It "adopts a critical stance towards the taken for granted ways in which we understand the World and ourselves" (Coyle, 2000, p. 252). Social constructionism posits that there is no such thing as an objective fact or truth, there are merely different perspectives of the World (Burr, 1995). Accordingly, the role of language is not to accurately represent the extralinguistic World, but to contribute to mutual understanding of it via social interaction (Bem and Looren de Jong, 1997). Thus, in the current context, social constructionism posits that the words used to describe any phenomena, for example 'emotion' and 'mood', and the phenomenon itself, are not exclusive of each other in the manner posited by folk psychology.

In order to link social constructionism to the issue at hand, an analogy may be helpful. It was mentioned above that a degree of shared knowledge, even complicity, between questioner and questioned was required to address certain philosophical problems. To illustrate the argument, consider an example from cosmology, that of the moon. The concept of the moon is shared by most humans. Most of us have seen it, and have witnessed or experienced its effects (its light, its influence on the tides, and possibly even its often-cited influence on the behaviour of animals and humans). We may also have seen film of men walking on it, seen it eclipse the sun, or seen parts of it on display in museums. It may be argued that for all but the most sceptical, there is ample evidence that the moon exists (this evidence relates to a *realist* perspective, the real moon exists in the real universe). Another concept, the 'black hole', has long been accepted as a phenomenon in cosmology. Most cosmologists accept that black holes exist (White and Gribbin, 1998). This is presumably because the concept of a black hole fits the, mostly mathematical, available evidence. Whether such a thing as a black hole *actually* exists is however problematic. The key question is whether the mathematical theories predicting black holes represent the real universe, or are in fact the only way for humans to explain a phenomenon of which we have no direct experience, one which may not behave in ways understood by contemporary science, and one whose presence we can only infer from the behaviour of other cosmological phenomena. Certainly no cosmologist has ever, or perhaps will ever, see or experience a black hole, and as such it is doubtful that their existence could be demonstrated empirically via any medium other than mathematics (and some would anyway argue that such evidence is not empirical). A black hole could thus be described as a social construct, a concept constructed to explain or describe a phenomenon, essentially to facilitate communication and understanding among cosmologists, who share a need for a concept to describe and explain that phenomena. On this basis, even if black holes exist in the conventional sense, they could defined as a social construct. However, because black holes are a social construct, a construct not based on any universal (species-wide) experience of *actual* black holes, it is possible that the term 'black hole' could apply to various phenomena. For example, independent social groups could attribute different characteristics to black holes; a group of cosmologists in the USA and a group of cosmologists in China could develop radically different representations on the basis of different data or as a result of working within different paradigms. Thus, without tangible, real objects to experience, a concept such as a black hole, or an emotion, whether real or not, may not have a single, universally accepted, representation, and thus when people discuss 'a black hole' or 'an emotion', they may not always mean the same thing.

Parkinson (1995) argued that to accept a realist approach toward emotion and mood, two questionable assumptions have to be made: first, that emotions and moods exist as a definable territory independent of our imposition of meaning, and second, that the labels we ascribe to such representations accurately reflect them. Certainly, emotion and mood, like black holes, are concepts constructed by groups of people to facilitate communication among them in relation to various experiences or observations of their own or other peoples' behaviour. Thus emotion and mood may not be separate and distinct phenomena (or phenomena at all) beyond the fact that we have chosen to construct them as such. It could be argued that one reason for the variability in research findings, opinion, and representations of emotion and mood is that the two are not consistently occurring biological realities, but socially constructed phenomena for which there exist as many representations as social groups who have defined them.

Emotion and Mood as Psychological Reality

Expounding a realist perspective, Searle (1995) argued that 'we live in exactly one world, not two or three or seventeen (p. 227). Midgley (1998) however argued that one world may be represented by several different maps:

> It is just as true to say that the World consists of lands and oceans, or of climatic zones, as that it consists of the territories of different nations... There is no bottom line. Our choice of terms depends on the purpose for which we want to analyse the World at the time. Indeed the simplest atlases sometimes contain just two maps, marked respectively 'Physical' and 'Political'. What would it mean to claim that one of these maps is, in some

absolute sense, less fundamental and needs to be reduced to the terms of the other? The fact that cities and national frontiers appear only on one of the maps, while mountain ranges appear only on the other, does not undermine the reality of either phenomenon. (p. 267)

Thus it might be argued that any defined distinction between emotion and mood might bare little relationship to biological reality. That, like the seemingly arbitrary lines drawn between nations on a map, it is a distinction convenient to human understanding and communication.

Continuing with a geographical theme, arguing that language does represent a tangible reality, Searle (1999) cites the 'fact' that the Atlantic Ocean contains salt water. He suggests that the Atlantic existed way before there was anyone to identify it as an ocean, that it contained water, or that this water contained salt. Searle's apparently simplistic argument is that it just because we have chosen words to label these phenomena does not mean that we have invented the phenomena. When the words 'Atlantic Ocean' are used in conversation, or any other form of communication, Searle argues that a common understanding of the concept among the communicators is almost guaranteed. Psychological phenomena such as emotion and mood are metaphysically more problematic than the Atlantic ocean; they are, for example, not directly observable. However, they are somewhat more concrete than black holes, in that we can at least experience them, and make certain assumptions about others' experience of them through their behaviour, their speech, facial expressions, posture, even through media such as film and literature. Whether social construct or biological reality, there are numerous consistencies in folk psychology theories of emotion and mood, consistencies alluded to by Burman and Parker (1993) who argued that 'psychological phenomenon have a public and collective reality, and we are mistaken if we think they have their origin in the private space of the individual' (p. 1). There is in everyday language a common understanding of, for example, anger, of what it means to be angry, how anger feels, how we react to our own anger, how we react to other people's anger, how they react to ours, situations in which anger is appropriate, situations in which it is not, methods to suppress anger or to increase it to elicit a desired effect. Not everyone experiences anger the same way, or responds to it in the same way, but there is a common thread - what Lazarus (1991) describes as a core relational theme - underlying all anger, that of the perception of an obstacle between an individual and that individual's goals. Anger, be it an emotion or a mood, like a black hole, is arguably a social construct, and like a black hole may also be a tangible biological reality. Either way, *it is certainly a psychological reality,* that is, there is a consistency in what the word 'anger' means in terms of human thought and behaviour. In everyday social interaction humans rely on consistencies like these to understand, to explain, and to predict human behaviour. It is argued that such consistencies allow examination of emotion and mood from the perspective of those who experience it, that is, from a realist, folk psychology perspective. In simple terms, accepting the fact that people say that emotion and mood are different things and the fact that they use the two words in different contexts (e.g., when an individual uses the phrase "he is moody" they are rarely trying to express the same sentiment as is implied by the phrase "he is emotional"), allows us to conclude that, unlike lifts and elevators, and like chalk and cheese, emotion and mood are distinct phenomena.

EMPIRICAL PROBLEMS IN INVESTIGATING EMOTION-MOOD DISTINCTIONS

It has been argued above that emotion and mood can be treated as distinct concepts. The psychology literature suggests that many criteria might distinguish between emotion and mood *conceptually,* however such conceptual distinctions will remain speculative unless some degree of empirical evidence can be presented. That is, a potential criterion is selected, a method of measuring that criterion is developed, and an analysis of the degree to which resultant data suggest that emotion and mood represent different levels of that criterion is performed. Beedie et al. (2005a) identified five general dimensions of emotion-mood distinctions, the 'potential criteria' alluded to above: structural (e.g., duration, intensity, stability); management (e.g., control, display); somatic (e.g., physiology, anatomy); objective context (e.g., cause, consequences); and subjective context (e.g., awareness of cause, 'aboutness'). In the next section, the potential for of each of these, plus one other often alluded to criterion, word meanings, in distinguishing empirically between emotion and mood are assessed. For ease of reading, the following section is formatted on the basis of (1) the *requirement* that would need to be satisfied for any criterion to distinguish emotion from mood empirically; (2) the *general premise* of the criterion in relation to emotion-mood distinctions; (3) the *arguments for* the criterion; and (4) the *arguments against* the criterion.

Linguistic Criteria: Taxonomies of Emotion and Mood Words

Requirement

To distinguish emotion from mood via a linguistic criterion would entail being able to say categorically that a state denoted by a certain word, e.g., 'anxious' is a mood while another state denoted by a different word, e.g., 'scared', is an emotion.

General Premise

Emotion and mood are both psychological constructs. A method often used to distinguish between constructs in many scientific disciplines is the development of a taxonomy, a process allowing the phenomena in question to be classified 'in such a way that it is possible to diagnose without any serious doubt whether or not some case fits the category in question' (Madge, 1969, p.44). Several phenomena could be classified in relation to emotion and mood. In fact, a well documented example of such a taxonomy is that of Lazarus's 'core relational themes' for emotion (1991). Similar taxonomies have been proposed by for example Ortony, Clore, and Collins (1988) who developed a taxonomy of the focus of emotions (e.g., 'prospect-based' and 'fortune of others' emotions) and Lormand (1985) who classified mood and 'non-mood' words (see also Clore, Ortony, and Foss, 1987; Davitz, 1969; Johnson-Laird and Oatley, 1989; Storm and Storm, 1987; Wierzbicka, 1992).

Argument For

In relation to distinguishing emotions from moods, the words used to refer to either construct arguably represent the obvious choice for such a taxonomy. Ortony et al. (1987) proposed that 'emotions are not linguistic things. However, the most convenient nonphenomonological access we have to them is through language' (p. 342). Words certainly provide a rich database from which to develop a taxonomy. Although no systematic approach to distinguishing between emotion and mood via a linguistic taxonomy has been published, several authors have conceptualised various discrete states as either moods or emotions. For example, Ekman (1994) stated that 'it seems evident that a mood potentiates a particular emotion (anger for irritability, positive emotions when in a euphoric mood, sadness when in a blue mood, fear when in an apprehensive mood)' (p. 57). Similar arguments have been proposed by Beck (1976); Ekman and Davidson (1994c); Frijda (1994); Isberg (2000); Lazarus (1994); Oatley and Jenkins (1992); and Zajonc (1994). It is thus tempting to speculate that every mood state may be denoted by a certain word, and be related to a specific emotion denoted by a different word, for example, 'anxious' and 'afraid', 'happy' and 'joyful', 'content' and 'relieved', 'hostile' and 'angry', 'excitable' and 'thrilled'.

Argument Against

There are several problems with a linguistic/taxonomic approach. The words proposed to denote moods by the authors cited above ('apprehensive', 'anxious' and 'irritable'), may have been selected because they are typically associated with low intensity states that tend to endure beyond a few seconds, making them *unlikely* candidates for emotions by generally accepted criteria. Many moods and emotions may be referred to by a number of words that describe increasing intensities of that state, for example, 'irritable', 'bad tempered', 'hostile', 'angry', 'furious', 'incensed' and 'outraged' refer to increasing intensities of the 'basic' emotion of anger, whilst 'worried', 'apprehensive', 'anxious', 'afraid', 'scared', 'terrified' and 'petrified' refer to increasing intensities of the basic emotion of fear. Words denoting high intensities of an emotion, such as 'outraged', 'terrified', and 'ecstatic' are rarely used to represent a mood. This is logical and consistent with generally accepted criteria. For example, a source of terror must represent a considerable threat to the survival of the organism, or one would not be terrified of it. Thus, one has to *do* something about the source of the terror, either by eliminating it or distancing oneself from it, or one must suffer the consequences of not taking such action. Thus terror, if it is to function in the way most theorists agree it should, that is by signalling an environmental threat and facilitating an appropriate response (Batson et al., 1992; Lazarus, 1994; LeDoux, 1998; Morris, 1992), should be intense, should facilitate immediate action, and consequently will be brief (it is brief because the action tendency, which constitutes part of the terror response, facilitates immediate distancing of the individual from the source of the terror, thus alleviating the need for the emotion to persist. One would understand that, if an object is so terrible, failure to achieve such a distance would probably have been fatal in the environment in which the species and their psychological processes evolved). Such a state satisfies many of the generally accepted criteria for an emotion, but few for a mood. In contrast, feeling 'anxious' may indicate that action of some sort is required but as the source of the anxiety, which may include a wide variety of factors ranging from lack of sleep through to feelings of inadequacy about life in general, is unlikely to be life threatening is not associated with any specific action tendency. Thus, not catalysing, and ultimately benefiting from, any direct activity aimed at alleviating its cause, the state may endure at a low intensity, colouring many other psychological processes, until it is convenient to search for, and attend to, the possible causes. Such a state satisfies many of the generally accepted criteria for a mood, and few for an emotion.

Such linguistic distinctions seem plausible. They are however unlikely to be supported empirically. If the words proposed to represent moods above, such as 'apprehension' and 'irritability', do indeed represent moods and not emotions, it is logical to assume that when an individual reports scores of '2', '3', '0', and '0' respectively to the items 'apprehensive', 'anxious', 'scared' and 'afraid' on a Likert format self-report mood scale, it should be possible to state with confidence that the individual is experiencing an anxious mood. However, we could not be confident in saying so for several reasons, ranging from the precise words that a respondent would habitually use to describe her or his feelings, to how the respondent conceptualises their present feelings. For example, the respondent may be apprehensive and anxious *about* an exam they are about to sit; these feelings of apprehension and anxiety may be *caused* by and *focussed on* the exam, they may dissipate after the exam, and they may not be colouring any other cognitive or perceptual processes. These are thus emotions by generally accepted criteria. The respondents may have placed a zero next to 'scared' and 'afraid' simply because these words seem to indicate extreme cases of fear which, according to their understanding of the words, they are not experiencing. Despite the fact that the words 'anxiety' and 'apprehension' may fit the criteria for moods as described above, in this case these words are more likely to be describing emotions. Ortony and Clore (1989) similarly doubt whether individual words represent either moods or emotions, and argued that the reason that terms denoting high intensity emotions are not often used to refer to moods, giving the impression of two mutually exclusive sets of emotion and mood words, is not that they cannot correctly be used to, but that the appropriate conditions for the eliciting of such moods is extremely rare.

Language is rarely used consistently (Ekman, 1994). There are probably sound *theoretical* bases for the argument that certain words refer specifically to either emotions or moods, but it is unlikely that these are reflected in practice. Semantic ambiguities are found in everyday speech and dictionary definitions and scientific classifications are not always reflected in common usage. A scientific taxonomy of emotion and mood based on such linguistic criteria is not likely to enable distinguishing the two states empirically.

Structural Criteria: Intensity, Duration, Clarity, Timing And Stability

Requirement

To distinguish emotion from mood via structural criteria would entail being able to state categorically that a state falling one side of some threshold value on a structural variable (e.g., duration, intensity) is an emotion, whilst if it falls on the other, it is a mood.

General Premise

There is general agreement that emotion and mood are distinct on several structural criteria. In the literature, the proposal that mood endures longer than emotion is the most frequently cited distinction between the two, a distinction which, on the surface, appears relatively simple to test empirically.

Arguments For

It would appear that structural criteria, which essentially define and describe the emotion or mood in space and time in the same way to that in which volume, frequency, duration and tone describe a musical note, would be the easiest to measure and evaluate of the six criteria currently under analysis. That is, to measure the duration of a state, be it by self-report (e.g., 'I was angry for about 5 seconds, then it subsided rapidly') or by physiological indices (e.g., the duration of a distinct pattern of neurological activity associated with an episode of anger) seems a relatively easy procedure. If for example, we know that a certain neurological pattern is associated with feelings of anger in a certain individual, we could measure the length of that pattern, its intensity, the time it takes to get to that intensity, how stable it is and how clearly defined it is in relation to other neural activity, and distinguish emotions from moods via these criteria.

Arguments Against

Many of the arguments against using a linguistic criterion to distinguish emotion from mood presented above apply equally to using a structural criterion. Most structural criteria by which emotion and mood may be distinguished cannot be said to be exclusive to either. For example, on the basis that the intensity of an emotion is proportional to the significance of the eliciting event, an event of low significance to the individual would be expected to elicit a low intensity emotion (e.g., mild surprise). However, to distinguish emotion from mood via the intensity of the state in question would entail assuming that a low intensity state, such as mild surprise, is a mood. Such an assumption ignores several other generally accepted criteria, that is, surprise is, by definition, both caused by and about a specific object, an object that the individual is by definition aware of - can you imagine a situation in which you are surprised by something you are not aware of? Surprise is also a short-lived state, the conditions that would elicit an enduring episode of surprise are also somewhat hard to imagine. Surprise therefore is classified as an emotion and not a mood by generally accepted criteria.

The two arguments above are however rendered relatively insignificant in the face of the seemingly unfeasible requirement that a threshold value be defined indicating at which point a quantitative change *within* the emotion or mood becomes a qualitative change *from* an emotion to a mood (or vice versa). In fact, the operationalisation of emotion-mood distinctions on the basis of structural distinctions is implausible for this reason alone. As well as requiring the defining of a threshold value, below which a state is an emotion and above which it is a mood (e.g., the time an emotion must endure before it becomes a mood), the problem is confounded by the fact that an individual may not necessarily be aware of certain structural factors, such as the moment of onset of a particular mood, rendering it impossible to know the duration of that mood. In fact, using structural criteria to distinguish emotion from mood implies that the two must exist on a continuum. Schimmack and Siemer (1998) argued:

> One might wonder why affect researchers should distinguish two types of affects if the distinction is merely a quantitative difference in intensity. Taxonomies usually make distinctions when phenomena are qualitatively different (birds vs. fish), but not for quantitative differences (big birds vs. small birds) (p. 10).

However, even if, contrary to the suggestions of Schimmack and Siemer, emotion and mood *do* exist on a continuum rather than as discrete phenomena, distinguishing the two via structural criteria is problematic; although certain states may be prototypical moods and others prototypical emotions (in a similar way to which water can be very hot or very cold), many may exhibit the characteristics of both, leading to a problem analogous to defining the temperature at which cold water becomes hot water. Such a criterion value for any structural variable would of course be controversial in the extreme, on this basis alone such a criterion is an unsuitable candidate for empirical research.

Management Criteria: Control and Display

Requirement
To distinguish emotion from mood via management criteria would entail being able to state categorically that a state that is manageable and not displayed is a mood and vice-versa.

General Premise
By generally accepted criteria, emotions are harder to control and more likely to be displayed than moods.

Argument For
It seems logical that the degree to which a subject is using any form of management strategy to modify either an emotion or mood can be assessed in one or both of two ways. First, direct observation of these management processes in response to an induced mood or emotion. For example, an induced mood, perhaps based on a stream of minor irritations, should result in manageable feelings of anger, while an induced emotion, perhaps based on an extremely frustrating scenario, especially when induced in a subject already in an angry mood, should result in un-manageable and displayed feelings of anger. Second, the self-report of that subject; for example, in the above situation, the subject should report manageable feelings of irritation and anger in response to the first induction, and un-manageable feelings of anger in response to the second. Thus, if the criteria of control and display do accurately represent distinctions between emotion and mood, to test the proposals empirically appears to be a fairly routine process. Having said this, such an experimental procedure would, perhaps somewhat problematically, require at least one other accepted and operationalised distinction between emotion and mood (in the case above, the inductions were based on the proposal that emotion and mood have differing causes).

Argument Against
The conceptual basis of the management criterion must be addressed. It is possible that the degree to which a feeling is either controlled and/or displayed is a function of other characteristics of emotion and mood, such as intensity and duration, rather than necessary distinctions in themselves. That is, it may be possible to control a mild or moderately intense feeling, but not a highly intense one, thus any state above a certain intensity would be unmanageable. Also, it may take time to consciously initiate a management strategy in response to a feeling (arguably more than a few seconds), thus any state shorter than this

minimum duration would be unmanageable. Thus, emotions may be unmanageable purely because they are too intense and too brief, as opposed to the fact that they are an emotion *per se*. Arguably, a less intense and more enduring emotion would be manageable. In support of this, it may be argued that most pathological moods, for example depression and mania, are intense and unmanageable, while many low intensity emotions (such as anticipation and surprise) are routinely suppressed by, for example a salesperson about to close a deal and not wishing to jeopardise it. Having said this, the proposals in the literature relating to the consequences of emotion and mood, especially that emotion biases behaviour (Davidson, 1994), would hint that a change in behaviour is a necessary consequence of an emotion, and certainly, much of the adaptive value of an emotion is based on its associated action tendency. In relation to *prototypical* cases of emotion and mood, it seems likely that the criteria of control and display hold true. It seems almost implausible that one could suppress the shock, and associated inclination to run, experienced in response to being barked at by a hitherto unseen large dog, whilst it is considered almost socially unacceptable – presumably on the basis that such feelings are controllable - to display irritation when, for example, waiting in a supermarket queue. There is however enough doubt that emotion and mood can be reliably distinguished on the basis of control and display to argue that the use of the criterion of Management is unlikely to reliably distinguish the two empirically.

Somatic Criteria: Anatomy and Physiology

Requirement

To distinguish emotion from mood via somatic criteria would entail being able to state categorically that a state associated with certain physiological processes or anatomical regions is an emotion whereas a state associated with different processes and sites is a mood.

General Premise

In many respects a criterion based on somatic patterning presents the most intuitively promising method for scientifically distinguishing emotion from mood. This is because, if it could be operationalised, it is the only criterion which removes any trace of subjectivity from the process. That is, if we *knew*, for example, that an angry mood is associated with a specific somatic pattern (perhaps involving activation of certain brain areas), while an angry emotion is associated with a *different* somatic pattern (perhaps involving endocrine processes that may be detected via blood indices) we would be able to state categorically that an individual is experiencing a certain emotion or mood without reference to that person's subjective report (although such a report would of course constitute a source of validity information).

Argument For

There is evidence that specific patterns of somatic or neural activity are associated with specific emotions; LeDoux (1998) argues that anger, fear, disgust, sadness, happiness and surprise can all be distinguished on the basis of different ANS responses; while Panksepp (1994) argues that certain neuropeptides are related to specific emotions or classes of emotion (corticotropin releasing factor with anxiety, vasopressin with male aggression, and the opioids with a variety of social processes). Also, research into the emotional characteristics of certain types of animals suggests that their respective emotion-based behaviour - predators tend to exhibit curiosity and aggression while herbivores exhibit fear, timidity and panic - may provide clues as to emotion- and mood-specific physiology (Panksepp, 1994).

There is in fact a great deal of promise in the use of new technologies in the investigation of such relationships; LeDoux (1994) stated that 'as more and more emotional processes are studied with the idea of identifying the underlying micro circuitry, more and more anatomical distinctions between different emotional responses will emerge' (p. 250-251). Thus, on the basis that distinct emotions may be distinguished via somatic indices, a basis for distinguishing emotion from mood may exist.

Argument Against

A significant and challenging difference between the process of discriminating different emotions from each other, and that of distinguishing emotion from mood is however evident. Put simply, there is general agreement about the conceptual difference between distinct emotions, for example, fear and anger have different antecedents or core relational themes (Lazarus, 1991), different experiential manifestations, and different consequences, such as 'flight' for fear and 'fight' for anger. Thus fear feels different to anger. This however is not the case with emotion and mood. That is, if we wish to associate a certain ANS response with an emotion, and a different ANS response with a related mood (e.g., the emotion of anger and an angry mood|), we must again have an *a priori* distinction between the two. For example, if a duration of 2 seconds were an accepted distinction – that is all emotions are less than 2 seconds in duration and all moods are equal to or longer than 2 seconds – we could state with a degree of confidence that a subject experiencing a pattern of ANS activity consistent with anger which endures for 5 minutes is in an angry mood, and our confidence would be increased if the subject described her or his self as 'being in an angry mood'. But if we do not have a criterion such as the 2 second duration above, 5 minutes of ANS activity consistent with anger is certainly anger, but could be either an emotion, repeated emotions, or a mood.

The above approach, though based on a common paradigm, of distinguishing between somatic correlates of two conceptually distinct states, represents only half the story in relation to somatic distinctions between emotion and mood. Although most theorists who have considered such distinctions have adopted this paradigm; for example, Panksepp (1994) talked of 'precipitous' arousal for emotion and 'milder and more sustained' arousal for mood (p. 86), it is possible that a conceptual distinction based on anatomical, physiological or neurological indices, as opposed to the corresponding correlates of existing distinctions, could be developed – essentially a somatic distinction between emotion and mood that was not dependent on another criterion. Such a distinction would not only have to be independent of other distinctions, but would also have to define emotion and mood, such as (to use an extreme simplification based on the non-academic responses cited by Beedie et al. 2005a), emotions are experienced exclusively in the heart, moods are experienced exclusively in the head. The likelihood of such a criterion being even proposed, let alone accepted, seems small at present.

Distinctions between emotion and mood based on somatic criteria (anatomical, neural, visceral) cannot be demonstrated empirically until at least one other conceptual criterion by which to distinguish between the two is established, or until such a conceptual distinction *actually defines* the difference between emotion and mood, as opposed to representing a correlate of another proposed distinction.

Objective Context: Causes and Consequences

Requirement

To distinguish emotion from mood via objective contextual criteria would entail being able to state categorically that a state caused by and resulting in a certain classification of factors is an emotion while one caused by and resulting in a different classification is a mood.

General Premise

Emotions are popularly seen as resulting from a single instigator of some significance to the individual, while moods are seen as being either the result of a series of less significant instigators, or of a factor(s) of which the individual may not be aware. Similarly, emotion seems to have behavioural consequences, while mood's may be more cognitive. As their causes and consequences differ, emotion and mood could be said to have distinct functions.

Arguments For

It is possible that classifications of such causes/situations and consequences could be developed, and episodes of emotion and mood could be distinguished via comparison with these (as mentioned above, Lazarus's 1991 'core relational themes' is, in fact, a classification of causes of emotions). For example, consider an observer attempting to assess whether a subject who reports 'feeling angry' is experiencing either an emotion or a mood. If the subject reports that the feelings were brought about by an incident earlier that day, and that every time the incident is remembered, renewed feelings of anger are accompanied by accelerated heart rate and slightly clenched fists and jaw, the observer would be able to see that all these factors fall into the (as yet hypothetical) classification 'causes and consequences of emotions', and assume that the emotion of anger is being repeatedly experienced by the subject. If the subject could not point to a specific cause for the feelings of anger, reported feeling 'generally' angry about several things, and does not seem physically agitated, the observer would be able to see that all these factors fall into the (also hypothetical) classification 'causes and consequences of moods'. Similarly, there is some basis for being able to observe that someone who is behaving nervously (i.e., sweating, trembling, shifting weight from foot to foot, speaking in short sentences, and perhaps even trying to put distance between themselves and a particular object or situation), is experiencing the emotion of anxiety (i.e., it is caused by something and resulting in a distinct pattern of somatic arousal that may diminish if distance is put between that something and the individual). On the other hand, someone whose verbal responses to a suggested plan are tinged with overly pessimistic predictions of failure, who is generally overcautious in accepting that plan, who may even admit to being anxious about the plan without being anxious about any specific aspect of it, may be in an anxious mood.

As highlighted above, Lazarus (1991), among others, has demonstrated that classification of distinct causes of emotions (and arguably moods) is a feasible task. His 'core relational themes' for emotion would certainly satisfy the 'causes' section of the classification 'causes and consequences of emotion' described above. Core relational themes for moods are likely to be related to their emotion counterparts, after all, anger, whether an emotion or a mood, is still anger. According to Lazarus, the core relational theme for the emotion of anger is having been slighted or demeaned. A core relational theme for the mood of anger could thus be either

a) repeated minor incidents of being slighted or demeaned, none of which on their own were significant enough to warrant an overt emotional response, b) the ongoing effects of residual somatic arousal and altered cognitive and perceptual processing as a result of an unresolved emotion of anger (i.e., the slight or demeaning event was not resolved or challenged at the time), or c) the cumulative effect of many diverse influences (e.g., biochemistry, weather, sleep, diet, etc) on cognitive and perceptual processes, causing the individual to experience feeling of anger as a result of a variety of events that would not normally cause anger in the absence of these diverse influences.

Arguments Against

There are limitations in using contextual distinctions. Such distinctions are, again, highly subjective; an event that elicits an emotion for one person may not do so for another. Also, it is perhaps not the *actual* cause that is likely to be the significant factor, but the *perceived* cause (an observer could not for example state categorically that a subject is experiencing the emotion of anger just because that subject was exposed to an anger-based emotion induction procedure – the stimulus may simply have been perceived as a minor irritant and to have either caused no response, or to have constituted one of a series of minor irritants that combined to form a mood). Consequences of emotions and moods are also likely to be highly individual. People can, for example, feel extremely angry without expressing overt anger, or feel only slightly angry while expressing intense anger.

Although a classification of causes and consequences of emotions and moods may present a first stage in distinguishing emotion from mood, it is likely to be limited in experimental settings by the above factors. It is perhaps the very subjectivity that has plagued this and the other criteria addressed above that should be examined as the most likely method of distinguishing emotion from mood.

Subjective Context: Awareness of Cause, Intentionality and Experience

Requirement

To distinguish emotion from mood via subjective contextual criteria would entail being able to state categorically that a *feeling* which *appears* to the individual to be caused by a certain group of factors and which *appears* to be about those factors is an emotion, whereas a state which *appears* to be neither caused by nor *about* anything in particular in which seems to influence thoughts in line with the affective orientation of that state, is a mood.

General Premise

It has been demonstrated that it is problematic to distinguish between emotion and mood empirically via the criteria of word meanings, structure, somatic processes, physiology, management, or objective context. Certainly, many of these criteria may be used to distinguish between the two once another *a priori* distinction is established, but it is doubtful that any represent the substantive difference between the two states *per se.* Certainly, according to many academic authorities, and most of the respondents to Beedie et al. (2005a), a mood is more than simply a low intensity, enduring, and relatively manageable emotion. However, to return to Schimmack and Siemer's (1998) argument above, there would surely be no need to classify feelings as either 'emotion' or 'mood' if the distinction between the two were merely a quantitative difference in intensity, duration or manageability.

The paragraph above implies that emotion and mood are substantially distinct phenomena, and that the distinctions between the two are more than just quantitative. Seemingly contradicting this position it has been proposed by several authors that corresponding emotions and moods do in fact *feel* identical to each other (e.g., Watson and Clark, 1994a); and on that basis it may be argued that at some level emotion and mood may be fundamentally the same thing. Although this at first seems counter-intuitive, it is surely not illogical to propose that anxiety felt in response to, for example an upcoming exam, *should* feel the same as anxiety felt for no apparent reason, or about life in general. From a folk psychology perspective, the fact that both states are labelled with the same word, 'anxiety', is compelling enough evidence. Indeed, one respondent reported in Beedie et al (2005a) stated 'I guess the difference for me is the degree to which the original feeling is felt and expressed that makes it either an emotion or a mood, but I get the sense that in their original form they may be the same thing'. This sentiment is not unlike that expressed by of Clore (1994), who explained how emotion and mood could feel the same but still be perceived as substantially different constructs:

> If the source of an emotion remains unconscious, the emotion may be experienced as part of one's reaction to almost anything, and hence may colour one's judgement of almost anything. If the source of an emotion is conscious, then its meaning will be constrained, and the range of judgements it colours will be limited. Hence not only is the conscious experience of emotion important, but also consciousness of its cause and also its meaning (p. 287)

Clore (1994) went on to make explicit the links between consciousness of cause and emotion, and unconsciousness of cause and mood. Similarly, Lormand (1985) argued that if moods are objectless because their objects are 'so general and vague as to escape notice' (p. 392) they may simply be unresolved emotions, that is, an emotion is resolved because its objects are not general and vague, but precise and clear. These two authors clearly believe that emotion and mood may be the same thing in biological terms, while representing different things in psychological terms. Significantly, *these differences are apparently determined by the subjective processes of the individual experiencing the state.* Seemingly addressing the issue some time ago, Arnold (1960) argued that the knowledge of the cause of a feeling cannot turn a mood into an emotion or vice versa, but there is no reason, given the complexity of the human organism, to argue that this is not at least a possibility. In fact, given the similarities between the two, the idea that emotion and mood are in fact two interpretations or perspectives of the same phenomena has some appeal. Certainly, Darwin (1872) highlighted that several organs and processes might serve more than one function (the mouth for example serves many), thus it would not be inconsistent with many other adaptive processes for emotion and mood to share the same fundamental form/processes while performing two different tasks. Nature also provides us with many examples of one phenomenon being 'changed into' another, apparently different, phenomenon through the action of certain contextual/environmental factors. For example, water becomes ice when certain environmental conditions are met. However, water and ice, although made of the same chemical components, are very different in appearance, behave in different ways, may be experienced very differently, and may have very different consequences. Despite the fact that water and ice are essentially the same material in a different form, these different forms determine that the two should be treated as different phenomena at all but the chemical level. It could be argued in response to Arnold's proposals above that emotion and mood, if they are the same at some level, may similarly be treated as the same only at that level of analysis (e.g., biological), while their subjective context-dependent differences determine that, like ice and water, they should be treated as different phenomena when analysed from other perspectives (e.g., psychological).

On the basis of the above argument, that emotion and mood are like water and ice, at some level the same phenomena, the key to distinguishing between them in empirical research may be to identify not how they differ biologically or 'physically', but how those individuals experiencing them tell them apart. It is certainly logical to assume that some aspect of an individual's subjective experience of emotion or mood indicates to that individual which of the two states they are experiencing or have just experienced. It is argued that an individual's experience of an emotion or a mood would be characterised by their awareness of the cause of the state and their awareness of what the state was about, or its *intentionality*.

Awareness of Cause: Arguments For and Against

Many theorists have suggested that an individual is aware of the real cause of an emotion whereas he or she may not be aware of the real cause of a mood (by 'real cause' it is implied that both emotions and moods are caused by certain factors, that is, although the causes of moods may be nebulous and extremely hard to identify, and therefore often misattributed along the lines 'I'm just in a bad mood for no particular reason', a mood does have a cause or set of causes, and does not just happen).

Awareness of cause cannot stand *alone* as a distinction between emotion and mood, as, although it has been proposed that we are aware of the causes of emotions but are not aware of the causes of moods, there may be exceptions. For example, an individual who loses their car keys and is late for work may subsequently be in a bad mood all day despite being aware of a distinct cause for that mood. Thus, in relation to awareness of cause, instead of stating that emotions have a cause of which the individual is aware while moods do not, it is perhaps more accurate to state that moods *do not necessarily have a cause of which we are aware*, but may have. However, it may be argued that the 'awareness of cause' criterion may have some utility in the discrimination of emotion from mood in that, although the cause of moods may or may not be obscure from the perspective of the individual, by generally accepted criteria, awareness of cause and object seems to be a defining characteristic of emotion. That is, a state of anxiety of which the individual is aware of a specific cause is probably an emotion but may be a mood. However, a state of anxiety which appears to have no specific cause is extremely unlikely to be an emotion.

Intentionality: Arguments For and Against

It has frequently been suggested that intentionality – that is, that is a relationship with 'something' - is one of the defining features of emotion. Emotions may serve to signal to the individual what that 'something' is, they are accompanied by somatic responses that may enable the organism to respond to that 'something', and may subside when the 'something' that caused them is removed or becomes familiar, only to reappear when the 'something' is remembered, or when a similar 'something' is anticipated or experienced. Moods on the other hand seem to have no specific cause or identifiable onset; they are described by several authors as *nonintentional* (e.g., Frijda, 1994; Lormand, 1985; Panksepp, 1994). They seem to be about nothing in particular, but may influence many diverse things, if not everything[2]. Moods seem to colour all our thoughts and feelings, our memories, hopes and predictions. Moods, although still transient states, also seem to endure despite changes in the immediate environment, changes which may be expected to initiate some related change in the emotions an individual would experience.

Certainly, by assuming that emotion is intentional and mood is non-intentional, many of the structural differences between the two may be explained. For example, if one knows the *object* of a state (i.e., what a state is about), one can address that state by distancing oneself from the object, dealing with the object, or changing one's perception of the object. The feeling (the emotion) associated with that object will dissipate once the object is so dealt with. When one does not know the object of the state, it is not possible to deal with it and so the state endures. Similarly, although it may seem a circular argument, the high intensity of an emotion, and the resultant effect on an individual's thoughts and behaviour, ensures that the state is intentional by forcing that individual to scan the environment for, and subsequently address, the object of the state before being able to resume ongoing activity (the object is serious enough to the interests of the individual to demand action, that is why the subsequent experienced state is of high intensity). Conversely, the low intensity of a mood may allow the individual to carry on as normal, as the cause of the state, although significant and causing a wide variety of effects on subjective experience, thoughts, and possibly behaviour, is not *critical* for the concerns of the individual. Therefore the resultant state is not of high enough intensity to interrupt ongoing activity and force the individual to seek out its object.

For intentionality to serve as a criterion by which to distinguish emotion from mood empirically, it would be necessary to demonstrate that all emotions are intentional and moods non-intentional. Schimmack and Siemer (1998) proposed that 'one advantage of intentionality as a criterion is that for most affect words the status of intentionality is stable. That is, all experiences of hate or jealousy are intentional, and none of the experiences of relaxation or tension are intentional' (p. 14). Certainly, as proposed by Brentano (1973), one has to hate, or be jealous *of*, something, and thus the emotions above are, and can only be, intentional. But this proposal could be countered with the argument that one can surely be in a relaxed or tense mood *about* something. Such claims are often made by, for example, athletes, politicians or performers when discussing their feelings in situations where emotions other than relaxation, such as anxiety or apprehension, would be expected (e.g., 'I'm very relaxed *about* the upcoming event, despite the current form of my opponent'). Thus, adopting a folk psychology approach, counter to Schimmack and Siemer's argument, relaxation can be intentional and thus an emotional response as well as a mood. It is clear from the linguistic analysis above that it is problematic to distinguish emotion from mood via the words used to describe them, thus it will be equally problematic to allocate intentionality to certain emotion words and not to certain mood words. Clearly, if intentionality were deemed the criterion by which to distinguish emotion from mood, all emotions would by definition be intentional irrespective of whether the word describing that emotion can also be used to describe a mood.

---

[2] Reisenzein and Schönpflug (1992) argued that, as moods are *about* many things, they are intentional.

Another potential problem in discussing intentionality is that it is often tempting to confuse the cause and object of a state. One can be in a relaxed mood *because* of completing a work-related project and being able to spend the weekend with friends, or a tense mood possibly *because* of not completing the project. But this argument talks of *causes* and not intentional objects. One is relaxed *because*, not necessarily *about*, having finished the work. One is probably consequently relaxed about many things; the mood has a variety of effects on subjective experience, cognitions, and possibly behaviour, it may endure for some time (possibly all weekend), at a relatively low intensity (one rarely feels *extremely* relaxed, at least not for a long period of time), and may endure well into one's working week. 'Relaxed' in this instance is a mood in the classical sense. Despite arguably having a clear *cause*, it is non-intentional.

It may thus be argued that intentionality could provide a criterion by which to distinguish emotion from mood empirically. That is, many popularly held or folk psychology beliefs pertaining to emotion and mood seem to be encapsulated in the concept of an emotion being about something in particular, while a mood may be about nothing in particular or many things in general, but rarely about one thing in particular. Emotion and mood may be substantially/biologically the same feeling initially, albeit with differences in intensity that determine the degree to which they register in consciousness and thus to which they interrupt ongoing activity, but the individual's subsequent appraisal of what the feeling is *about* determines how it is processed and labelled. If emotions are always intentional, then they will always have a focus (always be *about* something), and that focus is likely to be the cause of the emotion. If moods are nonintentional, then they will either not have a focus (be *about* nothing) or the focus could be something other than the cause, thus addressing the focus will not alleviate the mood.

Figure 5.0 is a simplified model of how a feeling of anxiety (which at Stage 1 is neither an emotion nor a mood) may 'become' either an emotion or a mood as the result of two factors; an individual's appraisal of the focus of the feeling (aboutness or intentionality), and their subsequent action. It is evident from Figure 5.0 that a highly intense feeling (depicted by heavy arrows) is unlikely to become a mood, while a low intensity feeling, which may not even register significantly in consciousness, is unlikely to become an emotion. Low to moderate intensity anxiety which is either misattributed or not addressed may endure as a mood, whereas misattributed intense anxiety is more likely to reoccur as another episode of intense anxiety (i.e., a repeated emotion) until it is resolved. Moderately intense anxiety can become either emotion or mood dependent on the individual's attribution as to the cause and focus of the feeling. For example, moderately intense anxiety caused by excessive caffeine consumption may persist and be experienced as a mood if anxiety is attributed to several issues, such as imminent exams, career, and financial problems. However, if the correct attribution were made, although the somatic symptoms would persist, they would no longer be interpreted as anxiety and a feeling experienced as the emotion of anxiety would have been resolved. It is also evident that even a correctly attributed feeling will persist if subsequent action does not resolve the cause/focus, or if no action is taken. An example would be an individual who is aware that their irritable mood is the result of hunger but who does not eat, allowing the mood to endure.

Clearly there are exceptions to these proposals. Even low intensity feelings such as mild surprise, although they would not interrupt ongoing activity in the same way as an intense feeling, may have an obvious cause and thus be easily resolved. Low intensity feelings may also motivate the individual to scan the environment for the cause of that feeling; for example, if one wakes up feeing slightly nervous, an immediate response may be to look ahead at the day's schedule to identify the possible cause of the nervousness. High intensity feelings may also endure if the cause is not correctly attributed or resolved. For example, a busy executive with little time for eating or relaxing may become highly irritable as a result of not eating, but incorrectly attribute these feelings to the poor performance of her or his staff, the failings of the company e-mail system, and their falling stock value, when, a sandwich might perhaps resolve the mood.

Despite the exceptions above, there by generally accepted criteria, a low intensity state which the individual says is about nothing in particular, many things, or everything in general, is a mood, whereas a moderate to high intensity state which the individual says is about something in particular is an emotion. Also, even a low intensity state which is about one thing in particular is probably a mild emotion, whereas a moderate to high intensity state which is about nothing in particular, many things, or everything, is an intense, possibly even disordered, mood.

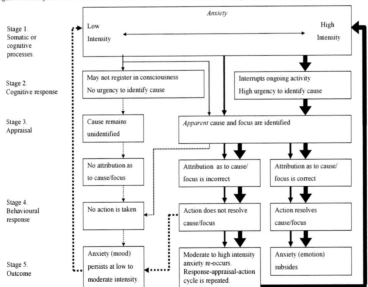

Figure 5.0. A subjective contextual model of emotion and mood: Possible outcomes for high, moderate and low intensity feelings of anxiety

Note: ➡️ high intensity anxiety,   = m~~odera~~te intensity anxiety,   = low intensity ~~anxie~~ty,
       = anxiety which will be labelled as mood as a consequence of the most recent stage of the model, i.e., the intensity is too low to register in consciousness, a misattribution as to cause/focus has occurred, there is no behavioural response, or the behavioural response is ineffective. To simplify the figure, all arrows represent possible paths for feelings of the intensity denoted by the size of the arrow *as well as* all feelings of lower intensities. That is, a low intensity feeling could follow the path of either a moderate or high intensity feeling, a moderate feeling could follow the path of a high intensity feeing, but high and moderate intensity feelings are unlikely to follow the path of moderate and low, or low intensity feelings respectively.

SUMMARY

The model presented above is speculative. It does however fit available data, is consistent with generally accepted distinguishing criteria, and might explain how one phenomenon, in this case anxiety, can be experienced as either emotion or mood depending on subjective contextual factors. This latter factor may be significant in reconciling the views of those who believe emotion and mood to be distinct and those who believe them to be one and the same. The model is based on a process of logical deduction as to which of several criteria was most likely to facilitate distinction between emotion and mood in research and practice. This does not mean that the criterion 'subjective context' is the only method by which this might be achieved, but perhaps the simplest at this point in time. The model certainly contradicts Arnold's (1960) argument that the knowledge of the cause of a feeling cannot turn an emotion into a mood, but is perhaps in keeping with Clore's (1994) more recent proposals.

As suggested in introducing the present chapter, the subjective contextual model is not conclusive, simply a step in the right direction. It does however differ from the theorising that has characterised the issue to this point in time in that it is testable, that is, it is a relatively simple task to develop self-report items to assess any individual's awareness of the perceived cause and focus of a state of, for example, anxiety or anger. Ongoing research using the recently developed Emotion and Mood Components of Anxiety Questionnaire (EMCA-Q), has already provided some empirical support for the model (Beedie et al., 2005b).

ACKNOWLEDGEMENTS

The author would like to thanks Professor Andy Lane and Professor Peter Terry for helpful comments on an earlier draft of this manuscript.

REFERENCES

Arnold, M. B. (1960). *Emotion and personality (volume 1): Psychological aspects*. New York: Columbia University Press.

Averill, J. R. (1996). Intellectual emotions. In R. Harre and W. G. Parrott (Eds.), *The emotions: Social, cultural and biological dimensions* (pp. 24-38). London: Sage.

Batson, C. D., Shaw, L. L., and Oleson, K. C. (1992). Differentiating affect, mood, and emotion. In M. S. Clarke (Ed.), *Emotion*. (pp. 294-326). Newbury Park: Sage.

Beck, A. T. (1976). *Cognitive theory and emotional disorders*. New York, NY: International Universities Press.

Beedie, C. J., Lane, A. M., and Terry, P. C. (2005a). Distinctions between emotion and mood. *Cognition and Emotion, 19,* 847-878.

Beedie, C. J., Lane, A. M., and Terry, P. C. (2005b). Development and Validation of the Emotion and Mood Components of Anxiety Questionnaire. ISSP 11th World Congress of Sport Psychology, Sydney Australia, 14-19th August.

Bem, S., and Looren de Jong, H. (1997). *Theoretical Issues in Psychology*. London: Sage

Brentano, F. (1973). Psychology from an Empirical Standpoint (A Rancurello, D. B. Terrell, and L. L. McAlister Trans). London: Routledge (Original work published 1874).

Burman, E., and Parker, I. (Eds.). (1993). *Discourse analytic research: Repertoires and readings of texts in action*: London: Routledge

Burr, V. (1995). *An introduction to social constructionism.* London: Routledge.

Clore, G. L. (1994). Why emotions are never unconscious. In P. Ekman and R. J. Davidson, R.J. (Eds.), *The Nature of Emotion,* (pp. 89-93). Oxford: Oxford University Press.

Clore, G. L., Ortony, A., and Foss, M. A. (1987). The psychological foundations of the affective lexicon. *Journal of Personality and Social Psychology, 53,* 751-766.

Coyle, A. (2000). Discourse analysis. In G. M. Breakwell, S. Hammond, and C. Fife-Shaw (Eds.), *Research methods in psychology* (pp. 251-268). London: Sage.

Darwin, C. R. (1872). *The expression of the emotions in man and animals.* London: Albemarle.

Davidson, R. J. (1994). On emotion, mood and related affective constructs. In P. Ekman and R. J. Davidson (Eds.), *The nature of emotion* (pp. 51-55). Oxford, England: Oxford University Press.

Davitz, J. R. (1969). *The language of emotion.* New York: Academic Press.

Ekman, P. (1994). Moods, emotions and traits. In P. Ekman and R. J. Davidson (Eds.), *The nature of emotion* (pp. 56-58). Oxford, England: Oxford University Press.

Ekman, P., and Davidson, R. J. (Eds.). (1994). *The nature of emotion.* Oxford, England: Oxford University Press.

Frijda, N. H. (1994). Varieties of affect: Emotions and episodes. moods and sentiments. In P. Ekman and R. J. Davidson (Eds.), The nature of emotion, (pp. 59-67). Oxford: Oxford University Press.

Frijda, N. H., Markam, S., Sato, K., and Wiers, R. (1995). Emotions and emotion words. In J. A. Russell and Jose-Miguel Fernandez-Dols (Eds.), *Everyday conceptions of emotion: An introduction to the psychology, anthropology and linguistics of emotion* (pp. 121-143). Amsterdam: Kluwer Academic Publishers

Grayling, A. C. (1982). *An introduction to philosophical logic.* Brighton: Harvester Press

Hospers, J. (1997). *An introduction to philosophical analysis.* London: Routledge.

Isberg, L. (2000). Anger, aggressive behaviour, and athletic performance. In Y. L. Hanin (Ed.), *Emotions in Sport* (pp. 113-134). Champaign, IL: Human Kinetics.

Johnson-Laird, P. N. and Oatley, K. (1989). The language of emotion: An analysis of a semantic field. *Cognition and Emotion, 3,* 81-123.

Lane, A. M., and Terry, P. C. (2000). The nature of mood: Development of a conceptual model. *Journal of Applied Sport Psychology, 12,* 16-33

Lazarus, R. S. (1991). *Emotion and adaptation.* New York: Oxford University Press.

Lazarus, R. S. (1994). The stable and the unstable in emotion. In P. Ekman and R. J. Davidson (Eds.), *The nature of emotion* (pp. 79-85). Oxford, England: Oxford University Press.

Lazarus, R. S. (2000). Cognitive-motivational-relational theory of emotion. In Y. L. Hanin (Ed.), *Emotions in Sport* (pp. 39-64). Champaign, IL: Human Kinetics.

LeDoux, J. (1994). Emotion processing, but not emotions, can occur unconsciously. In P. Ekman and R. J. Davidson (Eds.), *The Nature of Emotion,* (pp. 86-88). Oxford: Oxford University Press.

LeDoux, J. (1998). *The emotional brain.* London: Orion.

Levenson, R. W. (1994). Human emotion: A functional view. In P. Ekman and R. J. Davidson (Eds.), *The nature of emotion,* (pp. 123-126). Oxford, England: Oxford University Press.

Lormand, E. (1985). Toward a theory of moods, *Philosophical studies, 47,* 385-407.

Madge, J. (1969). *The tools of social science.* London: Longman.

Midgley, M. (1998). One world, but a big one. In Steven Rose (Ed.). *From brains to consciousness. Essay on the new sciences of the mind.* London: Penguin.

Morris, W. N. (1992). A functional analysis of the role of mood in affective systems. In M. S. Clarke (Ed.), *Emotion* (pp. 257-293). Newbury Park, CA: Sage.

Oatley, K., and Jenkins, J. M. (1992). Human emotions: Function and dysfunction. *Annual Review of Psychology, 43,* 55-85.

Ortony, A., and Clore, G. L. (1989). Emotions, moods, and conscious awareness. *Cognition and Emotion, 3(2),* 125-137.

Ortony, A., Clore, G. L., and Collins, A. (1988). *The cognitive structure of emotions.* Cambridge: Cambridge University Press

Ortony, A., Clore, G. L., and Foss, M. A. (1987). The referential structure of the affective lexicon. *Cognitive Science, 11,* 361-384.

Panksepp, J. (1994). Basic emotions ramify widely in the brain, yielding many concepts that cannot be distinguished unambiguously...yet. In P. Ekman and R. J. Davidson (Eds.), *The nature of emotion* (pp. 86-88). Oxford, England: Oxford University Press.

Parkinson, B. (1995). Ideas and realities of emotion. London: Routledge.

Schimmack, U., and Siemer, M. (1998). *Moods and emotions: Folk psychology's contribution to scientific taxonomies of affective experiences.* Unpublished Manuscript.

Searle, J. R. (1995). *The construction of social reality.* London: Allen Lane

Searle, J. R. (1999). *Mind, language and society.* London: Weidenfeld and Nicolson.

Semin, G. R. (1995). Social constructionism. In S. R. M. Hewstone, S. T. Hogg, H. T. Reis, and G. R. Semin (Eds.), *Blackwell encyclopaedia of social psychology* (pp. 544-546). Oxford, England: Blackwell.

Storm, C., and Storm, T. (1987). A taxonomic study of the vocabulary of emotions. *Journal of Personality and Social Psychology, 53,* 805-816.

Strongman, K. T. (1996). The Psychology of Emotion: Theories of Emotion in Perspective. Chichester: Wiley.

Watson, D., and Clark, L. A. (1994). Emotions, moods, traits, and temperaments: Conceptual distinctions and empirical findings. In P. Ekman and R. J. Davidson (Eds.), *The Nature of Emotion,* (pp. 89-93). Oxford, England: Oxford University Press.

White, M., and Gribbin, J. (1998). *Stephen Hawking: A life in science.* London: Penguin.

Wierzbicka, A. (1992). Talking about emotions: Semantics, culture, and cognition. *Cognition and Emotion, 6,* 285-319.

Zajonc, R. B. (1994). Evidence for non conscious emotions. In P. Ekman and R. J. Davidson (Eds.), *The nature of emotion* (pp. 293-297). Oxford: Oxford University Press.

In: Mood and Human Performance: Conceptual, Measurement...   ISBN 1-60021-269-7
Editor: Andrew M. Lane, pp. 89-118   © 2006 Nova Science Publishers, Inc.

Chapter 4

A TRANSACTIONAL MODEL OF MOOD

*Matthew J. Stevens**

School of Sport, Performing Arts and Leisure,
University of Wolverhampton, UK

ABSTRACT

This chapter reviews theories related to mood as a part of a dynamic transactional process. Early mood research investigated the interaction between mood and a second variable (often performance outcome), but recently there have been many calls for a more theoretical approach (Cerin, Szabo, Hunt, and Williams, 2000; Ekkekakis and Petruzzello, 2000; Ekkekakis and Petruzzello, 2002; Jones, 2003; Lazarus 2000a; Lazarus 2000b; Mellalieu, 2003). Moods are part of a continuous, transactional process between internal and external factors (Parkinson, Totterdell, Briner, and Reynolds, 1996), and the relationships with these factors will influence a performance and thoughts related to the performance.

A transactional process allows any of the variables to be antecedent, mediator, moderator, or consequence, at different points in the process (Lazarus, 2000c). This chapter examines previous models of mood and their associated theories. It identifies relationships between variables and proposes a transactional model of mood, incorporating personality traits, mood states, performance-related cognitions, emotions, and coping behaviours. Initial tests of the model, and implications of applying the transactional model in a field study are discussed.

INTRODUCTION – IDENTIFYING THE NEED FOR A TRANSACTIONAL APPROACH

Consider the following example; an experienced professional footballer has recently joined a team that plays in the top English league. He is playing in his first local derby. Before the game, he is told that the captain is injured and will not play, and he is given this

---

* sportpsychms@hotmail.com

responsibility. Under normal circumstances the player is very well suited to such a role, but unknown to anyone else his 1-week old baby has been taken ill that day. The team's sport psychologist is aware that many of the players are nervous. It is the first game between these teams in five years and there is an unusual amount of media attention. It is a knockout cup game, and crowd trouble has delayed the kick-off. Will the players still be nervous when the game starts and will these nerves continue during the game, and if so, how will this influence their performance? Will the stand-in captain be able to cope with the potentially distracting emotions caused by his baby's illness, or will he under perform? Should the sport psychologist encourage the players to regulate their emotions or should he or she intervene with an emotion control intervention?

As an applied scientist, a sport psychologist should draw on theory and research in an attempt to answer these questions. A wealth of published studies have has investigated relationships between emotional states and sport performance (see LeUnes and Burger, 2000), and the Journal of Applied Sport Psychology published a special edition on mood in 2000. However, despite the amount of research, a sport psychologist would struggle to locate research that has addressed the nature of mood changes in the build-up to, and during, competition (see Terry, 2000).

The vast majority of sport-based mood and emotion research has been cross-sectional, investigating relationships between mood states and various aspects of performance. Generally, these have been; differentiating athletes from non-athletes, differentiating between levels of achievement, and predicting performance outcome (see Beedie, Terry, and Lane, 2000). The usual 'mood-performance' research design is to investigate the 'interaction' between two variables at one point, for example pre-competition mood and a performance criterion. Acknowledged limitations of mood research are that mood can change between assessment and competition, and that some activities allow time for mood-fluctuation during the event, reducing the predictive capability of mood assessment (Beedie et al., 2000; Terry, 1995). Researchers tend to explore the relationships between or within the groups and usually other potentially influencing factors, such as performance expectations, personality, and ability of opponent are ignored.

Moods are proposed to influence our cognitive and behavioural responses to every day events (Morris, 1989). Similarly, our behaviour and thoughts can, in turn, influence our mood states (Thayer, 1996). Although the theory of mood has received some attention in the psychology literature, the nature of mood and the processes involved in how mood changes over time remain uncertain (Lane, Beedie, and Stevens, 2005; Mellalieu, 2003; Rusting, 1998). Until recently the theory of mood, affect, and emotion had received little attention in sport psychology literature (Lane and Terry, 2000). However, it has recently become a more popular topic of debate (Cerin, Szabo, Hunt, and Williams, 2000; Ekkekakis and Petruzzello, 2000; Ekkekakis and Petruzzello, 2002; Jones, 2003; Lazarus 2000a; Lazarus 2000b; Mellalieu, 2003).

Moods are suggested to be part of a continuous, transactional process between internal and external factors (Parkinson, Totterdell, Briner, and Reynolds, 1996). The transactional approach is different from an interaction approach; an interaction takes place when an aspect of the environment comes together with a person and produces a particular outcome (Parkinson et al., 1996). The transactional process is continuous over time, and although a particular interaction may cause an outcome, the transactional view assesses this not as the end product, but a by-product that will influence further interactions.

Interactions suggest a cause and effect relationship (where the environment and individual are causes), and centre on the effect at a particular point in time. Let us imagine that our football club's sport psychologist had administered a mood assessment one hour prior to the scheduled kick-off time, with the aim of finding a relationship between pre-competition mood and a self-referenced performance criterion. The initial mood assessment would not allow for any affective changes caused by the delayed start, by witnessing the crowd violence, or by having to change the warm-up routine. Nor would it be able to account for any emotional interactions experienced during the game, for example those caused by conceding a goal or having a player sent off.

This area of sport psychology research is in need of development. Would a pre-competition mood profile such as the Brunel Mood Scale (BRUMS: Terry, Lane, and Fogarty, 2003), or a measure of anxiety such as the CSAI-2 (Martens, Vealey, and Burton, 1990), or even a more personal Individual Zone of Optimal Functioning (IZOF: Hanin, 2000) approach have been able to detect the problem and predict how the players in our football team example would react to their emotions? Research adopting 'interaction' designs are limited, as it is not possible to establish a cause and effect relationship. To fully understand the nature of mood and emotion, not only should other constructs be included, but they must also be assessed over a period of time.

A transactional approach will not only consider the influence of the delayed start on mood, but also the contribution of other variables that have relationships with mood, such as personality, performance-related cognitions, and coping behaviours. The process will continue throughout the delay and into the competition. The transactional process is likely to include a number of distinct interactions, and may include a number of distinctly different emotions. For example, our footballer whose young baby was taken ill might be anxious about the illness. The delay to the start of the game might lead to frustration and anger because he will now get home later than anticipated. As time goes on, he could start to feel sadness/despair at the uncontrollable nature of the situation.

This example can also be used to highlight the individual nature of emotions, and the influence of personality and ambient mood on the interpretation of interactions. While the player above experienced a negative emotion caused by the delay, another player could recognise the potential distraction of having a delayed start, and make a conscious effort to focus himself on the task at hand. The emotions caused by these interactions could influence mood, which would alter the perception of further interactions. The transactional process will follow this through as the situation develops.

From a research perspective, there are a number of challenges. First, there is a lack of an accepted transactional model of mood within competition. Second, there is currently no method of assessment to allow for the differentiation between mood and emotion. Finally, there is no method available that will allow a continuous transactional assessment of mood and emotion during competition. The purpose of this chapter is to address the first issue by proposing a transactional model of mood.

WHAT ARE MOOD AND EMOTION?

The proposed primary function of mood is to adjust or bias cognition (Davidson, 1994). Unlike emotion, it generally has no specific cause, will have no object of direction, and will be relatively enduring (Parkinson et al., 1996). The feelings associated with a mood are often relatively weak (Parkinson et al., 1996), though there are occasions where individuals may experience more intense moods, such as depression (Brehm, 1999). Mood is a primary mechanism for altering information processing and our perception of external events. One could think of a mood state as a temporary trait (not to be confused with a personality trait), in that it predisposes a person to act in a particular way in a specific situation (Lazarus, 1994). For example, if a person in a bad mood spills a hot drink they are likely to react in an angry way, whereas a person in a good mood may laugh and make a joke of his or her clumsiness. Empirical evidence shows that we spend the majority of our lives in non-emotional states, though we are constantly experiencing mood (Watson, 1988; Clark, Watson, and Leeka, 1989). Davidson (1994, p.52) summarised mood as an "affective background, the emotional colour, to all that we do. [While] emotions can be viewed as phasic perturbations that are superimposed on this background activity. To the extent that moods are continually present, it can also be said that our cognitive processes are always biased or modulated".

In contrast, emotion serves to bias or alter action (Frijda, Kuipers, and ter Schure, 1989), and has been described as a multi-component response, resulting from an appraisal of some antecedent event, considered relevant to that person's goals (Frederickson, 2001). An emotion will result from a subjective appraisal of a person-environment interaction, where the event is perceived to influence one's goals, and will usually be accompanied by a tendency for action (Lazarus, 2000a). At an isolated point, the nature of an affective experience may be difficult to identify, though when assessing variables frequently in a short space of time it becomes an easier distinction to make. Generally, emotions are more intense feelings of shorter duration than moods (Parkinson et al., 1996). Emotions result from, and are focused on, specific environmental events and signal to an individual the state of the environment (Russell and Feldman Barrett, 1999). Emotion can be distinguished from mood on the basis of the perceived cause and directedness of the feelings (Parkinson et al., 1996; Stein, Trabasso, and Liwig, 1993). For example, if we experience an angry emotion, someone or something has made us angry, and we generally direct the emotion at that cause. If the cause of the emotion is removed, the emotion will decrease in intensity and possibly fade away altogether.

The emotional experience will depend on two factors; the appraisal of the situation, and the influence the interaction will have on the individual's goals (Arnold, 1970). Researchers generally support a two-stage appraisal process (Lazarus and Folkman, 1984; Vallerand, 1987). Primary appraisal is an immediate evaluation of an event that comprises three parts (Lazarus, 1991). First, the performer assesses whether or not there is 'goal relevance'. An emotion will only result if the person-environment interaction is relevant to a goal or concern. Second, the direction of the interaction is assessed as 'goal congruent' or 'incongruent'. Third, the extent of the 'ego involvement' is considered. For example, if the event involves self-esteem, then self-esteem related emotions such as pride and dejection may be evident (Lazarus, 1991). Primary appraisal is followed by secondary appraisal, which asks what can be done about the cause of the interaction and is linked to coping strategies (Lazarus and Folkman, 1984).

Vallerand (1987) put forward a similar appraisal process. He proposed that primary appraisal (or intuitive appraisal) involves minimal cognition and is akin to an almost automatic subjective assessment, for example when a footballer senses that he or she is not playing well. The second part of Vallerand's appraisal theory is termed reflective appraisal. This involves deliberate cognitive processing of internal and external information to cope with the interaction. Using the above example of our football team; when the match eventually started the opponents scored an early goal. Primary appraisal could have caused feelings of dejection and anger, but the secondary appraisal process would have highlighted those feelings as being debilitative of performance, and would only serve to direct attention away from the task. At this stage, adaptive coping strategies can be formed and a plan of action decided upon by the individual. Any interaction can be evaluated as obstructing, facilitating, or irrelevant to any current goal (Stein et al., 1993). Only those interactions that are relevant to an individual's concerns in such a way that they indicate a match or a mismatch with the expected rate of progress toward the attainment of goals will elicit emotions (Carver and Scheier, 1990; Frijda, 1992).

THE INTERACTIVE NATURE OF MOOD AND EMOTION

Given that a particular mood predisposes related emotions, it is reasonable to expect them to interact. Mood influences information processing, and will therefore, influence one's perception of an event and the appraisal process. Moods appear to lower the threshold for arousing those emotions that most frequently occur during a particular mood, "as if the person is seeking an opportunity to indulge the emotion relevant to the mood" (Ekman, 1994, p.57). In the same way as mood influences emotions, one can assume that emotions will influence mood (Frijda, 1994a). A coach whose team has just won a championship will experience positive emotions, which will then influence mood. Research in general psychology has shown that emotions such as pride and celebration have been shown to influence people to be generous to others even though they may have had nothing to do with the event (Frijda, 1994b).

Sport psychology is not alone in its struggle to understand mood; general psychology has also experienced difficulty in differentiating between the affective states of temperament, affect, mood, and emotion. Researchers have acknowledged that the terms emotion and mood are often used interchangeably (Lazarus, 1994), and although some theoretical suggestions have been put forward (as detailed above), particularly with regard to duration, intensity, and causation, it has been difficult to distinguish between the two in practical environments (Parkinson et al., 1996).

In response to the question, 'do you feel anxious?' an individual may indicate that they feel moderately anxious. This could mean that they have had a general feeling of anxiety since waking that morning with no particular cause, which would meet the criteria for an anxious mood. Alternatively, they might know that they are anxious because of an upcoming event, for which they are not sure if they have the necessary personal resources to cope with the demands of the task. This meets the criteria for an anxious emotion. In addition, the person could report that they always feel moderately anxious, which would indicate that they have an anxious temperament. For a researcher assessing mood or emotion states through questionnaires, it is usually impossible to make the distinction between affective constructs being experienced. (Beedie, Lane, and Terry, 2001; Beedie, Lane, and Terry, 2004; Ekkekakis and Petruzello, 2000; Lane, 2004; Lane and Terry, 2000).

Recently, Beedie and colleagues have pioneered a measure of anxiety that differentiates between mood and emotion (Beedie et al., 2001) using phrases rather than single-adjective items. For example, the item 'I feel anxious at the moment, but not for any one particular reason' is proposed to measure anxious mood, while the item 'I am anxious about not performing as well as I should in this event' is proposed to measure anxious emotion. A valid measure that can differentiate mood and emotion will enable researchers to monitor the transactional process more accurately.

A TRANSACTIONAL MODEL OF MOOD

Research into mood and emotion are usually considered isolated lines of investigation (Lane and Terry, 2000). However, the interactive nature of the constructs suggests that certain variables warrant inclusion in research designs (Lane and Terry, 2000; Lane et al., 2005; Mellalieu, 2003). To fully understand the nature of mood and emotion, not only should other constructs be included, but also assessed over a period of time. Lazarus (2000c) criticised research that has attempted to find a causal relationship in stress and coping, suggesting that a recursive frame of reference should be adopted in a transactional approach. This method allows any of the variables to be antecedent, mediator, moderator, or consequence, at different points in the process (Lazarus, 2000c).

Moderation infers that a relationship between variables holds for one group, but not for another (Baron and Kenny, 1986). For example, Lane and Terry's (2000) conceptual model of mood proposed that depressed mood 'moderates' the relationship between anger and performance. In the absence of depressed mood, anger is proposed to have a curvilinear relationship with performance, but when reported with depressed mood, it is proposed to have an inverse relationship with performance (Lane and Terry, 2000). In contrast, a model of mediation suggests that there is a genetic predisposition to behave in a certain manner, which may or may not manifest itself, depending on certain triggering environmental conditions (Collins, Maccoby, Steinberg, Heatherington, and Bornstein, 2000). For example, performers high in trait anxiety are likely to experience state anxiety in challenging situations.

The proposed model (Figure 1) promotes the longitudinal approach recommended by Lazarus (2000a), and shows that mood is part of a transactional process that is influenced by internal and external factors, and in turn influences the perception of these factors (Parkinson et al., 1996). The model has been developed using theories from general psychology and sport psychology. These theories, and previous models related to mood, emotion, and transactional processes that have contributed to the development of the proposed transactional model of mood are discussed below.

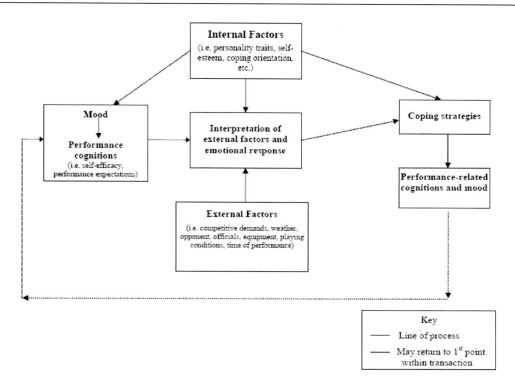

Figure 1. Proposed conceptual model of the transactional process through which mood states change

EARLY MODELS RELATED TO MOOD

An early conceptual model of the cognitive process experienced during competition was proposed by Martens (1977), and focused on the relationship between trait anxiety and competition-related state anxiety. Martens' model (Figure 2) suggested that behaviour is determined by an interaction between the person and the situation, with competition-related traits mediating the response to the stimulus. Within this model the external factors, whether expected or unexpected, were termed the 'objective competitive situation' (OCS). The athlete's perception of the OCS, was proposed to be mediated by internal factors such as personality, attitudes, abilities, and other interpersonal factors, and was called the 'subjective competitive situation' (SCS). The model proposes that the response to the SCS leads to the consequence, which is often considered as achieving or failing to achieve the goals set. This outcome is then proposed to influence future perception of the OCS. While Martens' model is transactional, it is relatively simplistic and required further development.

Prapavessis and Grove (1994) developed the model further by suggesting that it could be applied to similar psychological constructs, such as mood (Figure 3). Prapavessis and Grove (1994) proposed that certain personality traits had been either theoretically or empirically linked to mood states and these would mediate the performer's perception of the situation. The traits proposed to mediate this process were termed 'competitive-related traits' and included attributional-style, motivational orientation, self-confidence, and achievement tendencies.

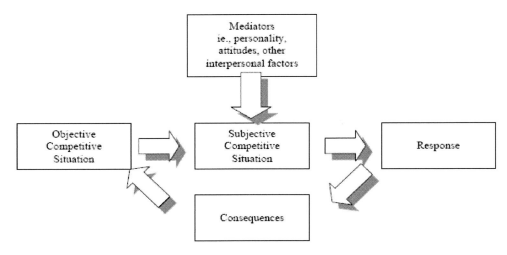

Prapavessis and Grove (1994, p.82)

Figure 2. Martens (1977) Competitive Process Model

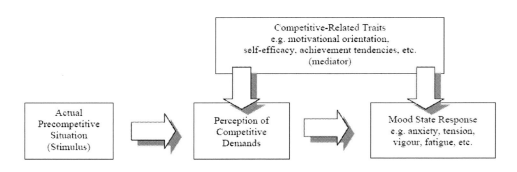

Prapavessis and Grove (1994, p.83)

Figure 3. Prapavessis and Grove's extension of Marten's Competitive Process Model

Prapavessis and Grove (1994) showed an example of an interaction between the situation and the person, but not a continuing transactional process. As the competitive environment changes, the competition-related traits would mediate the perceptions of the changes and as a result mood state might change. A number of these interactions would take place during a competition. Prapavessis and Grove (1994) also did not include short-term cognitions and their influence on the perception of the situation in the model. Regardless of stable personality traits, an athlete may react to a situation differently depending on their mood state. For example, an athlete experiencing problems away from sport may report depressed mood. This will be accompanied by confused, fatigued, and tense mood (Lane and Terry, 2000), which is likely to debilitate performance and influence performance expectations. Performers reporting depressed mood have been shown to set themselves unrealistically difficult performance goals (Cervone, Kopp, Schaumann, and Scott, 1994). Research has suggested that this is to provide an excuse for the expected failure (Beatty and Hewitt, 1995), or because only such a good performance will alleviate the negative mood (Cervone et al., 1994). Therefore, short-term cognitions are also likely to influence the perception of the actual pre-competitive situation and need to be included in the model. In addition, Prapavessis and Grove (1994) did not allow for coping behaviours in the model.

COPING AS PART OF THE TRANSACTIONAL PROCESS

Different attitudes towards coping may cause one athlete to respond differently to another, even if they share common personality traits, report a common mood state and experience the same event. Coping itself is proposed to be a transactional construct. The working model of coping as a transactional process (Figure 4, Hardy, Jones, and Gould, 1996) proposes that an individual's perception of environmental factors are influenced by their current psychological state, and the coping strategies used, influence performance, health, mood, and satisfaction.

The authors suggested that the process may then have two outcomes; either the stress is reduced and the athlete exits the process, or the athlete returns to the beginning of the model and re-assesses the situation. It is proposed that personality and motivational factors, as well as the athlete's coping traits influence the appraisal of the problem and the coping strategy used. Further, in studying coping, Folkman and Lazarus (1985) identified three criteria for assessing a process: a) it must be examined within a specific stressful encounter; b) what the person actually does must be described (not what they would do or usually do); and c) there must be multiple assessments during the encounter to assess changes over time.

Each of the models identified above have stated that personality traits mediate the perception of the environment, and in the case of the coping model, may influence all points where decisions can be made. Theory suggests that personality influences cognition, and therefore, the perception of events and their subsequent effect on the individual (Rusting, 1998; 1999). General psychology literature suggests that a model of mediation may best represent the underlying process that is responsible for emotional processing; however, the transactional approach suggests variables can mediate and moderate, depending on the stage in the process.

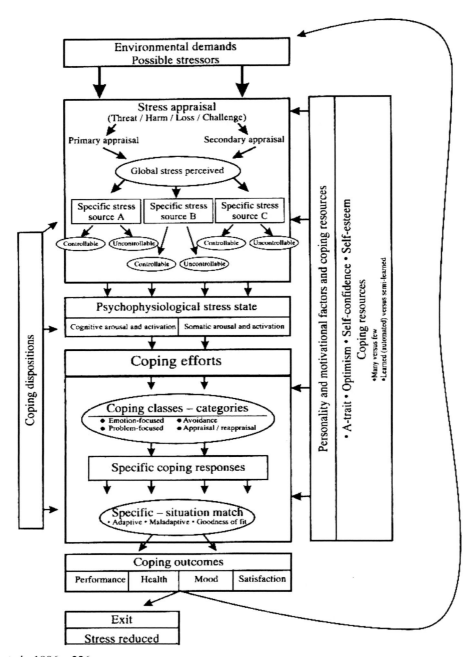

Hardy et al., 1996, p226

Figure 4. A working model of coping in sport

A CONTROL PROCESS VIEW OF AFFECT AS PART OF A TRANSACTION

In the general psychology literature, Carver and Scheier (1990) developed a theory to explain the nature of positive and negative affect and its relationship with self-regulation of actions. The authors suggested that humans operate through a hierarchical system of goals, with each subordinate level goal contributing to the attainment of the higher-level goal, with reference feedback at each level. The highest level, termed 'system concepts', concerns high level goals and values, such as those related to the global sense of the ideal self, or the idealised sense of a relationship or of a society. The next level is termed the level of principle control, which relates to adopting behaviours that are guided by the principles of the system concepts to which an individual aspires. Examples of principles are honesty, responsibility, and kindness. Principles are not specific behaviours; rather they are qualities that can manifest in a variety of different acts. Activities such as cooking a meal, or in sport, playing in a certain competition, are carried out at the program level. Programs are made up of a number of movement sequences, which are the lowest level of organisation. Carver and Scheier (1990) used the example (illustrated in Figure 5) of a person who attempts to conform to their ideal self by using the principle of kindness to guide his actions to achieve his high level goal of happiness. The program the authors used to illustrate the principle was shovelling snow off a neighbour's path.

The theory proposes that individuals compare the perception of their behaviour with the goal that is directing their actions. If the comparison denotes a difference between the internal value and the present action, then behaviour will be adjusted (Carver and Scheier, 1990). The model is related to mood through a feedback system that is related to each level of organisation.

It is suggested that behaviour continues as planned unless an individual faces an unexpected event (Carver and Scheier, 1990, see Figure 6). When efforts are disrupted, an individual will assess the likelihood of goal attainment with further effort. The obstacle can be either external, such as a weather conditions or officials, or internal, such as anxiety or a lack of ability. The theory suggests that a person will compare the current situation with previous situations and determine the probability of a successful outcome. If the individual is confident of success with a new strategy, he or she will continue the effort.

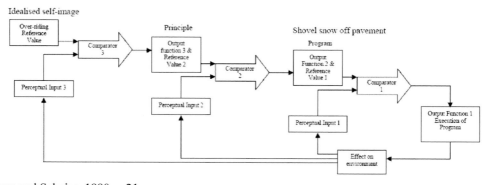

Carver and Scheier, 1990, p.21

Figure 5. The hierarchical organisation of control processes and affect

If the likelihood of failure is great the individual will begin to disengage from the activity. An individual's persistence and the point at which he or she disengages from an activity will be influenced by certain personality variables (identified here as confidence and hopefulness).

To relate Carver and Scheier's (1990) model to mood, if the perceived rate of progress toward the goal matches the internal standard there will be no change in mood state. However, if there is a discrepancy in the rate of progress when measured against the internalised standard for the rate of progress to goal attainment then there will be an affective change (Carver and Scheier, 1990). The authors used the term affect, and did not differentiate between mood and emotion (indeed, none of the models in this section make the distinction between mood and emotion); yet if we apply the accepted differences between the constructs, any immediate affective changes caused by a specific event are emotions. These emotional responses will interact with mood and may improve or deteriorate mood accordingly.

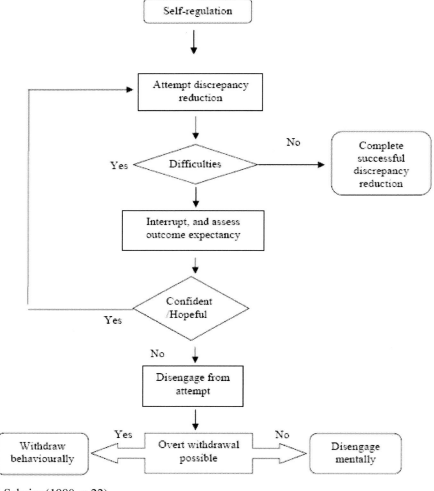

Carver and Scheier (1990, p.22)

Figure 6. Regulation of goal impediment process

Carver and Scheier (1990) conceded that much of the self-regulation is concerned solely with the program level, with little attention being paid to higher values. The structure of the process implies that if program goals are being attained then they are contributing to the acquisition of higher order goals. If the program goals are not being achieved, then new programs to achieve the higher goals need to be adopted, or the higher order goals need to be modified.

The authors acknowledged the role of the more cognitive-based secondary appraisal in modifying the initial reaction (Carver and Scheier, 1990). Comparisons with previous similar experiences, considerations of the effect of additional resources, other possible approaches, and information regarding social comparison are considered during this stage. The theory supports the notion that an emotional reaction will be an immediate consequence of an unexpected person-environment interaction, however, interventions may be employed in an attempt to reduce or eliminate the emotional episode. The process is transactional in that the outcome, or the subsequent emotion, is not viewed as the end product.

FACTORS THAT INFLUENCE EMOTIONAL REACTIONS

Goals and the reference value used to monitor progress toward the goals may be mediated by personality variables such as depression. Individuals reporting depressed mood tend to set goals that are too difficult (Beatty and Hewitt, 1995; Cervone et al., 1994). It is likely that the expected rate of progress used as a reference period for attaining these goals will also be unrealistic. Consequently, the individual will perceive himself or herself as making slow progress, causing a negative discrepancy between actual progress and desired progress and will result in a negative emotional episode. This will then serve to perpetuate the depressed mood. It is important to remember that these reference values can be changed as deemed necessary. For example, an athlete who becomes injured in the latter stages of a competition may be unable to achieve his or her goal, though until that point they had performed well. In this instance the performer may accept that the failure to achieve the goal was not within his or her control and re-assess the expected pace of progress to goal attainment.

Carver and Scheier (1990) acknowledged the potential influence of current mood on the perceptions relevant to meta-monitoring. These perceptions are determined by information regarding the situation at that time, and by information from memory (Carver and Scheier, 1990). An individual in a positive mood is more likely to view an unexpected event in a positive or neutral light compared to someone in a negative mood. A wealth of empirical evidence supports the notion that perception of a current situation can be biased by current mood, possibly through selective encoding (Forgas and Moylan, 1987).

A limitation to Carver and Scheier's (1990) theory is that if a goal is achieved at a rate equal to that of the internal standard there will be no change in affect (Crocker and Graham, 1995). In sport, the rate of progress is often limited by external factors, such as competition rules. For example, if the goal of a football team is to win a match, the team cannot win faster than the 90 minutes of the game. However, it seems logical that when achieving a goal that is important to a person's concept of their ideal self, some positive emotion will be experienced. Consider a tennis player who sets a goal of winning in three sets, but who actually takes five sets to achieve the goal. Goal attainment was reached a slower rate than the internal reference value. In these examples, the goal has still been achieved, which may still bring about some positive emotion because it is likely to contribute to the achievement of a higher order goal or goals (to win the competition, gain ranking points, etc.). Where sporting goals are achieved at a slower rate than the internal standard, the positive emotions may be dampened slightly as a result of the discrepancy.

The transactional model of mood (Figure 1) proposes that personality traits can also influence the perception of an event. Jones (1995) proposed that a number of personality variables, such as positive-negative affect, confidence, and perception of control mediated the perception of anxiety. Based on Carver and Scheier's (1988) control process theory, Jones developed a control model of debilitative and facilitative competitive state anxiety (Figure 7). When applying their theory to anxiety, Carver and Scheier (1988) proposed that anxiety would facilitate performance if the individual has positive expectations in being able to cope and in achieving the goal, otherwise anxiety will be perceived as debilitating performance.

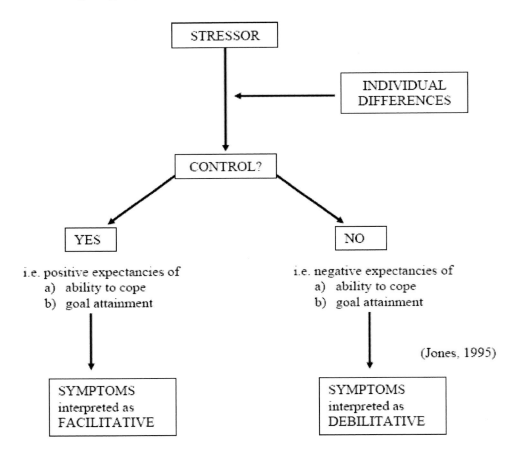

Figure 7. Jones' control model of debilitative and facilitative competitive state anxiety

Jones' model proposed that the performer's perceived degree of control over the environment and self, which is influenced by 'individual differences', would influence the perception of anxiety. Research has provided empirical support for the model (Jones and Hanton, 1996; Ntoumanis and Jones, 1998). While the model recognises the potential influence of personality variables on the perception of anxiety in any interaction, the 'individual differences' are not identified.

The proposed transactional model of mood (Figure 1) extends Jones' work by viewing the competitive situation as a dynamic and on-going process. For example, if a performer has positive expectancies for coping and goal attainment it is suggested that anxiety will be perceived as facilitative. However, if during the competition the environmental conditions change, the perceived ability to cope and to achieve goals may also change, and these changes result in a change to the perception of anxiety.

THE INTERACTION OF PERSONALITY AND MOOD TO INFLUENCE COGNITION

Rusting (1998) proposed three models to explain the organisation of the personality x mood structure and its influence on cognition (See Chapter 6 for a more in-depth analysis of personality x mood relationships). Figures 8 and 9 illustrate Rusting's models of moderation and mediation. She theorised, based on empirical evidence that an interaction between mood and personality combines to influence cognition. She noted that studies which consider personality x mood interactions "produce a more consistent pattern of findings than studies examining the effects of moods and traits separately" (Rusting, 1998, p.188). Rusting (1998) identified a lack of research in this area, particularly in field-settings.

Rusting (1999) found significant interactions between trait and state variables in studies where mood was induced in a controlled environment. Though Rusting's work (1998; 1999) established that an interaction does occur, the methods employed meant that the nature of the relationship remained unclear. Theoretical assumptions supported by empirical findings suggest that mood is mediated by personality. This notion also applies to coping behaviours, with a preferred coping style mediating actual coping behaviours. The transactional model proposed in this chapter advocates a mediation relationship with mood and performance-related cognitions at the start of a competition. However, since the model is transactional in nature, each variable can take on different functions (either antecedent, consequence, mediator, or moderator) at different points in the process (Lazarus, 2000c).

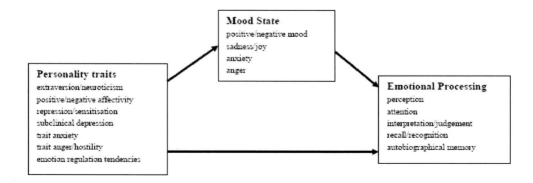

Figure 8. Rusting's model showing a mediation relationship

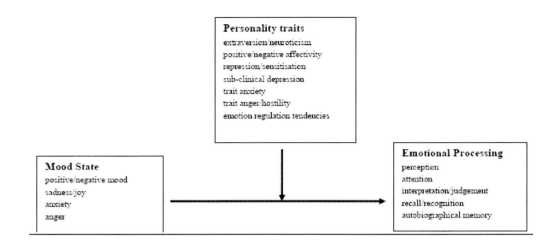

Figure 9. Rusting's model showing a moderation relationship

AN INTERACTION MODEL OF STRESS

Cerin et al. (2000) developed an 'interactional' model of stress as applied to a competition (Figure 10). The model identified the demands, constraints and opportunities of a competition, combined with personal and situational factors to influence the interpretation of person-environment interactions, emotional reactions, and coping behaviours. The model views the perception of stress, emotional reactions to an interaction, and coping behaviours as a 'part-whole' relationship. This is based on the notion that they are part of a process and the separation of the variables distorts the phenomena as they appear in nature (Lazarus, 1999).

Cerin et al. (2000) proposed personal factors, such as competitive trait anxiety, perfectionism, and perceived readiness, along with situational factors, such as environmental conditions and level of competition moderate the emotion/coping relationship. The acknowledgement of the stress model being part of a process that unfolds over time is a strength, since it recognises the transactional nature of the constructs involved.

The authors recognised that emotions may change focus rapidly, for example, feeling scared, then angry, then guilty, and finally distressed (Cerin et al., 2000), and it recognises that the behaviour or performance will influence the athletic competition. Yet it stops short of recognising the new cognitive state, which could alter the perception of any subsequent interactions. Therefore, although the authors recognised the temporal aspect of the model, they do not fully embrace the transactional nature of the variables, where each can be antecedent, mediator, moderator, or consequence at different points in time. Another limitation is the lack of mood and performance-related cognition variables, which should be incorporated with the personal factors. Mood is fundamental to the perception of person-environment interactions, and is a primary mechanism for altering information processing and the perception of external events (Lazarus, 1994).

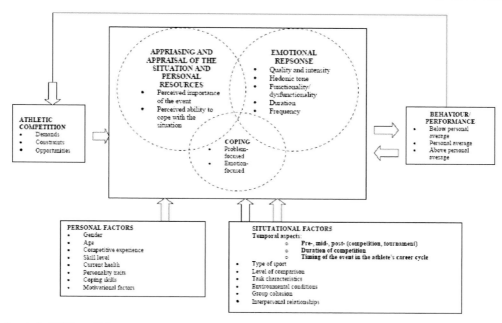

Cerin et al., 2000, p.606

Figure 10. Interactional model of stress as applied to athletic competition

Mellalieu (2003) identified the strengths of Cerin et al.'s (2000) model and included mood and attentional processing as additional variables. The author acknowledged the relationship between mood and the perception of external events, emotional reactions, and coping behaviour. Mellalieu also combined Janelle's (2002) work on information processing into his stress model. Janelle (2002) proposed that feelings of anxiety and high arousal would narrow the visual attention field. The consequence of a narrow field of attention is often missing relevant cues, which then debilitates performance (Easterbrook, 1959).

While Mellalieu has added an important dimension to the stress model, he placed mood on the opposite side of the model to personal factors, suggesting that mood and personality act independently on emotional processing. This is in contrast to Rusting's (1998) theoretical proposals and her empirical findings (Rusting, 1999), which have been given credence in the general psychology literature. It also overlooks the extensive body of research that has consistently found relationships between personality traits and mood (Costa and McCrae, 1980; Diener, 1984; Emmons and Diener, 1986; McFatter, 1994; Meyer and Shack, 1989; Nemanick and Munz, 1997; Watson and Clark, 1994).

The proposed transactional model (Figures 1 and 11) of mood allows for the interaction between personality and mood. While attention processing is not included as a separate variable, it is an acknowledged consequence. For example, an individual with a negative personality x mood interaction perceiving a negative event will be expected to be distracted by the cause of the emotion, or by the emotional episode itself. Attention will narrow or be directed towards irrelevant cues, causing relevant cues to be missed and performance to be impeded.

EXPLAINING THE TRANSACTIONAL MODEL OF MOOD

The transactional model of mood (Figures 1 and 11) proposes that certain personality traits will predispose individuals to experience certain moods, and will influence performance expectations (goals) and self-efficacy for goal attainment. At the first stage there are two components; stable internal factors, and transient states. The stable internal factors are personality traits that should remain relatively stable during the process.

Coping research has shown that personality and trait coping dispositions are related to coping behaviours adopted in stressful situations (David and Suls, 1999; Shewchuk, Elliott, MacNair-Semands, and Harkins, 1999; Watson and Hubbard, 1996). It is acknowledged that while coping disposition may mediate reactions to person-environment interactions, the situation and stressor may also influence the relationship (Shewchuk et al., 1999). Research has provided strong support for the notion that coping varies as a function of the situation (Dale, 2000; Gould, Eklund, and Jackson, 1993; Gould, Finch, and Jackson, 1993; Holt and Hogg, 2002; Johnson, 1997), and disposition x situation interactions have been shown to be effective predictors of coping behaviour (Bouffard and Crocker, 1992). The model proposes that the style of coping adopted is mediated by coping disposition. The model does not propose mediation of specific strategies, rather the adoption of specific styles of coping. For example, a preference for emotion- or problem-focused coping, or at more detailed level, a preference for distraction techniques or for seeking social support.

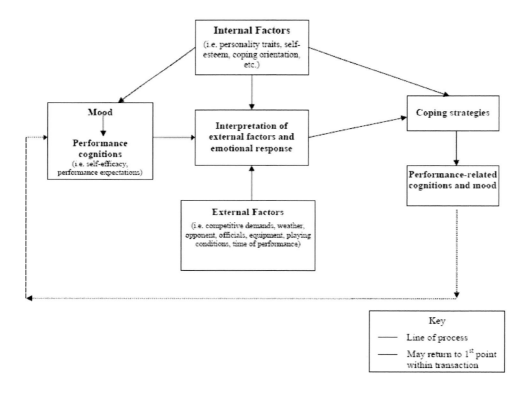

Figure 11. Proposed conceptual model of the transactional process through which mood states change

The transient states in the model can be split into two categories, performance-related cognitions and mood. Since the function of mood is to bias cognition there should be considerable correlation between the constructs. Performance-related cognitions represent a performer's thoughts directed toward to the competition, and include performance expectations, self-efficacy of goal attainment, and the amount of effort the individual intends to commit to attain the task. Goals can refer to the outcome (for example to win), to the performance (for example jumping a certain distance in the long jump), or to the actual processes in which the performer will engage (such as focusing on good technique in a jab for a boxer) (Hardy et al., 1996). The personality traits are proposed to interact with mood to influence cognitions, the interpretation of any external event, and coping behaviours.

The second part of the process takes place when a person-environment interaction occurs. An example of an unexpected situation might be failing to qualify for a final, or going a goal down against a perceived weaker opponent. As explained earlier, the process of interpretation comes in two stages, primary (or intuitive) and secondary (or reflective) appraisal (Lazarus and Folkman, 1984; Vallerand, 1987). Primary appraisal asks, "What is at stake for me in this encounter?" while secondary appraisal asks, "What can I do about the cause?"

A person-environment interaction perceived to be important to an individual's progress towards a goal will cause a discrepancy between the actual rate of progress and the internal standard and will result in an emotional response (Carver and Scheier, 1990). The direction and intensity of the emotion will correspond to size of the discrepancy (Crocker and Graham, 1995), which will be determined by the attributional process involved in the intuitive appraisal immediately following the event (Vallerand, 1987). The subtle differences between individuals in mood states, personality, and performance cognitions may cause different attributions and different emotional reactions.

Secondary appraisal compares previous experiences with the current situation and contemplates the possible outcome resulting from any coping intervention employed (Folkman, 1984). Coping has been defined as executing the response chosen as most likely to succeed during secondary appraisal (Carver, Scheier, and Weintraub, 1989). It is acknowledged that some performers may use denial as a way of coping and appear to not use any coping strategy. Carver et al. (1989) defined denial as the "refusal to believe that the stressor exists or of trying to act as though the stressor is not real" (p.270). In the first instance, refusing to believe the stressor exists will mean that the individual will not perceive it as an unexpected event and will continue in the same manner. Acting as though the stressor is not real is in itself a coping strategy, similar to restraint coping, which ignores the stressor until an appropriate opportunity to deal with the cause presents itself (Carver et al., 1989). Therefore, if an individual acknowledges the presence of a stressor, but claims to be taking no action, he or she is using the coping strategy 'denial'. A potential limitation testing the dynamic nature of coping is that a participant who is using denial may not report the stressful interaction as a part of the coping process.

The transactional model of mood suggests that the interpretation of the interaction and the subsequent emotional reaction will influence coping. The success of the coping strategy will influence mood state and may cause a re-evaluation of the performance-related cognitions. Goals could be changed, the intended effort may be reduced or increased, and the self-efficacy for goal attainment may decrease or increase. The model then returns to the beginning, with the adapted mood state and adapted performance cognitions (re-evaluated performance expectations, self-efficacy of achieving these goals, etc.) combining with the stable internal factors to influence the perception of any further person-environment interactions.

It has been suggested that intraperson variability over time is predictable, and should not be attributed to the change in the situations people encounter (Penner, Shiffman, Paty, and Fritzsche, 1994). A person who experiences an event that causes a negative discrepancy between the rate of perceived progress and the desired rate of progress to react in a similar way, regardless of the event causing the discrepancy. This model would agree with Penner and colleagues if mood were stable across the different events. The combination of a bad mood and the individual's personality traits could result in a different interpretation of an event compared to the combination of a positive mood and the individual's personality traits. For example, a tennis player may set herself the goal of winning a match in two sets. If she achieves the goal, she will maintain her current state and performance cognitions, as there have been no unexpected changes to her internally desired rate of progress. Should she lose the match, there will be a negative discrepancy in the rate of progress and will experience a negative emotion which will influence mood and performance cognitions. If the athlete wins more comfortably than expected there will be a positive discrepancy resulting in positive changes.

Although greater emotional reactions are proposed for goal-related events than for goal-unrelated events, unexpected interactions are sometimes not directly related to performance expectations. The tennis player may have the expectation of comfortably winning her first game in a tournament. She achieves the goal as expected, and therefore, maintains her mood state and performance cognitions. However, before her next game she is approached by a spectator, claiming to be a top coach from Europe, who criticises her negative approach to the game and suggests she attacks the net more often. This interaction is unexpected, and its interpretation may influence her current state. If the athlete is in a negative mood, she may internalise the comments, holding her lack of ability responsible for not playing an attacking game, resulting in a further decrease in mood and a change to her performance expectations. If she is in a very positive mood she may interpret the comments, coming from a person that she does not know, as irrelevant. She will ignore the comments, and therefore continue in the same state as if no interaction took place. Finally, she may reflect on her performance and agree with the spectator, deciding that a more attacking approach would benefit her game. This might result in a positive change to her current affective state and possibly more challenging goals being set.

MODERATOR, MEDIATOR, ANTECEDENT, OR CONSEQUENCE

According to Lazarus (2000c), variables that contribute to a transactional process can be antecedent, mediator, moderator, or consequence at different points in the process (Lazarus, 2000c). An example of how variables can be moderators and mediators can be illustrated with self-esteem. High self-esteem is associated with positive mood and low self-esteem associated with negative mood (Diener, 1984). Since self-esteem is the higher order construct it can be assumed to mediate the mood state. However, an athlete with high self-esteem but experiencing neutral or negative mood may perceive a person-environment interaction as a positive event in order to regulate mood and enhance performance-related cognitions (Smith and Petty, 1995). In contrast, an athlete experiencing the same mood state and performance-related cognitions but who has low self-esteem may perceive the same event in a negative manner (Smith and Petty, 1995). In this situation self-esteem acts as a moderator.

A further example can highlight the role of coping within the process. Trait coping can moderate the emotional reaction to an unexpected event. A person with a preference from emotion-focused coping might choose to vent their emotions (which is generally seen as debilitative to athletic performance), while an individual with a preference for problem-focused coping might initiate a plan to overcome the obstacle. In this case, the event could be identical, but the reaction is moderated by the trait coping variable. At this point the state coping strategy can be viewed as a consequence of emotional reaction. It can also be viewed as a contributing antecedent variable for a future mood state and performance-related cognitions.

PRACTICAL IMPLICATIONS OF TESTING THE TRANSACTIONAL MODEL OF MOOD

A limitation of a transactional model is that within the current assessment constraints of psychology a true transactional process cannot be measured since it requires many assessment points, and the nature of the assessments could distract from the process itself. Researchers in sport psychology can only assess a series of interactions during a competition, either retrospectively or during competition, and use a transactional model to guide the interpretation of the results.

There is considerable evidence from many areas of psychology to suggest that retrospective measures do not accurately represent measures taken in closer temporal proximity to the event. This has been evident in mood (Diener, Larsen, Levine, and Emmons, 1985; Rasmussen, Jeffrey, Willingham, and Glover, 1994; Terry, Stevens, and Lane, 2005; Winkielman, Knauper, and Schwarz, 1998), emotion (Tenenbaum and Elran, 2003), and coping research (Smith, Leffingwell, and Ptacek, 1999), which represent three fundamental components of the proposed transactional model. Research in other areas of psychology have also found that retrospective measures fail to accurately represent assessments taken in closer proximity to the event, including memory of medical history (Cohen and Java, 1995), memory of pain (Eich, Reeves, Jaeger, and Graff-Radford, 1985), and memory of childhood (Yarrow, Campbell, and Burton, 1970).

It is likely, when testing the transactional model, some time may have passed between an event causing an emotional reaction, and the assessment of the effect of that event on the individual, allowing time for a reflective appraisal to have taken place. This may be more relevant to athletic performance than assessing the immediate intuitive response, which might change in the few minutes following the interaction. The affective state that the athlete will experience during the next round, or until the next interaction, and the reasons for that state are of primary interest.

Carver and Scheier (1990) proposed that an interruption in the progress towards the goal might actually enhance mood. An unexpected interruption could slow perceived progress toward the goal and cause an immediate negative emotion, but once the interruption is removed, the new information received could rapidly enhance the progress toward the goal, which will result in a positive emotion. For example, a coach might stop a practice to give some advice. The performer might be frustrated that the coach has stopped them and initially experience a negative emotion, but based on the information given by the coach, the performer can make quicker progress than expected and a positive mood will result. This endorses the assessment of any change after the reflective, or secondary, appraisal stage.

TESTING THE TRANSACTIONAL MODEL

The initial tests for the transactional model of mood had to identify and assess specific variables. For example, the stable factors were assessed as extraversion, neuroticism, psychoticism, self-esteem, and trait coping disposition. Eysenck's Personality Questionnaire (Eysenck and Eysenck, 1975) was used to assess personality variables, although future research might consider using other personality variables, such as those based on the Five Factor Model (McCrae and Costa, 1985).

Mood and emotion was assessed using the BRUMS (Terry et al., 2003), but might equally be assessed with a different valid measure of mood. Indeed the development of a measure that is able to differentiate between mood and emotion constructs would add to a researcher's ability to interpret the results that are generated within a transactional process. Future research might also use a more ideographic measure of 'performance state', as offered by an IZOF approach (Hanin, 2000).

The initial test of the transactional model involved three stages. The first (using a sample of 61 high school athletes) provided support for the notion that personality trait combined with mood state variables are more accurate predictors of performance-related cognitions than personality or mood variables alone (Stevens, 2004). Performance-related cognitions included self-efficacy, and the amount of effort the individual intended to commit in the pursuit of the task.

The second investigation (Stevens, 2004) attempted to use the transactional process as a method of monitoring affective states in 21 youth footballers during a competitive football match. Adopting an ipsative-normative approach allowed within- and between-person comparisons. Interaction assessments were taken at four points, before, during, and after six competitions with the transactional model of mood being used to interpret the findings.

The findings generally supported theoretical assumptions. Extraversion was associated with pre-competition positive mood and neuroticism was associated with pre-competition negative mood, supporting the notion that personality traits mediate mood states. Individuals reporting high psychoticism scores tended to report negative mood states, and experienced large negative mood swings, particularly in the anger construct. Once again, the combination of personality and mood state variables accounted for a greater proportion of the variance in self-efficacy and intended effort than personality traits alone. Interestingly, the relationship between trait and state coping was not as strong as predicted. This result lends support to the notion that coping varies from situation to situation (Folkman and Lazarus, 1985), a finding that has received empirical support in sporting environments (Giacobbi, Lynn, Wetherington, Jenkins, Bodendorf, and Langley, 2004; Holt and Hogg, 2002; Johnson, 1997).

The third investigation (Stevens, 2004) used the transactional model of mood to explore the use of mental skills to aid coping with emotional episodes experienced in competitive football matches for seven youth footballers. After a baseline period, interventions were taught to the players who attempted to use them in competitive situations to maintain a positive affective state. Each competition was assessed using an ideographic design through a series of interactions and interpreted using the theory of the transactional model of mood. The data supported the findings of the previous two investigations and using the transactional process proved to be a useful and effective method for monitoring coping skills during competitions.

SUGGESTIONS FOR FUTURE WORK REGARDING THE TRANSACTIONAL MODEL OF MOOD

This chapter has proposed a theory related to mood as a transactional process. Future work must now test the model in a variety of activities and using a variety of sample populations. Although the transactional model has been developed and tested initially in a sport setting, it should not just be restricted to this environment. The model could be applied to a range of settings where individuals are working towards goals and unexpected events might cause emotional reactions, for example, educational and occupational environments.

The proposed model is not dependant upon certain measures being used to assess certain constructs. Any valid and reliable measure of personality, mood, emotion, coping, etc, could be employed. It is important that a researcher considers the impact of using a specific measure upon the process itself. Researchers might focus on developing valid and reliable measures for which brevity and simplicity in completion is a focus.

As research develops better understandings of 'newly identified' variables, we must consider the impact that they will have on the variables currently included in the model that we know have an impact on performance. Two chapters (Meyer and Zizzi, 2007; Devonport, 2007) in this book highlight recent work in the area of emotional intelligence (EI), and provide evidence of links between EI and personality, mood, and coping. Meyer and Zizzi's (2007) model, which is based on Lazarus and Folkman's (1984) transactional model of stress, shares similarities with the transactional model of mood proposed in this chapter. Incorporating EI within the transactional model of mood is certainly worthy of future development and investigation.

The development of a method for assessing a transactional process seems to be a long way off in the future, but this should still be a focus for research. It may require a combination of biofeedback and psychometric assessments, and the challenge for researchers is to develop accurate and reliable measures that do not distract from the task at hand. Although the appeal of retrospective assessments is attractive, in that it simplifies the task dramatically, there is too much evidence to show that moods and emotions reported retrospectively often do not accurately reflect the moods and emotions felt at a specific time for confidence to be had in this method (Diener et al., 1985; Rasmussen et al., 1994; Tenenbaum and Elran, 2003; Terry et al., 2005; Winkielman et al., 1998).

Criticisms of early mood research were that mood was only an effective predictor of performance for events lasting less than ten minutes (Beedie et al., 2000; Terry, 1995). Using the theory of the transactional model of mood, and making a number of interaction assessments, researchers can develop a clearer understanding of how mood changes during competition, and effectiveness of mood as a predictor of performance can be extended. Suggestions that an intra-individual stability in the way a person will react to events (Penner et al., 1994) would lend greater support to research being able to make effective predictions from pre-competition mood in ideographic investigations.

Although some researchers might argue that making a distinction between mood and emotion is not necessary in an applied setting because it is currently difficult to establish, from an applied perspective making that distinction is important. A sport psychologist working with athletes who are reporting high anxiety levels would benefit from knowing if the person is reporting an anxious mood or an anxious emotion, since they would require different interventions. Where a specific cause, or object of direction is present, the intervention is often easier to administer than when the reason for the affective state is unknown. The intervention might also vary, depending upon the cause of the emotion. Returning to our football example from the beginning of the chapter, the player who is anxious about his child would require a different intervention compared with a player who is anxious about the upcoming performance. A sport psychologist helping a player who is reporting competitive anxiety because they are playing in an unfamiliar position would ensure that the player understands what is expected of him in playing in that position, give reinforcement for their ability to cope with the demands of the task, and perhaps a relaxation technique to reduce any physiological tension. Whereas for the player whose child is sick, a quick phone call to the hospital or the child's mother to hear that everything is under control and the child is out of danger could alleviate the symptoms of anxiety.

Researchers must therefore continue in their efforts to develop a method of distinguishing between mood and emotion in assessment. Beedie et al. (2004) have started this task by developing a measure of anxiety that can make the distinction between mood and emotion. This research needs to be expanded to incorporate a wider range of moods and emotions.

CONCLUSION

Many of the early 'mood' studies in sport psychology yielded equivocal findings and were rightly criticised, often for methodological and conceptual limitations, which were a consequence of the lack of theory (Ekkikakis and Petruzello, 2000; Renger, 1993; Rowley, Landers, Kyllo, and Etnier, 1995, Terry, 2000). The urge for, and development of, more theoretically minded approaches (Ekkekakis and Petruzello, 2000; 2002; Lane and Terry, 2000; Lane et al., 2005) will help this area of sport psychology escape from the negative stereotype that some researchers have attached to it. It certainly is a challenging area of psychology, as those in general psychology will contest, but is not something to be shied away from.

Moods are frequently used by sportsmen and women in their analyses of performances ("I just felt really positive today", or "I was feeling down and that influenced the way I played"), and cannot be ignored when looking back on performances, or preparing for upcoming events. Nevertheless, as the transactional model of mood illustrates, there are also many other contributing factors. As applied sport psychologists, we know it is not as simple as ensuring that if one specific psychological construct (for example, self-efficacy) is under control then performance will be at the highest level. Researchers need to develop new theories and assessment techniques to conduct more transactional studies that will better reflect real-life scenarios.

REFERENCES

Arnold, M.B. (1970). *Feelings and Emotions: The Loyola Symposium*. New York: Academic Press.

Baron, R. M., and Kenny, D. A. (1986). The moderator-mediator variable distinction in social psychological research: Conceptual, strategic, and statistical considerations. *Journal of Personality and Social Psychology, 51*, 1173-1182.

Beatty, S., and Hewitt, J. (1995). Affective reactions to failure as a function of effort and depression. *Perceptual and Motor Skills, 80*, 33-34.

Beedie, C. J., Lane, A. M., and Terry, P. C. (2001). Distinguishing emotion from mood in psychological measurement: A pilot study examining anxiety [Abstract]. *Journal of Sports Sciences, 19,* 69-70.

Beedie, C. J., Lane, A. M., and Terry, P. C. (2004). Distinguishing emotion and mood components of pre-competition anxiety among professional rugby players [Abstract]. *Journal of Sports Sciences.*

Beedie, C. J., Terry, P. C., and Lane, A. M. (2000). The Profile of Mood States and athletic performance: Two meta-analyses. *Journal of Applied Sport Psychology, 12*, 49-68.

Bouffard, M., and Crocker, P.R.E. (1992). Coping by individuals with physical disabilities with perceived challenge in physical activity: Are people consistent? *Research Quarterly got Exercise and Sport, 63*, 410-417.

Brehm, J.W. (1999). The intensity of emotion. *Personality and Social Psychology Review. 3*, 2-22.

Carver, C. S., and Scheier, M. F. (1988). A control-process perspective on anxiety. *Anxiety Research. An International Journal, 1*, 17-22.

Carver, C. S., and Scheier, M. F. (1990). Origins and functions of positive and negative affect: a control process view. *Psychological Review, 97*, 19-35.

Carver, C.S., Scheier, M.F., and Weintraub, J.K. (1989). Assessing coping strategies: A theoretically based approach. *Journal of Personality and Social Psychology, 56*, 267-283.

Cerin, E., Szabo, A., Hunt, N., and Williams, C. (2000). Temporal patterning of competitive emotions: A critical review. *Journal of Sports Sciences, 18*, 605-626.

Cervone, D., Kopp, D.A., Schaumann, L., and Scott, W.D. (1994). Mood, self-efficacy, and performance standards: lower moods induce higher standards for performance. *Journal of Personality and Social Psychology, 67*, 499-512.

Clark, L.A., Watson, D., and Leeka, J. (1989) Diurnal variation in the positive affects. *Motivation and Emotion, 13*, 205-234.

Cohen, G., and Java, R. (1995). Memory for medical history: Accuracy of recall. *Applied Cognitive Psychology, 9*, 273-288.

Collins, W. A., Maccoby, E. E., Steinberg, L., Heatherington, E. M., and Bornstein, M. H. (2000). Contemporary research on parenting: The case of nature and nurture. *American Psychologist, 55*, 218-232.

Costa, P. T., and McCrae, R. R. (1980). Influence of extraversion and neuroticism on subjective well-being: Happy and unhappy people. *Journal of Personality and Social Psychology, 38*, 668-678.

Crocker, P.R.E., and Graham, T.R. (1995). Emotion in sport and physical activity: the importance of perceived individual goals. *International Journal of Sport Psychology, 26*, 117-137.

Dale, G.A. (2000). Distractions and coping strategies of elite decathletes during their most memorable performances. *The Sport Psychologist, 14*, 17-41.

Devonport, T.J. (2007). Emotional intelligence and the coping process amongst adolescent populations: A case study of student athletes. In A.M. Lane (ed.), *Mood and human performance: Conceptual, measurement, and applied issues* (pp. 167-188). Hauppauge, NY: Nova Science.

David, J.P., and Suls, J. (1999). Coping efforts in daily life: Role of Big Five traits and problem appraisals. *Journal of Personality, 67*, 265-293.

Davidson, R.J. (1994). On emotion, mood, and related affective constructs. In P. Ekman and R.J. Davidson (Eds.), *The nature of mood* (pp.51-55). Oxford: Oxford University Press.

Diener, E. (1984). Subjective well-being. *Psychological Bulletin 95*, 542-575.

Diener, E., Larsen, R.J., Levine, S., and Emmons, R.A. (1985). Intensity and frequency: Dimensions underlying positive and negative affect. *Journal of Personality and Social Psychology, 48*, 1253-1265.

Easterbrook, J.A. (1959). The effect of emotion on cue utilisation and the organisation of behaviour. *Psychological Review, 66*, 183-201.

Eich, E., Reeves, J.L., Jaeger, B., and Graff-Radford, .S.B. (1985). Memory for pain: Relation between past and present pain intensity. *Pain, 23*, 375-380.

Ekkekakis, P., and Petruzello, S.J. (2000). Analysis of the affect measurement conundrum in exercise psychology: I Fundamental issues. *Psychology of Sport and Exercise, 1*, 71-88.

Ekkekakis, P., and Petruzello, S.J. (2002). Analysis of the affect measurement conundrum in exercise psychology: IV. A conceptual case for the affect circumplex. *Psychology of Sport and Exercise, 3*, 35-63.

Ekman, P. (1994). Moods, emotions, and traits. In P. Ekman and R.J. Davidson (Eds.), *The nature of mood* (pp. 56-58). Oxford: Oxford University Press.

Emmons, R.A., and Diener, E. (1986). Influence of impulsively and sociability on subjective well-being. *Journal of Personality and Social Psychology, 50*, 1211-1215.

Eysenck, H.J., and Eysenck, S.B.G. (1975). *Manual for the Eysenck Personality Questionnaire*. San Diego: Educational and Industrial Testing Service.

Folkman, S. (1984). Personal control and stress and coping processes: A theoretical analysis. *Journal of Personality and Social Psychology, 46*, 839-852.

Folkman, S., and Lazarus, R.S. (1985). If it changes it must be a process: study of emotions and coping during 3 stages of a college examination. *Journal of Personality and Social Psychology, 48*, 150-170.

Forgas, J.P., and Moylan, S. (1987). After the movies: Transient mood and social judgements. *Personality and Social Psychology Bulletin, 13*, 467-477.

Fredrickson, B.L. (2001). The role of positive emotions in positive psychology: The broaden-and-build theory of positive emotions. *American Psychologist, 56*, 218-226.

Fridja, N.H. (1992). The laws of emotion. *American Psychologist, 43*, 349-358.

Frijda, N.H. (1994a). Emotions are functional, most of the time. In P. Ekman and R.J. Davidson (Eds.), *The nature of mood*, (pp. 112-123). Oxford: Oxford University Press.

Frijda, N.H. (1994b). Varieties of affect, emotions and episodes, moods and sentiments. In P. Ekman and R.J. Davidson (Eds.), *The nature of mood,* (pp. 59-67). Oxford: Oxford University Press.

Frijda, N.H., Kuipers, P., and ter Schure, E. (1989) Relations among emotion, appraisal, and emotional action readiness. *Journal of Personality and Social Psychology, 57,* 212-228.

Giacobbi, P.R. Jr., Lynn, T.K., Wetherington, J.M., Jenkins, J., Bodendorf, M., Langley, B. (2004). Stress and coping during the transition to University for first-year female athletes. *The Sport Psychologist, 18,* 1-20.

Gould, D., Eklund. R.C., and Jackson, S.A. (1993). Coping strategies used by U.S. Olympic wrestlers. *Research Quarterly for Exercise and Sport, 64,* 83-93.

Gould, D., Finch, L.M., and Jackson, S.A. (1993). Coping strategies used by National Champion figure skaters. *Research Quarterly for Exercise and Sport, 64,* 453-468.

Hanin, Y. (2000). Individual Zones of Optimal Functioning (IZOF) Model: Emotion-performance relationships in sport. In Y.L. Hanin (Ed.), *Emotions in sport* (pp.65-90). Champaign, IL: Human Kinetics.

Hardy, L., Jones, G., Gould, D. (1996). *Understanding psychological preparation for sport.* Chichester, UK: John Wiley and Sons.

Holt, N.L., and Hogg. J.M. (2002). Perceptions of stress and coping during preparations for the 1999 women's soccer World Cup Finals. *The Sport Psychologist, 16,* 251-271.

Janelle, C. M. (2002). Anxiety, arousal and visual attention: A mechanistic account of performance variability. *Journal of Sports Sciences, 20,* 237-251.

Johnson, U. (1997). Coping strategies among long-term injured competitive athletes. A study of 81 men and women in team and individual sports. *Scandinavian Journal of Medicine and Science in Sports, 7,* 367-372.

Jones, G. (1995). More than just a game: Research developments and issues in competitive anxiety in sport. *British Journal of Psychology, 86,* 449-478.

Jones, G., and Hanton, S. (1996). Interpretation of competitive anxiety symptoms and goal attainment expectancies. *Journal of Sport and Exercise Psychology, 18,* 449-478.

Jones, M.V. (2003). Controlling emotions in sport. *The Sport Psychologist, 17,* 471-486.

Lane, A.M. (2004). Emotion, mood, and coping in sport. Measurement issues. In D. Lavalle, J. Thatcher, and M. Jones (Eds). *Coping and emotion in sport,* (pp.253-269). Hauppauge, NY: Nova Science Publishers, Inc.

Lane, A. M., and Terry, P. C. (2000). The nature of mood: Development of a theoretical model with a focus on depression. *Journal of Applied Sport Psychology, 12,* 16-33.

Lane, A.M., Beedie, C.J., and Stevens, M.J. (2005) Mood Matters: A response to Mellalieu. *Journal of Applied Sport Psychology. 17,* 319-325.

Lazarus, R.S. (1991). *Emotion and adaptation.* New York: Oxford University Press.

Lazarus, R.S. (1994) The past and the present in emotion. In P. Ekman and R.J. Davidson (Eds.), *The nature of mood* (pp. 306-310). Oxford: Oxford University Press.

Lazarus, R.S. (2000a). Cognitive-motivational-relational theory of emotion. In Y.L. Hanin (Ed.) *Emotions in sport* (pp. 39-64). Champaign, IL: Human Kinetics.

Lazarus, R.S. (2000b). How emotions influence performance in competitive sports. *The Sport Psychologist,* 14, 229-252.

Lazarus, R.S. (2000c). Towards better research on stress and coping. *American Psychologist*, *55*, 665-673.

Lazarus, R.S., and Folkman, S. (1984). *Stress appraisal and coping*. New York, NY, Springer.

LeUnes, A., and Burger, J. (2000). Profile of Mood States research in sport and exercise psychology: Past, present, and future. *Journal of Applied Sport Psychology*, *12*, 5-15.

Martens, R. (1977). *The sport competition anxiety test*. Champaign, IL: Human Kinetics.

Martens, R., Vealey, R., and Burton, D. (1990). *Competitive Sports Anxiety Inventory-2*. Champaign, Ill; Human Kinetics.

McCrae, R.R., and Costa, P.T. (1985). Updating Norman's 'adequate taxonomy': Intelligence and personality dimensions in natural language and in questionnaires. *Journal of Personality and Social Psychology*, *49*, 710-721.

McFatter, R.M. (1994). Interactions in predicting mood from extraversion and neuroticism. *Journal of Personality and Social Psychology*, *66*, 570-578.

Mellalieu, S.D. (2003) Mood matters: But how much? A comment on Lane and Terry (2000). *Journal of Applied Sport Psychology*, *15*, 99-114.

Meyer, B.B., and Zizzi, S. (2007). Emotional intelligence in sport: Conceptual, methodological, and applied issues. In A.M. Lane (ed.), *Mood and human performance: Conceptual, measurement, and applied issues* (pp. 131-154). Hauppauge, NY: Nova Science.

Meyer, G.J., and Shack, J.R. (1989). Structural congruence of mood and personality: evidence for old and new directions. *Journal of Personality and Social Psychology*, *57*, 691-706.

Morris, W.N. (1989) *Mood: The frame of mind*. New Yourk: Springer-Verlag.

Nemanick Jr., R.C., and Munz, D.C. (1997). Extraversion and Neuroticism, trait mood and state affect: A hierarchical relationship? *Journal of Social Behaviour and Personality*, *12*, 1079-1092.

Ntoumanis, N., and Jones, G. (1998). Interpretation of competitive trait anxiety symptoms as a function of function of locus of control beliefs. *International Journal of Sport Psychology*, *29*, 99-114.

Parkinson, B., Totterdell, P., Briner, R.B., and Reynolds, S. (1996) Changing moods. The psychology of mood and mood regulation. London: Longman.

Penner, L.A., Shiffman, S., Paty, J.A., Fritzsche, B.A. (1994). Individual Differences in Intraperson Variability in Mood. *Journal of Personality and Social Psychology*, *66*, 712-721.

Prapavessis, H., and Grove, J.R. (1994). Personality variables as antecedents of precompetitive mood states. *International Journal of Sport Psychology*, *25*, 81-99.

Rasmussen, P.R., Jeffrey, A.C., Willingham, J.K., and Glover, T.L., (1994) Implications of the True Score Model in Assessment of Mood State. *Journal of Social Behaviour and Personality*, *9*, 107-118.

Renger, R. (1993). A review of the profile of mood states (POMS) in the prediction of athletic success. *Journal of Applied Sport Psychology*, *5*, 78-84.

Rowley, A.J, Landers, D.M., Kyllo, L.B., and Etnier, J.L. (1995). Does the iceberg profile discriminate between successful and less successful athletes? A meta-analysis. *Journal of Sport and Exercise Psychology*, *16*, 185-199.

Russell, J.A., and Feldman Barrett, L. (1999). Core affect, prototypical emotional episodes, and other things called emotion: Dissecting the elephant. *Journal of Personality and Social Psychology, 76,* 805-819.

Rusting, C.L. (1998). Personality, mood, and cognitive processing of emotional information: Three conceptual frameworks. *Psychological Bulletin, 124,* 165-196.

Rusting, C.L. (1999). Interactive effects of personality and mood on emotion-congruent memory and judgement. *Journal of Personality and Social Psychology, 77,* 1073-1086.

Shewchuk, R.M., Elliott, T.R., MacNair-Semands, R.R., and Harkins, S. (1999). Trait influences on stress appraisal and coping: An evaluation of alternative frameworks. *Journal of Applied Social Psychology, 29,* 685-704.

Smith, S.M., and Petty, R.E. (1995). Personality moderators of mood congruency effects on cognition: The role of self-esteem and negative mood regulation. *Journal of Personality and Social Psychology, 68,* 1092-1107.

Smith, R.E., Leffingwell, T.R., and Ptacek, J.T. (1999) Can people remember how they coped? Factor associated with discordance between same-day and retrospective reports. *Journal of Personality and Social Psychology, 76,* 1050-1061.

Stein, N.L., Trabasso, T., and Liwag, M. (1993). The representation and organization of emotional experience. In M. Lewis and J.M. Haviland (Eds), *Handbook of Emotions* (pp.279-300). New York: The Guildford Press.

Stevens, M.J. (2004). *Mood as a transactional process: Theory, measurement, and intervention issues.* Unpublished doctoral thesis. University of Wolverhampton, United Kingdom.

Tenenbaum, G., and Elran, E. (2003). Congruence between actual and retrospective reports of emotions for pre- and post-competition states. *Journal of Sport and Exercise Psychology,* 25, 323-340.

Terry, P.C. (1995). The efficacy of mood state profiling with elite performers: A review and synthesis. *The Sport Psychologist, 9,* 309-324.

Terry, P.C. (2000). Introduction to the special issue: Perspectives on mood and sport in exercise. *Journal of Applied Sport Psychology, 12,* 1-4.

Terry, P. C., Lane, A. M., and Fogarty, G. (2003). Construct validity of the Profile of Mood States-A for use with adults. *Psychology of Sport and Exercise, 4,* 125-139.

Terry, P. C., Stevens, M. J., and Lane, A. M. (2005). Influence of response time frame on mood assessment. *Anxiety, Stress, and Coping, 18,* 279-285.

Thayer, R. E. (1996). *The origin of everyday moods: Managing energy, tension, and stress.* Oxford, Oxford University Press.

Vallerand, R.J. (1987). Antecedents of self-related affects in sport: Preliminary evidence on the intuitive-reflective appraisal model. *Journal of Sport Psychology, 9,* 161-182.

Watson, D. (1988). Intraindividual and interindividual analyses of positive and negative affect: Their relation to health complaints, perceived stress, and daily activities. *Journal of Personality and Social Psychology, 54,* 1020-1030.

Watson, D., and Clark, L. A. (1994). *Manual for the Positive and Negative Affect Schedule (Expanded Form).* University of Iowa.

Watson, D., and Hubbard, B. (1996). Adaptational style and dispositional structure: Coping in the context of the five-factor model. *Journal of Personality, 64,* 737-774.

Winkielman, P., Knauper, B., and Schwarz, N. (1998). Looking back at anger: Reference periods change the interpretation of emotion frequency questions. *Journal of Personality and Social Psychology, 75*, 719-728.

Yarrow, M.R., Campbell. J.D., and Burton, R.V. (1970). Recollections of childhood: A study of the retrospective method. *Monographs of the Society for Research in Child Development, 35*, (5, Serial No. 138).

Chapter 5

VALIDITY OF THE BRUNEL MOOD SCALE FOR USE WITH UK, ITALIAN AND HUNGARIAN ATHLETES

Andrew M. Lane[1]*, Istvan Soos[2], Eva Leibinger[3], Istvan Karsai[4] and Pal Hamar[3]

[1]University of Wolverhampton, UK
[2]University of Sunderland, UK
[3]Semmeilweis University, Budapest
[4]University of Pecs, Hungary

ABSTRACT

The present study investigated the factorial validity of the Brunel Mood Scale for use with UK, Italian and Hungarian athletes. One thousand five hundred and eleven mood responses from athletes were analysed using Confirmatory Factor Analysis (CFA). CFA on the Italian, Hungarian and UK athletes were close to the .90 criterion for acceptable fit initially highlighted by Bentler (1990), but below the .95 fit index suggested by Hu and Bentler (1995). It is argued that CFA results lend some support for the proposed validity of an eight-factor and 32-item mood scale. However, as the fit index was marginal, further work was needed. Eight separate CFAs on each subscale indicated acceptable fit indices for each factor. As confusion is a cognitive rather than affective construct, we decided to remove confusion and re-analyse data on a 21-item and seven-factor scale. CFA results on the 21-item and seven-factor scale indicated fit indices over .90, hence an improvement over the 32-item version. In conclusion, the 21-item and 32-item BRUMS represent a theoretically and empirically supported approach to investigating mood for use in UK, Hungarian and Italian athletes.

* A.M.Lane2@wlv.ac.uk

INTRODUCTION

Demonstrating validity is fundamental to theory testing. Valid and reliable measures provide the backbone for assessing constructs whether it is for research or practice. Schutz (1994) emphasized the importance of extending validity to a different population. The inextricable link between theory testing and construct measurement suggests that thorough investigation of the validity of measures should be the first stages in the research process.

In a review of mood measures, Lane (2004) argued that one of the most prominent tools used to assess emotion and mood in sport psychology has been the Profile of Mood States (POMS: McNair, Lorr, and Droppleman, 1971, 1992). He acknowledged that the POMS has numerous limitations, one being that it was developed and validated for use in a clinical population and that it has a markedly unpleasant orientation. This said, the POMS is still a commonly used scale in research and practice alike. The POMS is proposed to assess six mood states: anger, confusion, depression, fatigue, tension, and vigour. A rigorous validation program of the 24-item Brunel Mood Scale for use with athletes has been conducted (Terry, Lane, Lane, and Keohane, 1999; Terry, Lane, and Fogarty, 2003). Face validity was developed over two stages involving samples of adolescents who rated the comprehensibility of items. Participants rated the extent to which items in the pool assessed the six mood states assessed in the POMS. They also assessed the relative ease in which participants could understand the meaning of the items. In 1999, Terry and colleagues argued that this work was fundamental to the validation program as a limitation of the POMS is that participants do not readily understand many items. Examples to illustrate this point include items such as 'Blue' and 'Grovely'. By starting the validation procedure with adolescents, this ensured that the level of education of participants would not restrict the generalizability of the measure. In addition, by starting with adolescents, this increases the likelihood that most participants would find items easy to understand, and therefore, reduce completion time. Completion time is a important concern for researchers interested in assessing mood states before competition, or any other achievement related context such as before an examination or before a job interview.

Given the proposal that validity is fundamental to theory testing it is important to describe the procedure used by Terry and colleagues in the development and validation of their scale. Terry et al. (1999, 2003) used confirmatory factor analysis to produce a 24-item 6-factor measure. The study conducted in 2003 confirmed factorial validity across different sample by using multisample confirmatory factor analysis. Results showed factorial invariance between items and factors and between factors across different four disparate samples. It is important to recognise the contribution of these studies to the literature as few questionnaires have been subjected to such rigorous tests. Terry et al. demonstrated that the relationship between the item and factor is consistent between different samples. Previous research has conducted confirmatory factor analyses on different samples and suggested that acceptable fit indices show factorial invariance. This is not necessarily the case as there can be subtle differences between samples that are not noticed simply because the researcher has not tested to find these differences. For example, an item might show a strong relationship with a factor in one study but a weak relationship in another study. If, for example, we find support for the integrity of the depression scale among athletes and students in two separate confirmatory factor analyses, we could tentatively assume support for the integrity of the scale between samples. However, we should test the extent to which items and factors are invariant before such a claim can be verified. It could be that there is a difference in the size of relationships between some items. For example, if the item 'downhearted' has a strong relationship (r = .80 for instance) with depressed mood among athletes but a weaker relationship among students (r = .5 for instance), this suggests that downhearted has a more prominent influence in the construct among athletes. Arguably, such a finding shows that there subtle differences between nature of the factor between different samples. The results of Terry et al that demonstrate factorial invariance represent an important step forward with regards to confirming the validity of the BRUMS.

Criterion validity is a second aspect of validity and tested by examining correlations between the target construct measured on one scale with the same target construct measured on a separate scale. Terry et al. (1999, 2003) tested the criterion validity of scales on the BRUMS through relationships with the PANAS (Watson, Clark, and Tellegen, 1988) and the State Anger-Expression Inventory (STAXI; Spielberger, 1991). Relationships were consistent with theoretical predictions, thereby providing evidence of criterion validity. Whilst this evidence provides support for the supposed validity of the BRUMS, it should be noted that there are several similarities between the scales. For example, there are shared items in the BRUMS and the PANAS. Participants reporting 'nervous' on one questionnaire should logically provide the same score on the second scale when the two scales are administered simultaneously. This is particularly pertinent for the BRUMS and PANAS as both are single adjective checklists. The STAXI differs and BRUMS should correlate as both are configured to a certain extent around the term 'angry'.

A limitation of the BRUMS that Lane (2004) recognised is that vigour is only positive mood construct assesses. Recent research has extended validation of the scale to include a calmness factor and a happiness factor (Lane and Jarrett, 2005) to produce a 32-item and eight-factor scale. The subscales of happiness and calmness were taken from the UWIST (Matthews, Jones, and Chamberlain, 1990). Eight mood dimensions are proposed to provide a more balanced assessment of positive mood and negative mood.

The purpose of the present study was to investigate the factorial validity of the 32-items BRUMS for use with UK, Hungarian and Italian students. As applied work tends to require participants to complete measures in conditions where brevity is paramount, a second purpose was to develop psychometrically measure with 3-items per factor. When considering developing external validity, Lane, Lane, and Matheson (2004) proposed that a researcher should select one of three options available. One option is to use a previously validated inventory on the new population and assume validity, and therefore conduct only a few validation checks. A second option is to cross-validate the measure. A third option is to develop a new measure from principles. Previous research has tended to use the first option (Schutz, 1994). If researchers are to use self-report measures to test theoretical links, the first step in this process should be to demonstrate the validity of measures used. We suggest that the second option should be conducted as a minimum requirement, and it is with this thought in mind that drives the present study.

METHOD

Translation from English to Italian and Hungarian

The second author translated the 32-item measure was translated from English into Hungarian. Two experts at the Physical Education and Sports Science Faculty, Semmeilweis University, Budapest, Hungary checked for accuracy and comprehensibility. It was further checked by an expert at the Institute of Physical Education and Sport Sciences, University of Pecs, Hungary. The questionnaire was translated into Italian using a similar procedure.

Participants

UK athletes were 664 (Male, $N = 416$; Female, $N = 248$: Age: $M = 21.11$, $SD = 3.44$). There were 540 responses from Italian athletes (Age: $M = 20.01$, $SD = 3.01$) and 307 responses from Hungarian athletes (Age: $M = 20.09$, $SD = 2.98$). Participants completed mood measures retrospectively before performance perceived as successful and a performance perceived unsuccessful.

Data Analysis

Following the recommendations of Byrne (2000), the hypothesized 32-item, eight-factor model of mood was first tested on each sample. Confirmatory factor analysis (CFA) using EQS V7 (Bentler and Wu, 1995) was used to test the model, which specified that items were related to their hypothesised factor with the variance of the factor fixed at 1. Consistent with theoretical predictions and previous empirical support, the latent factors anger, calmness, confusion, depression, fatigue, happiness, tension and vigour were allowed to correlate.

The choice of cut-off criteria used to evaluate model adequacy is a contentious issue. Some researchers favour a two-index strategy, with the indices selected on the basis of sample size, model complexity, and the distributional properties of the data (Hu and Bentler, 1999). We followed the approach of Byrne (1998, 2000) and Hoyle and Panter (1995).

Two incremental fit indices were used; the Comparative Fit Index (CFI: Bentler, 1990) and the non-normed fit index or Tucker-Lewis index (TLI: Tucker and Lewis, 1973). Incremental fit indices are based on comparisons between the hypothesised model and a null model (in which there are no relationships among the observed variables) and are not influenced by sample size. Kline (1998) proposed that values for the CFI and TLI of less than .90 indicate that the hypothesized model could be substantially improved, whereas Hu and Bentler (1999) suggested that, in most circumstances, values should approach .95. The fourth index used was the Root Mean Square Error of Approximation (RMSEA: Steiger, 1990), which indicates the mean discrepancy between the observed covariances and those implied by the model per degree of freedom, and therefore has the advantage of being sensitive to model complexity. A value of .05 or lower indicates a good fit and values up to .08 indicate an acceptable fit (Browne and Cudeck, 1993). Byrne (1998) described the RMSEA as "one of the most informative criteria in structural equation modelling" (p. 112).

RESULTS

Multivariate kurtosis indicated that assumptions of normal distributed were violated among Hungarian students (Mardia's coefficient = 197.39; Normalized Estimate = 37.07), Italian (Mardia's Coefficient = 241.40; Normalized Estimate = 60.13). Data were estimated using the ROBUST with the maximum likelihood estimation method.

CFA on the Italian, Hungarian and UK athletes are contained in Table 1. As Table 1 indicates, fit indices were close to the .90 criterion for acceptable fit initially highlighted by Bentler (1990), but below the .95 fit suggested by Hu and Bentler (1995). The RMSEA for all models was below .10 and therefore indicative of acceptable model fit. Factor loadings for the measure for each nationality are contained in Table 2. As Table 2 indicates, factor loadings were generally consistent across nationalities. There were inconsistent factor loadings for the items anxious, calm, composed, confused, exhausted, mixed-up, nervous, sleepy, and tired.

Relationships between mood states in each Nationality are contained in Table 3. Relationships between all pleasant mood states were all significant and positive. Vigour was more strongly related to happiness than to calmness in each nationality with especially large relationships among Italian athletes. Relationships between unpleasant mood states were all significant among Italian and Hungarian athletes. The general trend of significant relationships among unpleasant mood states was supported for UK athletes other than weak relationships between anger and fatigue, anger and tension, and tension and fatigue.

Table 1. CFA results for the 8-factor 32-item model of mood among Hungarian, Italian and UK Students

	Hungary	Italy	Mood All
Bentler-Bonett Normed Fit Index	.89	.89	.90
Bentler-Bonett Non-Normed Fit Index	.89	.86	.90
Robust Comparative Fit Index (RCFI)	.90	.90	.92
Root Mean-Square Error of Approximation (RMSEA)	.07	.07	.06
90% Confidence Interval of RMSEA	.06-.07	.07-07	06-.07

Table 2. Standardised factor loadings for the 32-item scale among Hungarian, Italian and UK athletes

Items	Factor loading	R^2	Factor loading	R^2	Factor loading	R^2
	Hungarian		Italian		UK	
Active	.89	.79	.79	63	.82	.68
Alert	.89	.80	.78	61	.79	.63
Angry	.76	.58	.69	49	.88	.78
Annoyed	.77	.59	.80	64	.88	.77
Anxious	.67	.45	.54	30	.86	.74
Bad tempered	.87	.76	.84	71	.87	.76
Bitter	.82	.67	.87	.75	.80	.65
Calm	.68	.47	.67	.45	.74	.55
Cheerful	.87	.76	.80	.64	.81	.66
Composed	.81	.65	.42	.18	.65	.43
Confused	.53	.28	.69	.48	.71	.50

Contented	.77	.59	.81	.66	.62	.39
Depressed	.81	.66	.75	.56	.84	.70
Downhearted	.71	.51	.77	.60	.83	.69
Energetic	.82	.68	.87	.75	.85	.73
Exhausted	.78	.61	.55	.30	.75	.56
Happy	.78	.61	.82	.67	.84	.70
Lively	.77	.59	.80	.64	.79	.63
Miserable	.72	.51	.83	.70	.79	.63
Nervous	.74	.55	.55	.31	.90	.81
Panicky	.72	.53	.70	.49	.81	.65
Relaxed	.70	.49	.76	.57	.83	.69
Restful	.62	.39	.72	.52	.62	.38
Satisfied	.69	.48	.79	.62	.71	.50
Sleepy	.69	.48	.59	.35	.81	.67
Tired	.84	.71	.60	.36	.92	.85
Uncertain	.75	.56	.76	.58	.70	.49
Unhappy	.73	.54	.84	.71	.84	.71
Worn-out	.85	.72	.74	.55	.82	.68
Worried	.78	.61	.74	.55	.79	.62
Mixed-up	.50	.25	.79	.63	.89	.80
Muddled	.79	.63	.71	.51	.92	.84

Table 3. Factor correlations among mood states among Hungarian athletes (all correlations are significant at p < .05)

	Vigour	Calmness	Happiness	Anger	Depression	Tension	Fatigue
Hungarian							
Calmness	.51						
Italian	.67						
UK	.43						
Happiness							
Calmness	.79	.75					
Italian	.94	.77					
UK	.67	.81					
Anger							
Calmness	-.62	-.44	-.64				
Italian	-.54	-.39	-.58				
UK	-.13	-.22	-.37				
Depression							
Calmness	-.60	-.35	-.62	.93			
Italian	-.65	-.48	-.65	.89			
UK	-.37	-.37	-.57	.75			
Tension							
Calmness	-.35	-.64	-.55	.64	.68		
Italian	-.44	-.71	-.45	.52	.61		
UK	.05	-.41	-.38	.33	.43		
Fatigue							
Calmness	-.46	-.37	-.48	.58	.71	.68	
Italian	-.55	-.50	-.47	.78	.88	.87	
UK	-.55	-.18	-.28	.27	.37	-.07	
Confusion							
Calmness	-.47	-.51	-.60	.69	.80	.99	.76
Italian	-.63	-.66	-.64	.63	.75	.94	.90
UK	-.27	-.38	-.46	.53	.74	.69	.25

CONCLUSIONS

CFA findings lend some support for the proposed validity of an eight-factor and 32-item mood scale. However, marginal fit indices, inconsistent factor loadings and relationships between mood states suggest further that work is needed. Therefore, the decision was to analyse each factor independently. This type of analysis provides some insight into the integrity of each mood state scale.

Confirmatory Factor Analysis on Each Mood State When Analysed Separately

The results of eight separate CFAs are contained in Table 4. Results for calmness, confusion, and depression showed acceptable fit indices. It should be noted that the RMSEA, which takes into account model complexity, tends to penalise simple models. With only 4-items in each mood state being analysed the models tested where simple. Therefore, it should not be too surprising that happiness, fatigue, tension and vigour showed acceptable fit indices for the NFI and CFI but poor indices for the RMSEA. The strategy was to use factor loadings to modify the questionnaire to produce a shortened scale.

Table 4. Confirmatory factor analysis for all mood states when analysed independently

	Anger	Calmness	Confusion	Depression	Fatigue	Happiness	Tension	Vigour
NFI	.94	.99	.99	.99	.97	.97	.99	.97
NNFI	.83	.97	.96	.97	.90	.92	.96	.90
CFI	.94	.99	.99	.99	.97	.98	.99	.97
RMSEA	.16	.07	.06	.06	.17	.13	.11	.19
90% Confidence intervals for RMSEA	.13-.18	.03-11	.03-.09	.03-.09	.14-.20	.10-.16	.09-.14	.16-.22

Factor loadings for each mood states are contained in Table 5. It should be stressed that these are the results of eight independent analyses. Anger demonstrated four items with moderate factor loadings, a result that somewhat contradicts summary fit indices which suggested a marginal fit. Factor loadings for other subscales indicated moderate to high factor loadings with all items showing acceptable values, findings that would be expected given the relatively high overall fit indices reported. The decision was made to remove the weakest loading item from each subscale and re-analyse data. A further decision was to remove confusion as a mood state.

It is highly questionable whether confusion is a mood state. The items 'confused, mixed-up, muddled and uncertain' are flavoured with cognitive rather than affective expression. Recent research removed confusion from a mood-regulation measure (Hewston, Lane, Karageorghis, and Nevill, 2005) for similar reasons. Beedie (2005) argued that confusion was not a mood state but a symptom of mood disorder. Beedie also raised an important question. He asked 'what mood states are relevant to sport? – confusion is not likely to be one of these subscales. Confusion items rarely appear in the items generated in Hanin's (2000) research. Recent research that developed an emotion scale for use in sport (Jones, Lane, Bray, Uphill, and Catlin, 2005) only included anger, anxiety, dejection, happiness and excitement, hence they also are likely to argue that confusion is a consequence of anxiety. Given the above arguments and research evidence, we decided to remove confusion and re-analyse data on a 21-item and seven-factor scale.

Table 5. Factor loadings for each mood subscale

	Factor loading	Error variance	R^2
Anger			
Angry	.90	.43	.81
Annoyed	.88	.45	.79
Bad tempered	.86	.49	.75
Bitter	.80	.60	.64
Calmness			
Calm	.72	.68	.52
Composed	.61	.79	.37
Relaxed	.85	.52	.73
Restful	.63	.76	.40
Confusion			
Confused	.69	.71	.48
Uncertain	.66	.74	.44
Mixed-up	.89	.43	.80
Muddled	.94	.33	.88
Depression			
Depressed	.86	.50	.74
Downhearted	.84	.53	.71
Miserable	.80	.60	.64
Unhappy	.80	.59	.64
Fatigue			
Exhausted	.72	.68	.52
Sleepy	.80	.58	.65
Tired	.94	.32	.89
Worn-out	.81	.57	.66
Happiness			
Cheerful	.80	.58	.65
Contented	.60	.79	.36
Happy	.86	.51	.74
Satisfied	.69	.72	.47
Tension			
Anxious	.87	.49	.75
Nervous	.92	.38	.85
Panicky	.78	.61	.62
Worried	.75	.65	.57
Vigour			
Active	.86	.51	.73
Alert	.82	.57	.67
Energetic	.82	.56	.68
Lively	.75	.66	.56

The 21-Item Seven Factor Mood Scale

CFA results on the 21-item and seven-factor scale are contained in Table 6. Results show fit indices have a marginal improvement in comparison to the 32-item questionnaire. With reference to acceptable fit indices argued as needed for acceptable fit by Hu and Bentler (1995), all CFA and RMSEA results are acceptable. For the UK sample, NFI and NNFI results are on the .95 limit, however, Hungarian and Italian results are marginally below the threshold. Factor loadings for the 21-item questionnaire are contained in Table 7.

Table 6. Confirmatory factor analysis for the 21-item and seven-factor scale

	Hungary	Italy	UK
Bentler-Bonett Normed Fit Index	.92	.92	.95
Bentler-Bonett Non-Normed Fit Index	.92	.93	.95
Comparative Fit Index (CFI)	.95	.95	.95
Root Mean-Square Error of Approximation (RMSEA)	.08	.08	.06
90% Confidence Interval of RMSEA	069-086	.071-.082	.060-.066

Table 7. Factor loadings for each mood subscale for the 21-item seven-factor scale among Hungarian, Italian and UK athletes

Item	Hungarian athletes Factor loading	R^2	Italian athletes Factor loading	R^2	UK athletes Factor loading	R^2
Active	.91	.84	.87	.75	.87	.76
Alert	.91	.83	.86	.74	.83	.70
Angry	.87	.75	.77	.59	.90	.82
Annoyed	.86	.75	.88	.77	.89	.80
Anxious	.76	.57	.68	.46	.87	.76
Bad-tempered	.79	.62	.79	.62	.84	.71
Calm	.69	.48	.69	.48	.75	.56
Cheerful	.90	.81	.80	.64	.83	.69
Composed	.80	.64	.41	.17	.67	.45
Depressed	.82	.68	.74	.54	.83	.69
Downhearted	.73	.54	.78	.62	.85	.72
Energetic	.78	.61	.82	.67	.80	.64
Happy	.80	.65	.79	.63	.85	.72
Nervous	.82	.68	.64	.41	.92	.85
Panicky	.66	.44	.67	.44	.77	.60
Relaxed	.69	.48	.69	.48	.79	.63
Satisfied	.67	.44	.76	.59	.68	.46
Sleepy	.72	.51	.65	.42	.81	.66
Tired	.86	.75	.62	.39	.95	.91
Unhappy	.72	.53	.81	.66	.82	.67
Worn-out	.82	.68	.73	.54	.79	.63

GENERAL DISCUSSION AND CONCLUSIONS

The present study has addressed two issues. The first is the development of a seven-factor measure of mood, that although based on the POMS model, assesses a greater number of positive mood states. The second aim was to extend validity to non-English speaking participants. Recent research has demonstrated the use of mood state monitoring in the response to stressful situations (Soos, Leibinger, Karsai, and Hamar, in press), and as Soos, Leibinger et al. outlined that there is a need to identify the extent to which students experience unpleasant and dysfunctional mood states in sport students in countries across Europe. A validated scale for use with students who speak a different language to English would be suitable for such a purpose.

Findings from the present study lend support for both the 32-item and 21-item seven-factor models. This contrasts with recent research that has attempted to validated a mood measure among Hungarian student-athletes. Soos, Lane, Leibinger, Karsai, and Hamar (2005) reported poor factorial validity for the Profile of Mood States Short-Form (POMS-SF: Grove and Prapavessis, 1992) among Hungarian athletes. Soos, Lane et al. also proposed that the POMS offered a limited conceptualisation of positive mood and used the Grove and Prapavessis (1992) 40-item version of the POMS to assess the six original factors (anger, confusion, depression, fatigue, tension, and vigour) and an esteem-related aspect of mood. Although obtaining a large sample size ($N = 623$), results indicated poor factorial validity for the hypothesised seven-factor model. It is therefore suggested that both the 32-item and 21-item extended BRUMS provide a stronger measure than the POMS-SF for use with Hungarian students.

An issue labelled at mood research driven by the POMS is the extent to which mood states experienced by athletes are captured in the scale. Recent research has developed a measure of emotion grounded in the experience of athletes. Jones et al. (2005) followed equally rigorous procedures as Terry et al. (1999) in assessing the comprehensively and contextual relevance of items. In stage one, 264 athletes completed an open-ended questionnaire to identify emotions experienced in sport and in the second stage, 148 athletes verified the item pool. Jones et al. grouped this list of items under five constructs; anger, anxiety, dejection, excitement and happiness. Subsequent development of the Sport Emotion Questionnaire (SEQ) through confirmatory factor analysis found evidence in support for the scale. Concurrent validity of the SEQ was explored through investigating relationships with the 24-item BRUMS. It is the relationships between the BRUMS and SEQ provide the most intriguing findings. Results indicate high correlations between depression-dejection ($r = .87$), anxiety-tension ($r = .93$), and the two anger scales ($r = .94$). Moderate relationships were evidenced for excitement and vigour ($r = .85$) and happiness and vigour ($r = .69$). A weak significant relationship emerged for dejection and fatigue: $r = .24$. Therefore, although Jones et al. (2005) started from a qualitative base, the resultant measure converges with the BRUMS for anger, depression and tension, which arguably according to Lane and Terry (2000) represent the most powerful mood states.

Although there is evidence to support the validity of the POMS in sport, it will not be without its critics. It has a markedly unpleasant orientation even though the present study has sought to provide a more even balance of pleasant and unpleasant mood states. Beedie (2005) further criticised the POMS as confusion is a cognitive state, that is either a consequence or antecedent of a mood state; fatigue and vigour and physiological states rather than mood states. In conclusion, the 21-item and 32-item BRUMS represent a theoretically and empirically supported approach to investigating mood for use in UK, Hungarian and Italian athletes.

REFERENCES

Beedie (2005). It's the POMS, it Measures Mood – Doesn't it? International Society of Sport Psychology (ISSP). *11th World Congress of Sport Psychology,* 15-19 August 2005, Sydney Convention and Exhibition Centre, Sydney, Australia.

Bentler, P. M. (1990). Comparative fit indices in structural models. *Psychological Bulletin, 107*, 238-246.

Bentler, P.M. (1995). *EQS structural equation program manual.* Encino, CA: Multivariate Software.

Bentler, P.M. and Wu, E.J.C. (1995). *EQS/Windows user's guide.* Encino, CA: Multivariate Software.

Browne, M. W., and Cudeck, R. (1993). Alternative ways of assessing model fit. In Bollen, K. A., and Long, J. S. (Eds.), *Testing structural equation models,* (pp.132-162). Newbury, CA: Sage.

Byrne, B.M. (1998). *Structural equation modelling with LISREL, PRELIS, and SIMPLIS: Basic concepts, applications and programming.* Mahwah, NJ: Lawrence Erlbaum.

Byrne, B.M. (2000). *Structural equation modelling with AMOS: Basic concepts, applications and programming.* Mahwah, NJ: Lawrence Erlbaum.

Grove, W.R., and Prapavessis, H. (1992) Preliminary evidence for the reliability and validity of an abbreviated Profile of Mood States. *International Journal of Sport Psychology, 23,* 93-109.

Hanin, Y. (2000). *Emotions in sport.* Champaign, IL: Human Kinetics.

Hewston, R., Lane, A. M., Karageorghis, C., and Nevill, A. M. (2005). The relationship between music, mood-regulation and coping style. *Journal of Sports Sciences, 22,* 175-176.

Hoyle, R. H., and Panter, A. T. (1995). Writing about structural equation models. In Hoyle, R. H. (Ed.), *Structural equation modeling: Concepts, issues, and applications,* (pp. 158-175). Newbury, CA: Sage.

Hu, L., and Bentler, P. M. (1999). Cutoff criteria for fit indexes in covariance structure analysis: Conventional criteria versus new alternatives. *Structural equation modelling, 6,* 1-55.

Jones, M. V., Lane, A. M., Bray, S. R., Uphill, M., and Catlin, J. (2005). Development of the Sport Emotions Questionnaire. *Journal of Sport and Exercise Psychology, 27,* 407-431.

Kline, P. (1998). *Handbook of psychological testing.* London: Routledge.

Lane, A. M. (2004). Measures of emotions and coping in sport. *In Coping and Emotion in Sport.* Pp255-271. Editors Lavallee, D., Thatcher, J., and Jones, M. Nova Science, NY.

Lane, A. M., and Jarrett, H. (2005). Mood changes following golf among senior recreational players. *Journal of Sports Science and Medicine, 4,* 47-51.

Lane, A. M., and Terry, P. C. (2000). The nature of mood: Development of a conceptual model with a focus on depression. *Journal of Applied Sport Psychology, 12*, 16-33.

Lane, H, J., Lane, A. M., and Matheson, H. (2004). Validity of the eating attitude test among exercisers. *Journal of Sports Science and Medicine, 3*, 244-253.

Matthews, G., Jones, D. M., and Chamberlain, A. G. (1990). Refining the measurement of mood: The UWIST Mood Adjective Checklist. *British Journal of Psychology, 81*, 17-42.

McNair, D. M., Lorr, M., and Droppleman, L. F. (1971). Manual for the Profile of Mood States. San Diego, CA: Educational and Industrial Testing Services.

McNair, D. M., Lorr, M., and Droppleman, L. F. (1992). Revised Manual for the Profile of Mood States. SanDiego, CA: Educational and Industrial Testing Services.

Schutz, R. W. (1994). Methodological issues and measurement problems in sport psychology. In S. Serpa, J. Alves, J., and V. Pataco (Eds.), *International Perspectives on Sport and Exercise Psychology*. (pp. 35-57). Morgantown, Fitness Information Technnology, Inc.

Soos, I., Lane, A. M., Leibinger, E., Karsai, I., and Hamar, P. (2005). Validity of the Profile of Mood States (SF) among Hungarian students. International Society of Sport Psychology (ISSP) 11th World Congress of Sport Psychology, 15-19 August 2005, Sydney Convention and Exhibition Centre, Sydney, Australia.

Soos, I., Leibinger, I., Karsai, I., and Hamar, P. (in press). Mood differences in university students in two countries. *Journal of Hospitality, Sport, Tourism, Leisure, Education.*

Speilberger, C. D. (1991). *Manual for the State-trait anger expression inventory*. Odessa, FL: Psychological Assessment Resources.

Steiger, J.H. (1990). Structural model evaluation and modification: An interval estimation approach. *Multivariate Behavioral Research, 25*, 173-180.

Terry, P. C., Lane, A. M., and Fogarty, G. (2003). Construct validity of the Profile of Mood States-A for use with adults. *Psychology of Sport and Exercise, 4*, 125-139.

Terry, P. C., Lane, A. M., Lane, H. J., and Keohane, L. (1999). Development and validation of a mood measure for adolescents: POMS-A. *Journal of Sports Sciences, 17*, 861-872.

Tucker, L. R., and Lewis, C. (1973). A reliability coefficient for maximum likelihood factor analysis. *Psychometrika, 38*, 1-10.

Watson, D., Clark, L. A., and Tellegen, A. (1988). Development and validation of brief measures of positive and negative affect: The PANAS scales. *Journal of Personality and Social Psychology, 54*, 1063-1070.

In: Mood and Human Performance: Conceptual, Measurement…   ISBN 1-60021-269-7
Edito: Andrew M. Lane, pp. 131-152   © 2006 Nova Science Publishers, Inc.

Chapter 6

EMOTIONAL INTELLIGENCE IN SPORT: CONCEPTUAL, METHODOLOGICAL, AND APPLIED ISSUES

Barbara B. Meyer[1] and Sam Zizzi[2]
[1]University of Wisconsin - Milwaukee
[2]West Virginia University

ABSTRACT

Over the past five years, sport psychology researchers and practitioners alike have become increasingly vocal in their suggestions that emotional intelligence (EI) may be an important construct in the sport domain (Botterill and Brown, 2002; McCann, 1999; Meyer, Fletcher, Kilty, and Richburg, 2003; Zizzi, Deaner, and Hirschhorn, 2003). Initial research has been valuable for preliminary insights, but the use of disparate theoretical frameworks and assessment techniques may serve to confuse rather than clarify the potential links between EI and sport. The need exists, therefore, to elucidate the theoretical and measurement underpinnings of the current research as well as provide further evidence of the efficacy of this construct in the sport domain. To that end, the purposes of the ensuing chapter are to: (a) provide a critical overview of the theoretical models and corresponding assessment tools typically used in EI research; (b) review the EI research conducted with leaders in health care and business, populations which may experience similar occupational challenges as leaders in sport, and; (c) summarize the results of two recent studies which describe the EI of coaches as well as the implications of this research for future study and professional practice.

INTRODUCTION

Interest in the multidimensional construct of intelligence has increased dramatically in recent years. Sternberg, Wagner, Williams, and Horvath (1995) suggested that 20% to 25% of the variance in real world performance is accounted for by cognitive (or general) intelligence which prompted intelligence psychologists to expand their conceptualization beyond the traditional analytical component in the hopes of identifying additional contributors to real world performance. The work of intelligence scholars Robert Sternberg and Howard Gardner has been instrumental in challenging the conventional notions of intelligence. Sternberg, for example, focused his research on identifying personal qualities that separate successful individuals from less successful individuals, regardless of intellect or cognitive ability (Sternberg, 1997a; Sternberg, 1997b; Sternberg et al., 2000). Sternberg suggests that *successful intelligence* is the combination of analytical, creative, and practical intelligences, and goes on to argue that an individual's ability to recall information is not synonymous with his/her use of that information to benefit self/others. Gardner's theory of multiple intelligences also challenges the notion that intelligence is a single general capacity inherent in every person (Gardner, 1983). Specifically, he identified several types of intelligence including linguistic, musical, logical-mathematical, spatial, bodily-kinesthetic, and personal (i.e., interpersonal and intrapersonal) intelligence. Although Gardner brought attention to the notion of personal intelligences, he devoted little attention to understanding the potential role of this type of intelligence in predicting success in various fields of human endeavor.

The conceptualization of multiple types of intelligence stimulated researchers to explore further the notion of various types or aspects of intelligence, leading to the identification of the construct now known as *emotional intelligence* (EI). Emotional intelligence, the ability to perceive, utilize, understand, and manage emotions in self and others (Salovey and Mayer, 1990; Salovey, Mayer, and Caruso, 2002) is popular with researchers and practitioners alike, and thought to be related to individual and group potential, satisfaction, and productivity (Salovey and Mayer, 1990; Sternberg et al., 1995).

Driven by economic interests and opportunistic desires to better understand the predictors of success and productivity beyond general intelligence, much of the early EI research was conducted in the corporate world and then in the health care domain. Results of this line of research suggest that appropriately regulated emotions may enhance on-the-job coping strategies (Jordan, Ashkanasy, and Hartel, 2002), collaborative conflict resolution (Jordan and Troth, 2002), work performance and employee health (Slaski and Cartwright, 2002, 2003), psychological well-being (Extremera and Fernandez-Berrocal, 2002; Schutte, Malouff, Simunek, McKenley, and Hollander, 2002), and healthy attitudes toward exercise as well as alcohol and tobacco use (Parker, Meyer, and Swartz, 2005; Trinidad and Johnson, 2002; Trinidad, Unger, Chou, and Johnson, 2004). The parallels identified between the business and sports worlds (Jones, 2002; Weinberg and McDermott, 2002) along with the knowledge that physical and mental health are important to athletic performance (Gould, Guinan, Greenleaf, and Chung, 2002; Mahoney, 2002; Wertheim, 2003), reinforce the need to examine the potential importance of EI in sport.

The emerging interest in EI among researchers and practitioners in applied sport psychology, in conjunction with the general lack of knowledge regarding EI-specific theoretical models and assessment techniques, prompt the foci of this chapter. That is, the purposes of this chapter are to:

a) Provide a critical overview of the theoretical models and corresponding assessment tools typically used in EI research;

b) Review the EI research conducted with leaders in health care and business, populations which may experience similar occupational challenges as leaders in sport (i.e., coaches), and;

c) Summarize the results of two recent studies which describe the EI of college and elite level coaches as well as the implications of this research for future study and professional practice.

OVERVIEW OF EMOTIONAL INTELLIGENCE MODELS AND ASSESSMENT TOOLS

The study of EI and the application of ensuing research results are complicated by the existence of multiple models and assessment inventories. In order for scholars and practitioners to determine the scientific significance of empirical research and/or determine which model and assessment inventory best informs professional practice, all parties must familiarize themselves with the aforementioned models and assessment techniques. Most of the research in the area of EI, the capacity for reasoning with the emotions of self and others, is informed by either the mixed or the ability model. Mixed models suggest that intelligence encompasses both mental abilities (e.g., emotional self-awareness, empathy, problem-solving, impulse control) and self-reported personality characteristics (e.g., mood, genuineness, warmth). The two most commonly used mixed models are those developed by Daniel Goleman and Reuven Bar-On.

Mixed Models

Although the conceptualizations of EI proposed by Goleman and Bar-On have their distinct nuances, both rely heavily on clusters of cognitive and/or noncognitive constructs to define the paradigm. The mixed model approach of integrating EI with other skills and personal characteristics, including personality traits, is presented below in a review of several specific configurations. As is demonstrated, the inclusion of personality-like traits contributes to difficulty in establishing EI as an independent construct.

Goleman's Model
According to Goleman (1995), EI includes "abilities such as being able to motivate oneself and persist in the face of frustrations; to control impulse and delay gratification; to regulate one's moods and keep distress from swamping the ability to think; to empathize and to hope" (Goleman, 1995, p. 34). The *abilities* referred to above represent 20 competencies that fall into four separate domains:

a) self-awareness (e.g., emotional awareness, accurate self-assessment, self-confidence);
b) self-management (e.g., trustworthiness, adaptability, organizational commitment, optimism);
c) social awareness (e.g., achievement drive, initiative, service orientation, leveraging diversity); and
d) social skills (e.g., communication, conflict management, leadership, collaboration, cooperation).

Although Goleman claims that his framework is based on *pure* ability, others disagree (Bar-On, 1997; Mayer, Caruso, and Salovey, 2000), suggesting that his conceptualization is based heavily in cognition, personality, motivation, emotions, neurobiology, and intelligence rather than one singular and distinct construct. Additional criticism exists due to questions about predictive validity, particularly for performance in the workplace (e.g., Druskat and Wolff, 2001). Further evaluation is made difficult because to date, little if any peer-reviewed research has been informed by Goleman's model or related measurement tool (Landy, 2005; Matthews, Zeidner, and Roberts, 2004).

The assessment inventory used by Goleman to inform his work, the Emotional Competence Inventory (ECI) – Version 2, is a self-report, 7-point Likert-type scale, which allows multiple individuals (i.e., self, manager, direct reports, and peers) to rate the person of interest on a series of behavioral indicators of EI. Concerns regarding the ECI begin with the suggestion that the inventory tests a different competence-based model than that proposed by Goleman in 1998, and continue with questions regarding the reliability and validity of the instrument (Matthews et al., 2004). In addition to reliabilities ranging from .59 (trustworthiness) to .82 (conscientiousness), further concerns suggest considerable overlap with constructs from the Big Five personality dimensions (Conte, 2005; Matthews et al., 2004). Given the dearth of published research utilizing the ECI, it is difficult to independently refute the aforementioned concerns. Unfortunately, the lack of publicly accessible data makes it difficult for Goleman to transition his work from the mainstream popular press to the peer reviewed academic press.

Bar-On's Model

Consistent with Goleman, Bar-On's mixed model approach suggests that EI is a multifactorial collection of trait and state characteristics. Bar-On defines EI as "… an array of noncognitive capabilities, competencies, and skills that influence one's ability to succeed in coping with environmental demands and pressures" (1997, p. 14), and goes on to identify five areas of functioning related to success (Bar-On, 1997, 2001):

a) intrapersonal (i.e., emotional self-awareness, assertiveness, self-regard, self-actualization, independence);
b) interpersonal (i.e., interpersonal relationships, social responsibility, empathy);
c) adaptability (i.e., problem solving, reality testing, flexibility);
d) stress-management (i.e., stress tolerance, impulse control); and
e) general mood (i.e., happiness, optimism).

Bar-On uses the Emotional Quotient Inventory (EQ-i: Bar-On, 1997) to measure EI.[1] The EQ-i is a 133-item self-report measure consisting of 15 subscales grouped into five higher-order dimensions, yielding but one overall measure of the construct. Test-retest reliability was .73 (Bar-On, 1997), suggesting a common association between scores over time. Although an r-value of .73 could be interpreted as adequate reliability, it should be noted that 47% of the variance is unexplained. Studies of concurrent validity suggest considerable overlap between the EQ-i and other psychological measures. Specifically, significant correlations were found between the EQ-i and psychological well-being (r =.54) as well as each factor of the Big Five

---

[1] Although a short form of the EQ-i (EQ-i:S) is now available (Bar-On, 2002), the original version has been used in most of the research to date. As such, the current critique will focus on this longer, original version.

personality dimensions (r = .16 to r = -.57) (Brackett and Mayer, 2001). Review of this convergent and discriminant validity data suggest that many items on the EQ-i pertain to personality attributes (e.g., emotional stability) (Bracket and Mayer, 2001; Conte, 2005; Dawda and Hart, 2000), so much so that it has been suggested that EI as conceptualized by Bar-On "may be a lower-level primary trait that could be placed below the Big Five in a multistratum model" (Matthews et al., 2004, p. 213).

Ability Model

Contrary to the mixed models described above, the ability model of EI conceptualizes the construct as a type of intelligence involving emotion, whereby "emotions govern, and often signal, motivated responses to situations" (Mayer, Salovey, and Caruso, 2004, p. 198). That is, EI involves an ability to recognize the meanings of emotions and their relationships, as well as the ability to use emotions to inform cognitive activities (e.g., reasoning, problem-solving) (Mayer, Salovey, Caruso, and Sitarenios, 2001). Proponents of the ability model conceptualize EI as:

> … the ability to perceive accurately, appraise, and express emotions; the ability to access and/or generate feelings when they facilitate thought; the ability to understand emotion and emotional knowledge; and the ability to regulate emotions to promote emotional and intellectual growth (Mayer and Salovey, 1997, p. 10).

This definition informs Mayer and Salovey's (1997) ability model, which consists of four skills or *branches*:

a) Branch 1 (i.e., perception and expression of emotion), which encompasses the ability to recognize and express one's physical states, feelings, and thoughts;
b) Branch 2 (i.e., assimilating emotion in thought), which consists of the ability to use one's emotions to prioritize thinking in productive ways;
c) Branch 3 (i.e., understanding and analyzing emotion), which encompasses the ability to label emotions and simultaneous feelings, and understand cognitions associated with shifts of emotion; and
d) Branch 4 (i.e., regulation of emotion), which consists of the ability to stay open to regulate emotions reflectively so as to promote emotional and intellectual growth.

These branches represent a hierarchical structure, in that logically it is difficult to manage emotions (Branch 4) if you cannot first understand how your emotions influence your thoughts (Branch 3). It is also suggested that abilities at the top of the hierarchy (i.e., Branch 4) interact with personality constructs. That is, "emotions are managed in the context of the individual's goals, self-knowledge, and social awareness" (Mayer et al., 2004, p.199).

Although the preceding conceptualization of EI as a hierarchical ability that can be developed or enhanced over time has been adopted by many researchers and practitioners world-wide, a specific operationalization and measurement of the construct has yet to be met with unanimity. An overview and critique of the four primary ability-based measures appears below, with self-report measures discussed first followed by performance-based measures. See Table 1 for a summary of the latter.

Table 1. Overview of EI Assessment Inventories and Their Psychometric Properties

Scale	Assesses	Assessment Type	Scales and Internal Reliability Coef.	Correlations with Big Five
Trait Meta-Mood Scale (TMMS: Salovey et al., 1995)	Ongoing process of reflecting, monitoring, evaluating, and regulating feelings associated with moods.	30-item self-report	Attention to emotion (α = .86) Emotional clarity (α = .88) Emotion repair (α = .82) Full scale (α = .82) *normed on 200 Americans	Attention to Emotion (.00-.27) Emotional Clarity (.14-.82) Emotion Repair (.19-.73) *Davies et al. 1998
Emotional Intelligence Scale (EIS: Schutte et al., 1998)	Perceptions of the extent to which an individual can identify, understand, harness, and regulate emotions in self and others.	33-item self-report	Emotion perception Utilizing emotion Managing self-relevant emotion Managing others' emotion Full scale (α = .90) *normed on U.S. college students	.09-.43 (Bracket and Mayer, 2003) .21-.54 (Schutte et al., 1998)
Multi-Factor Emotional Intelligence Scale (MEIS: Mayer et al., 1999)	Ability to perceive, assimilate, understand, and manage emotions in self and others.	402-item performance measure	Perceive emotions (α = .90 - .96) Assimilate emotions (α = .84 - .86) Understand emotions (α = .74 - .89) Manage emotions (α = .76 - .81) Full test (α = .90 - .96) *normed on U.S. adults	Perceive (.08 - .17) Assimilate (.07 - .17) Understand (.05 - .18) Manage (.13 - .24) Full test (.13 - .24) *Mayer et al., 2004
Mayer-Salovey-Caruso Emotional Intelligence Test (MSCEIT: Mayer et al., 2002)	Ability to perceive, assimilate, understand, and manage emotions in self and others.	141-item performance measure	Perceive emotions (α = .90 - .99) Assimilate emotions (α = .76 - .97) Understand emotions (α = .77 - .98) Manage emotions (α = .81 - .96) Full test (α = .91 - .98) *normed on U.S. adults	Perceive (.00 - .21) Assimilate (.09 - .21) Understand (.01 - .20) Manage (.08 - .39) Full test (.02 - .19) *Mayer et al., 2004

The Trait Meta-Mood Scale (TMMS: Salovey, Mayer, Goldman, Turvey, and Palfai, 1995). The TMMS is a 30-item self-report measure informed by early conceptualizations of the cognitive model of EI, and assesses an individual's perceptions in the following three areas: (a) attention to emotion, (b) emotional clarity, and (c) emotion repair. Inconsistencies abound regarding the psychometric properties of the TMMS. Although scale developers report adequate reliability, Matthews et al. (2004) suggest otherwise for the emotion repair scale. There is uniform concern for the validity of the instrument, in particular, the distinctiveness of certain subscales from Big Five personality factors (Ciarrochi, Chan, Caputi, and Roberts, 2001; Davies, Stankov, and Roberts, 1998; Matthews et al., 2004).

The Emotional Intelligence Scale (EIS: Schutte et al., 1998). The EIS is a 33-item self-report inventory informed by the work of Mayer and colleagues as well as the MEIS, which assesses an individual's perceptions of the extent to which s/he can identify, understand, harness, and regulate emotions in self and others. Although the inventory creators suggest that their survey is informed by the work of Mayer and colleagues, EI is conceptualized as a trait by the former and a state by the latter.

That said, it is not surprising that contradictory reports exist regarding the conceptualization and scoring of the inventory. While survey developers initially suggested that EI was a multidimensional construct with the EIS providing a score for general EI as well as a score for each of the four sub-factors (Schutte et al., 1998), they have more recently suggested that EI is a unidimensional construct with the EIS providing only an overall score of EI (Riley and Schutte, 2003; Schutte et al., 2002). The input of other researchers further confuses the issue, with some (Petrides and Furnham, 2000) supporting the multidimensional and others (Brackett and Mayer, 2003) supporting the unidimensional nature of the EIS. A possible reconciliation of these seemingly competing arguments would be conceptualization of the total as a higher-order construct.

Using the unidimensional conceptualization and 33-item inventory, adequate internal consistency reliability ($r = .87$ to $.90$) and test-retest reliability ($r = .78$) have been reported (Schutte et al., 1998). Similarly, results of a 69 sample meta-analysis (Van Rooy and Viswesvaran, 2004) indicate that the EIS had higher predictive validity than other EI measures examined (i.e., TTMS, EQ-i, ECI, and Multi-Factor Intelligence Scale [MEIS]). Although less related than the EQ-i, studies of concurrent validity suggest moderate correlations between the EIS and other personality measures (i.e., correlations range from $r = .09$ to $r = .43$) (Brackett and Mayer, 2003; Ciarrochi et al., 2001). Specifically, significant correlations were found between the EIS and psychological well-being as well as four factors of the Big Five personality profile (Brackett and Mayer, 2003). Examination of discriminant validity data yield contradictory results. The research of Schutte et al. (1998) suggests nonsignificant correlations between the EIS and four of the Big Five personality constructs while the research of Bracket and Mayer (2003) suggests that the EIS is not easily distinguishable from either personality or well-being.

While the EIS appears to be a better measure of EI than the aforementioned mixed model measures, the strong association with personality traits along with uncertainties regarding the dimensional structure prompt caution in interpreting results ensuing from its use. Similarly, the self-report nature of the EIS makes it susceptible to social desirability bias (Austin, Saklofske, Huang, and McKenney, 2004; Schutte et al., 1998), a fact which is exacerbated by relatively few reverse-keyed items and the lack of a lie-scale.

Performance-based measures. The two assessment inventories most frequently associated with the ability model are the Multi-Factor Emotional Intelligence Scale (MEIS: Mayer, Caruso, and Salovey, 1999) and the Mayer-Salovey-Caruso Emotional Intelligence Test (MSCEIT: Mayer, Salovey, and Caruso, 2002). Both are performance-based measures, the characteristics of which include: (a) testing for maximal performance, (b) utilization of external appraisal of performance, (c) minimal or nonexistent response bias, (d) long and complicated testing procedures, and (e) ability-like (Matthews et al., 2004).

The MEIS was developed first and consists of 402 items to measure overall EI and scores related to each of the previously identified four branches. Three alterative scoring procedures (e.g., consensual scoring, expert scoring, target scoring) are utilized to discriminate correct and incorrect answers (Mayer et al., 2000). Although adequate reliabilities have been reported for the total test (i.e., r = .90 to r= .96) as well as each of the four branches (i.e., r = .74 to r = .96) (Mayer et al., 2004), the prohibitive time needed to complete the MEIS (i.e., 2 hours) along with problems inherent in the type of scoring utilized, prompted the development of an equally reliable but less time-consuming ability measure.

The ensuing instrument, the MSCEIT, has gone through several iterations since its development in 2002. The most recent adaptation, the MSCEIT-Version 2, is a 141-item inventory designed to measure the four branches of EI. The MSCEIT yields among other things, a total score and four branch scores. The MSCEIT can be administered via pencil/paper booklet or on-line format. The correlation between response frequencies across the two measurement techniques is high (*r* = .98) (Mayer et al., 2003), suggesting that the forms of the test are largely indistinguishable.

Factor analysis calculations suggest that the MSCEIT has a factor structure consistent with the four-factor model of EI (Brackett and Mayer, 2001). Further analysis suggests a two week test-retest reliability of r = .86. Similarly, results suggest a lack of convergence between the MSCEIT and self-report (i.e., mixed model) EI measures (i.e., EIS, EQ-i), and discrimination between the MSCEIT and well-being scales as well as Big Five personality measures. Unlike correlations for the EQ-i and EIS reported above, correlations between the MSCEIT and the Big Five are weak, ranging from r = .03 to r = .28 (Brackett and Mayer, 2001; Conte, 2005). The results of multiple regression analyses using the Big Five as predictor variables and EI tests as the outcome variable further support the distinctiveness of the MSCEIT. Specifically, these data indicate that the Big Five predicted 38% of the variance in MSCEIT scores (2 significant predictors), 52% of the variance in EIS scores (4 significant predictors), and 75% of the variance in for EQ-i scores (5 significant predictors) (Brackett and Mayer, 2001).

Taken together, these data suggest that EI as measured by the MSCEIT exists as a construct that is distinct from personality variables as well as other mixed measures of the construct. Concomitantly, EI as measured by the MSCEIT is consistent with a true test of intelligence. That is, through expert or consensus scoring it is possible to determine *right* and *wrong* answers (Mayer, 2001; Mayer et al., 2004). In Branch 1 for example, a person is asked to view an abstract design and report the amount of emotional content the design contains (i.e., how much happiness, sadness, fear, etc.). According to test developers, correct answers in this branch may be surmised by evaluating the color (e.g., "... the swirling yellow, blue, and other colors suggest happiness, so the participant might be expected to indicate that happiness is present" [Mayer et al., 2000, p. 329]) and/or shape of the design (e.g., ... "the soft colors and shapes also suggest an absence of anger, so the participant might be expected to indicate that anger is mostly absent" [Mayer et al., 2000, p. 329]). Likewise in Branch 3, "if a person is asked, 'which two emotional experiences might blend together in the feeling of contempt?' some of the possible answers (e.g., anger and disgust) must be better than others (e.g., joy and challenge)" (Mayer et al., 2004, p. 200). Similarly in Branch 4, some alternatives for cheering-up a sad person (e.g., talking to some friends, seeing a violent movie, eating a big meal, talking a walk alone) have a higher probability of accomplishing the goal than others.

Given the differences in the theoretical models and concomitant measures of EI discussed above, it should come as little surprise that the same person may emerge from a testing session with a different EI profile depending on the assessment tool employed. Caution should be exercised, therefore, when interpreting EI data and applying EI results. Additionally, in an effort to advance both the scientific and applied literatures in EI, it may be prudent to consider the use of one fixed model and assessment inventory. Although likely to be controversial, the utility of such a suggestion can be seen in the literature review below.

RESEARCH IN THE HEALTH AND BUSINESS DOMAINS

Much of the EI research to date has been conducted in domains which inform and are informed by sport psychology. This research may be useful to researchers and practitioners alike as they continue to consider the utility of EI in understanding sport performance, participation patterns, and coaching behaviors. In the section that follows we review literature examining EI in the health and business professions, focusing specifically on the EI-leadership relationship and implications for leadership in sport (i.e., coaching). See Table 2 for a summary of the relationships between EI and performance outcomes in these two domains.

Emotional Intelligence and Leadership

Health professions. Informed by the Transactional Model of stress and coping (Lazarus and Folkman, 1984; Lazarus, 1990) as well as Salovey et al.'s suggestion that EI may be "critical for adaptive psychophysiological coping and subsequent well-being" (Salovey, Stroud, Woolery, and Epel, 2002, p. 613), researchers have recently begun to examine the relationship between EI and psychological well-being, health behaviors, and physical health. For example, higher EI (as measured by the TMMS) has been related to greater psychological adjustment and social adaptation, and decreased physical health problems among middle-aged Spanish women (Extremera and Fernandez-Berrocal, 2002) as well as less depression and anxiety among female breast cancer survivors (Schmidt and Andrykowski, 2004). Among overweight adults, Parker, Meyer, and Swartz (2005) found that individuals with average EI scores (as measured by the MSCEIT) recorded lower negative mood states and higher self-esteem, and engaged in almost twice as much daily walking as compared to individuals with below average EI scores. Results of this study portend the importance of EI to the research and professional practice of exercise and health psychologists.

Table 2. Relationships between EI and Performance Outcomes in Health and Business

Cite	Sample	Measure	Outcome	Positive, negative, or, or mixed results
HEALTH/WELL–BEING				
Extremera and Fernandez-Berrocal (2002)	99 middle-aged Spanish women	TMMS	EI related to increased psychological adjustment and reduced physical health problems.	Positive
Parker et al. (2005)	15 overweight adults from a large urban community	MSCEIT	Positive relationship between EI and PWB, obesity-related health, and physical activity participation.	Positive
Riley and Schutte (2003)	141 Australian adults from community and campus settings	EIS	Negative relationship between EI and alcohol- and drug-related problems Positive relationshipl between EI and coping with drug-related problems.	Positive
Schmidt and Andrykowski (2004)	210 female breast cancer survivors	TMMS	Negative relationship between EI and anxiety, depression, as well avoidant and intrusive cognitions.	Positive
Trinidad and Johnson (2002)	205 multi-ethnic middle school children from southern California	MEIS –student version	Negative relationship between EI and tobacco/alcohol use.	Positive
Trinidad et al. (2004)	416 multi-ethnic 6th graders from the Los Angeles area	MEIS- adolescent version	High EI predicted greater perceptions of the negative social consequences of smoking and greater confidence in refusing cigarette offers. High EI also predicted less likelihood of intending to smoke in the next year.	Positive
HEALTH PROFESSIONS				
Gertis et al. (2004)	380 Dutch nurses	EQ-i – Dutch version	Negative relatationship between EI and burnout and EI and psychopathology. No relationship between EI and absenteeism due to illness. Relationship between EI and coping behaviors	Mixed
Gertis et al. (2005)	380 Dutch nurses	EQ-i – Dutch version	Female nurses with high EI and lower social skills reported significantly less burnout than male or female nurses with other profiles. No relationship between EI and absenteeism due to illness.	Mixed

Cite	Sample	Measure	Outcome	+/-mixed
Pau and Croucher (2003)	213 dental students in the United Kingdom	EIS	Negative relationship between EI and perceived stress	Positive
Pau et al. (2004)	10 dental students with low EI and 10 dental students with high EI	Unstructured in-depth interviews	High EI students were more likely to adopt positive coping styles/behaviors in the face of stress while low EI students were more likely to engage in health-damaging behaviors	Positive
BUSINESS				
Jordan and Troth (2002)	139 students in an introductory management course	WEIP6[1]	Positive relationship between EI and likelihood/ability to engage in collaborative conflict resolution.	Positive
Kobe et al. (2001)	192 undergraduate students at a university in the U.S.	EQ-i	EI accounted for significant variance in leadership experiences, but did not add unique variance beyond that accounted for by social intelligence.	Negative
Slaski and Cartwright (2002)	320 middle managers for a major UK retailer	EQ-i	Positive relationship between EI and health, well-being, and management performance. Negative relationship between EI and subjective stress	Positive
Slaski and Cartwright (2003)	60 managers from a large retail chain in the UK	EQ-i	EI training resulted in significant increases in EI, health, and well-being.	Positive

[1] Workgroup Emotional Intelligence Profile-Version 6 (Jordan, Ashkanasy, Hartel, & Hooper, 2002)

The potential relationship between EI and health is further seen in the study of one particular type of health behavior -- substance use and abuse. In a study of ethnically diverse adolescents, Trinidad and Johnson (2002) found significant negative correlations between EI (as measured by the MEIS) and a general overall measure of tobacco and alcohol use, as well as specific tobacco and alcohol behaviors (e.g., trying a cigarette, smoking daily/weekly, drinking alcohol in the last week, etc.). In a follow-up study, researchers (Trinidad, Unger, Chou, and Johnson, 2004) reported that high EI was associated with factors that protect adolescents against smoking behavior. While the aforementioned results suggest a relationship between EI and substance use, they do not speak to *problematic* use, or abuse. To that end, Riley and Schutte (2003) report that lower EI (as measured by the EIS) was a significant predictor of alcohol- and drug-related problems among a sample of Australian adults. Their results also demonstrate that lower EI was strongly associated with poorer coping, which was significantly correlated to drug-related problems (e.g., loss of job, loss of friendships). Taken together, the results of these studies support the need for health care professionals to consider the potential influence of emotional states on health outcomes and health behaviors.

While the literature reviewed above suggests that EI may be related to physical and psychological well-being among individuals in a variety of healthy and health-compromised populations, recent attention has been devoted to the health and well-being of care providers themselves. For example, research and anecdotal evidence suggest high levels of stress among health care professionals may be related to decreased health and well-being, absenteeism, attrition, and sub-standard patient care (Gerits, Derksen, Verbruggen, and Katzko, 2005; Hatton et al., 1999; Rose, 1995). Thus, those individuals who work in professions with high rates of job stress may benefit from higher levels of EI in coping with that stress.

One of the largest bodies of literature involving health care providers examines the relationship between EI and burnout, and factors that may contribute to workplace performance and satisfaction. In a longitudinal study of nurses caring for individuals with mental retardation and severe behavioral problems, Gerits and colleagues (Gerits, Derksen, and Verbruggen, 2004; Gerits et al., 2005) used a Dutch version of the EQ-i to identify a negative relationship between EI and burnout. Similarly, results suggest that the fewest symptoms of burnout were reported by female nurses with a relatively high EI profiles. Concomitant measures in both studies offer insight into this relationship and the possible gender differences that may contribute to the findings. For example, coping style and social skills were identified as two variables of interest. The negative relationship between EI and depressive as well as avoidance coping, along with the positive relationship between EI and active coping, offers implications for training programs, despite the lack of further directional insight. Similarly, the finding that low levels of social skills appeared to buffer burnout among female nurses while problem-solving skills and stress tolerance appeared to buffer burnout among male nurses, suggests that training programs for health care professionals may benefit from the inclusion of some gender specific components.

As was the case with the nurses above, stress also emerged as a variable of interest in studies of British dental students. In a quantitative study, Pau and Croucher (2003) found an inverse relationship between EI (as measured by the EIS) and perceived stress. Their results also suggest that dental students with low EI cope less well with stress, and therefore experience more stress. That female dental students reported higher levels of perceived stress than male dental students reinforces the need to explore further issues related to gender, EI, and potential moderating variables. In a qualitative extension of the study cited above, it was suggested that EI may also play a role in the methods used to cope with stress in dental school (Pau, Croucher, Sohanpal, Nuirhead, and Seymour, 2004). Specifically, interviews with male and female students suggest that individuals with high EI utilize adaptive strategies for coping with dental school stress (e.g., reflection, social and interpersonal skills, organization, time management) while individuals with low EI utilize health-damaging strategies (e.g., alcohol and tobacco consumption). Given that leaders in sport and health care share similar job functions (e.g., manage conflict, provide vision, oversee hiring/firing) and expectations (e.g., objective success, subordinate satisfaction, balanced budget), and that elite level coaches report a high probability of experiencing job-related stress and/or burnout (Raedeke, Granzyk, and Warren, 2000), it makes sense to explore further the role of EI in sport leadership.

Despite the lack of experimental designs, results of the above studies examining EI and general as well as workplace health and well-being, point to the need for EI or related training in educational and/or career development programs. This suggestion is supported by research suggesting that the EI of medical school applicants is strongly related to their coursework in the social sciences and humanities (Carrothers, Gregory, and Gallagher, 2000). In addition to formal curricular requirements, there has been an ongoing call for informal educational experiences (e.g., in-service programs, continuing education programs, etc.) which address the importance of EI in health care as well as techniques for skill development (Duran, Extremera, and Rey, 2004; Evans and Allen, 2002; Gerits et al., 2004; Gerits et al., 2005; Wagner, Moseley, Grant, Gore, and Owens, 2002). Thus, with proper training, individuals in a variety of fields, including healthcare, business, and sport can learn to increase their social and emotional intelligence abilities (Cherniss, 2000). However, before we discuss the possible role of EI in coaches, let's examine the links with another field highly interested in effective leadership – namely, the business world.

Business and sport settings. As suggested previously, much of the anecdotal and empirical EI literature to date has focused on implications for the business world. A review of related research indicates that EI and appropriately regulated emotions in the workplace are thought to result in: (a) better coping strategies for dealing with job insecurity and job-related tension (Jordan, Ashkanasy, and Hartel, 2002), (b) enhanced ability to engage in collaborative conflict resolution (Jordan and Troth, 2002), (c) increased sales (Cherniss, 2000), (d) delivery of higher quality health care (Cherniss, 2000), (e) greater customer service and satisfaction (Ashkanasy, Hartel, and Daus, 2002; Salovey, Mayer, and Caruso, 2002), (f) enhanced health and improved work performance (Slaski and Cartwright, 2002, 2003), (g) better performance in job interviews (Ashkanasy et al., 2002), and (h) more effective and successful leadership (George, 2000; Palmer, Walls, Burgess, and Stough, 2000).

Given that both business and sport organizations share the purpose of achieving successful outcomes for their *shareholders*, it is reasonable to assume that some findings from the business literature may transfer to sport. Most importantly, it is the relationship between EI and leadership and its potential relevance for coaching, which may have the most meaningful link. In this next section, we provide an overview of the literature examining the relationship between EI and leadership, and identify implications for leadership in sport and the field of coaching.

In a recent synthesis of the leadership literature, George (2000, p. 1039) identified the following activities as among those essential for effective leadership:

- Development of a collective sense of goals and objectives and how to go about achieving them;
- Instilling in others knowledge and appreciation of the importance of work activities and behaviors;
- Generating and maintaining excitement, enthusiasm, confidence, and optimism in an organization as well as cooperation and trust;
- Encouraging flexibility in decision making and change;
- Establishing and maintaining a meaningful identify for an organization.

George also suggests that although the characteristics of effective leadership have been written about extensively, the role of emotions in leadership has been neglected. George's list of activities is supported by recent research (Kobe, Reiter-Palmon, and Rickers, 2001) involving 192 U.S. college students, which suggests that EI accounts for a significant amount of the variance in leadership experiences and that social and emotional aspects of leadership should be considered in both future empirical and applied endeavors. She as well as others (Caruso, Mayer, and Salovey, 2002; Kobe et al., 2001) support the notion that because the workplace is an emotion-laden domain, EI has the potential to contribute to leadership research and practice in many ways. For example, leaders must be able to communicate effectively, understand and interpret emotional reactions of co-workers, garner support for goals and initiatives, enact appropriate problem-solving and conflict resolution measures, manage change, and create a safe environment for a multi-cultural workforce. Overall, coaches are required to use a very similar skill set in their roles as the manager, tactician, and emotional leader of a sport team and not surprisingly, popular coach education programs include nearly all of the aforementioned key elements of leadership (Martens, 1987; Smith and Smoll, 1996). These task-oriented social skills have been shown to be effective in creating a more positive motivational climate that promotes adaptive participant behavior (Ames, 1992). Specifically, some EI research has suggested that effective managers are more likely than less effective managers to respond quickly to the needs of subordinate employees by adding or removing work challenges as needed to maximize individual motivation (Palmer et al., 2000). These data translate well to coaches because there is a constant need to monitor individual athlete progress on skills as well as to modify feedback and drills appropriately to ensure efficient athlete development. There is additional evidence that the sport environment is also emotion-laden, and that helping athletes recognize and manage these emotions is critical to facilitating successful sport performance (Hanin, 1995; 2000; Totterdell, 1999). Thus, due to the need for leaders to interact with and motivate others, promote goal-oriented behavior, and manage potentially stressful situations, evidence is building for the notion that business and sport leaders (i.e., coaches) may be more effective at their jobs if they have higher abilities in the personal and social dimensions of EI.

In addition to the EI-related cognitions and behaviors of leaders that directly influence group members as described above, it is important to recognize that EI may mediate the cognitions and behaviors of leaders, thereby having an indirect effect on member cognitions and behaviors. For example, in their two-stage model, Jordan, Ashkanasy, and Hartel (2002) suggest that an increased perception of job insecurity "results in two interrelated emotional reactions: lowered affective commitment and increased job-related tension" (p. 361). The resultant emotional reactions lead to negative coping *behaviors* such as those described earlier in the chapter. They go on to suggest that EI may moderate emotional reactions to job insecurity and ability to cope with the resultant stress. That is, leaders with high EI are more likely than leaders with low EI to experience practical reactions to job insecurity and adopt positive coping strategies. Consistent with the ability model as well as an abundance of anecdotal and empirical evidence (e.g., Cherniss, 2000; Caruso and Wolfe, 2001), the work of Jordan et al. (2002) reinforces the importance of EI training programs, which can facilitate management of emotions related to job insecurity and other workplace stressors.

At the elite level, the job climate of coaches can be quite unstable and stressful. With job security tied to objective performance of the team (e.g., wins / losses) as well as subjective evaluations of success (e.g., athlete GPA, athlete/fan satisfaction, attendance), coaches may experience significant job-related uncertainty and tension. Presumably, coaches with higher EI may tolerate these emotions better and make healthier coping choices as well as more effective decisions when faced with substantial stress and resultant negative mood states. As a potential role model for athletes, coaches are in a position to have a considerable impact on athlete's behavior by modeling emotionally intelligent responses to stressors. However, if coaches are unable to recognize and manage their own emotions and those of their athletes, anecdotal evidence from the business literature (Caruso et al., 2002) suggests that athletes may suffer from low satisfaction and be more prone to disengage from the team and their sport. These tentative, but encouraging links between EI and leadership processes and behavior have given rise to a new line of research regarding the role of EI in coaching.

Emotional Intelligence in Coaches

The importance of EI to the health, well-being, satisfaction, and performance of those in leadership positions is demonstrated above, as is the potential link between leadership issues in health care, business, and sport. While empirical evidence exists to support the aforementioned links between EI and leadership in the health care and business domains, there is a paucity of research in the area of EI and leadership in sport. In an effort to examine further the potential role of EI in coaching, data were collected to describe the EI of coaches working at the elite levels of sport. These data inform recommendations for future research and sport psychology applications.

College coaches. In a pilot study of college level coaches (Meyer, Kilty, Parker, Fletcher, Cole, and Davis, 2005), 19 individuals employed at NCAA Division I institutions across the United States completed an online version of the MSCEIT. Primary study results suggest that the total EI scores recorded by all of the coaches (M = 95.20) were not significantly different than the standardized norms recorded for the general population (M = 100), nor were branch scores recorded by all of the coaches (i.e., M = 93, 97, 95, and 99, respectively). Although no statistically significant gender difference in EI score between male and female coaches was found, a large effect size was noted (d = .76), suggesting that in larger samples, there may be a meaningful difference in the EI between male and female coaches. Concomitantly, the total EI score recorded by the male coaches (M = 89.27) were significantly lower than standardized population norm (M = 100). In terms of other coach subgroups, no significant differences in total EI were found between the coaches of the various sports (i.e., basketball, volleyball, soccer), nor between head coaches and assistant coaches.

Elite coaches. In an extension of the preceding study, 104 coaches from around the world working with athletes at various levels of competition (e.g., NCAA, professional, national amateur, etc.) completed an online version of the MSCEIT. Again, primary study results suggest that the total EI scores recorded by this group of coaches (M = 97.91) were not significantly different than standardized norms for the general population (M = 100). Unlike the college coaches studied above, however, the elite coaches recorded one branch score (i.e, Branch 1 – perceiving emotion) that was significantly lower than (M = 96.11) than population norms (M = 100). Although no statistically significant gender difference in EI score between male and female coaches was found, the total EI scores recorded by the male coaches (M = 97.38) were significantly lower than standardized population norms (M = 100). In terms of other coach subgroups, no significant differences in total EI were found between the coaches of the various types of sports (i.e., interactive, coactive), nor between head coaches and assistant/associate coaches. It should be noted, however, that the total EI scores recorded by the head coaches were significantly lower than standardized norms. These consistently lower scores in male coaches and head coaches at elite levels may be problematic given the aforementioned job responsibilities in sport leadership positions. It is unclear, however, at this point if this lower than average EI inhibits their objective or perceived coaching effectiveness. Previous authors have suggested that above average EI is likely to facilitate leadership effectiveness and team performance but that lower than average EI may not inhibit successful outcomes (Caruso et al., 2002).

Clearly, additional data must be collected before consistently sound contributions can be made to the scientific and applied literatures in the area of EI and sport leadership. If the results of follow-up studies suggest that male coaches consistently report lower EI scores than the general male population, for example, and if relationships are found between EI and other key sport leadership variables (e.g., athlete satisfaction, task cohesion, motivational climate), remediation and additional training may be necessary. Similarly, if follow-up data continue to indicate that coaches at the elite level experience difficulties in perceiving the emotions of self and others, awareness training could be integrated into their formal and/or informal coaching preparation. The implementation of an EI intervention is consistent with the ability model as well as research reviewed earlier in this chapter, which suggests that EI is a skill that can be learned and developed over time. Sport psychology professionals are encouraged to adopt an ability framework to their study and practice of EI, with an increased emphasis on program evaluation. With additional research coming from a similar paradigm, accumulated evidence may begin to illuminate the true role of EI in coach and athlete performance.

Suggestions for Future Research and Practice: Emotional Intelligence in Coaching

To continue to advance the study of EI in sport, coaching in particular, the following research suggestions are offered:

- Collect additional descriptive data with larger and more diverse samples to better understand the potential role of EI in sport leadership

- Compare relationship between EI scores and coaching styles or climates of coaches /teams at various competitive levels
- Explore the relationship of specific branches of EI as related to leader behavior or objective/subjective sport outcomes
- Conduct research to test the proposed links between EI, coping, social support, and stress responses
- Examine the relationships between coach EI and health as well as coach EI and health behaviors
- Examine the relationship between coach EI and his/her objective and subjective performance
- Evaluate the effect of EI training programs with male and female coaches
- Consider the use of an adapted model (Lazarus and Folkman, 1984) to further the understanding of the possible role of EI in sport psychology research and practice (see Figure 1)

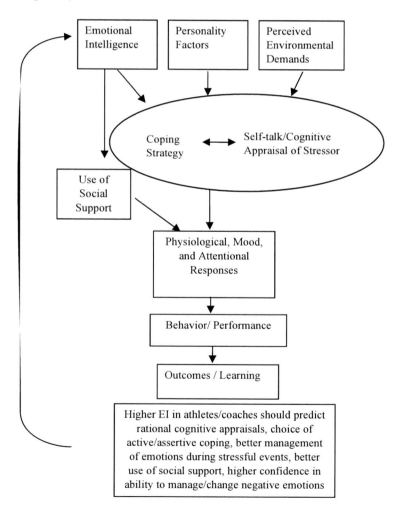

Figure 1. Possible Role of Emotional Intelligence in Sport

To advance the study of EI in sport, coaching in particular, the following professional practice suggestions are offered:

- Augment formal and informal coaching education programs with material on enhancing EI
- Include EI material as part of traditional PST programs offered to athletes and teams
- Integrate EI material into sport psychology graduate programs

REFERENCES

Ames, C. (1992). Achievement goals, motivational climate, and motivational processes. In G.C. Roberts (Ed.), *Motivation in sport and exercise* (pp. 161-176). Champaign, IL: Human Kinetics.

Ashkanasy, N. M., Hartel, C. E. J., and Daus, C. S. (2002). Diversity and emotion: The new frontiers in organizational behavior research, *Journal of Management, 28,* 307-338.

Austin, E.J., Saklofske, D.H., Huang, S.H.S., and McKenney, D. (2004). Measurement of trait emotional intelligence: Testing and cross-validating a modified version of Schutte et al.'s (1998) measure. *Personality and Individual Differences, 36,* 555-562.

Bar-On, R. (1997). *The Emotional Quotient Inventory (EQ-i): Technical Manual.* Toronto: Multi-Health Systems.

Bar-On, R. (2001). Emotional intelligence and self-actualization. In J. Ciarrochi, J.P. Forgas, and J.D. Mayer (Eds.), *Emotional intelligence in everyday life: A scientific inquiry* (pp. 82-97). New York, NY: Psychology Press, Inc.

Bar-On, R. (2002). *Bar-On Emotional Quotient Inventory: Short: Technical Manual.* Toronto: Multi-Health Systems.

Brackett, M., and Mayer, J.D. (2001, October). *Comparing measures of emotional intelligence.* Paper presented at the Third Positive Psychology Summit, Washington, DC.

Brackett, M., and Mayer, J.D. (2003). Convergent, discriminant, and incremental validity of competing measures of emotional intelligence. *Personality and Social Psychology Bulletin, 29,* 1147-1158.

Botterill, C., & Brown, M. (2002). Emotion and perspective in sport. *International Journal of Sport Psychology, 33,* 38-60.

Carrothers, R.M., Gregory, S.W., and Gallagher, T.J. (2000). Measuring emotional intelligence of medical school applicants. *Academic Medicine, 75,* 456-463.

Caruso, D.R., and Wolfe, C.J. (2001). Emotional intelligence in the workplace. In J. Ciarrochi, J.P. Forgas, and J.D. Mayer (Eds.), *Emotional intelligence in everyday life: A scientific inquiry* (pp. 150-167). New York: Psychology Press.

Caruso, D.R., Mayer, J.D., and Salovey, P. (2002). Emotional intelligence and emotional leadership. In M. Riggio (Ed), *Multiple intelligences and leadership: LEA's organization and management series* (pp 55-74). Mahwah, NJ: Lawrence Earlbaum.

Cherniss, C. (2000). Social and emotional competence in the workplace. In R. Bar-On, and J. D. A. Parker (Eds.), *The handbook of emotional intelligence: Theory, development, assessment, and application at home, school, and in the workplace* (pp. 433-458). San Fransisco, CA: Jossey-Bass.

Ciarrochi, J., Chan, A., Caputi, P., and Roberts, R. (2001). Measuring emotional intelligence. In J. Ciarrochi, J.P. Forgas, and J.D. Mayer (Eds.), *Emotional intelligence in everyday life: A scientific inquiry* (pp. 46-66). New York, NY: Psychology Press, Inc.

Conte, J.M., (2005). A review and critique of emotional intelligence measures. *Journal of Organizational Behavior, 26,* 433-440.

Davies, M., Stankov, L., and Roberts, R.D. (1998). Emotional intelligence: In search of an elusive construct. *Journal of Personality and Social Psychology, 75,* 989-1015.

Dawda, D., and Hart, S. D. (2000). Assessing emotional intelligence: Reliability and validity of the Bar-On Emotional Quotient Inventory (EQ-I) in university students. *Personality and Individual Differences, 28,* 797-812.

Druskat, V. U., and Wolff, S. B. (2001). Building the emotional intelligence of groups. *Harvard Business Review, 79,* 80-87.

Duran, A., Extremera, N., and Rey, L. (2004). Self-reported emotional intelligence, burnout and engagement among staff in services for people with intellectual disabilities. *Psychological Reports, 95,* 386-390.

Extremera, N., and Fernandez-Berrocal, P. (2002). Relation of perceived emotional intelligence and health-related quality of life of middle-aged women. *Psychological Reports, 91,* 47-59.

Evans, D., and Allen, H. (2002). Emotional intelligence: It's role in training. *Nursing Times, 98,* 41-42.

Gardner, H. (1983). *Frames of mind: The theory of multiple intelligences.* New York: BasicBooks.

George, J.M. (2000). Emotions and leadership: The role of emotional intelligence. *Human Relations, 53,* 1027-1055.

Gerits, L., Derksen, J.J.L., and Verbruggen, A.B. (2004). Emotional intelligence and adaptive success of nurses caring for people with mental retardation and severe behavior problems. *Mental Retardation, 42,* 106-121.

Gerits, L., Derksen, J.J.L., Verbruggen, A.B., and Katzko, M. (2005). Emotional intelligence profiles of nurses caring for people with severe behaviour problems. *Personality and Individual Differences, 38,* 33-43.

Goleman, D. (1995). *Emotional intelligence.* New York: Bantam Books.

Gould, D., Guinan, D., Greenleaf, C., and Chung, Y. (2002). A survey of U.S. Olympic coaches: Variables perceived to have influenced athlete performance and coach effectiveness. *The Sport Psychologist, 16,* 229-250.

Hanin, Y. L. (1995). Individualized zones of optimal functioning (IZOF) model: An idiographic approach to performance anxiety. In K. Henschen and W. Straub (Eds.), *Sport psychology: An analysis of athlete behavior* (pp. 103-119). Longmeadow, MA: Movement Publications.

Hanin, Y. L. (2000). *Emotions in sport.* Champaign, IL: Human Kinetics.

Hatton, C., Emerson, E., Rivers, M., Mason, H., Mason, L., Swarbrick, R., Kiernan, C., Reeves, D., and Alborz, A. (1999). Factors associated with staff stress and work satisfaction in services for people with intellectual disabilities. *Journal of Intellectual Disability Research, 43,* 253-267.

Jones, G. (2002). Performance excellence: A personal perspective on the link between sport and business. *Journal of Applied Sport Psychology, 14,* 268-281.

Jordan, P. J., Ashkanasy, N. M., and Hartel, C.E.J. (2002). Emotional intelligence as a moderator of emotional and behavioral reactions to job insecurity. *Academy of Management Review, 27(3)*, 361-372.

Jordan, P. J., and Troth, A. C. (2002). Emotional intelligence and conflict resolution: Implications for human resource development. *Advances in Developing Human Resources, 4*(1), 62-79.

Kobe, L.M., Reiter-Palmon, R., Rickers, J.D. (2001). Self-reported leadership experiences in relations to inventoried social and emotional intelligence. *Current Psychology, 20,* 154-163.

Landy, F.J. (2005). Some historical and scientific issues related to research on emotional intelligence. *Journal of Organizational Behavior, 26,* 411-424.

Lazarus, R.S. (1990) Theory-based stress measurement. *Psychological Inquiry, 1,* 3-13.

Lazarus, R.S., and Folkman, S. (1984). *Stress, appraisal, and coping.* New York: Springer-Verlag.

Mahoney, M.P. (2002). *Alcohol consumption and drug use among former major league baseball players.* Unpublished doctoral dissertation. Temple University.

Martens, R. (1987). *Coaches guide to sport psychology.* Champaign, IL: Human Kinetics.

Matthews, G., Zeidner, M., and Roberts, R. D. (2004). *Emotional intelligence: Science and myth.* Cambridge, MA: MIT Press.

Mayer, J. D. (2001). A field guide to emotional intelligence. In J. Ciarrochi, J.P. Forgas, and J.D. Mayer (Eds.), *Emotional intelligence in everyday life: A scientific inquiry* (pp. 3-24). New York: Psychology Press.

Mayer, J.D., Caruso, D.R., and Salovey, P. (1999). Emotional intelligence meets traditional standards for an intelligence. *Intelligence, 27,* 267-298.

Mayer, J.D., Caruso, D.R., and Salovey, P. (2000). Selecting a measure of emotional intelligence. In R. Bar-On and J.D.A. Parker (Eds.), *The handbook of emotional intelligence: Theory, development, assessment, and application at home, school, and in the workplace* (pp. 320-342). San Francisco, CA: Jossey-Bass Inc.

Mayer, J. D., and Salovey, P. (1997). What is emotional intelligence? In P. Salovey and D. Sluyter (Eds.), *Emotional development and emotional intelligence: Implications for educators (pp. 3-31).* New York: Basic Books.

Mayer J.D., Salovey P., and Caruso, D.R. (2002). *Mayer-Salovey-Caruso Emotional Intelligence Test (MSCEIT): User's manual.* Toronto: Multi-Health Systems.

Mayer, J.D., Salovey, P., and Caruso, D.R. (2004). Emotional intelligence: Theory, findings, and implications. *Psychological Inquiry, 15,* 197-215.

Mayer J.D., Salovey P., and Caruso, D.R., Sitarenios, G. (2003). Emotional intelligence as a standard intelligence. *Emotion, 1,* 232-242.

McCann, S. (1999). Emotional intelligence: The secret of athletic excellence. *Olympic Coach, 9,* 8-9.

Meyer, B. B., Fletcher, T. B., Kilty, K., and Richburg, M. J. (2003, October). *Emotional intelligence: Theoretical and applied implications for AAASP constituents.* Colloquium presented at the Association for the Advancement of Applied Sport Psychology, Philadelphia, PA.

Meyer, B.B., Kilty, K.A., Parker, S.J., Fletcher, T.B., Davis, N.W., and Cole, M.E. (2005, August). *The emotional intelligence of college athletes: An exploratory study.* Poster presented at the International Society of Sport Psychology 11th World Congress of Sport Psychology, Sydney, Australia, August 17.

Palmer, B., Walls, M., Burgess, Z., and Stough, C. (2000). Emotional intelligence and effective leadership. *Leadership and Organizational Development Journal, 22*, 5-10.

Parker, S.J., Meyer, B.B., Swartz, A.M. (2005, May). *Stress, coping, and obesity-related health: An exploratory study of emotional intelligence.* Poster presented at the University of Wisconsin-Milwaukee College of Health Sciences Research Symposium, Milwaukee, WI.

Pau, A.K.H., and Croucher, R. (2003). Emotional intelligence and perceived stress in dental undergraduates. *Journal of Dental Education, 67,* 1023-1028.

Pau, A.K.H., Croucher, R., Sohanpal, R., Muirhead, V., and Seymour, K. (2004). Emotional intelligence and stress coping in dental undergraduates – a qualitative study. *British Dental Journal, 197,* 205-209.

Petrides, K. V., and Furnham, A. (2000). On the dimensional structure of emotional intelligence. *Personality and Individual Differences, 29,* 313-320.

Raedeke, T.D., Granzyk, T.A., and Warren, A. (2000). Why coaches experience burnout: A commitment perspective. *Journal of Sport and Exercise Psychology, 22*, 85-105.

Riley, H., and Schutte, N.S. (2003). Low emotional intelligence as a predictor of substance-use problems. *Journal of Drug Education, 33*, 391-398.

Rose, J. (1995). Stress and residential staff: Towards an integration of existing research. *Mental handicap Research, 8,* 220-236.

Salovey, P., and Mayer, J. D. (1990). Emotional intelligence. *Imagination, Cognition, and Personality, 9,* 185-211.

Salovey, P., Mayer, J.D., and Caruso, D. (2002). The positive psychology of emotional intelligence. In C.R. Snyder, and S.J. Lopez (Eds.), *Handbook of positive psychology* (pp. 159-171). London: Oxford University Press.

Salovey, P., Mayer, J.D., Goldman, S., Turvey, C., and Palfai, T. (1995). Emotional attention, clarity, and repair: Exploring emotional intelligence using the Trait Meta-Mood Scale. In J.W. Pennebaker (Ed.), *Emotion, disclosure, and health* (pp. 125-154). Washington, DC: American Psychological Association.

Salovey, P., Stroud, L.R., Woolery, A., and Epel, E.S. (2002). Perceived emotional intelligence, stress reactivity, and symptom reports: Further exploration using the Trait Meta-Mood Scale. *Psychology and Health, 17,* 611-627.

Schmidt, J.E., and Andrykowski, M.A. (2004). The role of social and dispositional variables associated with emotional processing in adjustment to breast cancer: An internet-based survey. *Health Psychology, 23,* 259-266.

Schutte, N. S., Malouff, J. M., Hall, L. E., Haggerty, D. J., Cooper, J. T., Golden, C. J., and Dornheim, L. (1998). Development and validation of a measure of emotional intelligence. *Personality and Individual Differences, 25,* 167-177.

Schutte, N. S., Malouff, J. M, Simunek, M., McKenley, J., and Hollander, S. (2002). Characteristic emotional intelligence and emotional well-being. *Cognition and Emotion, 16,* 769-785.

Slaski, M., and Cartwright, S. (2002). Health and emotional intelligence: An exploratory study of retail managers. *Stress and Health, 18,* 63-68.

Slaski, M., and Cartwright, S. (2003). Emotional intelligence training and its implications for stress, health and performance. *Stress and Health, 19,* 233-239.

Schutte, N. S., Malouff, J. M, Simunek, M., McKenley, J., and Hollander, S. (2002). Characteristic emotional intelligence and emotional well-being. *Cognition and Emotion, 16,* 769-785.

Smith, R.E., and Smoll, F.L. (1996). *Way to go, coach! A scientifically-proven approach to coaching effectiveness.* Portola Valley, CA: Warde.

Sternberg, R. J. (1997a). The concept of intelligence and its role in lifelong learning and success. *American Psychologist, 52,* 1030-1045.

Sternberg, R. J. (1997b). *Successful intelligence: How practical and creative intelligence determine success in life.* New York: Plume.

Sternberg, R. J., Forsythe, G. B., Hedlund, J., Horvath, J. A., Wagner, R. K., Williams, W. M., Snook, S. A., and Grigorenko, E. L. (2000). *Practical intelligence in everyday life.* New York, Cambridge.

Sternberg, R. J., Wagner, R. K., Williams, W. M., and Horvath, J. A. (1995). Testing common sense. *American Psychologist, 50,* 912-927.

Totterdell, P. (1999). Mood scores: Mood and performance in professional cricketers. *British Journal of Psychology, 90,* 317-332.

Trinidad, D. R., and Johnson, C. A. (2002). The association between emotional intelligence and early adolescent tobacco and alcohol use. *Personality and Individual Differences, 32,* 95-105.

Trinidad, D.R., Unger, J.B., Chou, C.P., and Johnson, C.A. (2004). The protective association of emotional intelligence with psychosocial smoking risk factors for adolescents. *Personality and Individual Differences, 36,* 945-954.

Van Rooy, D.L., and Viswesvaran, C. (2004). Emotional intelligence: A meta-analytic investigation of predictive validity and nomological net. *Journal of Vocational Behavior, 65,* 71-95.

Wagner, P.J., Moseley, G.C., Grant, M.M., Gore, J.R., and Owens, C. (2002). Physicians' emotional intelligence and patient satisfaction. *Family Medicine, 34,* 750-754.

Weinberg, R., and McDermott, M. (2002). A comparative analysis of sport and business organizations: Factors perceived critical for organizational success. *Journal of Applied Sport Psychology, 14,* 282-298.

Wertheim, J. (2003, September 8). Prisoners of depression. *Sports Illustrated.*

Zizzi, S.J., and Deaner, H.R., and Hirschhorn, D.K. (2003). The relationship between emotional intelligence and performance among college baseball players. *Journal of Applied Sport Psychology, 15,* 262-269.

In: Mood and Human Performance: Conceptual, Measurement...   ISBN 1-60021-269-7
Editor: Andrew M. Lane, pp. 153-164   © 2006 Nova Science Publishers, Inc.

Chapter 7

MOOD STATES AND PERSONALITY

*Matthew J. Stevens**

School of Sport, Performing Arts and Leisure,
University of Wolverhampton

ABSTRACT

Recent research in general psychology has highlighted the link between moods, emotions, and personality traits yet sport psychology has long since banished personality focused research to the history books. As we begin to recognise that constructs such as mood and emotion are not isolated constructs, and are a part of a transactional process in which variables interact and take on different roles within an ongoing situation, we must realise that personality traits have an important influence on behaviour and cognition.

Findings consistently support associations between extraversion and positive mood (Costa and McCrae, 1980; Watson and Clark, 1984; Meyer and Shack, 1989), neuroticism and negative mood (Costa and McCrae, 1980; Watson and Clark, 1984; McFatter, 1994; Meyer and Shack, 1989), and the relationship between self-esteem and mood (Diener, 1984; Pelham and Swann, 1989). Further, models of proposing the nature of the personality x mood relationship have been put forward (Rusting, 1998; 1999). This chapter reviews some of the research that has identified links between personality traits and mood states, including the influence of mood-congruent and trait-congruent memory recall.

The relationships are important to sport psychologists investigating mood and using measures of mood in applied settings, since the personality can influence the interpretation of an event, the intensity and duration of a mood, and the effectiveness of any coping behaviours.

INTRODUCTION

Considerable research has investigated the relationship between mood and performance in a variety of sport and exercise activities and settings (LeUnes and Burger, 1998; LeUnes,

---

*E-mail: sportpsychms@hotmail.com

2000) and a great deal of early sport psychology research examined the relationships between personality constructs and performance (Weinberg and Gould, 2003; Vealey, 1992). But as noted in the Handbook of Sport Psychology, since the 1980s personality research within sport and exercise psychology seems to be dying out, and "personality is a dirty word" (Van den Auwelle, Nys, Rzewnicki, and Van Mele, 2001). Yet within general psychology, personality, defined as "more or less stable, internal factors that make one person's behaviour consistent from one time to another, and different from the behaviour other people would manifest in comparable situations" (Child, 1968, p.83), has continued to be investigated. Importantly, recent research has endorsed the notion that an individual's mood and emotional experiences are related to their personality traits (Rusting, 1998).

When considering the influence that mood and personality have on performance, is it right to investigate them independently as some researchers propose, or, does personality and mood interact to influence thoughts and behaviour? This chapter will hopefully shed some light on an area of sport psychology that has been ignored for too long.

PERSONALITY

Early investigations into personality suggested a number of factors make up an individual's personality. Researchers have proposed various numbers and types of factors (for example Cattell, 1946) though Eysenck and Eysenck (1968) suggested that two broad, higher-order factors (neuroticism and extraversion) incorporate the majority of lower-order factors. Research has supported the significance of these 'Big Two' higher-order factors (Watson and Hubbard, 1996).

A number of studies in general psychology have investigated the relationship between moods and personality traits, and have tended to assess personality using the Eysenck Personality Inventory (EPI: Eysenck and Eysenck, 1968), which assesses the construct in terms of neuroticism and extraversion. High neuroticism is characterised by feelings of fear, general emotionality, poor inhibition of impulse, sensitivity, and unhappiness (Costa and McCrae, 1985; Eysenck and Eysenck, 1968; Issever, Onen, Sabunku, and Altunkavnak, 2002), while, high extraversion is characterised by feelings of warmth, being affectionate, sociability, assertiveness, exhibitionism, and vigour (Depue and Collins, 1999). Eysenck and Eysenck (1975) later added a third dimension to their model of personality when they developed the Eysenck Personality Questionnaire (EPQ). Individuals reporting high psychoticism scores tend to be restless, irritable, aggressive, and are often unable to emotionally empathise with normal individuals. Table 1 illustrates the traits associated with the EPQ personality dimensions.

A more recent measure of personality was developed by Costa and McCrae (1985; 1992) is based on the Five Factor Model (FFM). In addition to neuroticism and extraversion, measures based on the FFM assess conscientiousness, agreeableness, and openness to experience. Openness to experience includes the appreciation of experience, aesthetic sensitivity, and intellectual curiosity (Costa and McCrae, 1985), and those high in openness tend to be imaginative and traditional (David and Suls, 1999). Agreeableness refers to an individual's orientation in terms of thoughts, feelings, and actions (Costa and McCrae, 1985), and individuals high in this construct are usually helpful and trusting (David and Suls, 1999).

Conscientiousness refers to preferences for structure, organisation, self-discipline, and motivation towards goal-directed behaviour (Costa and McCrae, 1985).

Table 1. Characteristics of personality traits included in Eysenck's personality system

Trait	Description
Neuroticism	Anxious, depressed, guilt feelings, tense, irrational, shy, moody, emotional.
Extraversion	Sociable, lively, active, assertive, sensation-seeking, carefree, dominant, surgent.
Psychoticism	Aggressive, cold, egocentric, impersonal, impulsive, antisocial, creative, tough-minded.

Adapted from Sher, Bartholow, and Wood, 2000, p. 819

Individuals high in conscientiousness are typically reliable, hard-working, and self-disciplined (David and Suls, 1999). Watson and Hubbard (1996) suggested that Eysenck's psychoticism factor could be separated into conscientiousness and agreeableness, and highlighted the similarities between the two theories. The authors noted that this enables findings to be translated into both FFM and Eysenck's terms.

MOOD AND PERSONALITY RESEARCH

Research within mood literature has tended to focus on relationships with neuroticism and extraversion. Extraversion has correlated with measures of positive affect, but is essentially unrelated to negative affect; whereas neuroticism is strongly correlated with negative affect, but is only weakly related to positive affect (Costa and McCrae, 1980; Watson and Clark, 1984). It should be noted that these studies, and the majority of studies investigating mood-personality relationships, have assessed a trait version of mood (an assessment of mood states experienced over a relatively long period of time), hence 'affect' is probably the term to use. An exception is a study carried out by Meyer and Shack (1989) who assessed trait mood using a "general" response set, and state mood using a "right now" response timeframe. In line with previous research, the authors concluded that extraversion is related to positive affect and neuroticism is related to negative affect.

McFatter (1994) found that the interaction of extraversion and neuroticism effectively predicted both PA and NA. The author stated that low extraversion and high neuroticism will result in low PA and high NA, while those low in neuroticism will exhibit a curvilinear relationship between PA and extraversion, and will be low in NA regardless of extraversion scores. Investigations into mood and personality using the FFM are more rare (Watson and Hubbard, 1996). One such study supported previous findings with respect to neuroticism and extraversion and found only minor correlation for agreeableness and conscientiousness (Watson and Clark, 1992). Openness was found to be largely unrelated to mood (Watson and Clark, 1992). The evidence is somewhat equivocal, however, findings generally support the notion that positive affect is related to extraversion and negative affect is related to neuroticism. In a sport sample, Lane (unpublished paper) found relationships between negative mood and neuroticism, and positive mood and extraversion, but in a later study, only the relationship for neuroticism and negative mood was significant (Lane, Milton, and Terry, 2005).

The equivocal nature of this research should not be surprising. Regardless of personality make-up, everyone will experience positive and negative moods of varying intensities at different times. However, within the 'affective' order, there are more stable (trait-like) temperaments, state moods, and unstable, briefly existing emotions. Many of the studies above assessed temperamental traits rather than transient moods, indicating a tendency towards a particular state and not an exclusivity of a particular mood state. Goldsmith (1994) suggested that temperaments increase the likelihood of a certain mood, but temperament is neither a pre-requisite nor a guarantee that such a mood will be experienced. The proposed link between extraversion and positive affect does not exclude this population from negative moods, merely that they will tend to report more positive moods than those reporting lower extraversion scores.

SELF-ESTEEM AND MOOD

Research into personality has tended to follow the trait tradition. An alternative conceptualisation of personality traits has been made in the social psychology literature. Self-esteem is a personal judgement of worthiness, which is expressed in the attitudes the individual holds towards him/herself (Coopersmith, 1967). It is widely agreed that self-esteem is an important construct across many psychology disciplines, including health psychology (Penninx, Tilburg, Boeke, Deeg, Kriegsman, and van Eijk, 1998), personality (Bushman and Baumeister, 1998), psychopathology (Ralph and Mineka, 1998), and social psychology, (Tesser, Felson, and Suls, 2000). Consequently, researchers have viewed the construct differently. Variations include self-esteem as a state or trait, as a primarily cognitive or affective structure, as a series of domain-specific evaluations or as a global evaluation of self-worth (Watson, Suls, and Haig, 2002).

Pelham and Swann (1989) proposed that when assessing self-esteem within a specific domain, an individual will not only ask 'how good am I?' but also 'is the attribute important?', 'how certain am I of possessing the attribute?', and 'how does my self-perception compare with my ideal self?' Despite its apparent potential for fluctuation, schema theory suggests that there will be some stability in an individual's evaluations (Markus, 1977), yet the subjective component of the construct means that it is different to, and more transient than Eysenck's personality traits and those in the FFM.

Research has shown that self-esteem is related to mood (Diener, 1984; Pelham and Swann, 1989). Diener (1984) stated that during periods of unhappiness a person would experience a concomitant reduction in self-esteem. The schema theory offers support for this occurrence, as a person suffering from negative mood will look for negative points to support his or her current self-schema and resist any inconsistent information, causing a further increase to negative mood and reduction in the perception of the self (Markus, 1977).

Empirical evidence has suggested that self-esteem has a strong negative correlation with neuroticism and negative affectivity, and a moderate to strong positive correlation with extraversion and positive affectivity (Watson et al., 2002). Since self-esteem, within the personality make-up, can be considered a less stable construct, a stronger relationship with state mood could be reasonably assumed when compared with the associations of mood with the higher order traits extraversion, neuroticism, and psychoticism.

MOOD AND PERSONALITY RELATIONSHIPS

Rusting (1998) initially proposed that there could be three types of model for the organisation of mood and personality relationships. First, the traditional view is that mood states and personality traits have independent effects on the processing of emotional stimuli. Second, personality traits moderate the relationship between mood states and emotional processing; and third, personality traits mediate mood, which in turn influences emotional processing.

Based on empirical evidence, Rusting (1998) proposed that the traditional view (mood and personality have independent effects on cognition) could be discounted and stated that there is an interaction between mood and personality, which influences cognition. For example, Mayer, Mamberg, and Volanth (1988) found that combined mood state and personality trait measures produced better predictions of performance than measures of mood states or personality traits alone. Rusting noted, studies that take into account personality x mood interactions "produce a more consistent pattern of findings than studies examining the effects of moods and traits separately" (1998, p.188). The next question should then be, does personality mediate moods, or does it moderate the mood-cognition relationship?

A model of mediation suggests that there is a genetic predisposition to behave in a certain manner, which may or may not manifest itself, depending on certain triggering environmental conditions (Collins, Maccoby, Steinberg, Heatherington, and Bornstein, 2000). For example, performers high in trait anxiety are likely to experience state anxiety in challenging situations. In contrast, a model of moderation infers that a relationship between variables holds for one group, but not for another (Baron and Kenny, 1986). For example, the relationship between anger and performance is proposed to be moderated by depression (Lane and Terry, 2000, see Chapter 1). Lane and Terry (2000) argued that anger in the absence of depression is externalised, and can be described as determination, but when combined with depression, the anger is internalised and detrimental to performance.

Rusting's (1998) proposed model of mediation (see Figure 1) shows that personality influences mood states, which in turn, contribute to how information is processed. For example, high extraversion and low neuroticism should mediate a positive mood state. When asked to recall any autobiographical event, a person in a positive mood is more likely to recall a positive memory than a negative memory. This phenomenon, which suggests that memories are more accessible when mood is similar to when the memories were originally encoded, is known as mood-congruent memory recall (Bower, 1981).

The research detailed above lends support to the notion that the personality-mood relationship is one of mediation. For example, extraversion mediates positive and neuroticism mediates negative affective constructs (Costa and McCrae, 1980; McFatter, 1994; Meyer and Shack, 1989; Watson and Clark, 1984; 1992).

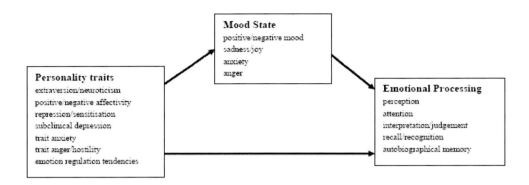

Figure 1. Rusting's model showing a mediation relationship

The model (Figure 1) also shows that personality has some direct influence on emotional processing (Rusting, 1998). This has been termed a trait-congruency effect (Derryberry and Reed, 1994; Reed and Derryberry, 1995). The authors found support for the notion that individuals high in neuroticism and low in extraversion responded faster to negative cues, whereas those low in neuroticism and high in extraversion responded faster to positive cues. Rusting and Larsen (1998) found further support for the trait-congruent effect of extraversion, but not for neuroticism. Given the proposed relationship between mood and these traits, this finding may be closely linked to mood-congruency. Further support for a mediation effect has been shown in studies investigating the influence of depression (as a stable personality trait) on emotional processing, which have generally found that depressed individuals are faster to identify negative words when compared to non-depressed individuals (i.e. Derry and Kuiper, 1981; Greenberg and Alloy, 1989). Similar effects have also been found for trait anxiety and repression/sensitisation (see Rusting for review, 1998).

Studies have also attempted to investigate potential moderating variables (see Figure 2). Within a mood-performance relationship these personality variables influence the perception of events and to what positive and negative changes are attributed.

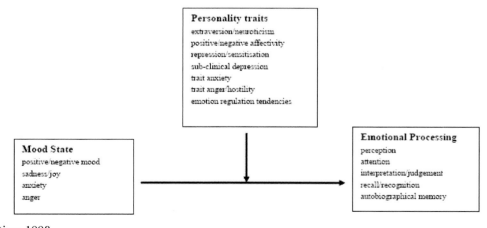

Rusting, 1998

Figure 2. Rusting's model showing a moderation relationship

Brown and Mankowski (1993) proposed that self-esteem moderates attribution, and found that those low in self-esteem responded to negative events in a negative manner and positive events in a positive manner, but those with high self-esteem showed different patterns. They tended to accept positive events and so reinforce the positive self-perception, but rejected negative events, or at least offset them, in an attempt to protect the positive self-perception (Brown and Mankowski, 1993). The authors found that appraisals of performance were more closely linked to mood states in people reporting low self-esteem compared to people reporting high self-esteem, and suggested that this was caused by mood-congruent memory recall.

Smith and Petty (1995) proposed that self-esteem and negative mood regulation expectancies would moderate the relationship between negative mood and memory recall. Smith and Petty (1995, p.1102) concluded that those with high self-esteem tend to engage in "counter-emotional thinking", whereas those with low self-esteem are prone to mood-congruent cognition. The differences in cognition may be a result of differences in the perceived ability to regulate mood. For example, those with low self-esteem may have low self-efficacy in their ability to successfully implement a mood regulating strategy, while those with high self-esteem are confident in their ability for mood repair. Alternatively, those with low self-esteem may have a negative self-schema and search for negative information to support their perception of the self, while those with high self-esteem, although in a negative mood, actually have a positive self-schema, and therefore, search for positive information.

These findings lend some support the notion that personality and mood interact. They also provide support for the notion that personality variables, such as self-esteem (Smith and Petty, 1995) and depression (Josephson, Singer, and Salovey, 1996), moderate the relationships between mood and cognitive processes. Yet, we also have evidence to support a model of mediation. So which explanation is correct? A limitation of this research is that they have often induced a particular mood state in the participants. The induction of mood may mask any mediation effect of personality on mood or cognition, and produce inaccurate findings. For this reason, findings of natural mood studies, where mood has not been manipulated might offer better support for the personality x mood interaction theories. Rusting (1998) noted that because mood is not manipulated in natural studies, personality variables might predispose individuals to experience their experimental mood states. Interestingly, studies investigating the interaction of mood and personality with regard to cognition in a natural environment have yielded more consistent findings than laboratory studies (Rusting, 1998).

Rusting (1999) attempted to investigate the interactive nature of personality and mood, and its combined effect on memory and judgement. She proposed that the effects of mood on cognitive processes depend on individual differences in emotion-related personality traits. In the first study, Rusting (1999) found support for a trait-congruency and mood-congruency effect. Extraversion, positive affectivity, and positive mood were significantly related to positive judgement and memory recall, while neuroticism, negative affectivity, and negative mood were significantly related to negative judgement and memory recall. Multiple regression analysis found that the trait-congruency effect was stronger than the influence of mood on cognition, and found no relationship between a personality x mood interaction and performance. However, the correlation between the personality and mood variables could have misled the results regarding the contribution that each made to the dependant variable (Rusting, 1999; Tabachnick and Fidell, 2001).

In the following investigation, Rusting (1999) induced mood in an effort to have more control over the contribution of the variables. Consistent with previous research, results found extraversion, positive affectivity, and positive mood were significantly related to positive judgement and memories, and neuroticism, negative affectivity. Negative mood states significantly related to negative judgement and memories. In this case, the effect of mood-congruency was stronger than in the first study, supporting the case for the mood induction. Support was also found for the significant contribution of personality x mood interactions in most of the tasks, but not all.

The results showed that individuals reporting high positive or negative personality traits demonstrated stronger mood-congruency effects than individuals reporting low scores on such traits (Rusting, 1999). In other words, in the negative mood group, individuals who were high in neuroticism or negative affectivity had greater access to negative information than those low in neuroticism or negative affectivity, suggesting that personality moderates the mood-congruency effect.

Though Rusting's work (1998; 1999) has established that an interaction does occur, the methods employed have meant that the nature of the relationship is unclear. Theoretical assumptions supported by empirical findings would suggest that mood is mediated somewhat by personality, but there is also evidence to suggest that personality can moderate a mood and cognition/performance relationship. By inducing mood in the second experiment, Rusting (1999) reduced the correlation between personality and mood states and was able to have more control over the multiple regression analysis, but these variables might correlate strongly because of a mediation effect.

Rusting (1999) noted that there is a need for investigations to assess the interaction of personality and mood on cognitive processes in the context of real-life situations. A limitation of much mood research, particularly in the sport and exercise field, is the restricted 'interaction' research design, which fails to take into account the influence of a range of variables and the effect of time (Parkinson, Totterdell, Briner, and Reynolds, 1996; Lane and Terry, 2000; Lane, Beedie, and Stevens, 2005; Stevens, 2007). A transactional approach assesses a series of interactions over time where each variable can take on different functions (in the case of personality mediator or moderator) at different points in the process (Lazarus, 2000).

Consider the following explanation. High extraversion and low neuroticism may mediate a tendency towards positive mood, which might be an optimal mood state for a certain individual to perform well. At this point the personality variable is mediator. Next consider two athletes, both reporting a facilitative pre-competition mood, who experience an early setback in the competition. One reports high extraversion, while the other reports high neuroticism. In this instance, personality can be moderator, with the extravert drawing on adaptive coping behaviours and maintaining a positive performance state, while the other competitor focuses on irrelevant cues and internalises their frustration and anger, leading to a decrease in the level of performance.

FUTURE DIRECTIONS AND CONCLUSIONS

It appears that the mediation/moderation arguments are not in competition with each other, and neither is incorrect. Rather, both are legitimate theories and the relationships explored do exist within different stages of a real-life transactional process. As Rusting (1999) and other researchers have found, laboratory studies where mood has to be induced for the sake of controllability and statistical analysis have serious limitations where personality and mood interactions are concerned. The relationships between some of these variables are very strong and to identify the unique contribution of each to any given outcome is very difficult, and using current methods, may not be possible.

Future research involving mood and performance should move away from the traditional single interaction design, and wherever possible, adopt a more 'real-life' transactional approach. It should also recognise the important contribution of personality traits within this process as events unfold over time. Not only the higher order personality traits such as extroversion and neuroticism, but also traits related to other areas of any transactional process model, such as coping disposition and self-esteem. Assessing such a model may bring new difficulties, but this does not mean that we should shy away from the challenge. It means that we should work to develop new techniques or methods to enable an accurate assessment of what is really happening within the process. As noted at the beginning of the chapter, sport and exercise psychology has recently tended to ignore this area of research, while general psychology has made great advances. Perhaps this an area where we can start to incorporate more ideas from other areas of psychology, and who knows, maybe start to lead the way.

REFERENCES

Baron, R. M., and Kenny, D. A. (1986). The moderator-mediator variable distinction in social psychological research: Conceptual, strategic, and statistical considerations. *Journal of Personality and Social Psychology, 51*, 1173-1182.

Bower G. H. (1981). Mood and memory. *American Psychologist, 36*, 129-148.

Brown, J. D., and Mankowski, T. A. (1993). Self-esteem, mood, and self-evaluation: Changes in mood and the way you see you. *Journal of Personality and Social Psychology, 64*, 421-430.

Bushman, B. J., and Baumeister, R. F. (1998). Threatened egotism, narcissism, self-esteem, and direct and displaced aggression: Does self-love or self-hate lead to violence? *Journal of Personality and Social Psychology, 75*, 219–229.

Cattell, R. B. (1946). *Description and measurement of personality.* Dubuque, IO: Brown Company Publishers.

Child, I. L. (1968). Personality in culture. In E.F. Borgatta and W.W. Lambert (Eds.), *Handbook of personality theory and research* (pp.79-98). Chicago: Rand McNally.

Collins, W. A., Maccoby, E. E., Steinberg, L., Heatherington, E. M., and Bornstein, M. H. (2000). Contemporary research on parenting: The case of nature and nurture. *American Psychologist, 55*, 218-232.

Coopersmith, S. (1967). *Antecedents of self-esteem.* San Francisco, CA: Freeman.

Costa, P. T., and McCrae, R. R. (1980). Influence of extraversion and neuroticism on subjective well-being: Happy and unhappy people. *Journal of Personality and Social Psychology, 38*, 668-678.

Costa, P.T., and McCrae, R.R. (1985). *The NEO Personality Inventory manual.* Odessa, FL: Psychological Assessment Resources.

Costa, P.T., and McCrae, R.R. (1992). *Revised NEO Personality Inventory (NEO-PI-R) and NEO Five-Factor Inventory (NEO-FFI) professional manual.* Odessa, FL: Psychological Assessment Resources.

David, J. P., and Suls, J. (1999). Coping efforts in daily life: Role of Big Five traits and problem appraisals. *Journal of Personality, 67,* 265-293.

Depue, R. A., and Collins, P. F. (1999). Neurobiology of the structure of personality: Dopamine facilitation of incentive motivation and extraversion. *Behavioural and Brain Sciences, 22*, 491-569.

Derry, P. A., and Kuiper, N. A. (1981). Schematic processing and self-reference in clinical depression. *Journal of Abnormal Psychology, 90*, 286-297.

Derryberry, D., and Reed, M.A. (1994). Temperament and attention: Orienting toward and away from positive and negative signals. *Journal of Personality and Social Psychology, 66*, 1128-1139.

Diener, E. (1984). Subjective well-being. *Psychological Bulletin 95*, 542-575.

Eysenck, H.J., and Eysenck, S.B.G. (1968). *Manual for the Eysenck Personality Inventory*. San Diego: Educational and Industrial Testing Service.

Eysenck, H.J., and Eysenck, S.B.G. (1975). *Manual for the Eysenck Personality Questionnaire*. San Diego: Educational and Industrial Testing Service.

Goldsmith, H. H. (1994).Parsing the emotional domain from a developmental perspective. In P. Ekman and R.J. Davidson (Eds.), *The nature of mood,* (pp. 68-73). Oxford: Oxford University Press.

Greenberg, M. S., and Alloy, L. B. (1989). Depression versus anxiety: Processing of self- and other-referent information. *Cognition and Emotion, 3*, 207-223.

Issever, H., Onen, L., Sabunku, H., and Altunkaynak, O. (2002). Personality characteristics, psychological symptoms and anxiety levels of drivers in charge of urban transportation in Istanbul. *Occupational Medicine, 55*, 297-303.

Josephson, B.R., Singer, J.A., and Salovey, P. (1996). Mood regulation and memory: Repairing sad moods with happy memories. *Cognition and Emotion, 10*, 437-444.

Lane, A. M. (unpublished paper). Relationships between mood states and personality among student athletes.

Lane, A. M., and Terry, P. C. (2000). The nature of mood: Development of a theoretical model with a focus on depression. *Journal of Applied Sport Psychology, 12*, 16-33.

Lane, A. M., Beedie, C. J., and Stevens, M. J. (2005). Mood matters: A response to Mellalieu. *Journal of Applied Sport Psychology, 17,* 319-325.

Lane, A. M., Milton, K. E., and Terry, P. C. (2005). Personality does not influence exercise-induced mood enhancement among female exercisers. *Journal of Sports Science and Medicine, 4,* 223-228.

Lane, A.M. (unpublished paper). Predicting mood from extraversion and neuroticism.

Lazarus, R.S. (2000). Towards better research on stress and coping. *American Psychologist, 55*, 665-673.

LeUnes, A. (2000). Updated bibliography on the Profile of Mood States in sport and exercise psychology research. *Journal of Applied Sport Psychology, 12*, 110-113.

LeUnes, A., and Burger, J. (1998). Bibliography on the Profile of Mood States in sport and exercise, 1971-1995. *Journal of Sport Behaviour, 21,* 53-70.

Markus, H. (1977). Self-schemata and processing information about the self. *Journal of Personality and Social Psychology, 35,* 63-77.

Mayer, J. D., Mamberg, M. H., and Volanth, A. J. (1988). Cognitive domains of the mood system. *Journal of Personality, 56,* 453-486.

McFatter, R.M. (1994). Interactions in predicting mood from extraversion and neuroticism. *Journal of Personality and Social Psychology, 66,* 570-578.

Meyer, G.J., and Shack, J.R. (1989). Structural congruence of mood and personality: evidence for old and new directions. *Journal of Personality and Social Psychology, 57,* 691-706.

Parkinson, B., Totterdell, P., Briner, R.B., and Reynolds, S. (1996).*Changing moods. The psychology of mood and mood regulation.* London: Longman.

Pelham, B.W., and Swann, W.B. (1989). From self-conceptions to self-worth on the sources and structure of global self-esteem. *Journal of Personality and Social Psychology, 57,* 672-680.

Penninx, B. W. J. H., van Tilburg, T., Boeke, J. P., Deeg, D. J. H., Kriegsman, D. M. W., and van Eijk, J. T. M. (1998). Effects of social support and personal coping resources on depressive symptoms: Different for various chronic diseases? *Health Psychology, 17,* 551–558.

Ralph, J. A., and Mineka, S. (1998). Attributional style and self-esteem: The prediction of emotional distress following a midterm exam. *Journal of Abnormal Psychology, 107,* 203–215.

Reed, M.A., and Derryberry, D. (1995). Temperament and attention to positive and negative trait information. *Personality and Individual Differences, 18,* 135-147.

Rusting, C.L. (1998). Personality, mood, and cognitive processing of emotional information: Three conceptual frameworks. *Psychological Bulletin, 124,* 165-196.

Rusting, C.L. (1999). Interactive effects of personality and mood on emotion-congruent memory and judgement. *Journal of Personality and Social Psychology, 77,* 1073-1086.

Rusting, C.L., and Larsen, R.J. (1998). Personality and cognitive processing of affective information. *Personality and Social Psychology Bulletin, 24,* 200-213.

Sher, K.J., Bartholow, B.D., and Wood, M.D. (2000). Personality and substance use disorders: A prospective study. *Journal of Consulting and Clinical Psychology, 68,* 818-829.

Smith, S.M., and Petty, R.E. (1995). Personality moderators of mood congruency effects on cognition: The role of self-esteem and negative mood regulation. *Journal of Personality and Social Psychology, 68,* 1092-1107.

Stevens, M. J. (2007). A transactional model of mood. In A. M. Lane (Ed.), *Mood and human performance: conceptual, measurement, and applied issues,* (pp. 89-118). PLACE: Nova Science Publishers.

Tabachnick, B. G., and Fidell, L. S. (2001). *Using Multivariate Statistics.* London: Harper and Row.

Tesser, A., Felson, R., and Suls, J. (Eds.). (2000). *Psychological perspectives on self and identity.* Washington, DC: American Psychological Association.

Van den Auwelle, Y., Nys, K., Rzewnicki, R., and Van Mele, V. (2001). Personality and the athlete. In R. N. Singer, H. A. Hausenblas, and C. M. Janelle (Eds.), *Handbook of Sport Psychology* (pp. 239-268). Chichester, UK: John Wiley and Sons.

Vealey, R.S. (1992). Personality and sport: A comprehensive view. In T.S. Horn (Ed.), *Advances in sport psychology* (pp. 25-59). Champaign, IL: Human Kinetics.

Watson, D., and Clark, L.A. (1984). Negative affectivity: The disposition to experience aversive emotional states. *Psychological Bulletin, 96*, 465-490.

Watson, D., and Clark, L.A. (1992). On traits and temperament: General and specific factors of emotional experience and their relation to the five-factor model. *Journal of Personality, 60*, 441-476.

Watson, D., and Hubbard, B. (1996). Adaptational style and dispositional structure: Coping in the context of the five-factor model. *Journal of Personality, 64*, 737-774.

Watson, D., Suls, J., and Haig, J. (2002). Global self-esteem in relation to structural models of personality and affectivity. *Journal of Personality and Social Psychology, 83*, 185-197.

Weinberg, R. S., and Gould, D. (2003).(3rd Ed.). *Foundations of Sport and Exercise Psychology*. Champaign, IL: Human Kinetics.

In: Mood and Human Performance: Conceptual, Measurement...   ISBN 1-60021-269-7
Editor: Andrew M. Lane, pp. 165-186   © 2006 Nova Science Publishers, Inc.

Chapter 8

EMOTIONAL INTELLIGENCE AND THE COPING PROCESS AMONGST ADOLESCENT POPULATIONS: A CASE STUDY OF STUDENT ATHLETES

Tracey J. Devonport[*]

School of Sport, Performing Arts and Leisure,
University of Wolverhampton

ABSTRACT

The present chapter will explore the contribution of emotional intelligence to the coping process, with a focus on adolescent populations. Following an introduction to these concepts, a review of research that seeks to enhance coping skills and behaviours amongst adolescent populations will be presented. This is followed by a review of an intervention intended to develop emotional intelligence amongst elite junior netball players. The chapter will conclude with recommendations intended to advance applied research within the emotional intelligence and coping domain. The emphasis placed on applied research within this chapter is driven by three important considerations. Firstly, a criticism of sport and exercise psychology research voiced by academics and sports personnel is the lack of applied research that strives to bridge the gap between theory and practice (Lazarus, 2001; Lane and Terry, 2000). Secondly, adolescence is a crucial stage in psychosocial development, and there are clear benefits of research that utilises theory with the intent to intervene for the benefit of participants. Finally, there is a need to extend present understanding of positive psychology (Frydenberg, 2002). Exploring the way in which individuals cope effectively, develop emotional intelligence and achieve success will increase understanding of positive psychology. As Frydenberg suggests *'genetics will make us better human animals but the promise of positive psychology is that it will make us better human beings'* (2002, P. vii).

---

[*] T.Devonport@wlv.ac.uk

STRESS AND COPING THEORY

Within the stress and coping literature, the Transactional Model of Stress and Coping conceptualised by Lazarus and Folkman (Lazarus and Folkman, 1984; Folkman and Lazarus, 1988; Folkman, 1997; Lazarus, 1991, 1993, 1999) is possibly the most widely accepted theoretical framework (Frydenberg and Lewis, 2004; Holt and Dunn, 2004; Kessler, 1998). This model views stress as a dynamic process whereby perceptions of environmental demands and perceived capability to respond to these demands, will determine the effects of a stressor. The process through which individuals interpret and respond to such interactions is known as cognitive appraisal. The cognitive appraisal of a stressor involves primary appraisal in which an individual determines the implications of a stressor for well-being, and secondary appraisal in which the capacity for minimising harm or maximising gains are considered, thus providing the cognitive underpinning for coping. The definition of coping most commonly used in research amongst adolescents (Compas, Connor-Smith, Saltzman, Thomsen, and Wadworth, 2001) is *constantly changing cognitive and behavioural efforts to manage specific external and/or internal demands that are appraised as taxing or exceeding the resources of the person* (Lazarus and Folkman, 1984, p. 141).

An evaluation of coping options and available resources occurs during secondary appraisal. This process may include an evaluation of social, physical, psychological and material assets (Lazarus and Folkman, 1984). For example, individuals assess perceived control over events, and decide what can or cannot be done to manage specific external and/or internal demands that are appraised as surpassing their resources (Affleck, Tennen, Pfeiffer, and Firfield, 1987). In addition, self-confidence in ability to execute courses of action or attain specific performance outcomes (Bandura, 1977, 1986, 1997) is proposed to influence task selection and the effort expended in task completion. This has implications for coping outcomes; it is not enough to possess the skills of competent coping, an individual must believe they have them (Roskies and Lazarus, 1980).

CONTRIBUTION OF EMOTIONAL INTELLIGENCE TO COPING

Contemporary coping literature is increasingly considering responses to those emotions, particularly negative emotions, elicited by stressful events (Lazarus, 2000). Lazarus (1999, 2000) emphasised the importance of considering emotions in stress and coping research suggesting that where there is stress, there are also emotions. These emotional responses occur as the stressful event unfolds (during the appraisal, coping and outcome phase), and influence continuing reappraisals and exchanges between the individual and environment (Riecherts and Pihet, 2000). Consequently, it has been suggested that emotional intelligence as a subset of the intelligence or personality domains (Bar-On, 1997; Mayer, Salovey, and Caruso, 2000), should be viewed as an important individual difference variable in coping research (Matthews and Zeidner, 2000). Emotional intelligence has been defined as *the ability to monitor one's own and other's emotions, to discriminate among them, and to guide one's thinking and actions* (Salovey and Mayer, 1990; p. 189). The Transactional Model (Lazarus, 1993; Lazarus and Folkman, 1984) suggests a possible conceptualisation of emotional intelligence as the psychological basis for adaptive coping, including the mastery of emotions, emotional growth, and both cognitive and emotional differentiation. In demanding and challenging environments, emotional intelligence competencies influence the selection and control of coping strategies directed towards the immediate situation. Regulation of coping operates in conjunction with self-referent cognitions concerning the personal significance of events, and of internal stimuli (metacognitions). Salovey, Bedell, Detweiler and Mayer (1999, p.161) suggest that emotionally intelligent individuals cope more successfully because they *'accurately perceive and appraise their emotional states, know how and when to express their feelings, and can effectively regulate their mood states'*.

Emotional Intelligence is becoming more widely recognised by sport psychology researchers and practitioners as an important construct in the sport domain (Mayer, Salovey, Caruso, and Sitaraneos, 2003; Zizzi, Deaner, and Hirschhom, 2003). Several theories exist that seek to explain the emotional intelligence paradigm, and all pursue an understanding of those abilities and traits related to recognising and regulating emotions in ourselves and others (Goleman, 2001). Three models proposed by Mayer and Salovey (1997), Bar-On (1997; 2000) and Goleman (1998) have generated the most interest in terms of research and application. Relatively speaking, emotional intelligence research is still in its infancy, and as such, it is unsurprising (and healthy) that emotional intelligence models have been subject to academic scrutiny. Locke (2005) suggests that the concept of emotional intelligence is invalid because it is not a form of intelligence, is defined broadly, and has no intelligible meaning. In two co-authored articles, Daus and Ashkanasy (2005) refute these claims and suggest that ability based models (in particular Mayer and Salovey, 1997) are deservedly attracting continued research interest in identifying the way in which individuals perceive, understand and manage their emotions. Whilst Daus and Ashkanasy (www.eqi.org/real_ei.htm accessed 6th October, 2005) are critical of the models proposed by Bar-On (1997; 2000) and Goleman (1998), they suggest that they may be useful for organisational development and interventions. This is because they offer a means by which to measure and develop emotional intelligence (Orme and Cannon, 2000). Furthermore, there is an increasing body of empirical support for the effectiveness of emotional intelligence interventions based on ability models (Cooper and Sawaf, 1998; Orme and Cannon, 2000).

The model of Emotional-Social Intelligence proposed by Bar-On (1997, 2000) specifically identifies a link with coping. Within this model Bar-On (1997, P.14) defines emotional intelligence as *'an array of non-cognitive capabilities, competencies, and skills that influence one's ability to succeed in coping with environmental demands and pressures.'* This model includes 1) the ability to be aware of, to understand, and to express oneself; 2) the ability to be aware of, to understand and relate to others; 3) the ability to deal with strong emotions and control personal impulses; and 4) the ability to adapt to change and to solve problems of a personal or social nature. Five main domains are identified within this model including intrapersonal skills, interpersonal skills, adaptability, stress management, and general mood (Bar-On, 1997). These five domains offer useful guidelines in terms of recognising emotional intelligence among adolescents, and understanding how it may impact their growth and development. As such emotional intelligence models may provide a useful basis for intervention based research.

THE CHARACTERISTICS OF ADOLESCENCE

During adolescence an individual is confronted by developmental (Fields and Printz, 1997; Hampel and Petermann, 2005; Piko, 2001; Renk and Creasey, 2003) academic, employment, and social stressors (Dugdale, Eklund and Gordon, 2002; Woodman and Hardy, 2001). Adolescent athletes concurrently experience additional stressors relating directly to the sport organisation (Anshel and Delany, 2001; Crocker and Isaak, 1997). The potential for these combined situational factors to be perceived as stressful may be exacerbated by the possibility that adolescents and young adults are still developing adaptive coping strategies and may be unable to cope with such pressures (Frydenberg and Lewis, 1993; Zeidner, 1990). Bebetsos and Antoniou (2003) looked specifically at age differences in athletes coping responses, their findings suggest that older athletes are better prepared to cope with adversity, and reported improved emotional self-control. Goleman (1995) completed a large-scale survey of parents and teachers and found evidence that there is a *"worldwide trend for the present generation of children to be more troubled emotionally than the last: more lonely and depressed, more angry and unruly, more nervous and prone to worry, more impulsive and aggressive" (p. xiii).* Whilst it is important to acknowledge that the methods used by Goleman have been criticised (Ashkanasy and Daus, 2005; Ciarrochi, Chan, Caputi, and Roberts, 2001; Daus and Ashkanasy, 2005), collectively results, such as these, indicate that there is a need to address the coping capacity and emotional health of children and adolescents.

Longitudinal and cross sectional studies suggest that the optimal time for coping interventions is during the psychosocial development of adolescence at 14-16 years of age (Compas, Malcarne, and Fondacaro, 1988; Frydenberg and Lewis, 2000; Groër, Thomas, and Shoffner, 1992). Adolescence is a crucial stage in the development of effective coping mechanisms, and changes at this stage in life are associated with the attainment of excellence across domains (Frydenberg and Lewis, 2002; Hampel and Petermann, 2005). The way in which adolescents cope with stress may mediate future psychopathology by habituating more versus less adaptive coping patterns (Compas et al., 2001). If coping competencies are enhanced this should lead to increases in psychosocial well-being, which could lead to better performance (Lazarus, 2000; Pensgaard and Duda, 2003) and positive experiences (Ntoumanis and Biddle, 1998). Regarding emotional intelligence, a number of researchers suggest that it is possible to develop social and emotional competencies over time, with sustained effort and commitment (Cherniss and Adler, 2000; Cherniss and Goleman, 2001; Goleman, 1998; Goleman, Boyatzis, and McKee, 2002). However, it is perhaps due to its relatively recent emergence that researchers have yet to rigorously explore the changeability of emotional intelligence. In one rare example, Bar-On (2000) found successively older cohorts tend to score higher on his scale of emotional intelligence, suggesting that it may be enhanced through life experience. Despite these findings, few studies have sought to apply theory with the intention of enhancing coping skills with even fewer studies seeking to enhance emotional intelligence (Lazarus, 2000; Van Rooy and Viswesvaran, 2004).

COPING INTERVENTIONS

If we accept the suggestions of Lazarus (1999, 2000) concerning the interdependence of stress and emotions, this should affect the types of coping interventions that researchers and applied practitioners develop. Coping interventions should also seek to enhance an individual's emotional intelligence as well as other coping competencies. In reviewing the coping interventions offered to adolescents, it is apparent that whilst there is a degree of variation (Ntoumanis and Biddle, 1998; Sandler, Wolchik, MacKinnon, Ayers, and Roosa, 1997), a common format does appear to exist. This consists of a) providing recipients with a rationale for the programme; b) modelling or demonstrating the procedure, c) having the participants rehearse or practice the skills, d) motivating the participants to transfer the learning via self-directed activities (Baker, 2001).

Regarding the content of interventions intended to facilitate the development of coping skills, most are based upon Lazarus's Transactional Model of Stress (Lazarus and Folkman, 1984). Within this model appraisal is an important first step in the coping process (Lazarus and Folkman, 1984; Folkman, 1997; Lazarus, 2000), as such the intention of interventions is to change an individual's appraisals concerning the nature of stress and their ability to cope with stress (Isrealasvili, 2002). The methods used vary and include cognitive/behavioural methods, emotional/cognitive methods and action theory approaches (Isrealasvili, 2002; Lazarus, 1991; Sandler et al., 1997). These will be reviewed in turn demonstrating that emotional intelligence is addressed to some extent within each approach.

A cognitive-behavioural approach to coping skills training is based on the principle that maladaptive emotions and behaviours are influenced by an individual's beliefs, attitudes and perceptions (Cormier and Cormier, 1998). As such, the focus of cognitive-behavioural interventions is learning to recognise, interrupt and replace maladaptive cognitions with adaptive ones. For example, Baker (2001) implemented a cognitive behavioural programme which consisted of four 45 minute sessions. Within these sessions older adolescents (16-19 years of age) were encouraged to identify self-defeating thoughts and replace these with self-improving thoughts. This intervention was partly teacher led (school teacher) and partly completed through self-instruction. Participants were asked to monitor the circumstances surrounding self-defeating thoughts, the level of emotion resulting from this, the self-improving thought used to replace self-defeating thoughts, and the level of emotion they felt having made this cognitive change. A ten-page training booklet was also provided to all participants to facilitate self-instruction. A review of the programme revealed improved cognitive self-instruction and self-reported state anxiety.

Regarding emotional-cognitive approaches, studies have found that encouraging positive appraisals leads to improved affect, especially when the participants can choose the exact appraisal to adopt (Wenzlaff and Lapage, 2000). Within sport psychology, studies have found that helping athletes think more positively leads to reduced performance anxiety during, or after competition (Arathoon and Malouff, 2004; Hanton and Jones, 1999; Maynard and Cotton, 1993; Maynard, Hemmings, Greenless, Warwick-Evans, and Stanton, 1999). For example, Arathoon and Malouff (2004) encouraged field hockey players to select one of five positive thoughts (e.g. Something you did well in a game) and one of six coping thoughts (e.g. We didn't win but we played well) following defeat. This intervention reduced the decrease in positive affect significantly when compared to a control group, supporting the contention that inducing realistic positive cognitions is an effective way to improve affect (Rexford and Wierzbicki, 1994).

Action theory addresses not only the cognitive and emotional aspects of a stress encounter, but also the motivational, behavioural, and contextual aspects (Isrealasvili, 2002; Young and Valach, 2000). Long-term goal directed systems are seen as affecting the various contexts that are part of coping process (Valach, Young, and Lynam, 2002). Isrealasvili (2002) contends that this offers a more comprehensive strategy in developing a person's ability to confront a stressful episode in life. It does so by addressing three aspects of action; the manifest behaviour of the individual, the conscious recognition that accompanies this manifest behaviour, and the social meaning in which the action is embedded (Young and Valach, 2000). Within action theory, intervention counsellors help individuals make sense of their actions by encouraging them to evaluate stressful stimuli differently, and equipping them with a wider range of coping skills. The traditional approach to coping skills acquisition is to acquaint a person with as many different coping styles as possible. Action theory assumes that coping is effective only if it adequately relates to the persons goals. Thus, interventions to promote coping should begin with a person's awareness of their goals and of the relationship between these goals and possible ways of coping.

REVIEW OF EMOTIONAL INTELLIGENCE INTERVENTIONS

Few published studies have sought to empirically apply and review emotional intelligence interventions. This is both interesting and surprising as there is a worldwide emergence of companies who specialise in optimising human performance within the workplace through the development of emotional intelligence. These include companies based in the United Kingdom, United States, Holland, Australia, Norway, Sweden, Canada, Mexico,   South   Africa   and   Ireland   (cited   on http://www.emotionalintelligencemhs.com/EITrainers.asp accessed 28th October 2005). These companies all appear to utilise Bar-On's Emotional Quotient Inventory (EQI) (Bar-On, 1997) as at least one measure of emotional intelligence within organizations. This inventory assesses five of emotional intelligence areas including 1) Intrapersonal skills (self awareness and self-management); 2) Interpersonal skills (social awareness and interpersonal relationship skills); 3) Stress management skills (the ability to manage and control emotions so they work for the individual not against them); 4) Adaptability (coping with situations and solving problems as they arise); and 5) General mood (the emotional skills that maintain motivation and positive outlook). It also contains two scales to assess the consistency and reliability of participant's responses which include the positive impression scale (designed to detect respondents providing an exaggerated positive or negative impression of themselves) and the inconsistency index (assesses consistency of responding to similar items).

A common approach seems to be adopted by these organisations in that they ask participants to complete the EQI (Bar-On, 1997) and subsequent interventions are based on the EQI scores. For example, Bar-On (2005) cites the work of a UK based company (EI world limited; Orme, 2003). This company administers the EQI (Bar-On, 1997), and interventions are then based on strengthening the weaker emotional and social intelligence factors identified by participants EQI scores. Similarly, a Swedish organisation (Skanska

Management Institute; Sjölund and Gustafsson, 2001) asks individuals to complete the EQI (Bar-On, 1997) before and after they participate in a workshop designed to strengthen the five competencies described in the Bar-On EQI.

Utilising a similar approach, Luskin, Aberman and DeLorenzo (2005) completed a yearlong project designed to measure the effect of emotional competence training on sales and quality of life. Participants were thirty-seven financial services advisors from two American Express Financial Services market groups. This project began with a one-day workshop which defined emotional competence, outlined the importance of aligning thoughts, emotions and behaviors, helped participants examine areas of weakness, and considered techniques for stress management. Subsequent to this workshop, an individual development plan (IDP) was created for each participant. The IDP was developed after evaluating the pre-test measures (including the EQI, Bar-On, 1997) and in consultation with the each participant's Group Vice President. Each IDP contained two or three action items that were presented as specific behavioral suggestions. The items were designed to help the participant develop areas of emotional competence in which they tested as weak. Results showed sales increased by an average of 25%, which compared to a corresponding 10% increase in sales for the market group reference samples. In addition, the stress levels of the thirty-six participants who completed the year-long training decreased 29% over the year of the project while their reported positive emotional states increased 24%. Quality of life, anger and physical vitality measures also demonstrated statistically significant positive change.

Within the research published to date, there is a lack of information regarding the specific content of emotional intelligence workshops and interventions. However, as many studies utilize the Bar-On model, it is likely that interventions are based on the following guidelines offered within this model (see Table 1).

**Table 1. Guidelines for emotional intelligence interventions
offered within the Bar-On model**

EI competency	Recommended interventions for low scores
Intrapersonal scale	Participants: Suggestions to improve intrapersonal skills. o Make a conscious effort not to compare yourself with others. Practice reaffirming your own uniqueness, and picture yourself as confident and self-assured. o Keep a personal journal of specific situations and the way you typically feel in those situations and why. o Make a conscious effort to be aware of your feelings, try to understand them and see if there are deeper meanings to those feelings. For example you may be angry because you are scared of losing something. o Practice conveying the way you feel to others, as well as the reasons behind those feelings. o Picture difficult situations and practice ways of approaching them more assertively. Be more aware when others are making unreasonable demands on you, and practice saying 'no' in such situations. Mentors suggestions to help participants: o Help the individual build on previous success so that they will gradually feel more confident, self assured and optimistic.

	o Help the individual to keep previous successful experiences in mind, no matter how trivial the success was.
	o Help the individual discriminate between past failures and present objectives.
	o Help the individual (continue to) set realistic and achievable goals.
	o Divide goals and objectives into more immediate tasks.
	o Enhance independent thinking by encouraging the employee to trust his or her own judgement or intuition when appropriate.
	o Provide training in assertiveness, presentation skills and management of others.
Interpersonal scale	Participants: Suggestions to improve interpersonal skills. o Practice looking at situations from the perspective of others by 'putting yourself in their shoes'. Picture what others would feel in these and other situations. o Make more of an effort to understand how others feel and why. Show more concern for other people. o Be more co-operative at home and work. Do things for others without thinking about what you will get in return. o Consider your relationship with others; decide what you can do to improve them. o Participate in a social skills training program that includes an emphasis on empathy development. o Practice the basic social skills that are vital to building good working relationships. Mentors suggestions to help participants: o Encourage participants to be considerate of the way others feel. o Encourage them to listen carefully to others to understand what they are saying/asking. o Encourage them to learn how to compromise and the importance of giving not just receiving. o Use job shadowing to improve their understanding of other staff member's work responsibilities. o Act as a role model to develop their sense of social responsibility. o Stress the importance of contributing to a group or team in which they operate. o Help them practice their communication.
Stress management scale	Participants: Suggestions to improve stress management skills. o Be proactive in stressful situations because there is always something you can do to improve the situation. o Prioritise your activities and don't leave things until last minute. o When you feel stressed, make an effort to relax, breathe deeply, relax your muscles, have a bath, get some rest. o Control your emotions rather than be controlled by them, make them work for you not against you. o Take 'time out' when tension builds up, and do something you really enjoy doing. Mentors suggestions to help participants: o Help the participant prioritise activities and better organise their work. o Help them develop simple time management techniques to avoid last minute rushing o Teach them to break tasks down into more manageable tasks. o Help them to become more conscious of their general health and make time for their relaxing hobby or exercise.

	o Encourage them to obtain adequate rest and to avoid excessive caffeine consumption. o Provide time management and relaxation training o Provide advice on anger management where appropriate
Adaptability scale	Participants: Suggestions to improve adaptability skills. o Practice examining the immediate situation rather than jumping to conclusions. o Change your overall approach when your usual way of doing things doesn't work. o Brainstorm as many solutions as you can when trying to solve problems. o Weigh the pros and cons of the outcomes of each possible solution before deciding on the best choice. Mentors suggestions to help participants: o Encourage them to improve their ability to accept change by sharing concerns with others and discussing solutions to the problem. o Stress that change is part of everyday reality, and emphasise the importance of flexibility and accommodating change. o Encourage them to develop different approaches to solving problems, to consider problems from different angles and to come up with a number of solutions to problems along with the pros and cons of each solution. o Prepare them in advance for change (when possible) and get them to consider their responses.
General mood	Participants: Suggestions to improve general mood. o Complain less, be more positive and try to enjoy yourself o Look at the brighter side of life o Practice being optimistic when coping with problems and difficult situations. o Base your approach to things on hope rather than fear. o Avoid things that make you sad. Mentors suggestions to help participants: o Help create a pleasant atmosphere at work, and make the workplace an enjoyable place to be and spend time. o Organise social activities for employees and their families from time to time. o Teach individuals to see that setbacks should be treated as experiences that are necessary steps to success and future happiness. o When goals are achieved, reward and celebrate this with praise and incentives o Encourage them to lead a balanced lifestyle stressing the importance of a personal life

Adapted from Bar-On (2002)

CASE STUDY OF AN EMOTIONAL INTELLIGENCE INTERVENTION

In reviewing the coping and emotional intelligence literature, it is apparent that there is a dearth of interventions across populations, but particularly amongst adolescents. Given the purported benefits of intervening with adolescents this void should be addressed. Clearly a goal of scientific research is to further knowledge with a view to enhancing social and emotional well-being. In view of these findings, I developed a longitudinal coping intervention that was applied to junior elite netball players. The intention was to increase the coping capacity and emotional intelligence of young athletes. The following provides an overview of the intervention specifically designed to develop emotional intelligence.

Devonport, Biscomb, Lane, Mahoney and Cassidy (2005) completed a series of focus groups and individual interviews in order to explore the sources of stress and coping strategies used by 33 elite junior netball players (aged 13-19 years). The qualitative comments offered by players exemplified the contribution of emotional intelligence to coping. Data indicated that collectively, players perceived factors such as self-confidence, positivity, assertiveness, emotional regulation and communication to impact upon their appraisal and coping. As a result of the qualitative data, emotional intelligence was addressed when developing a longitudinal intervention intended to assist athletes in developing coping competencies. The resultant 'emotional intelligence' pack was included in a 12-month coping intervention known as the 'mentor programme'.

The emotional intelligence pack contained a series of activities intended to address the subcomponents of emotional intelligence identified in Table 2. In addition to the emotional intelligence pack, the mentor programme also included packs intended to develop planning and organisational ability; goal setting; problem solving; and communication skills. Twelve players aged between 15–18 years, volunteered to take part in the mentor programme. Players were assigned a mentor who would help guide and support their progress through the coping packs. Mentoring has been described as a one-to-one developmental relationship where the mentor and mentee work together to establish goals, driven by the needs of the mentee (Linney, 1999; Ritchie, 1999). The literature suggests that effective mentors possess characteristics such as approachable, trustworthy, good communicator, friendly and exuding emotional intelligence (Goleman, 1995; Clarke, Harden, and Johnson, 2000). Since these characteristics are subjectively determined each player was encouraged to (and opted to) self-select a mentor.

A three-stage approach to the development of social and emotional competencies was adopted, based on the recommendations of Cherniss and Goleman (2001). Stage 1 involved preparation for change whereby mentors worked with participants to assess their personal strengths and limitations with regards to social and personal competencies. The aim was to identify those areas where mentor and athlete felt improvements could be made. As these competencies are mainly demonstrated in social interactions participants were encouraged to involve those who regularly interacted with them. This was to provide multiple ratings conducted of their socio-emotional competencies from different perspectives, e.g. parents, coach, team-mate, teacher etc. In addition to these multiple ratings, each participant also completed an EQI (Bar-On, 1997). The questionnaire responses were analysed and the results compared with population norms to identify strengths and areas for development. Each participant was then provided with modified guidelines for emotional intelligence interventions (see Table 1 for examples of interventions). The participant and mentor then reviewed these ratings and guidelines and used them to identify those competencies that were to be the focus of development.

The second stage of competency development was the training phase, firstly participants were encouraged to identify the competencies they wished to develop using the ratings from significant others and questionnaire results. They were then asked to establish short and long-term goals for development (using activities identified in Table 1). In social and emotional learning, regular practice was encouraged over a prolonged period of time in order to replace old behaviours/responses with new and more effective ones. Mentors had an important support role during this stage in that they were required to offer encouragement, feedback and opportunities for practice (see roles of mentor identified in Table 1).

The third and final stage was the transfer and maintenance of learned skills. Mentors were encouraged to help athletes reflect on any activities completed in applying and developing the learned skills, and to identify any barriers and facilitating factors for continued development. Developing social and emotional learning requires that athletes unlearn old habits of thought, feeling, and action that are deeply ingrained, and develop new more effective alternatives. As such this process required motivation, effort, time, support, and sustained practice.

Eighteen mentors and players (nine mentors, nine players), who took part in the mentor programme completed a semi-structured interview intended to explore and reflect upon their experiences. When reviewing the emotional intelligence pack, it became apparent that some players had failed to engage with it. This phenomenon is not uncommon in applied research. Albinson and Bull (1988) reported poor adherence rates to a relatively short mental skills training programme. This led Crocker (1989) to suggest that programme adherence is critical in the evaluation of any psychological intervention. Shambrook and Bull (2001) suggest that the lack of successful implementation by athletes indicates that a problem exists in convincing athletes to accept and employ psychological strategies.

When exploring the reasons why some participants failed to complete the emotional intelligence pack a range of explanations were offered. A number of players had entered the mentor programme because they had specific objectives for participation. Commonly this was because they wanted to develop their ability to plan and organise their time effectively. Once their objectives were achieved, some players felt there was no longer a need to progress through the other packs, as was evidenced with Jayne.

> Jayne (player): 'I'd say erm that I didn't think that it would help me this much but it really has because I've got out what I wanted which was to organise my time which is the bonus of all bonuses because how much less stressed its made me has been quite weird but it really works'

Alternatively, other players were deselected from the England junior squads, or acquired injuries during the mentor programme. For these individuals, the demands on their time reduced significantly and they no longer felt a need to continue with the mentor programme other than maintaining contact with their mentor.

> Tamsin (player): 'I didn't really continue it because I left county due to my exams at the beginning of the season so I was only really playing club so I didn't really feel any need to kind of continue with it 'cause I wasn't in England and I wasn't playing county so the kind of main pressures were off really so we stopped it'

> Mia (player): 'I used to get quite down about the fact that I couldn't play as well, and all the mentor packs focus on how to make playing better and that's why I didn't want anything to do with it and just forget about everything for that month'

Table 2. Aspects of emotional intelligence addressed within
the 'emotional intelligence' pack

Personal Competence

Self-awareness:
o *Emotional self-awareness:* recognizing emotions and their effects.
o *Accurate self-assessment:* knowing their strengths and limitations, seek out feedback and learn from mistakes, know where they need to improve and when to work with others who have complementary strengths.
o *Self-confidence:* a strong sense of self worth and capabilities. People with self-confidence present themselves with self-assurance, are decisive and able to make sound decisions despite uncertainties and pressures.

Self-management:
o *Adaptability*: flexibility in dealing with changing situations or obstacles, are open to new information and can let go of old assumptions and so adapt how they operate.
o *Emotional Self-control*: inhibiting emotions in order to meet group or organizational norms
o *Initiative:* take anticipatory action to avoid problems before they happen or take advantage of opportunities before they are visible to anyone else.
o *Achievement orientation*: an optimistic striving to continually improve performance taking more calculated risks and setting challenging goals.
o *Trustworthiness:* making others aware of personal values and principles, intentions and feelings, and acting in ways that are consistent with them.
o *Optimism*: a positive view of life and the future, can determine reactions to unfavourable events or circumstances; those with high achievement are proactive and persistent, have an optimistic attitude toward setbacks, and operate from hope of success.
o *Conscientiousness*: taking responsibility for personal performance, hold themselves accountable for meeting their objectives and are organized and careful in their work.

Social Competence

Social Awareness:
o *Empathy:* an awareness of others' emotions, concerns, and needs. The empathic individual can read emotional currents, and pick up on nonverbal cues such as tone of voice or facial expression.

Relationship Management:
o *Developing Others*: sensing people's developmental needs and helping them.
o *Conflict management:* spotting trouble as it develops and taking steps to calm those involved. Here the arts of listening and empathizing are crucial to the skills of handling difficult people and situations with diplomacy, encouraging debate and open discussion, and orchestrating win-win situations.
o *Influence*: getting others to agree with you. Those with this competence draw on a wider range of persuasion strategies than others do, including impression management and appeals to reason. At the same time, the influence competence requires them to be genuine and put collective goals before their self-interests; otherwise effective persuasion becomes manipulation.
o *Communication:* sending clear and convincing messages. They listen well, seek mutual understanding, and welcome sharing of information staying receptive to bad news as well as good.
o *Leadership*: inspiring and guiding groups and people, articulate and arouse enthusiasm for a shared vision and objectives, they step forward to lead as needed, regardless of position and lead by example.
O *Change catalyst*: recognize the need for change and remove barriers to change enlisting others to achieve change whilst modelling the change expected of others.

Adapted from www.eiconsortium.org/research/emotional_competence_framework.htm (accessed 16th December 2003)

An alternative explanation could be that highly emotionally intelligent individuals are aware of a need to enhance mood regulation skills, or they might perceive that additional training is not required. Alternatively, individuals low in emotional intelligence may be incapable of accurately assessing their emotional needs, or may not feel the need to develop emotional intelligence. One mentor believed that the player she was working with was sufficiently competent with EI, a view shared by the player and consequently, they did not complete the emotional intelligence pack. They did however suggest that the pack might be of use for other players.

> Gemma (mentor): 'It's just that we didn't see it as important for Kate (player), I think someone else might find it useful it depends on the person really'

The qualitative data also indicated that some players did not complete individual coping packs until they perceived a need to address the issue covered within them. For example, the first pack players were asked to complete was the planning and organisation pack, scheduled for completion over July – August 2004. Players and mentors would be contacted routinely (by the author), providing an opportunity to discuss any issues or difficulties they may have encountered. During these routine conversations it became apparent that one player had not engaged with the planning and organisation pack. She explained that because it was the summer, her commitments had reduced as she was between netball seasons. She continued by saying that she would start the planning and organisation pack when the commitments she faced started to place demands on her time. The author explained that this would mean that the time she had available to understand, implement and habituate the planning and organisation activities would be curtailed considerably if she was to wait for an occasion when she was under pressure. Following this conversation, she did engage with the pack and found it to be beneficial. The impact of perceived need was evidenced with the emotional intelligence pack in that that some players only addressed this pack when they perceived a need for it.

> Simone (player): I thought that was one of the best packs, because I think that is like most important especially in a teenage life because dealing with netball at this stage like this high level is quite hard especially at our age and like dealing with coursework and netball and if you've got a job and family members it's very hard, 'cause I remember last year before I started the pack I was like really emotional I just couldn't do anything and I used to argue with my Mum and stuff, … I think it's important to speak to somebody about how you're feeling … so I think it is like the best pack and I don't think it could be changed because I think everything is spot on it that pack… I read through the questions and it just showed me I suppose how to deal with other people, I wanted to move clubs last year and I didn't actually know how to tell my club and by reading this pack it actually helped me to realise that I've just gotta go and do it and not hold back and stay at a club that I'm not going to enjoy and get the benefits as much as I would at the other club'

These findings present a further explanation for the failure of some individuals to engage with the emotional intelligence pack. It could be that the benefits of completing coping packs either at all, or before they are required, are not immediately apparent. When reviewing the mentor programme the England netball talent co-ordinator felt that the benefits of the emotional intelligence pack might not have been apparent to players.

'But if they knew, I suppose it's about making it relevant to them, why is this going to help me get into the under 17's and under 19's ... so that they know that 'oh the selectors actually, this is some of the statements that the selector is actually looking at' they don't actually look at it when you have a trials or at a game but that's why we get them to come for the whole weekend and they're looking at what you're doing off the court, they're looking at which ones pick up the bibs and put them away, which ones support others which ones are, you know, blaming in the game, do they pull a face after the pass they made which was actually bad but the other person at the other end didn't catch it, ... and I don't think they even realised how much they were swayed by the emotions of the young people'

Consequently, when developing and implementing any coping intervention, including the development of emotional intelligence, it is critical that participants are aware in advance, of the benefits that may result from completion of the activities offered. The generalisability of the coping packs should also be emphasised in that the benefits offered by completing the activities are not exclusive to sport.

The issues presented here represent some of those that were overlooked when planning the intervention programme.It was only when they were identified by participants, that their importance for engaging and adhering with the packs became apparent. A great deal of time had been spent describing the objectives of the interventions at the expense of identifying the benefits. Had the benefits of the intervention been identified more clearly from the outset, this may have increased the perceived need to complete the coping activities before a challenging situation arose. That said, as players progressed through the packs, they commonly identified a number of long-term benefits for themselves.

Those players who did engage with the emotional intelligence pack produced a largely positive response to its content and format. Many individuals felt they had benefited from the activities contained within the pack. Conversely there were some who experienced difficulties in completing the recommended activities, or as already discussed, felt they did not have a need for it. The following excerpts offer an insight into the experiences of those who perceived benefits resulting from completion of the emotional intelligence pack.

Tamsin (athlete): 'Just kind of to differentiate between emotions and know what kind of emotions you're feeling you know to be able to deal with them, sometimes its quite hard to recognise what you're feeling it might be a mixture of things and I just think it's good to be able to recognise that and then go on from that and be able to deal with them'

Mia (player): 'It was quite good actually it made me open up quite a lot 'cause I tend to put up a guard and tend to act like I'm fine and it was good to talk about that, that was where it was good talking to someone, just talking about all those kinds of things and that was good just finding out how I am actually dealing with stuff really instead of just putting up a front'

Kelly (mentor): 'That ones deep 'cause it covers so many things doesn't it, I think sometimes you're looking at an athlete and you're just looking at them to be fit enough physically to play their sport but you don't always deal with the emotional side of it, but at the same time you see a lot of emotion in their sport so it's a very important part of what they do especially at that level'

Jasmine (mentor): 'Ellis (player) was always very concerned about how other people saw her I think rather than going onto the court and playing netball, so I think that was quite useful you know just reading that pack through you know how to cope with peoples reactions and you know people's confrontations, I thought that was quite useful that one'

The perceived benefits following completion of the emotional intelligence pack identified in the excerpts provided were numerous. Collectively the benefits identified included greater emotional awareness and control, more aware of the needs of others, enhanced ability to be assertive, to lead others, communicative, more positive, and more able to avoid and resolve conflict. Conversely, one player and mentor encountered difficulties when completing the emotional intelligence pack.

Helen (mentor): 'The only pack that really threw me was the emotional intelligence and I don't even know why it just seemed to, I don't know if it was the way it was set out or the way I was reading it, I felt like I had to read it over and over again just to try and absorb it... I just kind of felt that it was a bit too psychoanalysing and all that, it was that kind of getting into those realms and I just thought I'm not equipped to do this'

This mentor lacked confidence in her ability to utilise the emotional intelligence pack. She had experienced prolonged difficulties in encouraging her athlete to talk openly, and stopped completing the coping packs altogether following the difficulties she experienced with the emotional intelligence pack.

Helen (mentor): 'Her injury I actually found out through a third party, you know which just became equally frustrating because I really tried and I was contacting her, texting her, e-mailing her you know saying how are you, how's things and hope you're okay and give me a call and I'd find out, it might even be just little trivial things but I'd find out that she'd got a training weekend coming up that she hadn't told me about and it just seemed a real hard slog,. The people that she did confide in were people that she'd been around for years since she was young her club coach, which kind of made me think they would have been better placed or somebody in that arena would have been better placed to try and mentor her as well, or just had access to all of that information because I found it a real struggle to get it out of her'

The role of the mentor in modelling and developing emotional intelligence was demonstrated in a number of ways when reviewing the mentor programme. These included the demonstration of good interpersonal skills, self-awareness and control, and coping techniques. It is possible that when Helen was adopting a more autocratic approach taking responsibility for, controlling mentor programme activities, and initiating contact with Jodie (her athlete), this was rendering Jodie a passive recipient. This may not have been fulfilling the needs of Jodie. Alternatively, Ellis suggested that honesty and the ability to discuss issues openly with a mentor was influential on the success of the emotional intelligence pack.

Ellis (player): 'I had to be honest, and Jasmine (mentor) had to be honest with me and say 'look I don't think you do that, I think you do this' that's where you had to have a mentor that you could really kind of discuss with'

Helen (mentor) described the difficulties she had experiences in encouraging Jodie (her athlete) to talk honestly and openly. This appears to have created many of the difficulties Helen experienced in working through the emotional intelligence pack.

All players were able to describe the qualities they found to benefit the mentor-player relationship throughout the mentor programme. Commonly identified traits included approachable, fun, understanding, friendly, good listener and interested in sport. All athletes indicated that their mentors were invaluable, often acting as a 'sounding board' and thus providing emotional and instrumental support when faced with difficulties.

> Simone (player): 'You know you can go up and talk to them about anything 'cause I know I can, last year I was talking to Wendy (mentor) about anything and she was understanding about it, that was one of the most important things, you know that their approachable to talk to'

Helen described how her approach in working through the coping packs evolved as she progressed through the programme. She modified her approach when she perceived the autocratic approach was not working for her.

> Helen (mentor): 'I was just trying to find of ways of doing it that kept her interested and were beneficial to her rather than I think we started out and I sat with her and we went through the pack and it was kind of, I became a bit of a teacher, it started off like that and I started to grasp quite quickly that I could just see her glazing over and she wasn't really, I don't think that was what she was wanting to do'

It has been suggested that coping programmes should be conducted in a context that is sensitive to the needs of the individual, taking place in a setting where privacy and confidentiality are assured (Baker, 2001). Mia presented an example of poor mentoring practice, and arguably emotional intelligence. When selecting a mentor, players were encouraged to select an individual who was non-biased and did not have an invested interest in the player. Mia chose her PE teacher and described how their relationship changed as the mentor programme progressed.

> Mia (player): 'The only problem that I have talking to her now is that I'm scared of her primary interest being school netball, and when it's quite difficult to say no I cant go to training this week and she's like 'oh what are you doing instead?' Well nothing but I can't do too much training in a week 'cause that's what was happening, I was doing too much training and my tendons were just getting knackered from doing too much training'

Mia had just returned from injury and by insisting that she played in school tournaments her mentor was demonstrating a lack of empathy and social awareness. Mia was aware that these behaviours were inappropriate and the player-mentor relationship broke down as a result of this.

CONCLUSIONS

Both coping and emotional intelligence theories indicate that emotional intelligence should be addressed when developing the coping capacity of individuals. As Lazarus (1999, 2000) suggests where there is stress, there are also emotions. At present, there is public disagreement amongst emotional intelligence researchers as to what emotional intelligence is, and the theoretical model that best captures the concept. This has resulted in criticisms of emotional intelligence research, and this fragmentation is contributing to a failure on the part of some researchers in seeing the potential contribution of emotional intelligence research towards the development of positive psychology.

Following a review of interventions intended to enhance EI, it appears that many emotional intelligence researchers and practitioners utilise the Bar-On EQI (1997) to assess emotional intelligence. In interpreting the results of this questionnaire the Bar-On model then presents a series of intervention that may be utilised by those with low scores on particular emotional intelligence scales. In view of these findings regarding the development of coping and emotional intelligence, a longitudinal intervention was devised and applied with a group of junior elite netball players. The results of this study indicated that some mentors and players did not engage with the emotional intelligence pack. This was largely because they had met their objectives for entering the mentor programme (developing planning and organisational ability), or failed to see any benefits in completing the pack. Conversely, those who did engage with the pack (with one exception), perceived a number of benefits resulting from its completion. These included greater emotional awareness and regulation, enhanced ability to deal with and lead others and improved communication skills. Two main implications for future emotional intelligence interventions are proposed. Firstly, it is important that in addition to the objectives of emotional intelligence interventions, participants must also be immediately aware of the benefits that may be accrued across domains following the completion of emotional intelligence activities. Secondly, mentors should possess the qualities that enable them to effectively model emotional intelligence competencies and guide participants towards personal development. When these two considerations are met, participants are more likely to engage with, and adhere to emotional intelligence interventions.

At present there is an absence of research intended to develop emotional intelligence amongst individuals, in particular adolescents. This presents an exciting challenge for researchers in addressing this void. I believe the greatest rewards offered by applied research are those benefits accrued by participants, and in this respect emotional intelligence research has much to offer. Perhaps it is most fitting to conclude with the views of a recipient of emotional intelligence training; 'I found it really hard before this (the mentor programme and skills addressed) and then I'm using it, its more understanding I suppose, it is really hard when you just get into the talent programme as well, its quite scary so I think this has helped me a lot (Simone)'.

REFERENCES

Affleck, G., Tennen, H., Pfeiffer, C., and Firfield, J. (1987). Appriasals of control and predictability in adapting to chronic disease. *Journal of Personality and Social Psychology, 53,* 273-279.

Albinson, J., and Bull, S. J. (1988). *A mental game plan: A training program for all sports.* London, ON: Spodym.

Anshel, M. H., and Delany, J. (2001). Sources of acute stress, cognitive appraisals, and coping strategies of male and female child athletes. *Journal of Sport Behavior, 24,* 329-353.

Arathoon, S.M., and Malouff, J. M. (2004). The effectiveness of a brief cognitive intervention to help athletes cope with competitive loss. *Journal of Sport Behavior, 27,* 213 – 229.

Ashkanasy, N.M., and Daus, C. S. (2005). Rumours of the death of emotional intelligence in organizational behavior are vastly exaggerated. *Journal of Organizational Behavior, 26,* 441-452.

Baker, S.B. (2001). Coping-skills training for adolescents: Applying cognitive behavioural principles to psychoeducational groups. *Journal for Specialists in Group Work, 26,* 219-227.

Bandura, A. (1977). Self-efficacy: Toward a unifying theory of behavioral change. *Psychological Review, 84,* 191-215.

Bandura, A. (1986). *Social foundations of thought and action: A social cognitive theory.* Englewood Cliffs, NJ: Prentice Hall.

Bandura, A. (1997). *Self-efficacy: The exercise of control.* New York: W. H. Freeman.

Bar-On, R. (1997). *Bar-On Emotional Quotient Inventory: User's manual.* Toronto: Multi-Health Systems.

Bar-On, R. (2000). Emotional and social intelligence: Insights from the Emotional Quotient Inventory (EQ-i). In R. Bar-On and J. D. A. Parker (Eds.), *Handbook of emotional intelligence.* San Francisco: Jossey-Bass.

Bar-On, R. (2002). *Bar-On Emotional Quotient Inventory: Short: Technical manual.* Toronto: Multi-Health Systems.

Bar-On, R. (2005). The Bar-On model of emotional-social intelligence. In P. Fernández-Berrocal and N. Extremera (Guest Editors). Special Issue on Emotional Intelligence. *Psicothema, 17.*

Bebetsos, E., and Antoniou, P. (2003). Psychological skills of Greek badminton athletes. *Perceptual and Motor Skills, 97,* 1289-1296.

Cherniss, C., and Adler, M. (2000). *Promoting emotional intelligence in organizations.* Alexandria, VA: American Society for Training and Development.

Cherniss, C., and Goleman, D. (2001). Training for emotional intelligence (pp. 209-233). In C., Cherniss, and D., Goleman. *The emotionally intelligent workplace.* New York, Jossey-Bass.

Ciarrochi, J., Chan, A., Caputi, P., and Roberts, R. (2001). Measuring emotional intelligence. In J.V., Ciarrochi, J.P., Forgas, and J.D., Mayer (Eds.), *Emotional Intelligence in everyday life: A scientific inquiry.* Philadelphia, PA: Psychology Press.

Clark, R. A., Harden, S. L., and Johnson, W. B. (2000). Mentor relationships in clinical psychology doctoral training: Results of a national survey. *Teaching of Psychology, 27,* 262–268.

Compas, B.E., Connor-Smith, J.K., Saltzman, H., Thomsen, A.H., and Wadsworth, M. (2001). Coping with stress during childhood and adolescence: Progress, problems, and potential. *Psychological Bulletin, 127,* 87-127.

Compas, B. E., Malcarne, V. L., and Fondacaro, K. M. (1988). Coping with stressful events in older children and young adolescents. *Journal of Consulting and Clinical Psychology,* 56, 405-411.

Cooper, R., and Sawaf, A. (1998). *Executive EQ: emotional intelligence in business.* London: Orion.

Cormier, S., and Cormier, B. (1998). Interviewing strategies for helpers: Fundamental skills and cognitive-behavioural interventions (4th ed.). Pacific Grove, CA: Brooks/Cole.

Crocker, P. R. E. (1989). A follow up of cognitive-affective stress management training. *Journal of Sport and Exercise Psychology, 11,* 236-242.

Crocker, P. R. E., and Isaak, K. (1997). Coping during competitions and training sessions: Are youth swimmers consistent? *International Journal of Sport Psychology, 28,* 355–369.

Daus, C.S., and Ashkanasy, N.M. (2005). The case for the ability-based model of emotional intelligence in organizational behavior. *Journal of Organizational Behavior, 26,* 453-466.

Daus, C.S., and Ashkanasy, N.M. (2005). Will the real emotional intelligence please stand up? On deconstructing the emotional intelligence "debate". Available from www.eqi.org/real_ei.htm Accessed 6th October 2005.

Devonport, T. J., Biscomb, K., Lane, A. M., Mahoney, C. M., and Cassidy, T. (2005). Stress and coping in elite junior netball. *Journal of Sports Sciences, 22,* 162-163.

Dugdale, J. R., Eklund, R. C., and Gordon, S. (2002). Expected and unexpected stressors in major international competitive: Appraisal, coping, and performance. *The Sport Psychologist, 16,* 20-33.

Fields, L., and Prinz, R.J. (1997). Coping and adjustment during childhood and adolescence. *Clinical Psychology Review, 17,* 937-976.

Folkman, S., and Lazarus, R. (1988). *Ways of Coping Questionnaire Test Booklet.* Palo Alto, CA: Consulting Psychologists Press.

Folkman, S. (1997). Positive psychological states and coping with severe stress. *Social Science and Medicine, 45,* 1207-1221.

Frydenberg, E., and Lewis, R. (1993). Boys play sport and girls turn to others: age gender and ethnicity as determinants of coping. *Journal of Adolescence, 16,* 252-266.

Frydenberg, E., and Lewis, R. (2002). Adolescent well-being: Building young people's resources. In E. Frydenberg (ed.). *Beyond Coping: Meeting visions, goals and challenges.* Oxford: Oxford University Press, pp. 175-194.

Frydenberg, E. (2002). *Beyond coping; meeting goals, visions, and challenges.* Oxford: Oxford University press.

Frydenberg, E., and Lewis, R. (2000). Teaching coping to adolescents: when and to whom. *American Educational Research Journal, 37,* 727-745.

Frydenberg, E., and Lewis, R. (2004). Adolescents least able to cope: how do they respond to their stresses? *British Journal of Guidance and Counselling,* 32**,** 25 – 37.

Goleman, D. (1995). *Emotional intelligence.* New York: Bantam Books.

Goleman, D. (1998). *Working with emotional intelligence*. NY: Bantam.

Goleman, D (2001). Emotional intelligence: Issues in paradigm building. In C. Cherniss and D. Goleman (Eds.), *The emotionally intelligent workplace*, (pp. 13-26), Jossey-Bass: San Francisco.

Goleman, D. Boyatzis, R., and McKee, A. (2002). *Primal leadership: Realizing the power of emotional intelligence*. Boston: Harvard Business School Press.

Groër, M., Thomas, S., and Shoffner, D. (1992). Adolescent stress and coping: A longitudinal study. *Research in Nursing and Health, 15,* 209-217.

Hanton, S., and Jones, G. (1999). The effects of multimodal intervention program on performers: II. Training the butterflies to fly in formation. *The Sport Psychologist, 13,* 22–41.

Hampel, P., and Petermann, F. (2005). Age and gender effects on coping in children and adolescents. *Journal of Youth and Adolescence, 34,* 73-83.

Holt, N. L., and Dunn, J. G.H. (2004). Longitudinal idiographic analysis of appraisal and coping responses in sport. *Psychology of Sport and Exercise, 5,* 213-222.

Isrealasvili, M. (2002). Fostering adolescents' coping skills- An action approach. *Canadian Journal of Counselling, 36,* 211-220.

Kessler, T.A. (1998). The Cognitive Appraisal of Health Scale: development and psychometric evaluation. *Research in Nursing and Health, 21,* 73 – 82.

Lane, A. M., and Terry, P. C. (2000). The nature of mood: Development of a conceptual model with a focus on depression. *Journal of Applied Sport Psychology, 12,* 16-33.

Lazarus, R. S. (1991). *Emotion and adaptation*. New York: Oxford University Press.

Lazarus, R. S. (1993). Coping theory and research: Past, present and future. *Psychosomatic Medicine, 55,* 234-247.

Lazarus, R. S. (1999). *Stress and emotion: A new synthesis.* New York: Springer.

Lazarus, R. S. (2000). Toward better research on stress and coping. *American Psychologist, 55,* 665– 673.

Lazarus, R.S. (2001). Stress and Emotion: a new synthesis. *Human Relations, 54, 792-803.*

Lazarus, R. S., and Folkman, S. (1984). *Stress appraisal and coping*. New York: Springer.

Linney, B. J. (1999). Characteristics of good mentors. *Physician Executive, 25,* 70-72.

Locke, E. A. (2005). Why emotional intelligence is an invalid concept. *Journal of Organizational Behavior*, 26(4), 425-431.

Luskin, F., Aberman, R., and DeLorenzo, R. (2005, Jan.). The Training of Emotional Competence in Financial Advisors. Paper available from http://www.eiconsortium.org/research/training_of_emotional_competence_in_financial_advisors.htm (accessed 27/10/05).

Matthews, G., and Zeidner, M. (2000). Emotional intelligence, adaptation to stressful encounters, and health outcomes. In R., Bar-On., and J. D.A., Parker. (2000). *The handbook of emotional intelligence. Theory, development and application at home, school, and in the workplace.* San Francisco, Jossey-Bass.

Mayer, J. D., and Salovey, P. (1997). What is emotional intelligence? In P. Salovey and D. Sluyter (Eds). *Emotional Development and Emotional Intelligence: Implications for Educators* (pp. 3-31). New York: Basic Books.

Mayer, J., Salovey, P., and Caruso, D. (2000). Competing models of emotional intelligence. In Sternberg, R.J. (Ed.). *Handbook of Human Intelligence* (2nd ed.). New York: Cambridge University Press.

Mayer, J. D., Salovey, P., Caruso, D. R., and Sitaraneos, G. (2003). Measuring emotional intelligence with the MSCEIT V2.0. Emotion, 3, 97-105.

Maynard, I.W., and Cotton, P.G. (1993). An investigation of two stress management techniques in a field setting. *The Sport Psychologist, 7,* 375-387.

Maynard, I.W., Hemmings, B., Greenless, I.A., Warwick-Evans, L., and Stanton, N. (1999). Stress management in sport: A comparison of unimodal and multimodal interventions. *Anxiety, Stress, and Coping, 11,* 225-246.

Ntoumanis, N., and Biddle, S.J.H. (1998). The relationship of coping and its perceived effectiveness to positive and negative affect in sport. *Personality and Individual Differences, 24,* 773-778.

Orme, G. (2003). Emotional intelligence: The cutting edge of interventions in corporate and educational settings. Paper presented on the 29th May 2003 at the Nexus EQ conference, Halifax, Nova Scotia, Canada. Cited in Bar-On, R. (2005). The Bar-On model of emotional-social intelligence. In P. Fernández-Berrocal and N. Extremera (Guest Editors). Special Issue on Emotional Intelligence. *Psicothema, 17.*

Orme, G., and Cannon, K. (2000). Everything you wanted to know about implementing an EQ programme: 1 – Getting started. *Competency & Emotional Intelligence Quarterly,* 8, 19–24.

Pensgaard, A. M., and Duda, J.L. (2003). Sydney 2000: The interplay between emotions, coping, and the performance of Olympic level athletes. *The Sport Psychologist, 17,* 253-267.

Piko, B. (2001). Gender differences and similarities in adolescents' ways of coping. *The Psychological Record, 51,* 223-235.

Reicherts, M., and Pihet, S. (2000). Job newcomers coping with stressful situations: A micro-analysis of adequate coping and well-being. *Swiss Journal of Psychology, 59,* 303-316.

Renk, K., and Creasey, G. (2003). The relationship of gender, gender identity, and coping strategies in late adolescents. *Journal of Adolescence, 26,* 159-168.

Rexford, L., and Weirzbicki, M. (1994). An attempt to predict change in mood in response to Velten-like mood induction procedures. *Journal of Psychology, 123,* 285-294.

Ritchie, A. (1999). Professionalism through ALIA: outcomes from group mentoring programs. *Australian Library Journal,* 48, 160-177.

Roskies, E., and Lazarus, R.S. (1980). Coping theory and the teaching of coping skills. In P.O. Davidson and S.M. Davidson (Eds), Behavioural medicine: *Changing health lifestyles.* New York: Brunner/Mazel.

Sandler, I. N., Wolchik, S. A., MacKinnon, D., Ayers, T. S., and Roosa, M. (1997). Developing linkages between theory and intervention in stress and coping processes. In S. A. Wolchik and I. N. Sandler (Eds.), *Handbook of children's coping: Linking theory and research* (pp. 3–41). New York: Plenum.

Salovey, P., Bedell, B.T., Detweiler, J.B., and Mayer, J.D. (1999). Coping intelligently, Emotional Intelligence, and the coping process. In C.R. Snyder (Ed), *Coping: The Psychology of What Works* (pp. 141-160). New York: Oxford University Press.

Salovey, P., and Mayer. J. (1990). Emotional intelligence. *Imagination, Cognition, and Personality, 9,* 185-211.

Sjölund, M., and Gustafsson, H. (2001). Outcome study of a leadership development assessment and training program based on emotional intelligence. An internal report prepared for the Skanska Institute in Stockholm, Sweden. Cited in Bar-On, R. (2005). The Bar-On model of emotional-social intelligence. In P. Fernández-Berrocal and N. Extremera (Guest Editors). Special Issue on Emotional Intelligence. *Psicothema, 17.*

Shambrook, C. J., and Bull, S.J. (2001). *Adherence Issues in sport and Exercise.* Wiley, London.

Valach, L., Young, R.A., and Lynam, M.J. (2002). *Action theory: A primer in research in the social science.* Westport, CT: Preager.

Van Rooy, D. L., and Viswesvaran, C. (2004). Emotional intelligence: A meta-analytic investigation of predictive validity and nomological net. *Journal of Vocational Behavior, 65,* 71-95.

Wenzlaff, R.M., and Lepage, J.P. (2000). The emotional impact of chosen and imposed thoughts. *Personality and Social Psychology Bulletin, 26,* 1502-1514.

Woodman, T., and Hardy, L. (2001). A case study of organisational stress in elite sport. *Journal of Applied Sport Psychology, 13,* 207-238.

Young, R.A., and Valach, L. (2000). Reconceptualising career theory and research: An action-theoretical perspective. In A. Collin, and R.A. Young (Eds.), *The future of career* (PP.181-196). Cambridge, UK: Cambridge University Press.

Zeidner, M. (1990). Life events and coping resources as predictors of stress symptoms of adolescents. *Personality and Individual Differences, 11,* 693-703.

Zizzi, S.J., Deaner, H.R., and Hirschhom, D.K. (2003). The relationship between emotional intelligence and performance amongst college basketball players. *Journal of Applied Sport Psychology, 15,* 262-269.

In: Mood and Human Performance: Conceptual, Measurement...   ISBN 1-60021-269-7
Editor: Andrew M. Lane, pp. 187-200   © 2006 Nova Science Publishers, Inc.

Chapter 9

EMOTIONS AND EATING BEHAVIOURS IN EXERCISERS

*Helen J. Lane**

University of Wales, Newport, UK

ABSTRACT

This chapter explores relationships between perceptions of diet and emotional states. The research is focused on exercisers, a population that tend to emphasise diet, and therefore, the relationship between diet and emotion should be evaluated. The relative infancy of this line of research has led to researchers using measures developed initially for clinical samples. The chapter reviews the validity of a commonly used measure. A study is reviewed that demonstrated the limitations of the Eating Attitude Test for use with exercisers. A series of studies are presented that demonstrate the validity of a new measure of eating attitudes, developed specifically for use among exercisers. A theoretical model that investigates the nature of attitudes toward diet, particularly the interplay between healthy and unhealthy eating behaviours, dietary responses to emotions, the emotional consequences of eating and body image is presented. Studying relationships with emotional intelligence, eating attitudes and emotional responses to diet is proposed as a line of investigation for future research.

INTRODUCTION

Sport and exercise are emotional domains. Athletes experience a range of emotions before and after competition: Anxiety is experienced before competition starts with post-competition elation or depression following respective goal attainment (see Lane, Lane, and Firth, 2002). A wealth of research demonstrates enhanced mood following exercise (see Berger and Motl, 2000, for a review). Entwined in the relationship between sport and exercise and emotion are attitudes toward eating and subsequent eating behaviours. Evidence points to

---

* Helenlane1@yahoo.co.uk

people using food as a strategy to regulate unpleasant mood where individuals eat as a response to stress (Stevens and Lane, 2001; Thayer, Newman, and McLain, 1994). A phrase such as a 'comfort eater' has been used to describe an individual who eats as a strategy to enhance mood. Scientific research to investigate the nature of such relationships is lacking particularly among exercisers where the relationship between emotions, exercise, and diet can be positive. Participation in sport and exercise might prevent individuals developing strategies against eating problems in the same way that physical activity is associated with a number of health related benefits, of which some will be to experience positive emotions. By contrast, evidence also indicates that athletes represent a group particularly at risk of developing an eating disorder problem (Hausenblas and Carron, 1999; Smolak, Murnen, and Ruble, 2000). Therefore since exercise is associated with mood enhancement, it may be possible that dietary control might contribute positive affects following exercise, particularly among individuals who yield a great deal of personal satisfaction from using exercise as a part of a weight control regime. However, we also know that exercise is associated with maladaptive eating patterns, dysfunctional attitudes and unpleasant emotions. This chapter will firstly focus on constructs that influence eating behaviour with a view to identifying how eating behaviour, exercise and emotions are interlinked. Methodological issues in the study of eating behaviours are discussed with a view to developing a grounded measure. The chapter concludes with a theory to explain eating attitudes and emotions in future research.

Research shows that mood and eating attitudes are related. Terry, Lane, and Warren (1999) showed tension and depression was associated with disordered eating. Lane (2003) demonstrated that mood states, particularly depression, related to disordered eating, and importantly, relationships were consistent for males and females. These findings should be seen in conjunction with evidence showing individuals eat as a strategy to regulate mood (Thayer et al., 1994). Stevens and Lane (2001) found evidence to support the notion that athletes eat as a strategy to enhance positive mood and regulate negative mood among a sample of 107 athletes. When the two sets of studies are seen together, it could be argued that athletes or exercisers that seek to control weight through dieting could experience negative mood states due to changes in eating patterns. For example, Hall and Lane (2001) found mood deterioration in a sample of boxers engaging with weight loss strategies.

There appears to be circumstances under which sports participation constitutes a risk factor for certain elements of eating problems. Athletes may resort to dieting to improve performance or reach a specific weight. They may also have social pressure for thinness by other athletes or coaches, where the athlete may appraise their performance based on their perceived body shape and weight which in turn may trigger dieting. Athletic injury or illness has also been associated with dieting. It is suggested that if an athlete has some fear and anxiety of weight gain due to reducing training, this could trigger dieting if training tapers. This anxiety and fear of weight gain is not simply vanity, it is a belief than an increase in weight will affect their performance or/and in the case of a team sport, athletes could believe it may reduce their chance of being selected for the team.

The relationship between dieting and mood has been evidenced in a number of studies. Eating behaviours have been related to pleasant emotions such as happiness and unpleasant emotions. They can also be related to unpleasant emotions such as anger and depression (Arnow, Kenardy, and Agras, 1995; Healtherton and Baumeister, 1991; Macht and Simons 2000). A factor related to the eating-emotion link is the influence of stress and distress. A plethora of studies demonstrate that stress is related to eating behaviour. Research has shown that people regulate their eating behaviour as a way to cope with emotional distress (Polivy and Herman, 1999; Stice and Agras, 1999). Polivy and Herman (1999) found that stress suppresses eating in non-dieters, but increases eating in chronic dieters. These results suggest that dieters use overeating to mask their stress in other areas of their lives and in turn, attribute their stress or distress to their overeating rather than to more uncontrollable factors (Ball and Lee, 2002). In a recent study of stress, dieting and emotions among exercisers, Lane, Matheson, and Lewis (2004) highlighted that the reaction to stress was complex, but participant responses were largely supportive of the stress-diet relationship. For example, when these respondents were asked, "do you eat more or less when you are under stress?" The following examples from some of the interview scripts illustrate this point:

"It depends on the extend of the stress, if it is real extreme stress then I don't really eat much but if I'm slightly stressed then I eat more."

"Probably more and probably crap, stuff like choky bars. Yeah I might go for a quick fix like a packet of Maltesers or something"

"Well, if I have problems at work, I find that I come home and eat the nearest thing that is there and watch telly, it seems to release the tension and gives me a rest."

Solomon (2001) suggested that eating is not only a coping mechanism for stress but eating becomes a stressor in itself, and that a coping strategy specific for overeating is required. Solomon (2001) found that negative mood states were associated with social stressors, coping, calorie consumption, and weight control strategies. Solomon also reported that negative mood was associated with the interaction between the degree of weekly calorie consumption and the use of weight control strategies. Lane, Matheson, and Lewis (2004) found evidence to support the cycle of depression, body image and eating behaviour. The following quotes are illustrative findings:

"I feel really depressed when I overeat, but often the reason I overeat is when I'm depressed anyway. I'm a bit overweight and it makes me depressed among other things, but I have a terrible habit of eating lot of junk food when I'm depressed and then because I've eaten a lot of food I get even more depressed because I know it will make me fatter. However I notice if I exercise I don't get as depressed and because I'm not depressed, I eat healthier foods."

"I eat when I am depressed, which sometimes is quite a lot, I have put on a stone in one year"

"Yeah, when I'm depressed I eat, and when I am depressed I eat lots of really unhealthy foods like biscuits, chocolates and crisps, the sweeter and fattier the better and I keep eating even though I am full, I live to eat rather than eat to live. Well, I do just live to eat sometimes, I think it is only the fact that I exercise which has kept my weight down so I'm not obese."

"Yes, I seem to eat a lot more rubbish when I am depressed. I just love food and um, I'm happy eating it in a way as long as I know I'm going exercise but also in a way it does not make me feel that great because um, all the time I'm eating the rubbish I am also thinking I really should not be eating all this crap."

A powerful emotion related to dieting is disgust. Disgust sensitivity has been found to be higher in women with eating-disorders. Harvey, Troop, Treasure, and Murphy (2002) found evidence to demonstrate that females recovering from an eating disorder continued to report high levels of disgust to foodstuffs. Research has also found that fear is related to abnormal eating attitudes in response to high calorie foods and overweight body shapes (Harvey et al., 2002).

An argument frequently used to explain why athletes develop eating problems is based on an excessive focus on nutrition and weight loss. Research has proposed that sport could be a trigger factor for eating disorder symptoms especially when weight maintenance is critical. It is argued that in such cases, unpleasant emotional states will accompany disordered eating. Athletes in these sports may turn to 'unhealthy' weight control methods such as fasting, going on very low calorie diets and using diuretics to lose weight (Sundgot-Borgen, 1994). For example, Thiel, Gottfried, and Hesse (1993) reported a high frequency of eating disorder symptoms and even sub clinical incidences of eating disorders in low weight male wrestlers and rowers. There is, however, evidence that these weight loss behaviours and attitudes towards weight are transient and not long term. In a study of wrestlers, Dale and Landers (1999) found that although in-season, wrestlers are more weight-conscious than non-wrestlers, and out of season, these feelings change to similar levels as non-wrestlers.

Other factors contributing to eating disorders from athletes maybe an injury or illness. Injuries may cause a fear of weight gain in the individual due to reducing training which in turn might trigger dieting (Sundgot-Borgen, 1994; Thompson and Sherman, 1993). One retrospective study pointed out that a sudden increase in training load might induce a caloric deprivation in endurance athletes, which in turn may elicit biological and social reinforcements leading to the development of eating disorders (Sundgot-Borgen, 1994). By contrast, moderate exercise has been found to have a positive effective on disordered eating. Levine, Marcus, and Moulton (1996) demonstrated that a simple walking regimen, performed three to five times a week and aimed to expend 1,000 calories, was efficient in managing binge-eating disorders in a clinically diagnosed sample of obese women. They found that 71% of the experimental group abstained from binge eating by the end of the 6-month study. It is interesting to note that the exercise regime used by Levine et al. meets many of the criteria for mood enhancement proposed by Berger and Motl (2000). Thus, mood enhancement from exercise could have assisted in reducing binge-eating if exercise led to some individuals developing a greater sense of personal control.

METHODOLOGICAL ISSUES

The accuracy of previous studies assessing the nature of eating disorders in sport and exercise is problematic due to at least two interrelated methodological limitations. The first issue stems from the notion that neither athletes nor exercisers want to reveal disordered eating symptoms. The second methodological issue to consider is the relative validity of eating attitudes scales. The study of eating behaviours is complicated by studies that use clinical methods. These problems are briefly discussed, and then through qualitative research, an alternative measure that has been developed and validated is proposed which represents a feasible tool to investigate this under-researched area.

With reference to the first issue, eating disorders are not socially accepted ways to enhance performance or to improve body image among exercisers. It is suggested that if an athlete has some fear and anxiety of weight gain due to reducing training, this could trigger engaging in dieting behaviour. This anxiety and fear of weight gain is possibly brought about by a belief than an increase in weight will affect their performance. The worry of poor performance maybe linked to perceived attitudes of the coach on the importance of leanness for sport performance. The athlete may believe, rightly or wrongly, that the coach will not select them based on appearance or weight gain alone. Therefore, when they complete the inventory they may not tell the truth.

With reference to the second issue, existing eating attitude inventories have not been developed and validated with sport and exercise populations. The two most popular measures used in sport and exercise are the Eating Disorder Inventory (EDI: Garner and Olmstead, 1984) and the Eating Attitude Test (EAT; Garner and Garfinkel, 1979, EAT, Garner, Olmsted, Bohr, and Garfinkel, 1982). Both measures were developed for use with clinical samples. For example, the EAT was validated using female anorexia nervosa patients, ($n = 160$) and university students ($n = 140$). An example of why such a measure might be inappropriate for use in sport and exercise is given through the following example. An overweight exerciser who wants to lose weight may be dieting sensibly and spending a considerable amount of time thinking about the content and preparation of their food, but this is not indicative of an eating disorder. However, their score may be high on an eating disorder measure, as they probably would have high scores for pre-occupation for food, dieting, and avoiding fatty foods and sweets, all of which are items on the EAT. A second example is presented regarding a hypothetical athlete who wants to build up muscle and so is concerned about eating healthy food, but may have poor body image. In this case, a true reflection may not be gained from their score on the measure. Evidence of poor validity was demonstrated by Lane, Lane and Matheson (2004) in a study examining the validity of the EAT with exercisers.

In the study by Lane, Lane and Matheson (2004), confirmatory factor analysis (CFA) was used to test the factorial validity of the EAT. Lane, Lane and Matheson (2004) tested three models: a single-factor model (a global measure of eating attitudes, a three-factor model ('dieting', 'bulimia control and food pre-occupation', and 'oral control') and a four-factor model ('dieting', 'bulimia control', 'food pre-occupation', and 'oral control'). CFA results indicated that a four-factor model showed the best fit. However, it should be noted that five items showed poor factor loadings on all models and it was after the removal of these five items that a revised 21-item four-factor model showed acceptable fit indices. An important aspect of Lane et al's work is the distinction between bulimia and food-pre-occupation. Lane, Lane and Matheson found the factor 'bulimia and food pre-occupation' appeared to assess two constructs. Bulimics are likely to have pre-occupation with food, and thus the constructs will correlate. However, a pre-occupation with food is not necessarily an indicator bulimia. As suggested previously, individuals from an exercise population could interpret items differently to both individuals diagnosed with an eating disorder, and individuals from the general population. For example, the items 'I am aware of the calorie content of food I eat' and 'I avoid foods with sugar in them' on the EAT are proposed to assess an avoidance of fattening foods and a pre-occupation with being thinner, hence a potentially disordered attitude toward food. Among a sport and exercise population, knowledge of calorie content of food might be a reflection of good dietary practices, where the intention is to eat a low fat diet and high carbohydrate diet. Awareness of the caloric content is desirable when instigating an education-based intervention to promote a healthy lifestyle. Hence, a score of 'Always', rated as 3 on the EAT, might reflect a disordered attitude, or it could reflect increased knowledge of diet. If it does reflect increased knowledge, it clearly should not be included as an indicator of an eating disorder. In addition, the item 'I take longer to eat my meals' also might be conceptualized differently. Items that make a comparison to others can be problematic. In this instance, it depends on who they compare themselves to and what size meals they eat. The score reported to this item might also be reflection of an athlete eating larger meals than his/her associates. This might be entirely appropriate in order to balance the energy in - energy out equation. It is important for researchers to check whether items are understood by the participant-group under investigation because if the target population misunderstands items, they provide meaningless information.

In developing the EAT, items were developed by experts, with no qualitative checks on the extent to which participants from the target population on whom the measure would be used could understand the items. It is important to explore the nature of these items and factors. Interview techniques are suggested to be an effective approach to explore the nature of items, and identify factors not currently identified in the EAT. Lane, Lane and Matheson (2004) suggested that this should be the start of a comprehensive validation program of a measure of eating attitudes for use in exercise.

LANE, MATHESON, AND LEWIS 2004: QUALITATIVE EXPLORATION OF THE NATURE OF EATING ATTITUDES AMONG EXERCISERS

Interview techniques were used to explore the nature of eating attitudes among exercisers. Qualitative research was conducted over 2 stages. In stage 1, 16 under graduate third year students (Age range 20 – 35 years; Male $N = 9$, Female $N = 7$) volunteered to participate in focus groups. Two focus group sessions lasting 30-40 minutes in duration were conducted with 8 participants in each group. Themes were identified from the focus groups were used to generate the questions for interviews conducted on a one-to-one basis with individuals. In stage 2, 14 exercisers (Aged range 22 – 65 years; male $N = 8$, female $N = 6$) volunteered to participate in interviews of 30 to 40 minutes in duration. Data were transcribed, checked for accuracy and entered into INVIVO where the data were analysed by putting sections into categories or "nodes" and labelled. Themes and items were identified and a group of exercisers and a panel of experts then assessed the items for clarity, content, and construct validity. Any unclear, inappropriate items or problematic items were excluded.

Results identified six themes: 'Healthy and Unhealthy Eating Behaviours' (theme 1) which refers to what eating habits the participant has and what types of food the participant eats, for example, eating fatty foods. 'Weight Management' (theme 2) describes the methods used to keep their body in good shape such as fasting or by limiting calorie intake. 'Emotional responses to diet' (theme 3) describes cognitive concerns about food such as guilt about eating certain foods and being depressed after eating too much. 'Dietary responses to eating' (theme 4) refers to reasons that affect the amount eaten or type of food eaten. Examples include eating more when depressed, or eating more unhealthy foods when stressed. 'Knowledge of Food-Health Link' (theme 5) refers to factual knowledge of food and health.

'Body Image' (theme 6) described perceived body image. It is argued that themes 1, and 2 (Healthy and Unhealthy Eating Behaviours and Weight Management) are proposed to measure eating behaviours and eating attitudes. Themes 3, 4, 5 and 6 (Dietary responses to eating, Knowledge of Food-Health Link and 'Body Image) are related factors that would help to identify suitable strategies to encourage healthy eating behaviours and eating attitudes. These themes were used to develop a measure of eating behaviours and eating attitudes grounded in the experience of exercise participants.

DEVELOPMENT OF THE TEST OF EXERCISERS EATING SCALE (TEES)

Lane, Matheson and Lewis (2005) extended this study to produce a new measure of eating attitudes grounded in the experience of exercisers. Interview data were used to produce a pool of 130 items. Face validity and content validity were developed using a sample of exercisers and a sample of experts. Initially two regular exercisers rated the clarity of items, leading to four items being re-worded. Following the analysis of these data, a sample of 32 regular exercisers and 10 independent expert researchers (8 who have PhD's, and 2 who almost had completed their PhD's) from 5 UK Universities reviewed the 130 items for clarity. Participants placed items under one of the six themes described previously. They also highlighted items that were unclear. Data from both samples were analysed and an item was retained if 80% or more of the exercise participants agreed that the item reflected the proposed category. The remaining items were only included if 100% of the experts agreed that the item reflected the proposed category. Results indicated that after removing and revising the relevant items, 78 items were retained for further analysis. However, the decision was made to develop a separate scale for the food-health relationship theme as these items are more factual rather than perceptual in nature.

TEST OF FACTORIAL VALIDITY OF THE TEST OF EXERCISERS EATING SCALE (TEES)

The next stage in the research was to validate the new measure of eating attitudes and eating behaviour using confirmatory factor analysis. By using confirmatory factor analysis stronger items were retained and this result in a model of good fit. Three hundred and twenty-three regular exercisers completed the 78-item TEES. Confirmatory factor analysis indicated that 'Unhealthy eating behaviours' (5-items), 'Healthy eating behaviours' (3-items), 'Weight management' (5-items), Emotional responses to diet (5-items), 'Dietary responses to emotions' (5-items), and 'Body image' (5-items) showed acceptable fit indices when assessed independently. A 29-item and six-factor intercorrelated model showed acceptable fit indices (RCFI = 0.95, RMSEA = 0.07). The 29-item scale was administered to 937 exercise participants. Confirmatory factor analysis results indicated support for the hypothesized model (RCFI = .93, RMSEA = .06). Collectively, it is suggested that the six-factor TEES provides evidence of construct validity for assessing eating attitudes among exercisers. It is argued that these two studies produced a psychometrically robust 29-item questionnaire that assesses six-constructs related to eating attitudes among exercisers. An advantage of the

TEES is that the themes are grounded in the experience of exercisers. Future research should cross-validate the 29-item measure to a new sample and explore the nature of the factors identified.

Table 1. Factor loadings of the Test of Attitudes to Eating Among Exercisers

Item	Factor loading	Error variance
Unhealthy Eating Behaviours		
I eat lots of fatty foods	.729	.684
I eat lots of sweets and sugary foods	.615	.789
I eat a great deal of take-away food	.575	.818
I snack a lot on things like biscuits, crisps and chocolate	.684	.729
I eat lots of processed foods	.663	.749
I eat a lot of pre-cooked meals	.533	.846
Healthy Eating Behaviour		
Most days I eat more than three portions of fruit and/or vegetables	.674	.739
I eat a variety of fruits and/or vegetables	.862	.507
I eat lots of fresh, unprocessed foods	.701	.713
Weight Management		
I control my weight by limiting my calorie intake	.603	.798
I omit some foods from my diet to lose weight	.672	.741
I often change my diet in an attempt to lose weight	.660	.752
Sometimes I fast to lose weight	.473	.881
I control my weight by eating small portions of food	.532	.847
Emotional Responses to Diet		
I feel guilty if I eat too much	.794	.608
I feel guilty when I eat high calorie foods	.746	.666
I worry when I eat certain foods because I may gain weight	.814	.581
I feel disgusted with myself if I overeat	.736	.677
I feel disappointed with myself when I overeat	.807	.591
Dietary Responses to Emotions		
I eat more unhealthy foods when I am under stress	.669	.743
I eat more when I'm nervous	.695	.719
I eat unhealthy foods when I am depressed	.812	.584
When I'm angry, I often eat more	.681	.732
When I am tense I eat more	.823	.569
Body Image		
My stomach is too fat	.819	.574
I think I am overweight	.878	.478
I have too much fat on my arms	.744	.668
I have too much fat on my body	.862	.507
There are many parts of my body I would like to change	.722	.691

Table 2. Alphas, Descriptive, and Intercorrelations among subscales for the Test of Exercisers Eating Scale

	Alphas	M	SD	HB	WM	ECE	DRE	BI
Unhealthy Eating Behaviours	.80	2.46	0.89	-.36*	.21*	.21*	.46*	.41*
Healthy Eating Behaviour	.78	4.03	1.20		.28*	.24*	.13*	.12*
Weight Management	.73	2.69	1.01			.87*	.61*	.69*
Emotional Responses to Diet	.87	2.81	1.09				.69*	.71*
Dietary Responses to Emotions	.86	2.88	1.26					.67*
Body Image	.84	3.18	1.42					

* $p < .01$

As Table 2 indicates, all 15 relationships significantly correlated. Of principle interest are relationships between the emotional responses to diet and the dietary response to emotions which hint at a reciprocal relationship: individuals that feel stressed eat as a strategy to reduce stress, and the act of eating in turn becomes an additional stressor. Relationships between emotional responses to diet and reacting to unpleasant emotions by eating are complex. The role of healthy eating does not appear to influence this relationship. Healthy eating positively associated with both emotional responses to diet and dietary responses to emotions, and therefore suggesting that eating healthy foods when under stress does not prevent the unpleasant emotions-eating response-unpleasant emotions cycle. A factor that relates strongly to the emotional responses to diet is weight management, which is characterised by engaging in dieting behaviour. Relationships suggest that increased unpleasant emotions are experienced when engaging in weight-management behaviour, a finding consistent with those reported by Hall and Lane (2001). It should also be noted the relationship between weight management and dietary response to emotions is positive and therefore suggests that individuals engage in weight-management behaviours as a response to stress.

A factor that appears to be influential to dietary responses to emotions, emotional antecedents of eating, weight management and healthy and unhealthy eating patterns is body image. Body image is proposed to combine self-esteem and self-concept. Self-esteem refers to a cognitive evaluation of one's competencies. Self-esteem is proposed to be an appraisal of their body maybe based on their perceived shape and weight. Body dissatisfaction has consistently been related to dieting and depressive symptoms. Researchers have highlighted that physical exercise sometimes promotes positive body image and other times having detrimental effects (Hausenblas and Symons-Downs, 2001).

A MODEL OF THE FACTORS INFLUENCING EATING BEHAVIOURS

Having developed the measure, a model to explain factors influence eating attitudes (see Figure 1) is proposed which suggests that emotional responses to diet and emotional triggers toward dieting are mediated by perceptions of body image. Body image is proposed to be the crucial factor due to its link with weight-management; individuals with a positive body image are less likely to engage in weight-making behaviours. Given the link between poor diet and obesity, positive body image should reduce engaging in dieting as a response to stress, which in turn, reduces the potentially harmful effects of unpleasant emotions that stem from dieting.

Eating behaviour is influenced by the interaction between factors as depicted graphically in Figure 1.

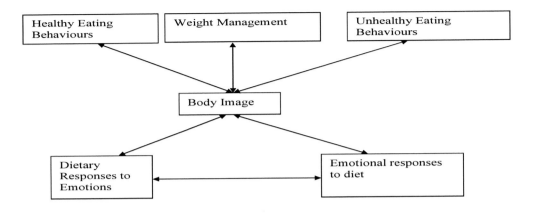

Figure 1. Proposed factors influencing eating behaviour

It is hypothesised that strategies to promote a positive body image will be associated with reduced weight-making behaviours, emotional responses to eating, and, eating as a response to stress. Healthy and unhealthy eating patterns will be associated with body image, but it is suggested that both are influenced by media, parents and other socialisation agents. Indeed, it is argued that developing knowledge of food might influence this relationship.

It appears that healthy and unhealthy eating patterns correlate with emotional responses to diet, dietary responses to emotion, and body image. The relationship between healthy and unhealthy eating, although inversely related and significant, is weaker than expected. Results suggest a greater degree of independence between these seemingly bi-polar scales than that should be reasonably expected. However, among exercisers, it is possible to analyse the internal thought processes associated with unhealthy and healthy eating behaviours. It seems contradictory that individuals should report eating five fresh fruit and vegetables per day and also report high eating fatty and processed foods. Individuals who use exercise to justify eating unnecessary calories in the form of unhealthy food choices, whilst at the same time, arguing to themselves that also eating food is necessary to sustain their exercise patterns. Although such thoughts could be justified, it is also possible to see how they lead to the development of unpleasant emotions, particularly through the mediating effect of body image. It is likely that unhealthy eating behaviours would negate the possibly desirable changes to body images that could result from exercise and healthy eating. Thus, whilst the individual engage in behaviours that could lead to a desirable body image, frustration and unpleasant emotions stem from unhealthy eating patterns.

In terms of developing a coherent framework to explain relationships between variables, it could be argued that body image is a central concept. When a harmonious balance between healthy eating, unhealthy eating, exercise and body image is attained, it is likely to be associated with positive emotions and using mood regulation strategies other than eating, possibly exercise (see Stevens and Lane, 2001; Thayer et al., 1994). In such circumstances, the inverse relationship between healthy and unhealthy eating would become more pronounced; individuals eating healthier food and abstaining from eating unhealthy food. This pattern of relationships is proposed in Figure 2. As Figure 2 suggests, unpleasant emotions and behavioural responses follow an inability to balance nutritional requirements via the balance between healthy and unhealthy eating.

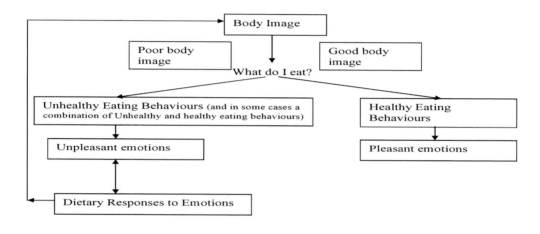

Figure 2. Model of eating behaviour and emotions

It is argued that individuals develop an awareness of these relationships. Developing a sense of personal control over this process is needed in order to break the cycle. The concept of emotional intelligence, which suggests that individuals are aware of experiential and personal factors on emotional states could be salient. Emotionally intelligent individuals will be aware of the emotional consequences of miscalculating healthy and unhealthy food choices.

Meyer and Zizzi (2007, this edition) reported the relationship between emotional intelligence and diet related indices. Parker, Meyer, and Swartz (2005) found that overweight individuals with average emotional intelligence recorded lower negative mood states and higher self-esteem. Highly emotional intelligent individuals also reported to engage in almost twice as much daily walking when compared with individuals with below average emotional intelligence scores. High emotional intelligence is also related to positive outcomes such as prosocial behaviour, parental warmth, and positive peer and family relations (Brackett, Mayer, and Warner, 2004; Salovey, Mayer, Caruso, and Lopes, 2001). Research has also found that emotional intelligence was associated with a high perceived ability to refuse cigarette offers (Trinidad, Unger, Chou, and Johnson, 2004), to avoid self-destructive deviant behaviours (Brackett and Mayer, 2003). Alcohol is considered the most widely used drug among athletes (O'Brien and Lyons, 2000), and its misuse by athletes is well documented (Hildebrand, Johnson, and Bogle, 2001; O'Brien and Lyons, 2000; Watson, 2002). Hildebrand et al. (2001) found that college students, who were either current athletes or former high school athletes, began drinking at an earlier age, consumed more alcohol more often, and engaged in binge drinking and other risk taking behaviours more frequently than did college students who had never been athletes. Wilson et al. (2004) suggested that the utilization of poor coping mechanisms might lead some groups of individuals to engage in higher levels of alcohol consumption. Wilson et al. (2004) found that correlations between alcohol behaviours and coping tactics varied by both gender and athletic status in college students. Arguably, the evidence presented by Parker et al. (2005) could be used to suggest that emotional intelligence could be a factor to reduce the likelihood of unpleasant psychological states and behaviours occurring. Emotionally intelligent people should choose short-term and long-term strategies to regulate emotion. Examination of such proposals should form the questions for future studies to try to answer.

FUTURE DIRECTIONS

Future research uses the measure developed to assess theoretically driven hypotheses made in the conceptual framework outlined in Figures 1 and 2, particularly the possible moderating factor of emotional intelligence.

REFERENCES

Arnow, B., Kenardy, J., and Agras, W. S. (1995). The Emotional Eating Scale: The development of a measure to assess coping with negative affect by eating. *International Journal of Eating Disorders, 18*, 79–90.

Ball K., and Lee C. (2002). Psychological stress, coping, and symptoms of disordered eating in a community sample of young Australian women *International Journal of Eating Disorders, International Journal of Eating Disorders, 31*, 71-81.

Berger, B. G., and Motl, R. W. (2000). A selective review and synthesis of research employing the Profile of Mood States. *Journal of Applied Sport Psychology*, 12, 69-92.

Brackett, M. A., and Mayer, J. D. (2003). Convergent, discriminant, and incremental validity of competing measures of emotional intelligence. *Personality and Social Psychology Bulletin*, 29, 1147–1158.

Brackett, M. A., Mayer, J. D., and Warner, R. M. (2004). Emotional intelligence and its relation to everyday behaviour. *Personality and Individual Differences, 36*, 1387–1402.

Dale, K.S., and Landers, D.M. (1999). Weight control in wrestling: Eating disorders or disordered eating? *Medicine and Science in Sports and Exercise*, 31, 1382-1389.

Garner, D. M., and Garfinkel, P. E. (1979). The eating attitudes test: An index of the symptoms of anorexia nervosa. *Psychological Medicine, 9*, 273-279.

Garner, D. M., Olmsted, M. P., Bophr, Y., and Garfinkel, P. E. (1982). The Eating Attitudes Test: Psychometric features and clinical correlates. *Psychological Medicine, 12*, 871-878.

Hall, C. J., and Lane, A. M. (2001). Effects of rapid weight loss on mood and performance among amateur boxers. *British Journal of Sports Medicine, 35,* 390-395.

Harvey, T ., Troop, N.A. Treasure,J. L., and Murphy, T. (2002). Fear, disgust, and abnormal eating attitudes: A preliminary study. *International Journal of Eating Disorders, 32,* 213-218.

Hausenblas, H. A., and Carron, A. V. (1999). Eating disorder indices and athletes: An integration. *Journal of Sport and Exercise Psychology, 2,* 230-258.

Hausenblas, H. A., and Symons-Downs, D. (2001). Body image and athletes. A meta-analysis. *Journal of Applied Sport Psychology,* 13, 323–339.

Heatherton, T. F., and Baumeister, R. F. (1991). Binge eating as an escape from self-awareness. *Psychological Bulletin,* 110, 86-108.

Hildebrand, K. M., Johnson, D. J., and Bogle, K. (2001). Comparison of patterns of alcohol use between high school and college athletes and non-athletes. *College Student Journal, 35,* 358-365.

Lane, A. M. (2003). Relationships between attitudes toward eating disorders and mood among student athletes. *Journal of Science and Medicine in Sport, 6,* 144-154.

Lane, A. M., Lane, H. J., and Firth, S. (2002). Relationships between performance satisfaction and post-competition mood among runners. *Perceptual and Motor Skills, 94,* 805-813.

Lane, H, J., Lane, A. M., and Matheson, H. (2004). Validity of the eating attitude test among exercisers. *Journal of Sports Science and Medicine*, 3, 244-253.

Lane, H. J., Matheson, H., and Lewis, N. (2004). A qualitative study of sport and exercise participants eating attitudes and eating behaviour. Paper presented at the British Association of Sport and Exercise Sciences Conference, Liverpool, September 5-7th 2004.

Lane, H. J., Matheson, H., and Lewis, N. (2005). Development of an Eating Attitude Measure Grounded in the Experience of Exercisers. Paper presented at the International Society of Sport Psychology (ISSP). *11th World Congress of Sport Psychology,* 15-19 August 2005, Sydney Convention and Exhibition Centre, Sydney, Australia.

Levine, M. D., Marcus, M. D., and Moulton, P. (1996). Exercise in the treatment of binge eating disorder. *International Journal of Eating Disorders, 19,* 171-179.

Macht, M., and Simons, G. (2000). Emotions and eating in everyday life. *Appetite,* 35, 65–71.

Meyer, B. B., and Zizzi, S. (2007). Emotional Intelligence in Sport: Conceptual, Methodological, and Applied Issues. In A.M. Lane (ed.), *Mood and human performance: Conceptual, measurement, and applied issues* (pp. 131-154). Hauppauge, NY: Nova Science.

O'Brien, C.P. and Lyons, F. (2000). Alcohol and the athlete. *Sports Medicine,* 29, 295-300.

Parker, S.J., Meyer, B.B., and Swartz, A.M. (2005, May). *Stress, coping, and obesity-related health: An exploratory study of emotional intelligence.* Poster presented at the University of Wisconsin-Milwaukee College of Health Sciences Research Symposium, Milwaukee, WI.

Polivy J., and Herman, C.P. (1985). Dieting and Binging: A causal analysis. *Americian Psychologist,* 40, 193 – 201.

Salovey, P., Mayer, J. D., Caruso, D., and Lopes, P. N. (2001). Measuring emotional intelligence as a set of mental abilities with the MSCEIT. In S. J. Lopez, and C. R. Snyder (Eds.), *Handbook of positive psychology assessment.* Washington DC: American Psychological Association.

Smolak, L., Murnen, S.K., and Ruble, A.E. (2000). Female athletes and eating problems: A meta-analysis. *International Journal of Eating Disorders* 27, 371-380.

Solomon, M. R. (2001). Eating as both coping and stressor in overweight control. *Journal of Advanced Nursing,* 36, 563-572.

Stevens, M. J., and Lane, A. M. (2001). Mood-regulating strategies used by athletes. Athletic Insight. *http://www.athleticinsight.com/Vol3Iss3/MoodRegulation.htm.*

Stice, E., and Agras, W. S. (1999). Subtyping bulimic women along dietary restraint and negative affective dimensions. *Journal of Consulting and Clinical Psychology,* 67, 460–469.

Sundgot-Borgen, J. (1994). Risk and trigger factors for the development of eating disorders in female elite athletes. *Medical Science in Sports Exercise,* 26, 414-419.

Terry, P. C., Lane, A. M., and Warren, L. (1999). Eating attitudes, body shape perceptions, and mood among elite rowers: effects of age, gender and weight category. *Journal of Science and Medicine in Sport, 2,* 67-77.

Thayer, R. E., Newman, R., and McClain, T. M. (1994). Self-regulation of mood: Strategies for changing a bad mood, raising energy, and reducing tension. *Journal of Personality and Social Psychology, 67,* 910-925.

Thiel, A., Gottfried, H., and Hesse, F. W. (1993). Subclinical eating disorders in male athletes. A study of the low weight category in rowers and wrestlers. *Acta Psychiatrica Scandinavica,* 88, 259–265.

Thompson, R. A., and Sherman, R. T. (1993). *Helping athletes with eating disorders. Champaign, IL: Human Kinetics.*

Trinidad, D. R., and Johnson, C. A. (2001). The association between emotional intelligence and early adolescent tobacco and alcohol use. *Personality and Individual Differences,* 32, 95–105.

Watson, J. C. (2002). Assessing the potential for alcohol-related issues among college student-athletes. Athletic Insight: The Online Journal of Sport Psychology, 4, *http://www.athleticinsight.com*

In: Mood and Human Performance: Conceptual, Measurement...   ISBN 1-60021-269-7
Editor: Andrew M. Lane, pp. 201-216   © 2006 Nova Science Publishers, Inc.

Chapter 10

COMPARISON OF THE PSYCHOLOGICAL EFFECTS OF EXERCISE AND HUMOR

*Attila Szabo**

National Institute for Sport Talent Care, Budapest, Hungary and
Faculty of Natural Sciences, University of Pécs, Hungary

ABSTRACT

The psychological effects of cycling and soap opera humour were investigated in 24 women. Participants were tested in two counterbalanced 20-minute conditions: 1) cycling at 60% of their maximal heart rate reserve and 2) watching an episode of the popular "Friends" series. Reports of 10 measures of affect were obtained 5 minutes before and after the treatments in the lab, as well as 30, 90, and 180 minutes following treatments outside the lab. An activity diary was used in the post-treatment period to assess life events possibly affecting the results. The findings revealed that the watching of a humourous soap could mimic the affective gain gathered with exercise from pre- to post-treatment with the exception of two measures: esteem and vigour. The treatment induced changes in anger, confusion, negative affect, and tension were similar after both treatments. However, fatigue and total mood disturbance were lower whilst vigour and positive affect were higher 30 and 90 minutes post-exercise, showing that the effects of exercise may last longer than the effects of humour. It is concluded that an episode of light-hearted humour could mimic some of the psychological benefits of exercise, but the duration of a number of positive changes are shorter than following exercise.

INTRODUCTION

Effects of Humor on Health

Anecdotal reports (Cousins, 1976; Sobel and Ornstein, 2005) suggest that humor has beneficial effects on physical and mental health. While in science controversy exists about the universality, specificity, and consistency of the positive effects of humor (Martin, 2001), the

---

* Correspondance: Attila Szabo, Ph.D. E-mail: draszabo-office@yahoo.com

therapeutic application of humor has emerged and it is growing rapidly (Zand, Spreen, and La Valle, 1999). Indeed, there are more than 100 references of works linking humor with health and wellness (AATH, 2005).

It is believed that humor yields both physical and psychological benefits (Berk, 2001). Martin (2001) has recently reviewed the empirical connection between humor and domains of physical health. His analysis revealed that humor has analgesic effects that are possibly linked to levels of emotional arousal *regardless of the emotional response*, because stimuli that induced negative emotions were also found to have analgesic effects. Although humor is an important topic in psychoneuroimmunology, Martin (2001) concluded that the connection between humor and immunity is weak, because there are many inconsistencies in the published research. Further, Martin (2001) suggested that a good sense of humor was related to lower blood pressure in women whilst the opposite effects were seen in men. Finally, Martin's review unexpectedly reveals that sense of humor is either unrelated or it is *inversely* related to longevity. The overall conclusions of Martin's (2001) review shed doubt on the overoptimistically prophesized connection between humor and physical health.

The connection between humor and mental well-being appears to be somewhat better substantiated. There is convincing evidence for numerous psychological benefits of humor. For example, several reports suggest that humor may reduce or positively mediate certain affective *states*, such as levels of anxiety (Abel, 1998; Cann, Holt, and Calhoun, 1999; Houston, McKee, Carroll and Marsh, 1998; Moran, 1995; Moran and Massam, 1999; Smith, Ascough, Ettinger, and Nelson, 1971; White and Winzelberg, 1992; Yovetich, Dale, Hudak, 1990), tension (Moran and Massam, 1999; Newman and Stone, 1996; Wooten, 1996), and depression (Beck, 1997; Danzer, Dale, and Klions, 1990; Overholser, 1992; Porterfield, 1987; Thorson, Powell, Sarmany-Schuller, and Hampes, 1997). Most of experimental evidence stems from studies that have adopted an acute (single bout) of humor intervention.

As humor occurs, and it is most effective, in real-world situations, there is need to investigate the validity of humor triggered in laboratory studies. Humor in laboratory studies may be the independent variable that is a stimulus subject to cognitive interpretation. Lack of understanding could lead to dissociation from the stimulus or overt (artificial laughter) or covert (no laughter) responses in social environments. This in turn triggers ambiguity about the correctness of the response (i.e., laughter or no laughter) and may result in negative affect (manifested through tension) related to uncertainty about the response. However, most laboratory research is conducted on an individual basis (non-social context) in which the cognitive interpretation determines the funniness or appeal of the humorous material. This evaluation is dependent on a multidimensional sense of humor (Thorson and Powell, 1993) that includes production, coping with, liking, and approving the humor stimulus. The outcome of the evaluation places the humor stimulus on a continuum ranging from 'extremely funny' to 'not funny at all' that leads to bipolar emotional responses with euphoric feelings at one end and negative emotions at the other end. Finally, these responses, depending on their direction as well as intensity, trigger a chain of physical reactions starting either with laughter/smile (eustress), or tension, uneasiness, and even anger (distress) if the humor is perceived as offensive or hurting. Therefore, in laboratory research it must be ensured that the humor stimulus is perceived as positive, funny, and appealing to the participants studied (refer to Figure 1).

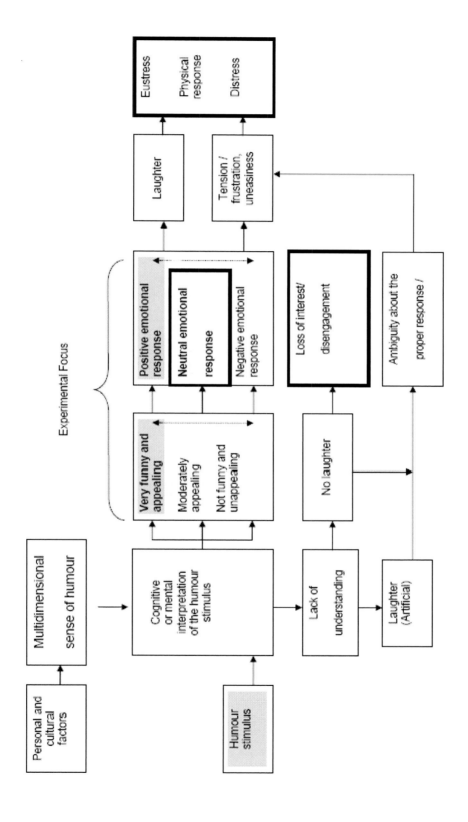

Figure 1.

SIMILARITY IN THE AFFECTIVE BENEFITS
OF HUMOR AND EXERCISE

The acute positive psychological response to appreciated humor is thought to be similar to the response to aerobic exercise (Berk, 2001; Sobel and Ornstein, 2005). Physically, humor that triggers laughter is speculated to result in increased heart rate, reduced muscle tension, increased oxygenation of the blood, and even the release of endorphins (Fry, 1994). It was also speculated that laughter might not be necessary for the release of endorphins since that may occur with a smile also (Kuhn, 1994). The analogy between humor and exercise culminates in Fry's (1992) note that a few minutes of intense laughter could produce physical benefits that are similar to 10-15 minutes of ergometer cycling or rowing.

Psychologically, the effects of exercise are also similar to that of humor. For example, several relatively recent literature reviews concluded that aerobic exercise reduces state anxiety, which is paralleled by positive changes in affect (Berger and Motl, 2000; Biddle, 2000; Biddle and Mutrie, 2001; Ekkekakis and Petruzzello, 1999; O'Connor, Raglin and Martinsen, 2000; Scully, Kremer, Meade, Graham and Dudgeon, 1998). The implication of such a consensus is that exercise is now prescribed for improving mental health (Biddle, Fox and Boutcher, 2000; Morgan, 1997). From another perspective, however, the mental health benefits of exercise could not be universally enjoyed by all, but only by a small fraction of the population that is both able and willing to engage in exercise. This segment of the population probably excludes many elderly and disabled people (Berk, 2001). However, these people could still benefit from various forms of low grade physical activities. Therefore, in appraising the mental health benefit of exercise the actual definition of exercise is important.

In light of the current knowledge about the mental benefits of appreciated humor, it is tempting to prescribe a bout of humor as a limited alternative to a bout of exercise. However, even though the psychological effects of humor and exercise appear to be similar, only few studies made a direct comparison between the two behavioral interventions. Such a planned experimental comparison of the effects of humor and exercise is warranted on theoretical basis. The effects of both, humor and exercise were linked to release and binding of the endogenous opioids (i.e., beta-endorphins) that trigger temporary feelings of euphoria and pain relief (Berk, 2001; Fry, 1992; Sobel and Ornstein, 2005; Steinberg and Sykes, 1985). The distraction theory (Morgan, 1985) also may be a common denominator between humor and exercise since both could results in brief distraction from the routine, hence yielding a 'time-out' effect that could generate psychological gains. Indeed, preliminary results of a study that included three exercise treatments and a humor treatment as control support this conjecture (Snowball and Szabo, 1999). A third, more plausible, explanation may be that psychological gains occur with many personally satisfying experiences (Parente, 2000; Sandlund and Norlander, 2000) and these leisure activities could, of course, include both humor and exercise.

RECENT STUDIES COMPARING THE ACUTE PSYCHOLOGICAL EFFECTS OF HUMOR AND EXERCISE

The first study to compare the acute affective benefits of aerobic exercise and humour was published in the form of an abstract by Snowball and Szabo (1999). These authors revealed that psychological well-being has improved at least as much after a stand-up comedy humour as after three different forms of aerobic exercises (cycling, rowing and running) performed in laboratory at participants' 70% of maximal heart rate reserve. Interestingly, no changes were seen after a control video condition, showing participants geographical sceneries. Therefore, this study was a first to establish that when examining acute psychological benefits, a 30-minute bout of humour may be as good as 30 minutes of aerobic exercise.

In a subsequent study, Szabo (2003) tested the hypothesis that 20-minutes of humour could result in affective benefits comparable to those of a 20-minute bout of aerobic exercise. Using a within-participants research design, Szabo tested 39 university students at a weekly interval for three weeks: running/jogging at self-selected pace, watching a humorous stand-up comedy, and watching a documentary video. Mood and state anxiety were determined 5-minutes before and after each treatment by using the Subjective Exercise Experience Scale (McAuley and Courneya, 1994) and the Spielberger State Anxiety Inventory (Spielberger, Gorsuch, and Luchene, 1970). While the control (documentary) condition did not have significant impact on affect, both humour and exercise have yielded ratings of reduced psychological distress and increased positive well-being. Surprisingly, however, humour exerted greater anxiety-lowering effect than exercise. Based on these results, Szabo carefully and tentatively concluded that a brief session of stand-up comedy humour could induce positive psychological changes that are *at least comparable,* if not superior, to the effects of exercise.

In a more recent laboratory study, Szabo, Ainsworth, and Danks (2005) examined the effects of aerobic exercise in contrast to a light hearted humour, which consisted of the popular "Friends" television series, and an equal duration New Age music appreciation session. In this within-participants experiment the authors tested 20 women four times at weekly intervals. The volunteers were exposed to four 20-minute treatments in a counterbalanced order: 1) stationary cycling at 50% of their maximal heart rate reserve, 2) watching the humorous video, 3) listening to music, and 4) only sitting quietly. Participants' state anxiety and profile of mood states were measured 5-minutes before and 5-minutes after each treatment. Statistically significant decreases in state anxiety were observed in all four conditions. The total mood disturbance also decreased in all but the sitting quietly (control) condition. Their effects sizes, reflecting the meaningfulness of the intervention-induced changes, were highest in response to the light-hearted humour session, followed by music and exercise. Szabo et al. (2005) concluded on the basis of these results that the acute psychological benefits of humour and even music are comparable, if not superior, to the psychological benefits of a bout of aerobic exercise. Indeed, to this point all research shows that the immediate psychological effects of humour and exercise are very similar.

Based on the limited number of studies, practitioners and even investigators may conclude that it is possible to prescribe a session of favored humor instead of exercise when the focus is solely on psychological benefits. This is an attractive speculation for many who cannot or do not want to exercise. However, one unresolved dilemma triggers a note of caution before making any recommendation and that is the lack of knowledge about the *magnitude* and, perhaps more importantly, the *duration* of the psychological benefits of these two behavioural interventions. A further complication arises in comparing the duration of the effects of the two interventions because the keeping of the participants in the laboratory for a prolonged period (i.e. up to 3 hours) may result in frustration canceling out any psychological changes due to the interventions. Possibly, the only solution to this problem is to adopt a mixed laboratory experiment and in-situ field study research design whereby participants go back into their natural environment after exposure to the treatments and continue with their normal daily routine. At various intervals they would then receive an experimenter-delivered signal to complete the same questionnaires that they did complete in the laboratory. This method would allow the researcher to gauge the same variable not only pre- and post-intervention in the lab, but also after various intervals outside laboratory. The external validity of such method could be expected to be high since after a bout of exercise in the gym, for example, people do go back into their usual life routine.

In the subsequent sections, an original piece of research is presented. This research combines laboratory research with an experience sampling -based field study to compare the magnitude and the duration of the psychological benefits of exercise and humor. Like in the previous studies by the author, a within participant design was used in which participants serve as their own control in relation to both experimental period and experimental condition. Again, an episode of the Friends series was used as this programme is proposed to represent light-hearted humor and something that most individuals will have everyday-access. Pilot studies showed high preference for this form of humor.

LABORATORY AND FIELD RESEARCH COMBINED

Method

Participants

Twenty-five university students were recruited through a campus-wide call for female volunteers to participate in the study. This sample size was determined on the basis of a power analysis that indicated that using a 95% confidence interval with a moderate (target) effects size ($d = .50$) there was an 80% chance of detecting statistically significant effects. All participants signed an informed consent form before taking part in the study. Their mean age was 19.5 years ($SD=1.1$). All participants reported to be in good health, belonged to the Caucasian ethnic group and were native speakers of English. All reported regular involvement in some form(s) of physical activity at least once per week. One participant did not show up for her scheduled tests. Therefore, the final sample consisted of 24 women. For the proposed design the minimum sample size was calculated to be N=20 (Schutz and Gessaroli, 1987). As a consequence of losing one participant, the power was slightly reduced from 80% to 78%.

Materials

Momentary psychological states were assessed with two instruments. The first was a shortened version of the Profile of Mood States (POMS) inventory (Grove and Prapavessis, 1992). This version of the POMS is a 40-item questionnaire that has seven subscales: anger, confusion, depression, esteem, fatigue, tension and vigor. The respondents are required to indicate how they feel at the moment of completion on a 5-point rating scale, ranging from 0 (not at all) to 4 (very strongly). Five subscales measure negative moods while two gauge positive moods. The POMS also yields a "total mood disturbance" (TMD) score, which is obtained by subtracting the sum of the ratings on the positive subscales from the sum of the ratings on the negative subscales (Grove and Prapavessis, 1992). Reliability coefficients originally reported for the seven subscales of this version of the POMS ranged between Cronbach α = .66 to .95.

The second instrument used for measuring affect was a modified version of the Well-Being Questionnaire (WBQ) employed by Gauvin and Szabo (1992). This instrument contained six positive (happy, pleased. energetic, joyful, relaxed, and enjoyment or having fun) and eight negative (angry or hostile, irritated, frustrated, guilty, stressed, depressed or blue, unhappy, and worried or anxious) mood states that are rated on a 7-point Likert scale ranging from *not at all* to *extremely much*. Diener and Emmons (1985) reported that such mood adjectives represent the dimensions of positive affect (PA) and negative affect (NA) and have high internal consistency (Cronbach α = .90). Thus, the WBQ yielded general measures of PA and NA that complemented the eight other dependent measures generated with the POMS.

The exercising equipment was a Monark (Model: 824E ERGOMEDIC) ergometer. Participants' heart rate during exercise was monitored with a Polar (Model: PolarBeat GBR 161302 B) heart rate monitor. A commercially videotaped episode of the "Friends" (Series 5, Episode 14; Warner Brothers Television, 1999) series was the humour selected as the humour intervention for this study. A pilot study comprising 10 female university students were shown several humorous materials, including stand-up comedy, candid camera, and comic soap episodes. They were asked to indicate their preference on the basis of familiarity and humour content as well as on the basis of personal appeal. These young women came from the same student population as the participants in the current research. The humorous video was presented with a Philips (Model: VIDEOPLUS) colour TV and VCR combined unit.

An open-ended *activity diary,* covering three post-intervention periods (5 to 30, 30 to 60 and 60 to 180 minutes), was used to tap the activities participants undertook after leaving the lab. It was conjectured that this information would be beneficial in identifying stressful (both positive and negative) events that could substantially influence the data. To ensure that participants would not forget completing this diary and the questionnaires at the specified times, they were all given a Motorola (Model: MINI *Call*) pager. This pager was used to send signals to the participants to complete the questionnaires at three post-experimental periods after they have left the laboratory (i.e., 30, 60, and 180 minutes).

Procedure

Each participant was tested twice in a counterbalanced order. The two test-sessions were scheduled at least one week apart and at about the same time of the day. All tests were performed between 9.00 and 16.00 h. In both sessions participants completed the POMS and the WBQ five minutes before and five minutes after the interventions in the laboratory, as well as 30, 90, and 180 minutes after interventions, upon the signal received from the pager, outside the laboratory. The latter questionnaires were returned along with the pager and the completed activity diary to the experimenters within 48 hours following testing. The two interventions consisted of cycling on an ergometer at 60% maximal heart rate reserve (MHRR), which was calculated by using the *Karvonen formula* (MHRR = [(220 - age) – resting heart rate] * .60 + resting heart rate (Karvonen, Kentala, and Mustala, 1957), and watching the humorous episode of *Friends*. Both treatments lasted for 20 minutes in a humidity and temperature-monitored laboratory. In the cycling session, participants were given a 2-min warm-up and a 2-min cool-down that was contained within the total of 20-minute exercise period. They were asked to maintain their heart rates within the 10% range of their 60% MHRR throughout the exercise session. This exercise intensity appears to be optimal for psychological benefits (Ekkekakis and Petruzzello, 1999). To maintain target exercise intensity, each participant received continuous feedback from the heart rate monitor that was also visible to the experimenter. The contact between the participant and the experimenter was limited to the greeting period at the beginning and the debriefing period at the end of each session. During the actual test-phase the participants were left alone in the laboratory while the experimenter continuously observed them via a one-way mirror from an adjacent observation room.

Data Analyses

The Statistical Package for Social Sciences (SPSS) software (version 11.0) was used for the analysis of the data. The main test consisted of a two (experimental conditions) by five (data collection periods) multivariate repeated measures analysis of variance (MRM-ANOVA) using the method described by Schutz and Gessaroli (1987). This test provides reasonable power and guards against Type I error. In parallel with the multivariate analysis, the test also calculates the univariate effects for each dependent measure as part of its SPSS routine. Since the assumption of sphericity was violated in the current data, the Greenhouse-Geisser correction method (Field, 2000) was applied for all the univariate tests, even though Schutz and Gessaroli (1987) consider this method rather conservative. The statistically significant interactions were followed-up with Tukey's *honestly significant difference* (HSD) test (Vincent, 1999), because it is more powerful than the Bonferroni method when a large number of comparisons are made. On the other hand, the significant main effects were followed-up with *simple contrasts* that could be generated, and Bonferroni corrected, in conjunction with the SPSS repeated measures ANOVA tests.

RESULTS

The MRM-ANOVA yielded significant multivariate main effects for condition and period (Wilks' Lambda = .278, $F (10, 14) = 3.64$, $p < .01$, and Wilks' Lambda = .326, $F (40, 316.6) = 2.73$, $p < .01$, respectively) as well as a significant condition by period interaction

(Wilks' Lambda = .450, F (40,316.6) = 1.86, $p <$ .01). Subsequently, the univariate ANOVAs were examined for the 10 dependent measures. Since Mauchly's test of sphericity violation (Field, 2000) was found to be significant in seven out of ten cases, the Greenhouse-Geisser correction method was used in all univariate repeated measures ANOVAs. The means and standard deviations for all dependent measures in the five periods of the two experimental sessions are illustrated in Table 1.

Table 1. Illustrates the means and standard deviations (in brackets) of 10 dependent measures at five periods in two experimental conditions

Measure	Condition	Pre-5-min	Post-5-min	Post-30-min	Post-90-min	Post-180-min
Anger	Exercise	2.3 (2.3)	0.6 (1.0)	0.7 (1.0)	1.6 (2.2)	1.8 (2.7)
	Humor	2.2 (2.6)	1.0 (1.9)	1.3 (1.4)	2.0 (2.6)	1.5 (2.1)
Confusion	Exercise	2.5 (3.1)	1.4 (2.3)	2.0 (2.6)	1.9 (2.5)	2.3 (2.4)
	Humor	2.5 (2.3)	1.5 (1.8)	2.5 (2.2)	1.9 (2.8)	2.4 (2.0)
Depression	Exercise	1.2 (1.6)	0.7 (1.6)	1.0 (1.6)	1.5 (2.4)	1.3 (2.0)
	Humor	1.5 (3.1)	1.0 (2.1)	0.8 (1.5)	1.4 (3.1)	1.2 (1.7)
Esteem	Exercise	10.9 (2.2)	13.3 (2.1)	11.6 (2.4)	10.7 (2.1)	11.0 (2.3)
	Humor	10.4 (1.7)	11.4 (1.8)	10.5 (2.3)	10.0 (1.8)	10.6 (2.2)
Fatigue	Exercise	5.8 (3.7)	4.8 (3.7)	3.8 (2.8)	4.3 (3.0)	5.6 (3.8)
	Humor	6.3 (4.2)	4.5 (4.0)	5.6 (3.0)	6.6 (4.0)	5.7 (3.7)
Negative Affect	Exercise	12.7 (3.6)	9.8 (2.0)	11.3 (4.3)	11.3 (3.5)	12.8 (4.6)
	Humor	13.6 (6.1)	11.0 (4.4)	12.3 (4.4)	13.3 (6.6)	13.0 (4.9)
Positive Affect	Exercise	18.5 (5.1)	22.3 (5.6)	21.2 (6.6)	20.2 (5.5)	18.1 (7.0)
	Humor	18.5 (6.3)	22.1 (5.8)	17.6 (6.1)	16.1 (5.5)	17.3 (6.6)
Tension	Exercise	3.4 (2.3)	1.0 (1.3)	1.9 (2.3)	1.5 (1.6)	2.5 (3.2)
	Humor	3.1 (2.5)	1.0 (1.8)	2.6 (3.3)	2.6 (3.0)	2.9 (3.7)
TMD	Exercise	-2.2 (9.3)	-15.2 (7.8)	-11.0 (12.2)	-8.2 (13.1)	-3.6 (12.5)
	Humor	-.9 (12.8)	-10.2 (9.6)	-4.0 (10.2)	-.09 (15.0)	-2.8 (13.0)
Vigor	Exercise	6.3 (3.2)	10.1 (3.7)	8.7 (4.2)	8.2 (3.9)	6.2 (4.5)
	Humor	6.4 (3.5)	6.7 (3.2)	5.4 (3.1)	4.1 (3.2)	5.9 (3.9)

The univariate repeated measures ANOVA results, based on Greenhouse-Geisser adjusted degrees of freedom, confirmed a significant condition by period interaction for five out of ten measures (Figure 2, A-E): esteem (F (3.03, 69.70) = 2.99, $p <$ .04); fatigue (F (3.14, 72.16) = 2.63, $p <$ .05); positive affect (F (2.40, 55.29) = 3.48, $p <$ .03); vigour (F (3.26, 68.75) = 6.97, $p <$ .001; and total mood disturbance (F (3.26, 75.08) = 2.82, $p <$ .04). These interactions were followed up with Tukey's HSD pairwise comparisons in which the alpha was set to .05.

Since the condition by period interaction was only confirmed for five measures, the main effects were examined for the remaining five dependent variables. Repeated measures ANOVAs, using Greenhouse-Geisser correction, yielded significant *period* main effects for four out of five measures: negative affect (F (3.77, 72.04) = 11.24, $p <$ .001), anger (F (2.38, 54.81) = 8.67, $p <$ .001), tension (F (2.50, 57.56) = 6.86, $p <$ .001) and confusion (F (3.19, 73.43) = 3.03, $p <$ .03). For the depression subscale of the POMS the period main effect did not reach the set level of statistical significance, but a trend was evident is this measure as well (F (2.79, 64.08) = 2.20, $p <$ .10). These results, including between period differences, are shown in Figure 3 (A-E).

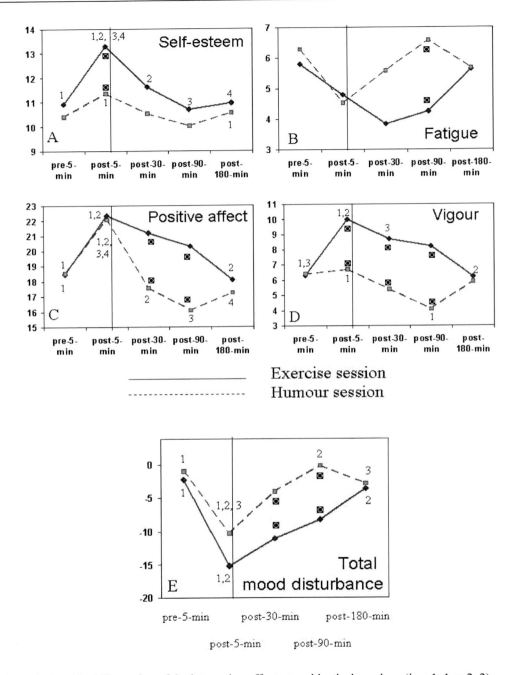

Figure 2. Graphical illustration of the interaction effects: two identical numbers (i.e., 1, 1 or 2, 2) represent statistically significant "within-treatment" effects between those periods where the numbers appear, whereas the ◙ symbol identifies "between treatments" differences that were found to be statistically significant (Tukey's tests, p< .05). The vertical line at post-5-min. marks the separation between the periods in and out of the lab. The continuous line represents the exercise session whereas the interrupted line stands for the humour session.

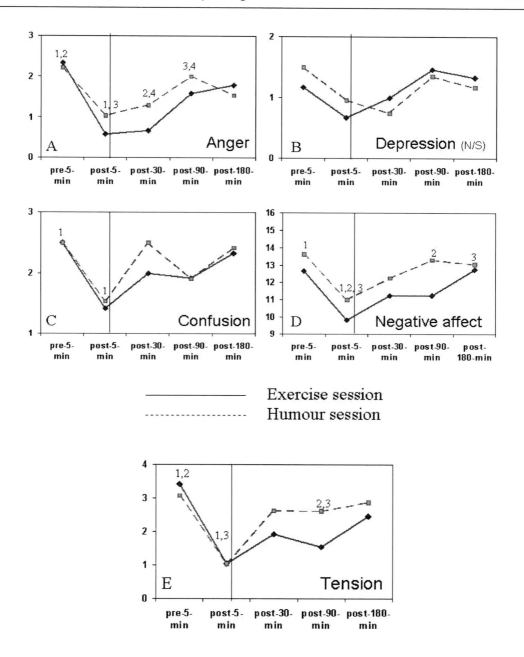

Figure 3. Graphical illustration of the period main effects: identical numbers identify the statistically significant (Bonferroni corrected simple contrasts, p< .05) session period differences that occurred in both treatments. (Separate lines are used to illustrate the similarity in the pattern of changes in both treatments.) The vertical line drawn at post-5-min marks the separation between the lab and the outside laboratory sampling periods. The continuous line represents the exercise session whereas the interrupted line stands for the humour session

Examination of the Activity Diaries

The activity diaries, completed upon the reception of every pager signal, were content analyzed. No affect-mediating or stressful events were reported by any of the participants after either experimental condition. Therefore, it was assumed that participants undertook relatively similar patterns of activities after both exercise and humour sessions and that residual effect in affect after both test sessions was primarily due to the previous experimental intervention.

DISCUSSION

The results of this study agree with previous research findings that both acute exercise (Berger and Motl, 2000; Biddle, 2000; Biddle and Mutrie, 2001; Ekkekakis and Petruzzello, 1999; O'Connor et al., 2000; Scully et al., 1998) and an episode of humour (Abel, 1998; Beck, 1997; Cann et al., 1999; Danzer et al., 1990; Houston et al., 1998; Moran, 1995; Moran and Massam, 1999; Newman and Stone, 1996; Overholser, 1992; Porterfield, 1987; Smith et al., 1971; Thorson et al., 1997; White and Winzelberg, 1992; Yovetich et al., 1990; Wooten, 1996) have positive psychological effects. The current results also expand on past research findings by revealing that light-hearted humour stemming from the watching of a humorous TV soap has similar psychological effect to a bout of moderate aerobic exercise. However, the positive changes in affect, resulting from exercise, last longer than the positive effects of humour. In the current study the magnitude of the affective changes seen from pre- to post-intervention in both conditions was not different with the exception of *esteem* and *vigour*. These measures could be associated with feelings of accomplishment (esteem) and exercise-induced vitality (vigour) that could not be generated with the passive form of humour intervention.

Therefore, it appears that the acute affective benefits of exercise and humour may be mediated via different mechanisms. The former, could result from a combination of a brisk tension relief after exercise accompanied by feelings of self-efficacy and/or accomplishment. In contrast, humour may result in tension relief, or relaxation, and possible distraction from mundane tasks and/or concerns. Indeed, the completion of an exercise session also results in residual physiological changes, such as enhanced circulation and decreased tension, through which the exerciser feels invigorated and reports feeling positive until total recovery from exercise-induced activation takes place.

This explanation could account for the observed differences in some measures that were statistically significantly different between exercise and humour sessions at 30 and at 90 minutes following the interventions. These measures were: Positive affect, vigour, total mood disturbance, and at 90 minutes only fatigue (Figure 2 B-E). Such findings could be interpreted as evidence for longer persistence of the positive changes resulting from exercise in contrast to humour in at least some of the measured indices.

It should be appreciated that this study was of composite nature, including both a controlled laboratory experiment and a field study (separated by the vertical line in the plots included in Figures 2 and 3) following the participants' departure from the laboratory. The majority of research to date relies on pre- to post-treatment measurements because once the participants leave the laboratory control over environmental influences fades away. However, such studies are necessary because in the real life situation when the person leaves the gym or the counseling room the same environmental influences will affect the "treated" person. More precisely, the participants return into their *natural world*. Therefore, the experimenter could only assume that there may be a similar set of activities, ensuing in similar situational effects, following both interventions (i.e., humour and exercise). This assumption was justified in this study on the basis of the information extracted from the participants' activity diaries.

The magnitude and the pattern of changes in negative affect, anger, confusion, tension and a similar but non-significant trend in depression were identical in both humour and exercise sessions (Figure 3, A-E). These findings suggest that negative mood has decreased equally in response to both treatments. Indeed, anger decreased after the two interventions and remained significantly lower even after 30 minutes in contrast to the pre-treatment scores. Although not significant statistically, a trend in lower post-intervention depression scores was also evident. Confusion decreased from pre- to post-interventions only. Negative affect decreased from pre-to post-intervention, but it was no longer significant 30 minutes after the treatments. Therefore, it may be concluded that favourable changes in measures of negative affect occur in response to both humour and exercise intervention. However, measures of negative affect may have been low from the beginning (i.e. a floor effect). While the magnitude of the effects generated by the two treatments appeared to be equal, their duration was limited to the immediate post-intervention period lasting at best up to 30-minutes (i.e., decreased anger).

Some limitations of the current study need to be addressed as well. First, studying only young female students raises a question mark with regard to the generalizability of the results to other populations. Second, no manipulation check for humor (or laughter) was made as humor material was chosen through a pilot study based on a sample from the same population. Yet any effect the overlooking of manipulation check may have had, would only minimize (rather than amplify) the humor's effects. Third, a no-intervention control group was not present (that is highly difficult to select since research has shown that even simply sitting quietly has an affect-improving effect (Focht and Hausenblas, 2001; Jambor, Rudisill, Weekes, and Michaud, 1994; Raglin and Morgan, 1987)). Last, some researchers could critique the study for not testing individual sense of humor that in some instances may have an impact (Porterfield, 1987). However, in this research we used a pilot study through which it was assured that the humor used was funny and appealing (regardless of sense of humor or laughter) for this population. Thus the experimental focus was placed on the (pre-tested and not simply assumed) ascertained positive impact of the humor stimulus.

In summary, this research demonstrates that compared to pre-intervention scores both behaviours, humour watching and aerobic exercise, have beneficial psychological effects. In the case of measures of negative affect, anger, confusion and tension these effects were restricted to the immediate post-intervention period lasting up to 30 minutes and were of equal magnitude after both humour and exercise sessions. In the case of esteem and vigour positive changes from pre- to post-treatment were seen only after the exercise session and these effects were limited to the 5-minute post-exercise period in esteem but they lasted up to 90-minutes post-exercise in case of vigour. Positive affect increased and total mood disturbance decreased after both interventions but the positive effects were sustained 30 and/or 90 minutes respectively, after exercise only. These results show that some of the positive effects of exercise last longer than that of humour.

CONCLUSION ABOUT THE PSYCHOLOGICAL EFFECTS OF EXERCISE AND HUMOR

It may be concluded that light-hearted humour could mimic the immediate (post-treatment) positive psychological changes induced by a single bout of moderate aerobic exercise. However, favourable changes in some positive states of affect like esteem and vigour may only be triggered by exercise. These feelings may be related to the active accomplishment provision aspects of exercise and could not be seen during passive watching of humour. Also, the duration of some of the positive changes seen with both interventions appear to last longer after exercise than after humour. It is recommended that future research should examine further the acute mental benefits of humour. However, in light of the well-established physical health benefits of exercise, in addition to favourable psychological benefits, exercise should be recommended whenever possible. Finally, future research with focus on maximizing the psychological benefits may wish to examine whether the psychological effects of humour and exercise may be additive.

REFERENCES

AATH. (2005). *Purpose of the Association for Applied and Therapeutic Humour.* Retrieved July 13, 2005, from *http://www.aath.org/ezine/index.html#topic03*.

Abel, M.H. (1998). Interaction of humour and gender in moderating relationships between stress outcomes. *The Journal of Psychology*, 132, 267-277.

Beck, C.T. (1997). Humor in nursing practice: a phenomenological study. *International Journal of Nursing Studies*, 34, 346-352.

Berger, B.G., and Motl, R.W. (2000). Exercise and mood: A selective review and synthesis of research employing the Profile of Mood States. *Journal of Applied Sport Psychology*, 12, 69-92.

Berk, R.A. (2001). The active ingredients of humor: Psychophysiological benefits and risks for older adults. *Educational Gerontology*, 27, 323-339.

Biddle, S.J.H. (2000). Emotion, mood and physical activity. In S.J.H. Biddle, K.R. Fox, and S.H. Boutcher (Eds.), *Physical activity and psychological well-being* (pp. 63-87). London: Routledge.

Biddle, S.J.H., and Mutrie N. (2001). Psychology of physical activity. London: Routledge.

Biddle, S.J.H., Fox, K.R., and Boutcher, S.H. (Eds). (2000). *Physical activity and psychological well-being.* London: Routledge.

Cann, A., Holt, K., and Calhoun, L.G. (1999). The roles of humor and sense of humor in responses to stressors. *HUMOR: International Journal of humor Research*, 12, 177-193.

Cousins, N. (1976). Anatomy of an illness (as perceived by the patient). *New England Journal of Medicine*, 295, 1458-1463.

Danzer, A., Dale, J.A., and Klions, H.L. (1990). Effects of exposure to humorous stimuli on induced depression. *Psychological Reports*, 66, 1027-1036.

Diener, E., and Emmons, R.A. (1985). The independence of positive and negative affect. *Journal of Personality and Social Psychology*, 47, 1105-1117.

Ekkekakis, P., andPetruzzello, S.J. (1999). Acute aerobic exercise and affect: Current status, problems and prospects regarding dose-response. *Sports Medicine*, 28, 337-374.

Field, A. (2000). Discovering Statistics Using SPSS for Windows. London: SAGE.

Focht, B.C., andHausenblas, H.A. (2001). Influence of quiet rest and acute aerobic exercise performed in naturalistic environment on selected psychological responses. *Journal of Sport and Exercise Psychology*, 23, 108-121.

Fry, W. F. Jr. (1992). The physiological effects of humor, mirth, and laughter. *Journal of the American Medical Association*, 267, 1857-1858.

Fry, W. F. Jr. (1994). The biology of humor. *HUMOR: International Journal of humor Research*, 7, 111-126.

Gauvin, L., andSzabo, A. (1992). Application of the experience sampling method to the study of the effects of exercise withdrawal on well-being. *Journal of Sport and Exercise Psychology*, 14, 361-374.

Grove, J.R., and Prapavessis, H. (1992). Preliminary evidence for the reliability and validity of an abbreviated Profile of Mood States. *International Journal of Sport Psychology*, 23, 93-109.

Houston, D.M., McKee, K.J., Carroll, L., and Marsh, H. (1998). Using humor to promote psychological well-being in residential homes for older people. *Aging and Mental Health*, 2, 328-332.

Jambor, E.R., Rudisill, M.E., Weekes, E.M., andMichaud, T.J. (1994). Association among fitness components, anxiety, and confidence following aerobic training and aquarunning. *Perceptual and Motor Skills*, 78, 595-602.

Karvonen, M., Kentala, K., and O. Mustala, O. (1957). The effects of training heart rate: a longitudinal study. *Annales Medicinae Experimentalis et Biologiae Fenniae*. 35, 307-315.

Kuhn, C.C. (1994). The stages of laughter. *Journal of Nursing Jocularity*, 4, 34-35.

Martin, R.A. (2001). Humor, laughter, and physical health: Methodological issues and research findings. *Psychological Bulletin*, 127, 504-519.

McAuley, E., andCourneya, K. S. (1994). The Subjective Exercise Experience Scale (SEES): Development and preliminary validation. *Journal of Sport and Exercise Psychology*, 16, 163-177.

Moran, C.C. (1995). Short-term mood change, perceived funniness, and the effect of humor stimuli. *Behavioral Medicine*, 20, 32-38.

Moran, C.C., and Massam, M.M. (1999). Differential influences of coping humor and humor bias on mood. *Behavioral-Medicine*, 25, 36-42

Morgan, W.P. (1985). Affective beneficence of vigorous physical activity. *Medicine and Science in Sports and Exercise*, 17, 94-100.

Morgan, W.P. (Ed.). (1997). *Physical activity and mental health*. Washington DC: Taylor and Francis.

Newman, G.A., and Stone, A.A. (1996). Does humor moderate the effects of experimentally-induced stress? *Annals of Behavioral Medicine*, 18, 101-109.

O'Connor, P.J., Raglin, J.S., andMartinsen, E.W. (2000). Physical activity, anxiety and anxiety disorders. *International Journal of Sport Psychology*, 31, 136-155.

Overholser, J.C. (1992). Sense of humor when coping with life stress. *Personality and Individual Differences*, 13, 799-804.

Parente, D. (2000). Influence of aerobic and stretching exercise on anxiety and sensation-seeking mood state. *Perceptual and Motor Skills*, 90, 347-348.

Porterfield, A.L. (1987). Does sense of humor moderate the impact of life stress on psychological and physical well-being? *Journal of Research in Personality*, 21, 306-317.

Raglin, J.S., and Morgan W.P. (1987). Influence of exercise and quiet rest on state anxiety and blood pressure. *Medicine and Science in Sports and Exercise*, 19, 456-463.

Sandlund, E.S., and Norlander, T. (2000). The effects of tai chi chuan relaxation and exercise on stress responses and well-being: An overview of research. *Journal of Stress Management*, 7, 139-149.

Schutz, R.W., and Gessaroli, M.E. (1987). The analysis of repeated measures designs involving multiple dependent variables. *Research Quarterly for Exercise and Sport*, 58, 132-149.

Scully, D., Kremer J., Meade, M.M., Graham, R., and Dudgeon, K. (1998). Physical exercise and psychological well-being: A critical review. *British Journal of Sports Medicine*, 32, 111-120.

Smith, R.E., Ascough, J.C., Ettinger, R.F., and Nelson, D.A. (1971). Humor, anxiety, and task performance. *Journal of Personality and Social Psychology*, 19, 243-246.

Snowball, J., and Szabo, A. (1999). Anxiety, affect and exercise: Preliminary evidence lends support to the Distraction Hypothesis. *Journal of Sport Sciences*, 17, 67-68.

Sobel, D. S., and Ornstein, R. (2005). Good humor, good health. Retrieved July 13, 2005, from *http://www.healthy.net/scr/article.asp?lk=P8andId=193*.

Spielberger, C.D., Gorsuch, R.L., and Luchene, R.E. (1970). *Manual for the state-trait anxiety inventory.* Palo Alto, CA: Consulting Psychologists.

Steinberg, H., and Sykes, E.A. (1985). Introduction to symposium on endorphins and behavioural processes: Review of literature on endorphins and exercise. *Pharmacology Biochemistry and Behavior,* 23, 857-862.

Szabo, A. (2003). The acute effects of humor and exercise on mood and anxiety. *Journal of Leisure Research,* 35(2), 152-162.

Szabo, A., Ainsworth, S.E., and Danks, P.K. (2005). Experimental comparison of the psychological benefits of aerobic exercise, humor, and music. *Humor: International Journal of Humor Research,* 18, 235-246.

Thorson, J.A., and Powell, F.C. (1993). Development and validation of a multidimensional sense of humor scale. *Journal of Clinical Psychology*, 49, 13-23.

Thorson, J.A., Powell, F.C., Sarmany-Schuller, I., and Hampes, W.P. (1997). Psychological health and sense of humor. *Journal of Clinical Psychology*, 53, 605-619.

Vincent, W.J. (1999). *Statistics in kinesiology.* Champaign, IL: Human Kinetics

White, S., and Winzelberg A. (1992). Laughter and stress. *HUMOR: International Journal of humor Research,* 5, 343-355.

Wooten, P. (1996). Humor: An antidote for stress. *Holistic Nursing Practice*, 10, 49-56.

Yovetich, N.A., Dale, J.A., and Hudak, M.A. (1990). Benefits of humor in reduction of threat-induced anxiety. *Psychological Reports*, 66, 51-58.

Zand, J., Spreen, A.N., and La Valle, J.B. (1999). *Smart medicine for healthier living.* Garden City Park, NY: Avery Publishing.

In: Mood and Human Performance: Conceptual, Measurement... ISBN 1-60021-269-7
Editor: Andrew M. Lane, pp. 217-231 © 2006 Nova Science Publishers, Inc.

Chapter 11

MOOD STATE CHANGES DURING AN EXPEDITION TO THE SOUTH POLE: A CASE STUDY OF A FEMALE EXPLORER

Juliette C. Lloyd[1], Charles R. Pedlar[1]*,
Andrew M. Lane[2] and Greg P. Whyte[1]
[1]English Institute of Sport
[2]School of Sport, Performing Arts and Leisure,
University of Wolverhampton, UK

ABSTRACT

Solo travel to the Poles represents a significant physiological and psychological challenge, requiring a large volume of arduous exercise in extreme conditions. The case study presented investigated mood state changes of a female explorer travelling solo and unaided to the South Pole. During the 44-day expedition, the explorer logged the distance covered each day and the duration of time spent performing physical work. Mood assessments using the Brunel Mood Scale (BRUMS) indicated a period of high tension at the beginning of the expedition; a slight increase in anger at the end of the trip, a progressive reduction in vigour and increase in fatigue set against a backdrop of relatively stable confusion and depression scores. This account may be applicable when planning future expeditions of this nature as it highlights the nature of mood states during adverse conditions. Teaching athletes mood regulation strategies to help them cope with extreme negative mood could not only enhance the quality of their expedition but also improve performance.

---

* Address correspondence to Charles Pedlar, St Mary's College High Performance Centre, Waldegrave Road, Twickenham, TW1 4SX, UK charles.pedlar@eis2win.co.uk

INTRODUCTION

"First you fall in love with Antarctica, and then it breaks your heart." - Kim Stanley Robinson" (taken from *http://www.70south.com/resources/quotes* April 11th 2005)

"Polar exploration is at once the cleanest and most isolated way of having a bad time which has been devised... There are many reasons which send men to the Poles, and the Intellectual Force uses them all. But the desire for knowledge for its own sake is the one which really counts and there is no field for the collection of knowledge which at the present time can be compared to the Antarctic. Exploration is the physical expression of the Intellectual Passion. And I tell you, if you have the desire for knowledge and the power to give it physical expression, go out and explore. If you are a brave man you will do nothing: if you are fearful you may do much, for none but cowards have need to prove their bravery. Some will tell you that you are mad, and nearly all will say, 'What is the use' For we are a nation of shopkeepers, and no shopkeeper will look at research which does not promise him a financial return within a year. And so you will sledge nearly alone, but those with whom you sledge will not be shopkeepers: that is worth a good deal. If you march your Winter Journeys you will have your reward, so long as all you want is a penguin's egg."
(taken from http://www.gdargaud.net/Humor/QuotesPolar.html *April 11th 2005)*

An Antarctic expedition represents one of the most fearsome challenges of all the feats of human endurance. The quotations above indicate some of the emotions and coping strategies used by explorers during an expedition. The present study assessed mood state responses during a polar expedition to the South Pole. Completing a solo expedition to the South Pole is akin to attaining a hugely important personal goal; the goal is difficult to achieve and contains a number of factors that are beyond the control of the individual. The individual is aware the challenge will be physically demanding and will involve dealing with extreme environmental conditions, but will only know the true extent to which factors are influential during the expedition. This, of course, makes preparation difficult.

There are aspects of studying mood changes during an Antarctic expedition relevant to the study of mood in other achievement settings. Arguably an Antarctic expedition is a unique experience, however, it could be said that each individual's pursuit of a highly important personal goal represents a personal Antarctic expedition. Athletes seeking to achieve Olympic medals are faced with difficult tasks; factors that will be highly important to success are not fully understood until the competition is underway. It is not surprising that the preparation for such challenges involves athletes undergoing intense training. Indeed, the study of mood state responses to intense training among athletes who treat sport competition seriously reveals that some athletes experience highly disturbed responses (Jurimae, Maestu, Purge, Jurimae, and Soot, 2002; Morgan, Brown, Raglin, O'Conner, and Ellickson, 1987; Raglin, 2001). It is with this in mind that the present study seeks to explore mood state responses to intense and persistent exercise in extreme conditions. A recent review of mood responses in extreme conditions highlighted that performing exercise under extreme conditions is psychologically stressful with increased negative mood (Lane, Terry, Stevens, Barney, and Dinsdale, 2004).

The study of mood in extreme environments should consider how mood states could change during repeated bouts of exercise. The expected trend is for unpleasant mood states to increase during an expedition. Previous research investigating mood state changes during performance indicates that the greatest variation occurs in fatigue and vigour (Lane, Whyte,

Shave, Barney, Wilson, and Terry, 2003; Lane, Whyte, Shave, and Wilson, 2003). A reduction in vigour and increase in fatigue is a normal response to hard exercise (Berger, Motl, Butki, Martin, Wilkinson, and Owen, 1999; Hooper, MacKinnin, and Hanrahan, 1997). Although the vigour-fatigue relationship typically shows an inverse relationship, Lane and Terry (2000) pointed out that this tends to be moderate in strength. A further exploration of the vigour-fatigue relationship shows that in some cases, vigour and fatigue appear unrelated. For example, research shows that exercise is associated with increased vigour and increased fatigue (Lane, Mills, and Terry, 1998; Lane, Firth, and Terry, 2002). It is possible that the relationship between fatigue and vigour is low following a single bout of long intense exercise. Lane, Whyte, George, Shave, Barney, and Terry (2004) found that individuals used self-talk to maintain a sense of vigour as a strategy to offset running fatigue during marathon performance. It is interesting to note that when marathon runners were asked how they felt at the worst part of the race, many reported feelings of vigour and fatigue simultaneously. Whilst this seems contradictory, evidence suggested that runners used self-talk to maintain vigour as a strategy for coping with increasing sensations of fatigue linked to running a marathon. Therefore, it is important to investigate vigour and fatigue as independent factors and explore the extent to which vigour can buffer potentially debilitating perceptions of fatigue.

Research to explore changes in other mood states during a single bout of intense exercise tends to show less variation. Changes in other unpleasant mood states such as depression and tension tend to be small (Pierce, 2002). However, Lane, Whyte, Shave, and Wilson (2003) demonstrated the interactive effects of depression on the fatigue and vigour scores. Using Lane and Terry's (2000) framework for using Profile of Mood States (McNair, Lorr, and Droppleman, 1971), they indicated that when participants reported symptoms of depressed mood these small scores were reflected in much larger reductions in vigour and extreme increases in fatigue. Depressed mood was also associated with increases in anger, tension and confusion, and therefore contributes to an overall unpleasant and de-motivating mood profile.

Repeated bouts of intense exercise have been associated with negative mood states (Berger et al., 1999; Hooper et al., 1997; Lehmann, Lormes, Opitz-Gress, Steinacker, Netzer, Foster, and Gastmann, 1997). Previous research has emphasised the value in rest when athletes conduct repeated bouts of intense exercise (Lehmann et al., 1997). It is clearly difficult to take adequate rest during an Antarctic expedition, and therefore, research should expect to observe a mood profile associated with overtraining. However, given that extreme explorers expect to experience a negative mood profile during performance at extreme environments, they should have coping strategies in place before starting and therefore mood profiles could be similar to those reported by Lane et al. (2004) in their marathon study. Collectively, the aim of the study was to explore mood state changes to performing in extreme conditions. These data are part of a larger study that investigated relationships between sleep profiles and mood states during the expedition (Pedlar, Lloyd, Lane, Dawson, Emegbo, Stanley, and Whyte, 2006). This chapter focuses on mood data whereas Pedlar et al. focus on the interaction between sleep and mood.

Method

Participant and Background

The participant was a 43-year-old female polar explorer. This was her third expedition to the South Pole, which was undertaken solo.

Mood

The Brunel Mood Scale (BRUMS: Terry, Lane, Lane, and Keohane, 1999, Terry, Lane, and Fogarty, 2003) which assesses anger, confusion, depression, fatigue, tension, and vigour was used. The scale is a derivative of the Profile of Mood States (McNair, Lorr, and Droppleman, 1971, 1992). Anger items include "Bad-tempered" and "Angry"; Confusion items include "Muddled" and "Uncertain"; Depression items include "Depressed" and "Miserable"; Fatigue items include "Sleepy" and "Tired"; Tension items include "Anxious" and "Panicky"; and Vigour items include "Lively" and "Energetic". Items are rated on a 5-point scale anchored by "not at all" (0) and "extremely" (4). Validation of the BRUMS involved 3,361 participants ranging in age from 12-39 years (Terry et al., 1999, 2003).

Performance

The explorer logged the distance covered each day and the duration of time spent performing physical work.

RESULTS

Data were collected from November 3rd 2003 until January 22nd 2004, with the expedition arriving at the South Pole on January 13th, which was the 44th day. Data collection started 20 days before the expedition commenced. There were days when data collection did not take place due to difficult and often unforeseen conditions. For example, no data were collected on Christmas day. Ten sets of mood scores were collected before the expedition started and 33 sets of data were completed during the expedition.

Mood scores during the pre-expedition phase indicate vigour scores tended to fluctuate, reducing progressively for three days, rebounding to the maximum score before yo-yoing and finishing on a relatively low score before the expedition commenced (see Figure 1). Scores for anger, confusion, depression, fatigue and tension remained relatively low with increases in all states on the final completion, five days before the expedition started.

Given the physically demanding nature of the task, a more stable mood state for vigour in particular was desirable. Vigour is a mood state that indicates the ability to use emotional states in an energising way, something that should be a desirable state during performance.

Each day following wake up, the athlete spent approximately 2 hours decamping before the daily activity pattern began. The daily program involved periods of intense physical effort lasting for two or more hours interspersed with inactive periods of rest of between 10 and 15 minutes duration. The day ended with a further two hours making camp, eating and preparing for sleep. Figure 2 shows the mileage covered during the expedition. As Figure 2 illustrates, the distance covered was typically around 10 miles per day in the first half of the expedition and nearer 20 miles per day in the latter half. It should be noted that there was a steady increase in miles covered nearing the end of the expedition.

Mood state changes are analysed by coupling related mood states.

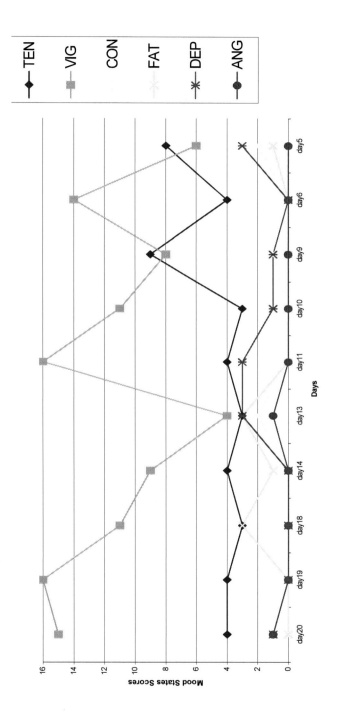

Figure 1. Mood States Scores during Preparation

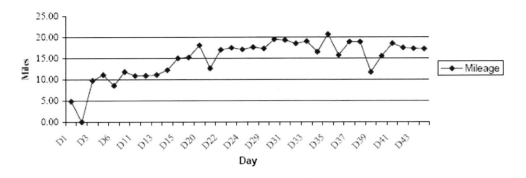

Figure 2. Mileage covered during the expedition

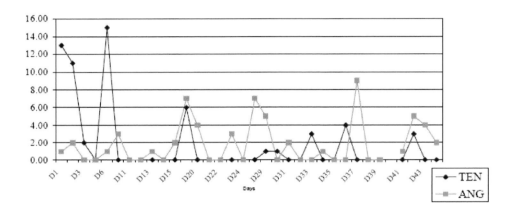

Figure 3. Tension and Anger during the expedition

Tension and Anger

Tension remains relatively stable throughout the expedition (see Figure 3); however, at the beginning of the expedition, days 1, 2 and 6 in particular, it is high. It is possible to explain high tension at the beginning of any expedition due to the uncertainty of a number of factors. These include factors beyond the control of the individual such as the weather, the course, equipment failure and also, the response to these factors, something that is under the control of the individual. Research indicates that tension is associated with uncertainty about coping with task demands (see Lane, 2001). As Figure 3 demonstrates, tension and anger increased sharply on Day 17. Referring to the qualitative diary, on this day the participant discovered that she had lost her vital Argos system (communication/navigation device) and, was going to have to re-trace her steps and find it. During the three subsequent days, mood and performance scores reflect this incident: Mood = increased depression, anger, vigour, and tension scores; Performance = a record mileage recorded. It is also interesting to note that this incident triggered a period of high vigour and low fatigue, but other mood scores returned to their pre-incident level. In her qualitative diaries around this time, she describes enforcing a positive state of mind to prevent her morale spiralling down.

It is worth noting that the days where anger is particularly high are day 17 (Argos incident), day 25 and day 37. Day 37, again she describes being chronically tired, falling asleep whilst "on haunches peeing"; and falling asleep while marching. Further, towards the end of the expedition, it turned into a 'race' situation as the participant was trying to race another woman to become the first solo female to get to the South Pole. Frustration of feeling that goal attainment was unlikely might explain some of anger scores.

Vigour and Fatigue

A closer examination of vigour scores indicates that there appears to be a great deal of fluctuation even though there was a steady decline as the expedition progressed (see Figure 4) for vigour on days 12, 13, 25 and 31. In the qualitative diaries, these days are associated with missing home (husband and son), a telephone call home; noticing how much weight she has lost and feeling massively tired. Vigour is high on days 14, 15, 22, 23, 24, 26, 34. After this time, vigour scores reduce and never return to these levels. It appears from the accompanying diary that the participant successfully counteracted the onset of fatigue with high vigour scores throughout the expedition.

Fatigue scores during the expedition are contained in Figure 4. Looking in more detail, this mood state fluctuates widely throughout the expedition, not surprisingly given the relationship between fatigue and work. Fatigue is particularly high on day 12, (notes missing husband and son in diary); day 20, (record mileage of 44nm/36 hrs, following Argos incident); day 25; day 32; and day 36. Day 32 describes being chronically fatigued in the diary, and how this is affecting her negatively (and dangerously i.e. badly cutting her finger in the tent). On day 41 she describes being "reliant completely on mindset now – body is useless".

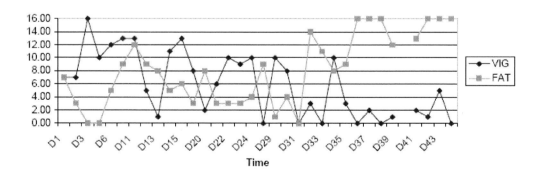

Figure 4. Vigour and Fatigue during the expedition

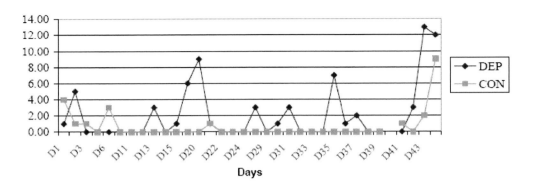

Figure 5. Depression and Confusion during the expedition

Confusion and Depression

Confusion scores (see Figure 5) remain low throughout the expedition apart from the last day when the score soars. Day 44 was arrival day and in the diary, she describes feeling disappointment (at having been beaten to the post), being confused at arrival (unclear where she should go) and feeling like a trespasser because of the lack of any attention upon arrival.

Depression scores remain low apart from day 17 (Argos incident), day 35 and day 43. On day 35 she describes in her diary how her mood changes to despondency, she is shouting at herself a great deal; both of her stoves refuse to work and she has an evening of disaster in the tent where she knocks them both over. It should be noted that the day after, she finds out that someone else has beaten her to the Pole. Her depression score remains high on arrival day.

FURTHER ANALYSIS

In order to try to elucidate some trends from the dataset, it was subjected to further analysis. A comparison of mood data before and after the expedition (see Table 1) indicated a significant overall effect (Wilks Lambda $_{6,36}$ = .63, p < .01, Eta^2 = .37). Table 1 indicates that tension and vigour scores were significantly higher before the expedition and fatigue and anger scores were significantly higher during the expedition.

Given the proposed influence of depressed mood state scores on other mood states, data were re-analysed by depression scores. To do this, data from the depression subscale were coded zero (for all days in which the participant reported zero for each depression item) and depression (days where the participant reported 1 or more on the depression subscale). This approach to analysing depression scores has been advocated by Lane and Terry (2000).

As Table 2 indicates, the overall multivariate effect with depressed mood was associated with increased anger and reduced vigour. There was no difference in other mood states, particularly fatigue that increased significantly during the expedition and tension that was high before the expedition.

Table 1. A comparison of mood state scores before and after the expedition

| | Pre-expedition (n = 10) | | Expedition (n = 33) | | | | |
	M	SD	M	SD	F	P	Partial Eta2
Anger	0.20	0.42	1.82	2.44	4.28	0.04	0.09
Confusion	0.50	0.85	0.67	1.76	0.08	0.78	0.00
Depression	0.80	1.23	8.03	5.34	0.69	0.41	0.02
Fatigue	1.20	1.32	2.15	3.52	17.79	0.00	0.30
Tension	4.60	2.12	1.79	3.90	4.73	0.04	0.10
Vigour	11.00	4.24	6.00	4.89	8.48	0.01	0.17

Wilks Lambda $_{6,36}$ = .63, $p < .01$, Eta^2 = .37

Table 2. Mood state by depression scores before and during an Antarctic expedition

| | No-depression (n =21 | | Depression (n =23) | | | | |
	M	SD	M	SD	F	P	Eta 2
Anger	0.67	1.35	2.18	2.68	5.38	0.03	0.12
Confusion	0.24	0.70	1.00	2.07	2.56	0.12	0.06
Fatigue	6.14	5.28	6.55	6.04	0.05	0.82	0.00
Tension	1.71	3.42	3.14	3.97	1.58	0.22	0.04
Vigour	8.81	5.02	5.59	4.91	4.52	0.04	0.10

Wilks' lambda $_{5,37}$ = .88, $p < .05$, Eta^2 = .32

A comparison of correlations among mood states by depressed mood conditions are contained in Table 3. Relationships among mood states when experienced independently of depressed mood are in bold on one side of the diagonal, with relationships between mood states when experienced with some depressed mood scores in italics on the other diagonal. As Table 3 indicates, consistent relationships were found for the inverse relationship between fatigue and vigour ($r = -.62$, and $r = -.74$). However, relationships between mood states differed significantly. When participants experienced depressed mood, anger correlated significantly with fatigue ($r =.46$), a relationship that was weak in the absence of depressed mood ($r = -.13$). In addition, tension and confusion were closely associated when reporting depression (.80), but showed a weak relationship when independent of depression ($r =.14$).

Table 3. A comparison of relationships among mood states between depressed and non-depressed scores (non-depressed in bold, depressed in italics)

	Anger	Confusion	Fatigue	Tension	Vigour
Anger		0.04	-0.13	-0.04	0.12
Confusion	-0.12		-0.04	0.80*	0.14
Fatigue	0.46*	0.28		-0.27	-0.74*
Tension	-0.23	0.14	-0.35*		-0.27
Vigour	-0.34*	-0.21	-0.62*	0.32*	

* $p < .05$

An analysis of mood state responses by depressed mood scores indicated the influence of depressed mood on the other mood states. The typical response to extreme exercise is increased fatigue, something that occurred regardless of depression. However, when the participant reported feeling depressed, anger correlated with fatigue, whereas fatigue and anger were unrelated in the absence of depression. Lane and Terry (2000) suggested that depression tends to generate an overall negative psychological state. Anger is a powerful mood state and can heighten determination under certain conditions (Lane and Terry, 2000). Anger could be motivating if channelled externally. In the present study, the combination of anger, depression and fatigue represent a potentially debilitating state and not conducive to motivated behaviour.

DISCUSSION

An aim of the study was to explore mood state changes associated with performing in extreme conditions. The present study represents a case study where the explorer reached some of her goals. She successfully completed a solo expedition to the South Pole, but failed in her attempt to become the first female solo explorer to achieve this goal. This should be seen in contrast to mood state responses in which the athlete did not reach the goal. Goal achievement is an aspect of mood dynamics. Using Carver and Scheier's (1990) control process model, which proposes that positive perceptions of goal attainment are associated with positive mood, it is speculated that the explorer maintained a belief that goal attainment was possible, and therefore, this positive evaluation of perceived ability to overcome task difficulty would have influenced the interpretation of mood states.

A discussion of the mood dynamics during the expedition leads to looking at the pre-expedition phase, the early part of the expedition and the latter part of the expedition. It is interesting to observe that statistical analysis of pre and during expedition mood states indicates significant differences in anger, fatigue, tension and vigour but no differences in confusion and depression. During the pre-expedition period, increased tension is expected given the demands of the task. Previous research has demonstrated that tension is related to performance expectation (Lane, 2001). Anger in the present study tends to increase at certain parts of the expedition, although mainly near the end. As expected, the greatest variation in mood states occurred in vigour and fatigue with high levels of fatigue and low levels of vigour experienced over the latter part of the expedition (see Figure 4). The relative stability of depression during the pre-expedition and early expedition phase should be set against the huge variation in other mood states. Lane and Terry (2000) argued that depressed mood is the most important mood dimension and have sought to determine whether increased depression activates other mood states, or whether increased depression is the end point of increases in other mood states (see Lane et al., 2003). Towards the end of the expedition depression increases sharply, coupled with other unpleasant mood states.

Mood states during the latter part of the expedition warrant discussion against Lane and Terry's (2000) proposals on the influence of depression on the other mood states and mood-performance relationships. It should be noted that this research informs on the nature of mood states responses not only to extreme environmental conditions, but also on the nature of mood itself. A key feature of Lane and Terry's work is that depressed mood is associated with unpleasant mood profile and de-motivated behaviour. In the present study, motivated behaviour (see Figure 2) occurred regardless of an overall unpleasant mood profile. Clearly, previous research has demonstrated significant mood-performance relationships (Beedie, Terry, and Lane, 2000). Lane and Chappell (2001) found evidence to show that mood and performance were related in some individuals and not others. We suggest that inconsistent mood-performance relationships can be explained through applying the proposal that the reason mood influences performance is based on the notion that affective content of mood serves a signal function (Lane and Terry, 2000). Mood states themselves do not *cause* poor performance, but contribute information that increases the likelihood of behaviour. In the present study, during the latter part of the expedition the explorer behaved independently of mood states, demonstrating highly motivated behaviour against a backdrop of highly unpleasant mood states. The explorer chose to ignore the affective content of mood when deciding behaviour patterns, a result which suggests that teaching athletes mood-management strategies could be desirable. The explorer in the present study seems highly competent in being able to ignore the information from mood states, something that some athletes in the study by Lane and Chappell (2001) were clearly unable to manage.

Once an athlete has recognised that a mood warrants changing, numerous cognitive and behavioural strategies could be used (Thayer, Newman, and McLain, 1994). Thayer et al. (1994) investigated how people attempt to change bad moods. Common strategies included relying on social support, such as talking to someone, cognitive strategies, such as thinking positively or redirecting attention, distraction techniques, such as listening to music or engaging in pleasant activities, or exercising. The most effective strategies for changing a bad mood were assessed by the sample, and by a panel of 26 psychotherapists. Both groups agreed that active mood management strategies, which included relaxation, stress management, engaging in cognitive activities, and exercise, were most effective strategies. In addition, both groups judged seeking pleasurable activities and distraction as the second most effective category.

Stevens and Lane (2001) used the methodology developed by Thayer et al. (1994) on a sample of 107 athletes. Consistent with findings of Thayer et al. (1994), Stevens and Lane (2001) found that individuals use a range of behavioural and cognitive techniques to alter their mood. Although strategies such as 'change location', 'exercise', and 'listen to music' were strategies common to each mood identified in the POMS, there is a great deal of variation within each of these strategies. Listening to music can be used to increase energy or evoke feelings of relaxation depending on the music that is being listened to.

Gross and his colleagues (Gross, 1998; Gross and John, 2003; Richards and Gross, 2000) have consistently found that cognitive reappraisal is a more positive regulation technique than expressive suppression. Cognitive reappraisal is a deliberate cognitive change that involves interpreting a potentially emotion-eliciting situation in a way that will change the emotional experience and subsequent mood (Lazarus and Alfert, 1964). For example, an athlete training at altitude might view the training as a positive experience to benefit performance instead of dwelling on the difficulty of the task. Expressive suppression involves the inhibition of ongoing emotionally expressive behaviour (Gross, 1998).

Cognitive reappraisal is a more positive strategy to adopt as it is antecedent-focused and so acts as an early intervention, thus reducing the intensity of the experience and reducing the likelihood of a negative behaviour (Gross and John, 2003). Suppression is response-focused and so comes later in the process when mood (and often behaviour) has already changed. It may mask the mood, but may not actually help in reducing the intensity of the feelings. Suppression requires a conscious effort to direct cognitive resources to managing the response, which has been shown to decrease access to memory for the details of the unfolding emotion-eliciting situation while reappraisal was found to put no negative demands on cognitive capacity (Richards and Gross, 2000). Suppression has also been shown to have negative impact on positive moods, by decreasing the intensity of those experiences (Gross and Levenson, 1997).

Recent research has addressed how such strategies can be used to regulate mood. It has been proposed that possibly the most effective strategy for regulating mood is to focus on events that will occur in the future rather than events that occurred in the past (Persson and Sjöberg, 1985; Totterdell, Parkinson, Briner, and Reynolds, 1997). For example, athletes who feel unusually fatigued following training at altitude are more likely to improve their mood by focusing on the process of acclimatisation rather than remembering how they felt after a similar session performed at in a normal training and competitive environment. Focusing on the future and setting achievable goals through acclimatisation should lead to improved mood (Carver and Scheier, 1990). Thus it is suggested that as well as discovering a baseline mood profile for each individual athlete, practitioners should attempt to establish which mood management strategies are favoured, and which are the most effective strategies for the athlete's different moods at different times.

Those working with polar explorers to try to find effective mood management strategies may struggle to do much of their work "in the field" given the unusual and extreme nature of such challenges. Whilst lessons could be taken from previous or similar events, it may be helpful to draw on the experiences of others. One explorer who has given us much insight into the psychological strategies employed on polar expeditions is Pen Hadow, who in 2003, became the first person to walk unaided to the North Geographic Pole. Hadow documented his trip, via The Times newspaper and his book: "Solo. The North Pole: Alone and Unsupported" (Hadow, 2004). Studying these sources gives us an insight into some of the mood management strategies he employed and describing these may provide useful for others. Hadow seemed to have used three strategies for managing his mood. Firstly, he focused on the future a great deal; secondly he used positive talk and thirdly he employed distractions to take his mind away from *"the endless drudgery of putting one foot in front of the other"* (Hadow, 2003, p.228). Focusing on the future (Persson and Sjöberg, 1985; Totterdell et al., 1997) is shown to be an effective strategy for regulating Hadow's mood. In his book, he describes how he used this strategy. *"Almost every day there was a reason for having another milestone, if not in days or weeks, then in miles or degrees of latitude or even days of the month. And if those failed there were always special family occasions..., national holidays or anniversairies....That way, I always had a reason to be positive and looking forward to the day ahead"* (Hadow, 2004, p.271).

Hadow spoke to himself to lift his mood. *"If something good has happened...I've found that if I verbalise it, it carries much more weight than if I just think it. It can change my mood and make me feel better"*. (The Times, April 8th 2003). He also found that speaking to others (Thayer et al. 1994) helped. He spoke to people on the phone but he was aware of the potentially negative effects of this strategy, fears he conveyed to the Times correspondent just before his departure. *"You know I'll be very vulnerable...If you tell me that everyone's getting fed up with my slow progress, it could really tip me over the edge. So it would be great if you could end each conversation on an up-beat note"*. The people whom he did speak to throughout his trip were his "team" and it was these conversations that seemed to have had the greatest positive effect. *"There's been a big development with my verbalising, and it's having an even bigger impact upon my attitude and mood. Now I have The Team – my skis, ski poles and my sledge – and I talk to them at least once an hour. I'm not being funny; I'm really struck by it"* (The Times, April 8th, 2003). It is perhaps because these conversations were one-way that they were so effective and this distinction would be an interesting area of future study.

Distraction (Thayer et al., 1994) was the third mechanism used for mood management. In the following quote we see how Hadow using this skill to prevent him from slipping into a negative mood state. *"When I see the worst rubble field ahead of me..before I have the chance to get angry, I start to think beautiful thoughts, I conjure an image of a very cool man...with a huge Afro hairdo, and he's in a recording studio, leaning over a huge deck of sliding knobs. Some artist is singing away and he's pushing all the knobs to the top level and saying: 'I'm blocking all this out and I'm just gonna listen to the music.' That mechanism distracts me from all the things that might have followed: hatred of the icy world you're going through; the feeling that someone's trying to stop you getting to the Pole, that the world's against you. Within minutes you can spiral into deep depression"* (The Times, April 8th 2003).

CONCLUSION

This study demonstrates that it is possible to conduct a scientific study in adverse conditions and highlights the nature of mood states changes during adverse conditions. It is argued that teaching athletes mood regulation strategies to cope with extreme negative mood could not only enhance the quality of the experience from the perspective of the explorer, but also improve performance.

REFERENCES

Beedie, C. J., Terry, P. C., and Lane, A. M. (2000). The Profile of Mood States and Athletic Performance: Two meta-analyses. *Journal of Applied Sport Psychology, 12*, 49-68.

Berger, B. G. Motl R. W. Butki B. D. Martin D. T. Wilkinson J. G., and Owen D. R. (1999). Mood and cycling performance in response to three weeks of high-intensity, short-duration overtraining, and a two-week taper. *The Sport Psychologist, 13*, 444-457.

Carver, C. S., and Scheier, M. F. (1990). Origins and functions of positive and negative affect: a control process view. *Psychological Review, 97*, 19-35.

Gross, J.J. (1998). Antecedent- and response-focused emotion regulation: Divergent consequences for experience, expression, and physiology. *Journal of Personality and Social Psychology, 74* 224-237.

Gross, J.J., and John, O.P. (2003). Individual differences in two emotion regulation processes implications for affect, relationships, and well-being. *Journal of Personality and Social Psychology, 85*, 348-362.

Gross, J.J., and Levenson, R.W. (1997). Hiding feelings: The acute effects of inhibiting positive and negative emotions. *Journal of Abnormal Psychology, 106*, 95-103.

Hadow, P. (2004). *Solo. The North Pole - alone and unsupported.* Penguin Books Ltd., London

Hooper, S. L., Mackinnon L. T., and Hanrahan S. (1997). Mood states as an indication of staleness and recovery. *International Journal of Sport Psychology, 28,* 1-12.

Jurimae, J., Maestu, J., Purge, P., Jurimae, T., and Soot, T. (2002). Relations among heavy training stress, mood state, and performance for male junior rowers. *Perceptual and Motor Skills, 95,* 520-526.

Lane, A. M. (2001). Relationships between perceptions of performance expectations and mood among distance runners; the moderating effect of depressed mood. *Journal of Science and Medicine in Sport, 4,* 235-249.

Lane, A. M., and Chappell, R. H. (2001). Mood and performance relationships at the World Student Games basketball competition. *Journal of Sport Behavior, 24,* 182-196.

Lane, A. M., Firth, S., and Terry, P. C. (2002). Mood changes following exercise. Paper presented at the *XXV International Congress of Applied Psychology*, Singapore.

Lane, A. M., Mills, M., and Terry, P. C. (1998). Mood regulation among corporate workers: effects of exercise on mood. *Journal of Sports Sciences, 16,* 92.

Lane, A. M., Terry, P. C., Stevens, M. J., Barney, S., and Dinsdale, S. L. (2004). Mood responses to athletic performance in extreme environments. *Journal of Sports Sciences, 22,* 886-897.

Lane, A. M., Whyte, G. P., George, K., Shave, R., Barney, S., and Terry, P. C. (2004). Marathon: A fun run? An investigation of mood state changes among runners at the London Marathon. Paper presented at the annual conference for the British Psychological Society, Imperial College, April 15th-17th, 2004.

Lane, A. M., Whyte, G. P., Shave, R., and Wilson, M. (2003). Mood state responses during intense cycling. *Journal of Sports Sciences, 21,* 352-353.

Lane, A. M., Whyte, G. P., Shave, R., Barney, S., Stevens, M. J., and Wilson, M. (2005). Mood disturbance during cycling performance at extreme conditions. *Journal of Sports Science and Medicine, 4,* 52-57.

Lane, A. M., Whyte, G. P., Shave, R., Barney, S., Wilson, M., and Terry, P. C. (2003). Mood disturbance during cycling performance at altitude. *Medicine and Science in Sports and Exercise, 35,* S162.

Lazarus, R.S., and Alfert, E. (1964). Short-circuiting of threat by experimentally altering cognitive appraisal. *Journal of Abnormal and Social Psychology, 69,* 195-205.

Lehmann, M. J., Lormes W., Opitz-Gress A., Steinacker J. M., Netzer N., Foster C., and Gastmann U. (1997). Training and overtraining: an overview and experimental results in endurance sports. *Journal of Sports Medicine and Physical Fitness, 37*(1), 7-17.

McNair, D. M., Lorr, M., and Droppelman, L. F. (1971). *Manual for the Profile of Mood States.* San Diego, CA: Educational and Industrial Testing Services.

McNair, D. M., Lorr, M., and Droppelman, L. F. (1992). *Revised Manual for the Profile of Mood States.* San Diego, CA: Educational and Industrial Testing Services.

Morgan, W.P., Brown, D,R., Raglin, J.S., O'Conner, P.J. and Ellickson, K.A. (1987) Psychological monitoring of overtraining and staleness. *British Journal of Sports Medicine,* 21, 107-114.

Pedlar, C. R., Lloyd, J. C., Lane, A. M., Dawson, J., Emegbo, S., Stanley, N., and Whyte, G. P. (2006). Sleep profiles and mood state changes during an expedition to the south pole: a case study of a female explorer. Manuscript under review.

Persson, L., and Sjöberg, L. (1985). Mood and positive expectations. *Social Behavior and Personality, 13*, 171-181.

Pierce, E. F. (2002). Relationship between training volume and mood states in competitive swimmers during a 24-week season. *Perceptual and motor skills, 94*, 1009-1012.

Raglin, J. S. (2001). Psychological factors in sport performance: The mental health model revisited. *Sports Medicine, 31*, 875-890.

Richards, J.M., and Gross, J.J. (2000). Emotion regulation and memory: The cognitive costs of keeping one's cool. *Journal of Personality and Social Psychology, 79,* 410-424.

Stevens, M.J., and Lane, A.M. (2001). Mood-regulating strategies used by athletes. *Athletic Insight, 3. www.athleticinsight.com/vol3lss/copingissue.htm.* (accessed July, 2003).

Terry, P. C., Lane, A. M., and Fogarty, G. (2003). Construct validity of the Profile of Mood States-A for use with adults. *Psychology of Sport and Exercise, 4*, 125-139.

Terry, P. C., Lane, A. M., Lane, H. J., and Keohane, L. (1999). Development and validation of a mood measure for adolescents: POMS-A. *Journal of Sports Sciences, 17*, 861-872.

Thayer, R.E., Newman, R., and McClain, T.M. (1994). Self-regulation of mood: Strategies for changing a bad mood, raising energy, and reducing tension. *Journal of Personality and Social Psychology, 67*, 910-925.

Totterdell, P., Parkinson, B., Briner, R., and Reynolds, S. (1997). Forecasting feelings: The accuracy and effects of self-predictions of mood. *Journal of Social Behavior and Personality, 12*, 631-650.

In: Mood and Human Performance: Conceptual, Measurement...   ISBN 1-60021-269-7
Editor: Andrew M. Lane, pp. 233-244   © 2006 Nova Science Publishers, Inc.

Chapter 12

THE PERCEIVED RECOVERY-STRESS STATE AS A MARKER OF TRAINING AND PERFORMANCE STRESS IN HIGHLY TRAINED ROWERS

Jaak Jürimäe and *Toivo Jürimäe*

Centre of Behavioural and Health Sciences,
University of Tartu, Tartu, Estonia

ABSTRACT

It is well known that peak athletic performance depends on the proper manipulation of training volume and intensity as well as providing adequate rest and recovery between training sessions. The Recovery-Stress Questionnaire for Athletes (RESTQ-Sport) measures stress and recovery at the same time, and may therefore be more effective than the previously used Borg ratio scale or the Profile of Mood States, which both focus mainly on the stress component. Longitudinal studies in athletes have demonstrated that the RESTQ-Sport can sensitively monitor stress and recovery processes in training camps and throughout the season. A dose-response relationship has been demonstrated between training volume and the somatic components of stress and recovery in rowers. These results suggest that RESTQ-Sport is a potential tool for monitoring the training of elite athletes. The RESTQ-Sport can also monitor stress and recovery processes in rowers approaching for the major competitions. Through utilization of the RESTQ-Sport, athletes and coaches can be informed of the importance of daily activites and how these activities are related to recovery-stress state of an athlete compared with the frequently used one-item Borg scale or POMS, which generally measure the stress related behaviour and, therefore, may not be sufficient in high performance areas.

---

[*] Associate Professor Jaak Jürimäe, PhD, Institute of Sport Pedagogy and Coaching Sciences, Centre of Behavioural and Health Sciences, 18. Ülikooli St. University of Tartu. Tartu 50090. ESTONIA. Email: jaakj@ut.ee

INTRODUCTION

The evaluation of the current state of an athlete, i.e., of current trainability and of the diagnosis of possible overload and overtraining, is possibly one of the most complicated tasks in sports science (Mäestu, Jürimäe, and Jürimäe, 2005). Training physiological adaptations should be organized in periods of stressful heavy training to induce sufficient training response followed by a period of reduced load to allow recovery and an increase in performance (Kellmann and Günther, 2000). Arguably the most straightforward way of training monitoring is to evaluate the sport-specific performance of the athlete (Mäestu et al., 2005). However, this can sometimes be rather complicated, because of the specificity of athletic event (e.g., team sports, weather conditions, long-distance events, etc). The complexity of the goals of training may also be a problem, because different capacities (e.g., aerobic, anaerobic, strength, etc.) of the athlete have to be developed and improved (Mäestu et al., 2005). Furthermore, training is not only repetitive physical exercise, but regular regeneration is also an integral part of successful training programme (Kellmann and Günther, 2000; Mäestu et al., 2005). The monitoring process is effective only if it has profound scientific foundations. To date, different clinical, metabolic and hormonal parameters, including the psychologically-related monitoring of stress and recovery, have been used in training monitoring (Mäestu et al., 2005). However, there is still a lack of appropriately designed investigations concerning the reliability of different parameters for monitoring training and especially regeneration of elite athletes during different periods of training (Mäestu et al., 2005). The aim of the current review is to deal with the psychometric monitoring of different training periods in elite athletes with special emphasis on rowers.

SELECTED PSYCHOMETRIC INSTRUMENTS FOR THE ASSESSMENT OF MOOD STATE

The relationship between stress and sport performance is well documented in athletes (Jürimäe, Mäestu, Purge, Jürimäe, and Sööt, 2002; Kellmann and Günther, 2000; Mäestu et al., 2005). Stress is defined as an unspecific reaction-oriented syndrome that is characterised by a deviation from the norm in a biological/psychological state of the organism (Janke and Wolffgramm, 1995) and it should be treated dealing with psychological, cognitive behavioural/performance, emotional and social aspects of the problem. Stress is accompanied by emotional symptoms like anxiety and anger, elevated activation in the central and autonomic nervous system, humoural responses and behavioural changes (Kellmann and Günther, 2000). However, it has been argued that stress is needed to initiate the process of adaptation in athletes. An increase in performance is only achieved when athletes optimally balance training stress with adequate recovery (Rowbottom, Keast, and Morton, 1998). There is a dose-response relation between training volume and mood disturbances (Raglin, 1993), with increases in training volume that parallel elevations in mood disturbances (Morgan, Brown, Raglin, O`Conner, and Ellickson, 1987). Improvements in mood occur when training volume is decreased (Raglin, 1993; Morgan et al., 1987).

To date, the research concerning training monitoring and mood states has used: 1) the one-item Borg ratio scale (Borg, 1998), which was developed to subjectively measure the intensity of the exercise; 2) the Profile of Mood States (POMS; McNair, Lorr, and Droppelman, 1992), which measures a range of mood states of which five are unpleasant and is positive; and 3) the Recovery-Stress Questionnaire for Athletes (RESTQ-Sport; Kellmann and Kallus, 2001), which allows measuring both subjectively perceived stress and recovery. In addition, athletes can record in their training logs subjective ratings of fatigue, stress, sleep, and muscle soreness on a scale of 1 to 7 from very, very low, or good, (1) to very, very high, or bad, (7) (Hooper and Mackinnon, 1995; Jürimäe, Purge, Mäestu, and Jürimäe, 2004). Athletes may also record training enjoyment, and health together with causes of stress, incidence of ilness, and injuries (Hooper and Mackinnon, 1995; Jürimäe et al., 2004). Taken together, it appears that there are many different ways to assess subjectively athlete responses to training programmes.

Borg`s Rating of Perceived Exertion (RPE; Borg, 1998) has widely been used in sport research to measure the level of perceived exertion of an individual. For example, a highly consistent relationship between Borg ratio scale perceptions of exertion on a rowing ergometer and heart rate has been found (Marriot and Lamb, 1996). However, when the RPE was used as a mean of producing an appropriate training heart rate, it was satisfactory only at the higher intensities of effort (i.e., ratings 15 and above) (Marriot and Lamb, 1996). In another study, Snyder, Jeukendrup, Hasselink, Kuipers and Foster (1993) argued that changes in the ratio of RPE and blood lactate concentration were found to be a reliable predictor of overreaching in athletes. However, it has to be considered that the one-item construction of the Borg ratio scale cannot assess different aspects of stress and recovery (Kellmann, 2002). Furthermore, it is difficult to interpret what causes the change of the Borg scale after standardized exercise and, therefore, proper intervention is complicated. Accordingly, the one-item Borg ratio scale is not suitable for monitoring training and mood state in elite athletes (Kellmann, 2002).

The POMS, with its multidimensional approach, takes more dimensions into account and has extensively been used to study the relationship between training stress and mood state in athletes (Kellmann, 2002; Mäestu et al., 2005). POMS was initially developed as an economical method of identifying and assessing transient, fluctuating affective state (McNair, Lorr, and Droppelman, 1992). It is a 65-item Likert-format questionnaire and yields a global measure of mood, consisting of tension, depression, anger, vigour, confusion, and fatigue. An overall score is computed by summarising the five negative mood states and subtracting the positive mood state (vigour) (McNair et al., 1992). A dose-response relation between mood disturbances and training stress is prevalent (Raglin, 1993). For example, Morgan et al. (1987) measured mood states of swimmers throughout the season. At the beginning, the swimmers exhibited the "iceberg profile", an indicator of mentally healthy state. Increased high level of training was accompanied by such feelings as tension, fatigue, anger, depression, loss of vigour and well-being (i.e., mood disturbances). After reducing the training intensity, swimmers demonstrated the "iceberg profile" again (Morgan et al., 1987). This dose-response relationship between training and mood disturbance is well documented also in rowers (Kellmann, 2002; Mäestu et al., 2005). However, it should be taken into account that five of the six scales of POMS measure the negative mood characteristics (tension, anger, fatigue, depression and confusion) and, therefore, POMS only vaguely reflects recovery processes. Berger and Motl (2000) argued that a decrease in a negative mood state might not necessarily indicate mood benefits. Furthermore, although low vigour and high fatigue scores on the POMS do reflect a need for recovery, it is not clear which specific recovery strategy is needed (Kellmann, 2002). Taken together, when using POMS as the psychometric tool to monitor the mood state of athletes, the main focus is on stress-related behaviour and it might be not appropriate to evaluate the recovery of athletes.

Concerning the perspective of a biopsychological stress model from Janke and Wolffgramm (1995), recovery and stress should be treated using a multidimensional approach. Restricting the analysis to the stress dimension alone is insufficient, especially in high-performance areas, since the management of training intensity and volume is tightly linked to outstanding performance (Kellmann, 2002; Mäestu et al., 2005). The RESTQ-Sport (Kellmann and Kallus, 2001) has been reported as one of the few questionnaires with which one may address the full complexities of stress and recovery (Kenntä and Hassmen, 1998). In contrast to the POMS, the RESTQ-Sport assesses mood oriented stress- and recovery-associated activities. The main advantage of RESTQ-Sport over POMS is that it allows specific intervention strategies, which are complicated with the POMS that measures the mood state itself (Kellmann and Günther, 2000; Kellmann and Kallus, 2001). Specifically, the recovery-stress state indicates the extent to which persons are physically and/or mentally stressed, whether or not they are capable of using individual strategies for recovery as well as which strategies are used (Kellmann and Günther, 2000). The RESTQ-Sport was created to get distinct answers to the questions "How are you?" (Kellmann, 2002) and addresses physical, subjective, behavioural and social aspects using a self-report approach (Kellmann and Kallus, 2001). The RESTQ-Sport is constructed in a modular way including 12 scales of the general Recovery-Stress Questionnaire and additional 7 sport-specific scales (19 scales with four items each plus one warm-up item) (Table 1) (Kellmann and Kallus, 2001).

Table 1. Subscales of RESTQ-Sport, one representative item, subscale orientation, Cronbach á, and test-retest repeatability for Estonian version of the questionnaire

No	Subscale	Example	Orientation	á	r
1	General Stress	I felt depressed	Stress	0.91	0.75
2	Emotional Stress	I was in bad mood	Stress	0.91	0.74
3	Social Stress	I was upset	Stress	0.95	0.79
4	Conflicts/Pressure	I felt under pressure	Stress	0.72	0.84
5	Fatigue	I was overtired	Stress	0.75	0.75
6	Lack of Energy	I had difficulties in concentrating	Stress	0.81	0.76
7	Somatic Complaints	I felt physically exhausted	Stress	0.74	0.81
8	Success	I was successful in what I did	Recovery	0.77	0.79
9	Social Relaxation	I had fun	Recovery	0.93	0.75
10	Somatic Relaxation	I felt physically relaxed	Recovery	0.78	0.82
11	General Well-Being	I was in good mood	Recovery	0.91	0.80
12	Sleep Quality	I had a satisfying sleep	Recovery	0.83	0.76
13	Disturbed Breaks	I could not get rest during the breaks	Stress	0.81	0.63
14	Emotional Exhaustion	I felt burned out by my sport	Stress	0.87	0.75
15	Fitness/Injury	I felt vulnerable to injuries	Stress	0.73	0.83
16	Being in Shape	I recovered well physically	Recovery	0.93	0.81
17	Burnout/Personal Accomplishment	I dealt with emotional problems in my sport very calmly	Recovery	0.87	0.76
18	Self-Efficacy	I was convinced that I performed well	Recovery	0.86	0.79
19	Self-Regulation	I pushed myself during performance	Recovery	0.78	0.82

The theory behind this questionnaire is that an accretion of stress in everyday life, coupled with weak recovery potential, will cause a variation of the psychophysical general state (Kellmann, 2002). A Likert-type scale is used with values ranging from 0 (never) to 6 (always), indicating the frequency of the stress- and recovery-related mood states, social activities, performance, and specific physical states during the past three days/nights. The mean of each scale can range from 0 to 6, with high scores in the stress-associated activity scales reflecting intense subjective stress, whereas high scores in the recovery-oriented scales mirror plenty recovery activities (e.g., social activities, vacation, sauna, etc.) (Kellmann and Kallus, 2001). The process of recovery cannot just take place through the elimination of stress, rather it is characterized by an active personalized process that must take place in order to reestablish psychological and physical strength.

THE PERCEIVED RECOVERY-STRESS STATE IN ATHLETES DURING TRAINING

It is well established that appropriate training is needed for improved performance. However, the extent and content of the training may often lead to inappropriate training responses of the athlete and in the long-term, to overtraining syndrome (Kellmann and Kallus, 2001). It is well known that peak athletic performance depends on the proper manipulation of training volume and intensity as well as providing adequate rest and recovery between training sessions (Kellmann, 2002; Mäestu et al., 2005). Longitudinal studies in athletes have demonstrated that the RESTQ-Sport can sensitively monitor stress and recovery processes in training camps and throughout the season (Kellmann and Günther, 2000; Kellmann and Kallus, 2001; Mäestu, Jürimäe, and Jürimäe, 2003; Mäestu et al., 2005). In addition, a dose-response relationship has been demonstrated between training volume (i.e., daily rowed kilometres) and the somatic components of stress and recovery in rowers (Jürimäe et al., 2002; Kellmann and Günther, 2000; Mäestu, Jürimäe, Kreegipuu, and Jürimäe, 2006; Purge, Jürimäe, and Jürimäe, 2005). These results together suggest that RESTQ-Sport is a potential tool for monitoring the training of elite athletes.

Success in rowing is determined overwhelmingly by the amount of training time spent on the water in the form of low-intensity endurance rowing (Jürimäe et al., 2004; Mäestu et al., 2005). In our study, we investigated the usefulness of the RESTQ-Sport for monitoring training during rapidly increased training volume in junior rowers (Jürimäe et al., 2002). The training volume during the six-day training period amounted to 21.2 ± 2.2 hours, which was equivalent to an average increase in training load by approximately 100% compared with their average training during the preceding four weeks, while the intensity remained relatively unchanged. A high training volume was indicated by elevated scores on the subscales of stress and simultaneously almost all recovery-associated measures were decreased. Significant changes were found for scores on the Fatigue (from 2.1 ± 0.6 to 3.5 ± 0.8; $p < 0.003$) and Social Relaxation (from 3.7 ± 0.9 to 2.5 ± 0.8; $p < 0.003$) subscales of the questionnaire. The raised scores for Fatigue indicated the heavy training period response to athletes` perceived fatigue ratings and as the same time the performance was significantly dropped, a state of short-term overreaching might have been achieved. Similarly to the results of our study, the values of the Fatigue subscales have been reported to increase relatively early in parallel with increased training volume, while the scores of General Stress are stable and low for a relatively long period (Kellmann and Kallus, 2001).

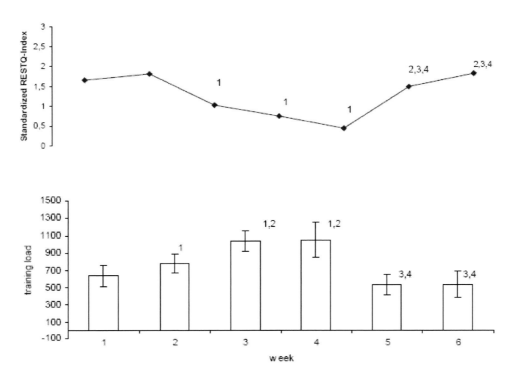

Figure 1. Training load and Standardized RESTQ index during a six-week training cycle (compiled from Mäestu et al., 2003, 2006). Numbers indicate the significantly different (p<0.05) training load from pointed week

However, the increased mean on the Social Relaxation subscale suggested that the emotional, physical, and social aspects of recovery may not have been adequate during the heavy training camp. A significant decrease on the Social Relaxation subscale demonstrated a drop in social activities during this training period. In general, this suggests that athletes should be aware of the importance of recovery in the training process. This is even more important in a training camp, where the focus is on monotonous high load practice (Kellmann and Günther, 2000). Adequate recovery during phases of heavy training allows the adaptation of the athlete to stress and prevents overtraining (Raglin, 1993).

The results of our other study with senior rowers revealed that different subscales of the RESTQ-Sport demonstrated a clear dose-response relationship with training volume (see Figures 1 and 2) during high loaded training cycle and the following recovery period (Mäestu et al., 2003, 2006). Specifically, this study with Estonian national level rowers lasted for six weeks and consisted of the reference week followed by three week high training volume phase (50% increase in training volume compared to the reference week) and two week recovery period (90% of training volume of the reference week). The training regimen remained similar during each week of the study and only training volume was manipulated during the study period. The questionnaire was administered to athletes after every week and in addition to different subscales, the standardized scores for Stress and Recovery were calculated (Kellmann and Kallus, 1999). The scores of stress-related subscales (subscales 1 to 7, 13, 14 and 15) were summed and divided by the number of subscales representing the Standardized Stress. The same procedure was used for the recovery-oriented subscales (subscales 8 to 12, 16, 17, 18 and 19) resulting a Standardized Recovery. In addition, the Standardized Stress as well as Standardized Recovery scores were converted to standardized values by subtracting the global sample mean and dividing the difference by the standard deviation. In this way, a standardized recovery and stress score could be obtained on a common scale, which allowed computing a difference between stress and recovery (Standardized RESTQ-Index; Kellmann and Kallus, 1999). It is speculated that higher values for the RESTQ-Index indicate that the athlete is in a more optimal recovery-stress state. The results of our study indicated that RESTQ-Index was negatively correlated with training volume ($r = -0.39$; $p < 0.008$); and high training volume was accompanied by lowered levels of RESTQ-Index and vice versa, lowered training volume during recovery period was indicated by higher RESTQ-Index (see Figure 1) (Mäestu et al., 2006). This index can be interpreted as a kind of athletes´ resource measure (Kellmann and Kallus, 1999) and could be used as an indicator of athletes´ recovery-stress state and may, therefore, be more understandable to use for athletes and coaches to monitor the impact of different trainings to the athletes´ current state. In accordance with our results, Kellmann and Kallus (1999) have demonstrated that the RESTQ-Index is decreased dramatically before the overtraining state was diagnosed, while increased RESTQ-Index was found in an athlete who won European Championships on a mountain bike. However, it still remains unclear how much the RESTQ-Index must decrease and/or how long the lowered RESTQ-Index can be tolerated before athlete shows the signs of overtraining. The changes in Standardized Stress score in current investigation were similar and as expected, a significant increase during high volume training period and a significant decrease following recovery period occurred. However, the Standardized Recovery score decreased during high volume training period but no significant improvement was followed during recovery period. It could be suggested that recovery activities, in general, were not enough during the recovery period. This is also supported by evidence showing that only the subscale of Success was significantly improved during the recovery period compared with the high training volume period indicating that athletes should also focus on recovery periods as essential parts of the whole training programme. Accordingly, using the RESTQ-Sport coaches can be informed how athletes spend their time when not training, and how this period may affect their state. If an athlete shows a negative recovery profile, solutions can be derived to make some intervention in order to improve athlete`s recovery potential in order to better cope with different stressors.

The RESTQ-Sport can sensitively monitor stress and recovery processes also in rowers approaching for the major competitions (Kellmann and Günther, 2000). In our recent study, we investigated the usefulness of this questionnaire for monitoring performance in elite rowers participating in World Cup series and how the recovery-stress state of rowers participating in double and quadruple scull boat classes is represented by a final result in competitions (Purge et al., 2005). Rowers took part in three World Cup competitions, which were held in June and July with a three week training period between each competition and were preparing for major competitions of the year, which was held in August. Double scullers were more experienced, while rowers in quadruple sculls took part for the first time at that level of international competitions.

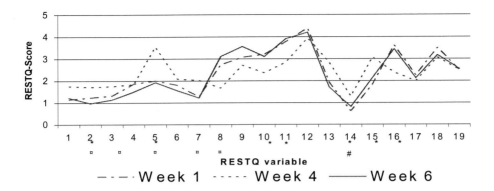

*- Significant difference between the first and the fourth week; ¤ - significant changes between the fourth and the sixth week; # - significant difference between the first and the sixth week.

1- General Stress, 2-Emotional Stress, 3-Social Stress, 4- Conflicts/Pressure, 5-Fatigue, 6- Lack of Energy, 7-Somatic Complaints, 8-Success, 9-Social Relaxation, 10- Somatic Relaxation, 11- General Well-Being, 12- Sleep Quality, 13- Disturbed Breaks, 14-Emotional Exhaustion, 15- Fitness/Injury, 16- Being in Shape, 17- Burnout/Personal Accomplishment, 18- Self-efficacy, 19- Self-regulation

Figure 2. RESTQ-Sport variables after the first, the fourth and the sixth week of a six-week training cycle (compiled from Mäestu et al., 2003, 2006)

Generally, the performance of double scullers in three World Cup series met their expectations, while the performance in quadruple scullers was as expected in the first two World Cup competitions (Table 2). Rowers in both boat classes continued training with relatively high load during this period. In double scullers, the decrease in the RESTQ-Index from World Cup 1 to World Cup 3 was accompanied by the increased loss for winning boat time (World Cup 1: +3.1%; World Cup 2: +4.8%; World Cup 3: +9.6%). Similarly, Kellmann, Kallus, and Kurz (1996) found a close relationship between the recovery-stress state and performance in competition of swimmers. While the Standardized Stress score did not change from World Cup 1 to World Cup 2 and a moderate increase occurred only before World Cup 3 (by 14.3%) in double scullers, quadruple scullers demonstrated a constant increase in the Standardized Stress value from World Cup 1 to World Cup 3. This indicates that rowers in quadruple sculls were more stressed, as the Standardized Recovery value remained almost unchanged during three World Cup competitions for quadruple scullers. According to these results, it can be speculated that the training and competition load for the rowers competing in quadruple sculls might have been too hard for them to cope with, since they finished in the 10th place in World Cup 3 competitions. Probably, they were in an overreaching state (i.e., Jürimäe et al., 2002) before World Cup 3, which was reflected by increases in perceived stress and also measured catabolic hormone concentration (Purge et al., 2005).

Table 2. Performance and Standardized RESTQ-Sport scores in rowers during World Cup competitions (adopted from Purge et al., 2005)

	World Cup 1	World Cup 2	World Cup 3
Double Scullers			
Place	2	6	5
Standardized Stress	1.9±1.0	1.8±0.4	2.1±0.3
Standardized Recovery	2.7±0.2	2.3±0.1*	2.2±0.4*
RESTQ-Index	0.9±1.1	0.5±0.5	0.1±0.1*
Quadruple Scullers			
Place	4	2	10
Standardized Stress	1.4±1.1	1.7±1.0	2.0±1.5
Standardized Recovery	2.9±1.4	2.8±1.7	2.9±1.8
RESTQ-Index	1.5±1.8	1.1±2.3	0.8±3.0

* Large difference from World Cup 1, Effect Size> 1.0.

An interesting finding of this study was the decrease in the RESTQ-Index in quadruple scullers accompanied by a large increase in the Standardized Stress score. The RESTQ-Index worsened in double scullers because of inadequate recovery activities as indicated by a large decrease in the Standardized Recovery score between World Cups 1 and 3. This demonstrates that double scullers coped with training and competition stress better than quadruple scullers and their relative loss to the winning boat in World Cup 3 was accompanied by inadequate recovery between training sessions and competition races. This further shows that athletes should be aware of the importance of recovery in the training process and especially during competition period (Kellmann and Kallus, 1999; Kellmann and Günther, 2000). The knowledge of the importance of active recovery gives an athlete more responsibility for their own activities. Furthermore, these different results in rowers of double and quadruple scullers demonstrate the importance of assessing perceived stress and recovery at the same time. The advantage of using the RESTQ-Sport is that it gives us a detailed picture of the rowers´ state. Concrete solutions to potential problems can be derived only from the up-to-date recovery-stress profile (Kellmann and Kallus, 2001). The profile can be used to derive specific intervention strategies. The results also demonstrated to athletes and coaches the importance of daily activites on their mood state and how these activities are related to their performance in international competitions. Similarly to our study, studies in German rowers suggest that before important competitions athletes become more sensitive about certain activities, and perceive their environment differently, although the coaches´ views did not change (Kellmann and Kallus, 1999).

In summary, through utilization of the RESTQ-Sport, athletes and coaches can be informed of the importance of daily activites and how these activities are related to recovery-stress state of an athlete compared with the frequently used one-item Borg scale or POMS, which generally measure the stress related behaviour and, therefore, may not be sufficient in high performance areas. While the RESTQ-Index could be used as an athlete´s resource measure, Standardized Stress and Standardized Recovery scores reflect an athlete's extent of stress and recovery separately.

MULTI-LEVEL APPROACH IN TRAINING MONITORING

There is a cascade of various responses to training monitoring. However, it is also evident that only some of the parameters are reliable and specific enough. The monitoring of training adaptation in a period of heavy training stress and the current adaptation state of an athlete appears to be a very complex task (Mäestu et al., 2005). For example, the hypothalamus has an important role in integrating different stress influences and the answers from the hypothalamus are expressed via the endocrine system, the autonomic nervous system and the behaviour (Barron, Noakes, Lewy, Smith, and Millar, 1985). Such integration involves information from autonomic nerve system afferents, direct metabolic effects, hormones and also different information from different brain centres (Mäestu et al., 2005). In accordance with this, the subscales of Physical Complaints, Fatigue and General Stress (Mäestu et al., 2003) as well as Conflicts/Pressure (Jürimäe et al., 2002) were highest with highest training load, elevated cortisol concentrations and high creatine kinase activity (Mäestu et al., 2005). Sleeping Quality, Personal Accomplishment, Self-Efficacy and General Well-Being were lowest with the high training volume (Jürimäe et al., 2002; Mäestu et al., 2003). Furthermore, cortisol has been found to be related to all of the stress subscales (except Disturbed Breaks) of the RESTQ-Sport after three week high volume training in rowers (Mäestu et al., 2003). In addition, we have found that cortisol is correlated with Standardized Stress score ($r=0.76$; $p<0.001$) and the RESTQ-Index ($r=-0.59$; $p<0.001$), while creatine kinase activity is related to Standardized Recovery score ($r=-0.45$; $p<0.001$) during high training load in rowers (Mäestu et al., 2005). It is well known that creatine kinase activity increases following exercise of high muscular strain because of muscle cell leakage and/or damage, and the morning levels represent mainly the creatine kinase release during the previous days and normalization of the creatine kinase activity demonstrates a reduced muscle stress.

In summary, there appears no single marker of training monitoring and possible overtraining in elite athletes. In addition to the assessment of perceived recovery-stress state, some blood biochemical markers should also be included to the evaluation of the current state of an athlete. However, the exact mechanism by which the brain senses metabolic imbalance and fatigue in athletes is still speculative. Future studies are needed in the area of elite training monitoring.

REFERENCES

Barron, J.L., Noakes, T.D., Lewy, W., Smith, C., and Millar, R.P. (1985). Hypothalamic dysfunction in overtrained athletes. *Journal of Clinical Endocrinology and Metabolism*, *60*, 803-806.

Berger, B.G., and Motl, R.W. (2000). Exercise and mood: A selective review and synthesis of research employing the Profile of Mood States. *Journal of Applied Sport Psychology*, *12*, 69-92.

Borg, G. (1998). *Perceived Exertion and Pain Rating Scales*. Champaign, IL: Human Kinetics.

Hooper, S.L., and Mackinnon, L.T. (1995). Monitoring overtraining in athletes. Recommendations. *Sports Medicine*, *20*, 321-327.

Janke, W., and Wolffgramm, J. (1995). Biopsychologie von Stress und Emotionalen Reaktionen: Ansätze Interdiziplinärer Kooperation von Psychologie, Biologie und Medizin [Biopsychology of stress and emotional responses: starting points of an interdisciplinary cooperation of psychology, biology, and medicine]. In: G. Debus, G. Erdmann, and K. Kallus (Eds.), *Biopsychologie von Stress und Emotionalen Reaktionen* [Biopsychology of stress and emotional reactions (pp. 293-349). Göttingen: Hogrefe.

Jürimäe, J., Mäestu, J., Purge, P., Jürimäe, T., and Sööt, T. (2002). Relations among heavy training stress, mood state, and performance for male junior rowers. *Perceptual and Motor Skills, 95*, 520-526.

Jürimäe, J., Purge, P., Mäestu, J., and Jürimäe, T. (2004). Heavy training stress in male rowers: effects on circulatory responses and mood state profiles. *Kinesiology, 36*, 213-219.

Kellmann, M. (2002). Psychological assessment of underrecovery. In: M. Kellmann (Ed.), *Enhancing Recovery: Preventing Underperformance in Athletes* (pp. 35-55). Champaign, IL: Human Kinetics.

Kellmann, M., and Günther, K.D. (2000). Changes in stress and recovery in elite rowers during preparation for the Olympic Games. *Medicine and Science in Sports and Exercise, 32*, 676-683.

Kellmann, M., Kallus, K.W., and Kurz, H. (1996). Performance predictions by the RESTQ. *Journal of Applied Sport Psychology, 8(*S), S22.

Kellmann, M., and Kallus, K.W. (1999). Mood, Recover-Stress State and Regeneration. In: M. Lehmann (Ed.), *Overload, Performance Incompetence, and Regeneration in Sport.* (pp. 101-117). New York: Plenum.

Kellmann, M., and Kallus, K.W. (2001). *The Recovery-Stress Questionnaire for Athletes. User Manual.* Champaign, IL: Human Kinetics.

Kenntä, G., and Hassmen, P. (1998). Overtraining and recovery. *Sports Medicine, 6*, 79-92.

Mäestu, J., Jürimäe, J., and Jürimäe, T. (2003). Psychological and biochemical markers of heavy training stress in highly trained male rowers. *Medicina Dello Sport, 56*; 95-101.

Mäestu, J., Jürimäe, J., and Jürimäe, T. (2005). Monitoring of performance and training in rowing. *Sports Medicine, 35,* 597-617.

Mäestu, J., Jürimäe, J., Kreegipuu, K., and Jürimäe, T. (2006). Changes in perceived stress and recovery during heavy training in highly trained male rowers. *The Sport Psychologist, 20, 24-39.*

Marriot, H.E., and Lamb, K.L. (1996). The use of ratings of perceived exertion for regulation exercise levels in rowing ergometry. *European Journal of Applied Physiology, 72*, 267-271.

McNair, D., Lorr, M., and Droppelmann, L.F. (1992). *Profile of Mood States Manual.* San Diego: Educational and Industrial Testing Service.

Morgan, W.P., Brown, D.R., Raglin, J.S., O`Connor, P.J., and Ellickson, K.A. (1987). Physiological monitoring of overtraining and staleness. *British Journal of Sports Medicine, 21*, 107-114.

Purge, P., Jürimäe, J., and Jürimäe, T. (2005). Changes in recovery-stress state and performance in elite rowers during preparation for major competitions. *Perceptual and Motor Skills, 101*, 375-381.

Raglin, J.S. (1993). Overtraining and staleness: psychometric monitoring of endurance athletes. In: R.N. Singer, M. Murphey, and L. Tennant (Eds.), *Handbook of Researh in Sport Psychology* (pp. 840-850). New York: Macmillan.

Rowbottom, D.G., Keast, D., and Morton, A.R. (1998). Monitoring and preventing of overreaching and overtraining in endurance athletes. In: R.B. Kreider, A.C. Fry, and M.L. O`Toole (Eds.), *Overtraining in Sport* (pp. 47-66). Champaign, IL: Human Kinetics.

Snyder, A.C., Jeukendrup, A.E., Hesselink, M.K.C., Kuipers, H., and Foster, C. (1993). A physiological/psychological indicator of overreaching during intensive training. *International Journal of Sports Medicine, 14*, 29-32.

In: Mood and Human Performance: Conceptual, Measurement...   ISBN 1-60021-269-7
Editor: Andrew M. Lane, pp. 245-259   © 2006 Nova Science Publishers, Inc.

Chapter 13

RELATIONSHIPS BETWEEN MOOD STATES AND MOTOR PERFORMANCES: WHAT CAN YOU LEARN FROM HIGH ALTITUDE

Benoît Bolmont[*]

Department of Sport *Science*s, LIMBP - Emotions-Actions (EA 3940)
University of Metz
Université de Metz, UFR *Science*s Fondamentales Appliquées
Campus Bridoux, Avenue Général Delestraint
57070 Metz-Borny, France

ABSTRACT

A complex relationship has been highlighted between Emotion and Action, and emerged as a new research theme. Among extreme environments, high altitude is well known to induce behavioural and mood disturbances including anxiety and alterations in cognitive functions, such as mental and reasoning processes and psychosensorimotor skills. The effects of high altitude, simulated or actual, on mood states and human motor performances are reviewed, and relationship between psychological states and motor performances at high altitude is discussed. To take into account this interplay between mood states including anxiety, personality traits and human performances could be essential to consolidate security and success of missions in extreme environments, and to improve quality of life and maybe human capacities. Finally, an environmental stressor, such as high altitude simulated, which has mainly provided the evidence of a significant interplay between the psychological states and the motor performances, could constitute a model to understand mechanisms by which moods including anxiety may improve, maintain or increase the human performances in normal condition.

---

[*] Tel/ Fax: 33 387 378 671 / 33 387 378 603; bolmont@univ-metz.fr

INTRODUCTION

The relationship between emotion and cognition has been widely investigated (Damasio, 1994). Positive or negative moods have been found to interact with several domains of cognition, in particular attention, memory, reasoning, problem solving and decision making (Ashby, Isen, and Turken, 1999; Isen, Daubman, and Nowicki, 1987). Although Darwin first described a functional link between varying motivational states of emotional reactivity and specific postural responses (Darwin, 1872), a complex relationship has been highlighted between emotion and action (Bolmont, 2005; Bolmont, Gangloff, Vouriot, and Perrin, 2002; Bolmont, Thullier, and Abraini, 2000; Eysenck, 1992; Lane, Terry, Stevens, Barney, and Dinsdale, 2004; Lane, Whyte, Shave, Barney, Stevens, and Wilson, 2005; Wada, Sunaga, and Nagai, 2001), and emerged as a new research theme (Bolmont et al., 2000; Eysenck, 1992; Lane et al., 2004; Terry, 2005). Indeed, several studies examine the influence of mood states and anxiety on various human motor performances (Bolmont, 2005; Bolmont et al., 2000; Eysenck, 1992; Raglin, 1992). Conversely, others investigate the effects of motor performances on mood states (Lane, Milton, and Terry, 2005; Lane et al., 2004; Reed, 2005). Because individual differences, such as personality traits or physiological responses play a major role in mood responses, the relation between emotion and action remains ambiguous and widely discussed.

Among stressors, extreme environments, such as high altitude, deep diving, polar stations, space flight and few industrial jobs constitute useful tools for the investigation of the processes of adaptation of the nervous system, brain function and balance patterns between emotion and action. Although long-term isolation at an Antarctic station might have a 'salutogenic' or health enhancing effect (Rivolier, Goldsmith, Lugg, and Taylor, 1988), generally, environmental conditions are well known to induce both physiological and psychological disturbances including behavioural and mood changes. Among such situations, high altitude is characterized by hypobaric hypoxia. At heights of more than 3000m, the arterial oxyhaemoglobin saturation decreases frankly and may produce a set of physiological and psychological disorders, known as Acute Mountain Sickness (AMS) (Carson, Evans, Shields, and Hannon, 1969). In addition to the AMS symptoms, which include breathlessness, headache, insomnia, dizziness and abnormal tiredness, exposure to high altitude further induces behavioural and mood disturbances. Mood disturbances include anxiety and alterations in cognitive functions, such as mental and reasoning processes and psycho-sensorimotor skills (Abraini, Bouquet, Joulia, Nicolas, and Kriem, 1998). For a given altitude, AMS symptoms show maximal amplitude during the first or second day of exposure and then recede rapidly but reappear if climbing continues too fast. The number, severity, rapidity of onset, and duration of high altitude symptoms vary between individuals and are related to both level of altitude and rate of ascent (Bahrke and Shukitt-Hale, 1993; Shukit and Banderet, 1988). The effects of high altitude, simulated or actual, on various functions of the central nervous system such as moods and human motor performances, will be reviewed briefly in both first of the first sections. A third section examines the effects of mood states including anxiety on motor performances at high altitude. Finally, the relationship between moods and human performance is discussed.

MOOD STATES, ANXIETY AND PERSONALITY AT HIGH ALTITUDE

As suggested by Nelson (1982), the critical altitude for psychological changes seems to be 4000-5000 m (Figure 1) (Tune, 1964). Although, sleepiness is a frequent symptom at lower altitudes (Shukit and Banderet, 1988), it seems less perceptible compared to over symptoms at higher altitudes (Bahrke and Shukitt-Hale, 1993). Indeed, as Figure 1 indicates, exposure to high terrestrial elevations may produce adverse changes in mood states, such as increases in euphoria, irritability, hostility, depression, and anxiety (Bahrke and Shukitt-Hale, 1993; Banderet, 1977; Barach and Kagan, 1940; Bolmont, Thullier, and Abraini, 2000; Nicolas, Thullier-Lestienne, Bouquet, Gardette, Gortan, Richalet, and Abraini, 2000; Van Liere and Stickney, 1963). As suggested by Houston (1983), euphoria, which is characterized by a feeling of self-satisfaction and a sense of power and followed later by depression (Banderet, 1977; Jobe, Shukitt-Hale, Banderet, and Rock, 1991; Shukit and Banderet, 1988, Shukitt-Hale, Rauch, and Foutch, 1990; Van Liere and Stickney, 1963), could lead to dangerous consequences. With time, participants may become quarrelsome, irritable and apathetic (Banderet, 1977; Van Liere and Stickney, 1963).

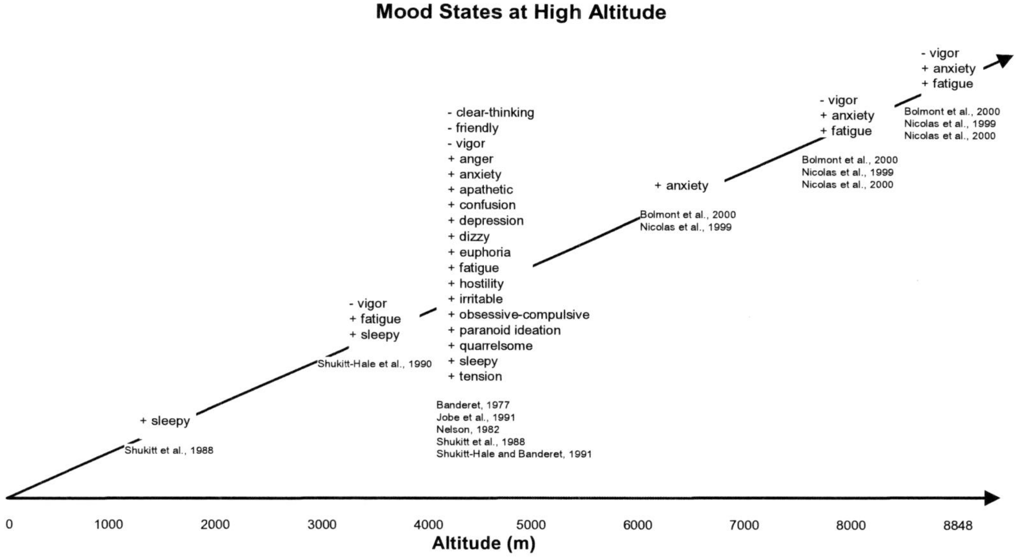

Figure 1

Studies using the Clyde Mood Scale have shown that although no mood changes were observed at 1600 m (the staging site), at an actual altitude of 4300 m (Pikes Peak, Co), volunteers become less friendly and clear thinking, more sleepy and dizzy, and happier than at 200 m (baseline) (Banderet, 1977; Shukit and Banderet, 1988). It should be noted that participants under treatment strategy (acetazolamide and staging) were more friendly, less sleepy and dizzy, but no improvement on the clear-thinking factor was observed. Participants treated with dexamethasone were less sleepy, dizzy, depressed, and anxious than placebo-treated subjects at 4300 m (Jobe et al., 1991).

Among the psychological changes, experiments have also reported that a feeling of generalized fatigue, which is not related to the amount of work performed (Van Liere and Stickney, 1963), could be the first mood change at altitude (Shukit and Banderet, 1988). Indeed, as expected, fatigue and vigour were found to be adversely affected at altitude (Banderet, 1977; Nicolas et al., 2000; Shukit and Banderet, 1988; Shukitt-Hale et al., 1990). During a climb to moderate altitude (3630m) over a period of 7 days, climbers were less vigorous and more fatigued over time by the changes in altitude (Shukitt, Banderet, and Sampson, 1990). In a simulated climb of Mount Everest (Everest-Comex 97), mood states in eight volunteers decompressed in a chamber over 31 days to the altitude of 8848m were assessed by the Profile of Mood States (POMS: McNair, Lorr, and Droppleman, 1971) at different stages of ascent. The results of this study indicated that of the six POMS factors, only significant changes in scores on vigour and fatigue have been assessed at 8000 m and 8848 m. Although length of confinement could have contributed to alterations in rated the vigour and the fatigue, it has been suggested that adverse mood changes mainly resulted from the effect of altitude rather than confinement. These findings differ somewhat from previous studies at actual altitude (Shukitt et al., 1990; Shukitt-Hale et al., 1990) that have shown that adverse changes in rated the fatigue and the vigour may occur at altitudes as low as 3630 m (Shukitt et al., 1990). However, a simulated ascension experiment 'only' inflicted hypoxia, whereas expeditions in actual altitude further impose additional stresses, such as energy expenditure, cold and danger due to climbing, which could have mainly effects on the mood states. Support for this suggestion is previous data showing that adverse environmental conditions (Shukitt-Hale et al., 1990) may constitute a potential source of mood disorders.

As far as anxiety is concerned, significant increases occurred at actual altitudes of 4300 and 5000 m (Nelson, 1982) and at simulated altitudes of 6500 m, 8000 m and 8848 m (Nicolas, Thullier-Lestienne, Bouquet, Gardette, Gortan, Joulia, Bonnon, Richalet, Therme, and Abraini, 1999). The participant's feeling of danger in extreme environments (Abraini, 1997) and the adverse environmental factors other than just the level of altitude (Shukitt-Hale et al., 1990) may induce anxious reactions in subjects exposed to such conditions. Although it has been suggested that stress of isolated duty cannot produce psychiatric disorders in healthy people (Meichenbaum and Novaco, 1985), the development of severe anxiety responses has been shown to occur possibly in normal participants and individuals showing an anxious guilt. Furthermore, low-self control and emotional instability are associated with depressive anxious guilt, and frustration (Cattel and Sheier, 1958).

PSYCHOLOGICAL CHANGES DURING A PROLONGED EXPOSURE TO ACTUAL HIGH ALTITUDE

A prolonged isolation and confinement at high altitude is associated with stress. In such extreme environmental situations, studies have demonstrated that social environment is the most potent source of stress rather than physical environment (Lantis, 1968). This social environment is further characterized by a lack of privacy, boredom due to the lack of environmental stimulation and interaction with the same limited number of individuals, and reductions in the gratification of the "basic" human needs of affection and feeling of personal significance. Individuals who stayed at an altitude of 2300 m for a year or more, without a break at lower levels, often became somewhat irritable. At various altitudes (sea level, 3810 m, and 5000 m) during a 35-days mountaineering expedition to Denali, participants became more hostile, constrictive, anxious, obsessive-compulsiveness, paranoiac, and depressed (Nelson, 1982). It seems than personality traits play a crucial role in the success of prolonged isolation and confinement experiments. Extroverts are less successful at adapting to experimental confinement (Miyashiro and Russell, 1974) or prolonged isolation in extreme environments (Biesner and Hogan, 1984) than introverts. Furthermore, experiments in other extreme environments, such as deep diving, have reported that any adverse psychological symptoms remain at the individual level and are relatively transient (Abraini, Ansseau, Martinez, Burnet, Wauthy, and Lemaire, 1995; Bugat, 1987, 1989). Paradoxically, in spite of these extreme situations, some investigators have suggested that long-term isolation in an extreme environment may have a health-enhancing effect (Rivolier et al., 1988). Support for the existence of this "Salutogenic" effect (Antonovsky, 1987) has come from empirical studies of Antarctic Winter-over personnel (Palinkas, 1986, 1991). Elsewhere, the work emanating from crisis theory (Lindemann, 1979) and stress inoculation training (Meichenbaum and Novaco, 1985) also supports the notion that stressor agents can provide psychological growth rather than a risk to psychological health and well-being.

HUMAN PERFORMANCES AT HIGH ALTITUDE

In 1937, McFarland (1937) noted that exposure of un-acclimatized humans to altitudes above 3660 m affects their general well-being and capacity for carrying out essential tasks. Fine and Kobrick (1978) reported that many kinds of performance are altered at an altitude higher than 4000 m (Bahrke and Shukitt-Hale, 1993; Tune, 1964), and the deterioration becomes progressively more marked with increase in altitude (Luft, 1961). Exposure to high altitude further induces adverse changes in cognitive functions, such as mental and reasoning processes (Bahrke and Shukitt-Hale, 1993; Hornbein, 1992; Stamper, Kinsman, and Evans, 1970; Tune, 1964), attentional (Dunlap, 1919) and visual (Bouquet, Gardette, Gortan, Therme, and Abraini, 2000; Stivalet, Leifflen, Poquin, Savourey, Launay, Barraud, Raphel, and Bittel, 2000; Tune, 1964). It also affects concentration (Van Liere and Stickney, 1963) and working memory (Bahrke and Shukitt-Hale, 1993; Shukitt-Hale, Stillman, Welch, Levy, Devine, and Lieberman, 1994). It may also alter postural stability (Fraser, Eastman, Paul, and Porlier, 1987), sensory motor coordination (Dunlap, 1919), eye-hand coordination (Chiles, 1971), neuromuscular control (Garner, Sutton, Burse, McComas, Cymerman, and Houston, 1990), psychosensorimotor and motor skills (Bahrke and Shukitt-Hale, 1993; Bouquet, Gardette, Gortan, and Abraini, 1999; Silber, 2000; West, 1986), and complex auditory or visual reaction time (Fowler and Kelso, 1992; Fowler and Lindeis, 1992). However, other studies have not found alteration in reaction time (Abraini, 1997; Bouquet et al., 1999), and disturbance in motor skills, such as finger tapping (Kramer, Coyne, and Strayer, 1993), which involves fairly simple and well-practiced skills. Thus, it seems that motor complex tasks, which require high cognitive processes, would be more sensitive to hypoxia than simple tasks with the idea that automatic processes developed in learning are resistant to hypoxic stress

(Abraini, Ansseau, Bisson, de Mendoza, and Therme, 1998). Although sensory receptor or muscular dysfunctions due to a direct effect of high altitude cannot be excluded (Garner et al., 1990), the effect of exposure to high altitude on psychomotor performance has central rather than peripheral origins because performance decrements in psychomotor skills had similar patterns and time courses to those of reasoning processes (Abraini et al., 1998; Bouquet et al., 1999). In addition, although at altitudes of 4000 m or below, studies have not found decrements in learning of performance in tasks of spatial orientation (Denison, Ledwith, and Poulton, 1966), logical reasoning and serial choice reaction time (Paul and Fraser, 1994), high altitude has been shown to produce learning deficits (Abraini et al., 1998; Bouquet et al., 1999; Denison et al., 1966). The most clear-cut effect is an increased learning time (Abraini et al., 1998). The psychomotor skills learning are altered as a function of the task complexity (Abraini et al., 1998; Hornbein, 1992; Sharma, Malhotra, and Baskaran, 1975; Shukitt-Hale, Banderet, and Lieberman, 1991). Such impairments could be the consequence, at least in part, of high cognitive function disruptions, such as strategic learning and working memory processes (Abraini et al., 1998; Bouquet et al., 1999; Lieberman, Protopapas, and Kanki, 1995). Finally, a prolonged exposure at high altitude could alter ability to execute coordinated muscle movements (Sharma et al., 1975). Psychomotor performance was adversely affected both in terms of speed as well as accuracy (Sharma et al., 1975). Beyond ten months, trauma of stress is reduced and there is a progressive recovery in such performances, which could result from a learning effect or physiological and psychological acclimatisation achieved. Thus, a continued practice and psychological training probably may compensate deficits in human activity.

RELATIONSHIPS BETWEEN PSYCHOLOGICAL STATES AND HUMAN PERFORMANCES AT HIGH ALTITUDE

Disturbances in psychological mood and behaviour after exposure to altitude have been recognised for many years (Heber, 1921; Wilmer and Berens, 1918) and the investigations of the effects of adverse mood changes on human performance could be essential for the group survival. A depressive type of reaction as suggested by Shephard (1956) may operate at altitude from the very beginning that affects not only the speed but also the accuracy of performance (Sharma et al., 1975). In a more recent investigation, military personnel have completed the POMS at multiple points before and after participating in a 30-day, cold weather, high-altitude field training exercise. Anger and fatigue scores were comparable to adult male psychiatric outpatient norms. Bardwell, Ensign, and Mills (2005) suggested that a rigorous training in challenging environments may results in enduring negative moods that approach levels of clinical significance and may have implications for readiness for duty and performance of critical tasks.

PERSONALITY TRAITS AND PERFORMANCES IN REACTION TIME AND PSYCHOMOTOR ABILITY

In the 'Everest-Comex 97' experiment, which consisted of a 31-day gradual decompression in a hypobaric chamber from sea level to 8848 m equivalent altitude, eight experienced male climbers performed psychomotor (pegboard test) and binary visual choice reaction time tasks, and completed the POMS and the Y1 form of the Spielberger State-Trait Anxiety Inventory (Spielberger, 1983). Measurements were taken at different periods of the experiment including at sea level and at several stages of ascent. Traits of personality and anxiety were assessed before the simulated climb using the Sixteen Personality Factors Questionnaire (16PF; (Russel and Karol, 1933) and the Y2 form of the Spielberger State-Trait Anxiety Inventory (Spielberger, 1983).

Results indicated two significant negative correlations between reaction time, but not psychomotor ability, with both factors A and G of the sixteen Personality Factors Questionnaire, two personality traits that range, respectively, from 'reserved' to 'outgoing' and from 'expedient' to 'conscientious' (Bolmont, Bouquet, and Thullier, 2001). This suggests that Factor A and Factor G are related to, and perhaps, modulate performance in reaction time but not in psychomotor ability. Cautiously, we have suggested that individuals with personality traits such as 'outgoing' or 'conscientious' could have, at hypoxic situations, slight disadvantages in processing information for stimulus-response tasks that mainly require automatic abilities. Conversely, this supports that individuals with personality traits such as 'reserved' or 'expedient' could have slight advantages in the processing of such tasks. These data partly agree with previous studies in which introverts have been shown to be more successful in adapting to stressful environmental conditions than extroverts (Miyashiro and Russell, 1974). It should be noted, however, that previous researchers have found climbers scored significantly differently on Factor A and Factor G compared to control participants (Magni, Unger, Valfre, Cesari, Polesel, De Leo, Rizzardo, and Gallucci, 1985). Thus, our results may not reflect general processes of adaptation but specific characteristics of climbers.

Interestingly, results have also indicated two significant positive correlations between the climbers' mean performance in reaction time and scores on trait-anxiety and changes in anxiety levels (Bolmont et al., 2000, 2001). These results suggest that trait-type anxiety, like state-type anxiety, could lead to an improvement in reaction time, but not in psychomotor ability. State-anxiety is defined as an acute emotional response that may occur in stressful situations, whereas trait-anxiety is a personality trait referring to individual differences in the proneness of a person to experience anxiety reactions. Trait-anxiety and state-anxiety are often discussed as either distinct concepts or as a continuous single concept. As a consequence, although some studies have suggested that either only trait-anxiety or only state-anxiety scores could be associated with performance (Fox and Houston, 1983), other studies have suggested, in the frame of a continuous single concept of anxiety that either trait- or state-anxiety scores could be associated with performance (Head and Lindsey, 1983). In this way, trait-anxiety and state-anxiety which are highly and positively correlated (Nicolas et al., 1999), and positively associated with performance in reaction time, would be closely linked and organized on a *continuum*, rather than distinct. Moreover, our results are consistent with studies suggesting that anxiety could lead performers to invest additional effort in a task (Peretti, 1998), and to yield a sort of 'sensation seeking', allowing individuals to develop hyperadaptative behavioural processes (Sanders, 1983), so that performance could be maintained or enhanced with no deficit on simple tasks requiring automatic abilities. Alternatively, although trait-anxiety and state-anxiety generally are often thought to reduce attentional resources (Wilken, Smith, Tola, and Mann, 1999), in agreement with the hypervigilance theory, state- and trait-anxiety could have, in the present study, favoured or maintained at its basal level the processing of information in visual reaction time task.

Furthermore, the differences of sensitivity to chronic hypoxia between performances may be also regarded according to numerous theoretical studies that lead to the assumption that anxiety and memory could be two closely linked concepts. Indeed, studies have evidenced that state-anxiety would induce working memory deficits (Darke, 1988), and that anxious participants would show an implicit, but not an explicit, memory advantage (MacLeod and McLaughlin, 1995). Interestingly, performance in reaction time, which was significantly correlated with anxiety and not clearly sensitive to chronic hypoxia under our experimental conditions, depends greatly, as a stimulus-response ability, on the integrity of implicit memory and basal ganglia-sensorimotor system functions (Mishkin, Malamut, and Bachevalier, 1984). Conversely, performances in psychomotor ability (manual dexterity), which impaired significantly as altitude increased (Abraini, Bouquet, Joulia, Nicolas, and Kriem, 1998) and showed no significant correlation with state-anxiety, have been shown to depend greatly on the integrity of explicit memory and frontal lobe systems functions (Mishkin et al., 1984).

MOOD STATES AND PERFORMANCES IN REACTION TIME AND PSYCHOMOTOR ABILITY

Significant negative correlations were also found between performance in psychomotor ability and fatigue, and visual reaction time and three of the six POMS factors: tension, hostility, and confusion. These results suggest that adverse changes in tension, confusion, hostility, or fatigue could lead to an altered performance (Bolmont, Thullier, and Abraini, 2000). Results supporting adverse changes in mood states could influence performance negatively, may be arranged in good agreement with a previous study demonstrating that hostility, tension, and ideation at altitude occur concurrently with performance decrements (Nelson, 1982). Among the significant correlations between performances and moods, it should be noted that a higher correlation was found between psychomotor ability and fatigue. Therefore, one might think that muscular effort needed to perform the manual dexterity task could be responsible for the decrements of performance. However, although such a muscular discomfort or dysfunction cannot be excluded, it may be noted that fatigue, as measured by the POMS, is a symptom of central rather than peripheral origin (McNair et al., 1971). In this way, the relationship between psychomotor ability and fatigue would reflect a slowing of the information processing and motor strategy needed to perform the psychomotor task. Support for this may be obtained from a previous study that has evidenced no neuromuscular impairment at similar altitudes and conditions in a hypobaric chamber (Garner et al., 1990). In addition, further support for this suggestion is that no decrements were found in reaction time task, which includes an important motor component.

CONCLUSION

High altitude constitutes a particular extreme environment susceptible to disturb human capacities. Thus, it seems to be reducing to consider independently physiological and psychological processes. In accord with these relations, for instance, previous studies have proposed that state-anxiety could constitute a good predictor of susceptibility to AMS (Missoum, Rosnet, and Richalet, 1992), and have also evidenced correlations between mood states including anxiety and altitude symptoms showing similar time-courses (Bahrke and Shukitt-Hale, 1993; Nicolas et al., 1990; Shukitt-Hale et al., 1990). Moreover, relationships between AMS symptoms and psychomotor function suggest possible similarities in pathogenesis of AMS and psychomotor dysfunction at altitude (Silber, 2000). In addition, personality traits play a major role in the occurrence of mood states and the processes of adaptation. As a consequence in a holistic perspective, the correlations between human performances, mood states including anxiety and personality traits have mainly provided evidence of significant relationships at high altitude (Bolmont et al., 2000, 2001). Adverse changes in mood states, mainly tension, hostility, fatigue and confusion could modulate performance negatively. Increase in fatigue may alter performance in complex tasks with high information content, whereas increases in tension, hostility and confusion may disturb performances in more simple tasks involving well-practiced skills. In spite of complexity of anxiety and moods, which may be arranged in a single construct (Bolmont and Abraini, 2001), state-anxiety and trait-anxiety organized on a continuum could favor, or at least not alter, the processes of information of relatively simple tasks, such as reaction time. Moreover, the analysis of personality traits suggests that it could mediate performance in reaction time requiring automatic abilities, but not psychomotor ability. Individuals with personality traits such as 'outgoing' or 'conscientious' could have slight disadvantages in processing information for stimulus-response tasks. Conversely, individuals with personality traits such as 'reserved' or 'expedient' could have slight advantages in the processing of such tasks. It should be emphasized that our results were assessed in a small sample of only male climbers exposed to simulated and not actual high altitude, using psychometric and not clinical techniques. In addition, because participants, experimental designs, levels, conditions and duration of exposure and methods of assessment vary highly between studies, it is difficult to compare them and to draw a uniform synthesis. However, research is needed to consider interplay between mood states including anxiety, personality traits and human performances. Whether a great deal of studies have mentioned potential relationship between stress, well-being, tension and human performances, few studies have investigated and discussed the relationship between performances and moods in extreme environments. Since this interdependence is crucial in normal conditions (Bolmont, 2005; Hainaut and Bolmont, 2005, 2006; Lane et al., 2004; Lane, Whyte, Terry, and Nevill 2005), it should be taken into account to consolidate security and success of missions in extreme environments. Indeed, although, rate of adaptation appears to be highly individualized (Terry, 2005), adaptations to extreme conditions could be enhanced (Lane et al., 2004). If one considers that the effects of environmental change may influence psychological functioning before they affect physiological factors (Kobrick and Johnson, 1991), monitoring of mood, which have been found to reflect environmental change (Bahrke and Shukitt-Hale, 1993) and also predict athletic performance (Beedie, Terry, and Lane, 2000) could be used as an indicator of the adverse effects of environmental stress (Lane et al., 2004). As a consequence, Lane et al. (2004) proposed a guide for using mood to assess the effects of adverse conditions so that interventions can be implemented to ensure functional mood states. Future research should develop such practical guidelines and adapt batteries of tests used in varied normal conditions and susceptible to predict for each individual reactions in extreme conditions and effects on performances. To take into account this relationship between personality traits, mood states and human performances could improve the quality of life and human capacities. However, although studies are divided (Abraini, Bouquet, Joulia, Nicolas, and Kriem, 1998; Anooshiravani, Dumont, Mardirosoff, Soto-Debeuf, and Delavelle, 1999; Cavaletti, Garavaglia, Arrigoni, and Tredici, 1990; Cavaletti, Moroni, Garavaglia, and Tredici, 1987; Cavaletti and Tredici, 1992; Clark, Heaton, and Wiens, 1983; Garrido, Castello, Ventura, Capdevila, and Rodriguez, 1993; Nelson, 1982; West, 1986; West and Lahiri, 1984), extreme environments characterized by stressful conditions could have disturbing or irreversible effects. Thus, such environments remain really hostile and dangerous for human beings.

REFERENCES

Abraini, J.H. (1997). Inert gas and raised pressure: evidence that motor decrements are due to pressure per se and cognitive decrements due to narcotic action. *Pflügers Archives European Journal of Physiology, 433,* 788-91.

Abraini, J.H., Ansseau, M., Bisson, T., de Mendoza, J.L., and Therme, P. (1998). Personality patterns of anxiety during occupational deep dives with long-term confinement in hyperbaric chamber. *Journal of Clinical Psychology, 54,* 825-30.

Abraini, J.H., Ansseau, M., Martinez, E., Burnet, H., Wauthy, J., and Lemaire, C. (1995). Development of anxiety symptoms during a deep diving experiment. *Anxiety, 1,* 237-241.

Abraini, J.H., Bouquet, C., Joulia, F., Nicolas, M., and Kriem, B. (1998). Cognitive performance during a simulated climb of Mount-Everest: Implications for brain function and central adaptive processes under chronic hypoxic stress. *Pflügers Archives European Journal of Physiology, 436,* 553-9.

Anooshiravani, M., Dumont, L., Mardirosoff, C., Soto-Debeuf, G., and Delavelle, J. (1999). Brain magnetic resonance imaging (MRI) and neurological changes after a single high altitude climb. *Medicine and Science in Sports and Exercise, 31,* 969-972.

Antonovsky, A. (1987) *Unravelling the mystery of health,* Jossey-Bass.

Bahrke, M.S., and Shukitt-Hale, B. (1993). Effects of altitude on mood, behaviour and cognitive functioning: A review. *Sports Medicine, 16,* 97-125.

Banderet, L.E. (1977). Self-rated moods of humans at 4300 m pretreated with placebo or acetazolamide plus staging. *Aviation, Space, and Environmental Medicine, 48,* 19-22.

Barach, A.L., and Kagan, J. (1940). Disorder of mental functioning produced by varying the oxygen tension of the atmosphere. *Psychosomatic Medicine, 2,* 53-67.

Bardwell, W.A., Ensign, W.Y., and Mills, P.J. (2005). Negative mood endures after completion of high-altitude military training. *Annals of Behavioral Medicine, 29,* 64-69.

Beedie, C.J., Terry, P.C., and Lane, A.M. (2000). The Profile of Mood States and athletic performance: two meta-analyses. *Journal of Applied Sport Psychology, 12,* 49-68.

Biesner, R.J., and Hogan, R. (1984). Personality correlates of adjustment in isolated work groups. *Journal of Personality Research, 18*, 491-496.

Bolmont, B. (2005). Role and influence of moods including anxiety on motor control. In A.V. Clark (Ed.), *Causes, Role and influence of Moods States*, Nova Science Publisher, New York, pp. 56-73.

Bolmont, B., and Abraini, J.H. (2001). State-anxiety and low moods: evidence for a single concept. *Physiology & Behavior, 74*, 421-424.

Bolmont, B., Bouquet, C., and Thullier, F. (2001). Relationships of personality traits with performance in reaction time, psychomotor ability, and mental efficiency during a 31-day simulated climb of Mount Everest in a hypobaric chamber. *Perceptual and Motor Skills, 92*, 1022-1030.

Bolmont, B., Gangloff, P., Vouriot, A., and Perrin, P.P. (2002). Mood states and anxiety influence abilities to maintain balance control in healthy human subjects. *Neuroscience Letters, 329*, 96-100.

Bolmont, B., Thullier, F., and Abraini, J.H. (2000). Relationships between mood states and performances in reaction time, psychomotor ability, and mental efficiency during a 31-day gradual decompression in a hypobaric chamber from sea level to 8848 m equivalent altitude. *Physiology & Behavior, 71*, 469-476.

Bouquet, C., Gardette, B., Gortan, C., Therme, P., and Abraini, J.H. (2000). Color discrimination under chronic hypoxic conditions (simulated climb "Everest-Comex 97"). *Perceptual and Motor Skills, 90*, 169-179.

Bouquet, C.A., Gardette, B., Gortan, C., and Abraini, J.H. (1999). Psychomotor skills learning under chronic hypoxia. *Neuroreport, 10,* 3093-3099.

Bugat, R. (1989). Stress et plongée profonde. *Neuropsy, 2*, 93-102.

Bugat, R. (1987). Suivi psychologique à la plongée profonde. *Med Sub Hyp, 6*, 132-144.

Carson, R.P., Evans, W.O., Shields, J.L., and Hannon, J.P. (1969). Symptomatology, pathophysiology, and treatment of acute mountain sickness. *Fed Proc, 28,* 1085-1091.

Cattel, R.B., and Sheier, I.H. (1958). The nature of anxiety: A review of thirteen multivariate analyses comprising 814 variables. *Psychological Reports, 4,* 351-388.

Cavaletti, G., Garavaglia, P., Arrigoni, G., and Tredici, G. (1990). Persistent memory impairment after high altitude climbing. *International Journal of Sports Medicine, 11,* 176-178.

Cavaletti, G., Moroni, R., Garavaglia, P., and Tredici, G. (1987). Brain damage after high-altitude climbs without oxygen. *Lancet, 1*, 101.

Cavaletti, G., and Tredici, G. (1992). Effects of exposure to low oxygen pressure on the central nervous system. *Sports Medicine, 13*, 1-7.

Chiles, W.D. (1971). Combined effect of altitude and high temperature on complex performance. *Office of Aviation Medicine*, Oklahoma City.

Clark, C.F., Heaton, R.K., and Wiens, A.N. (1983). Neuropsychological functioning after prolonged high altitude exposure in mountaineering. *Aviation, Space, and Environmental Medicine, 54*, 202-207.

Damasio, A. R. (1994). *Descartes' error.* New York: Avon Books.

Darke, S. (1988). Effects of anxiety on inferential reasoning task performance. *Journal of Personality and Social Psychology, 55,* 499-505.

Darwin, C. (1872). The expression of the emotions in man and animal, Murray, J.

Denison, D.M., Ledwith, F., and Poulton, E.C. (1966). Complex reaction times at simulated cabin altitudes of 5,000 feet and 8,000 feet. *Aerospace Medicine, 37*, 1010-1013.

Dunlap, K. (1919). Psychological research in aviation. *Science, 49*, 94.

Eysenck, M.W. (1992). *Anxiety: The cognitive perspective*. Lawrence Erlbaum.

Fine, B.J., and Kobrick, J.L. (1978). Effects of altitude and heat on complex cognitive tasks. *Human Factors, 20*, 115-122.

Fowler, B., and Kelso, B. (1992). The effects of hypoxia on components of the human event-related potential and relationship to reaction time. *Aviation, Space, and Environmental Medicine, 63*, 510-516.

Fowler, B., and Lindeis, A.E. (1992). The effects of hypoxia on auditory reaction time and P300 latency. *Aviation, Space, and Environmental Medicine, 63*, 976-981.

Fox, J.E., and Houston, B.K. (1983). Distinguishing between cognitive and somatic trait and state anxiety in children. *Journal of Personality and Social Psychology, 45*, 862-870.

Fraser, W.D., Eastman, D.E., Paul, M.A., and Porlier, J.A. (1987). Decrement in postural control during mild hypobaric hypoxia. *Aviation, Space, and Environmental Medicine, 58*, 768-772.

Garner, S.H., Sutton, J.R., Burse, R.L., McComas, A.J., Cymerman, A., and Houston, C.S. (1990). Operation Everest II: neuromuscular performance under conditions of extreme simulated altitude. *Journal of Applied Physiology, 68*, 1167-1172.

Garrido, E., Castello, A., Ventura, J.L., Capdevila, A., and Rodriguez, F.A. (1993). Cortical atrophy and other brain magnetic resonance imaging (MRI) changes after extremely high-altitude climbs without oxygen. *International Journal of Sports Medicine, 14*, 232-234.

Hainaut, J.-P., and Bolmont, B. (2005). Effects of mood states and anxiety as induced by the video-recorded Stroop Color-Word Interference Test in simple response time tasks on reaction time and movement time. *Perceptual and Motor Skills,101(3)*, 721-729.

Hainaut, J.-P., and Bolmont, B. (2006). State-Anxiety differentially modulates Visual and Auditory Response Times in Normal and Very Low Trait-Anxiety Subjects. *Neuroscience Letters, 395(2)*, 129-132.

Head, L.Q., and Lindsey, J.D. (1983). The effect of trait anxiety and test difficulty on undergraduates' state anxiety. *Journal of Psychology, 113*, 289-293.

Heber, A.R. (1921). Some effects of altitude on the human body. *Lancet, 1*, 1148-1150.

Hornbein, T.F. (1992). Long term effects of high altitude on brain function. *International Journal of Sports Medicine, 13 Suppl 1*, S43-45.

Isen, A.M., Daubman, K.A., and Nowicki, G.P. (1987) Positive affect facilitates creative problem solving. *Journal of Personality and Social Psychology, 52*, 1122-1131.

Jobe, J.B., Shukitt-Hale, B., Banderet, L.E., and Rock, P.B. (1991). Effects of dexamethasone and high terrestrial altitude on cognitive performance and affect. *Aviation, Space, and Environmental Medicine, 62*, 727-732.

Kobrick, J.L., and Johnson, R.F. (1991). Effects of hot and cold environments on military performance. In R. Gal and A.D. Mangelsdorff (Eds.), *Handbook of Military Psychology*, Wiley, New York, pp. 215-32.

Kramer, A.F., Coyne, J.T., and Strayer, D.L. (1993). Cognitive function at high altitude. *Human Factors, 35*, 329-344.

Lane, A.M., Milton, K.E., and Terry, P.C. (2005). Personality does not influence exercise-induced mood enhancement among female exercisers. *Journal of Sports Sciences and Medicine, 4,* 223-238.

Lane, A.M., Terry, P.C., Stevens, M.J., Barney, S., and Dinsdale, S.L. (2004). Mood responses to athletic performance in extreme environments. *Journal of Sports Sciences, 22,* 886-897.

Lane, A.M., Whyte, G.P., Shave, R., Barney, S., Stevens, M., and Wilson, M. (2005). Mood disturbance during cycling performance at extreme conditions. *Journal of Sports Sciences and Medicine, 4,* 52-57.

Lane, A.M., Whyte, G.P., Terry, P.C., and Nevill, A.M. (2005). Mood, self-set goals and examination performance: the moderating effect of depressed mood. *Personality and Individual Differences, 39,* 143-53.

Lantis, M. (1968). Environmental stresses on human behavior. Summary and suggestions. *Archives of Environmental Health, 17,* 578-585.

Lieberman, P., Protopapas, A., and Kanki, B.G. (1995). Speech production and cognitive deficits on Mt. Everest. *Aviation, Space, and Environmental Medicine, 66* 857-864.

Lindemann, E. (1979). *Studies in Crises Intervention.* Jason Aronson, 1979.

Luft, U.C. (1961). *Altitude sickness.* Bailliere, Tindal and Cox.

MacLeod, C., and McLaughlin, K. (1995). Implicit and explicit memory bias in anxiety: a conceptual replication. *Behavioral Research Therapy, 33,* 1-14.

Magni, G., Unger, H.P., Valfre, C., Cesari, F., Polesel, E., De Leo, D., Rizzardo, R., and Gallucci, V. (1985). Personality factors, psychological distress and "illness behavior" in patients before heart surgery. *Minerva Psichiatrica, 26,* 11-20.

Mc Nair, D.M., Lorr, M., and Droppleman, L.F. (1971). *Manual for the Profile of Mood States,* Educational and Industrial Testing Service, San Diego (CA), 1971.

McFarland, R.A. (1937). Psycho-physiological studies at high altitude in the Andes. *Comparative Psychology, 23-24,* 191-220.

Meichenbaum, D., and Novaco, R. (1985). Stress inoculation: a preventative approach. *Issues Mental Health Nursing, 7,* 419-435.

Mishkin, M., Malamut, B.L., and Bachevalier, J. (1984). *Memory and habits: two neuronal systems.* Guilford Press.

Miyashiro, C.M., and Russell, D.L. (1974). Experimental participation as a source of stimulation in sensory and perceptual deprivation studies of stimulus-seeking behavior by introverts and extraverts. *Perceptual and Motor Skills, 38,* 235-238.

Nelson, M. (1982). Psychological testing at high altitudes. *Aviation, Space, and Environmental Medicine, 53,* 122-126.

Nicolas, M., Thullier-Lestienne, F., Bouquet, C., Gardette, B., Gortan, C., Joulia, F., Bonnon, M., Richalet, J.P., Therme, P., and Abraini, J.H. (1999). An anxiety, personality and altitude symptomatology study during a 31-day period of hypoxia in a hypobaric chamber (experiment 'Everest-Comex 1997'). *Journal of Environmental Psychology, 19,* 407-414.

Nicolas, M., Thullier-Lestienne, F., Bouquet, C., Gardette, B., Gortan, C., Richalet, J.P., and Abraini, J.H. (2000). A study of mood changes and personality during a 31-day period of chronic hypoxia in a hypobaric chamber (Everest-Comex 97). *Psychological Reports, 86,* 119-126.

Palinkas, L.A. (1991). Effects of physical and social environments on the health and well-being of Antarctic winter-over personnel. *Environmental Behavior, 23,* 782-799.

Palinkas, L.A. (1986). Health and performance of Antarctic winter-over personnel: a follow-up study. *Aviation, Space, and Environmental Medicine, 57,* 954-959.

Paul, M.A., and Fraser, W.D. (1994). Performance during mild acute hypoxia. *Aviation, Space, and Environmental Medicine, 65,* 891-899.

Peretti, C.S. (1998). Anxiety and cognition disorders. *Encephale, 24,* 256-259.

Raglin, J.S. (1992). Anxiety and sport performance. *Exercise and Sport Sciences Reviews, 20,* 243-274.

Reed, J. (2005). Acute Physical Activity and Self-Reported Affect: A Review. In A.V. Clark (Ed.). *Causes, Role and Influence of Mood States,* Nova Science Publisher, New York, 2005, pp. 91-113.

Rivolier, J., Goldsmith, R., Lugg, D.L., and Taylor, A.J.W. (1988). *Man in the Antarctic.* Taylor and Francis. UK.

Russel, M.T., and Karol, B.L. (1933). The 16 PF fifth edition administrator's manual (French version). *Institute for Personality and Ability Testing,* 1993.

Sanders, A.F. (1983). Towards a model of stress and human performance. *Acta Psychologica, 53,* 61-97.

Sharma, V.M., Malhotra, M.S., and Baskaran, A.S. (1975). Variations in psychomotor efficiency during prolonged stay at high altitude. *Ergonomics, 18,* 511-516.

Shepard, R.J. (1956). Physiological changes and psychomotor performance during acute hypoxia. *Journal of Applied Physiology, 9,* 343-351.

Shukitt, B.L., and Banderet, L.E. (1988). Mood states at 1600 and 4300 meters terrestrial altitude. *Aviation, Space, and Environmental Medicine, 59,* 530-532.

Shukitt, B.L., Banderet, L.E., and Sampson, J.B. (1990). The Environmental Symptoms Questionnaire: Corrected computational procedures for the alertness factor. *Aviation, Space, and Environmental Medicine, 61,* 77-78.

Shukitt-Hale, B., Banderet, L.E., and Lieberman, H.R. (1991). Relationships between symptoms, moods, performance, and acute mountain sickness at 4,700 meters. *Aviation, Space, and Environmental Medicine, 62,* 865-869.

Shukitt-Hale, B., Rauch, T.M., and Foutch, R. (1990). Altitude symptomatology and mood states during a climb to 3,630 meters. *Aviation, Space, and Environmental Medicine, 61,* 225-228.

Shukitt-Hale, B., Stillman, M.J., Welch, D.I., Levy, A., Devine, J.A., and Lieberman, H.R. (1994). Hypobaric hypoxia impairs spatial memory in an elevation-dependent fashion. *Behavioral Neural Biology, 62,* 244-252.

Silber, E. (2000). Upper limb motor function at 5000 metres: determinants of performance and residual sequelae. *Journal of Neurology, Neurosurgery, Psychiatry, 69,* 233-236.

Spielberger, C.D. (1983). *Manual for the State-Trait Anxiety Inventory* (Form Y) (Self-Evaluation Questionnaire), Palo Alto, CA: Consulting Psychologists Press (1983).

Stivalet, P., Leifflen, D., Poquin, D., Savourey, G., Launay, J.C., Barraud, P.A., Raphel, C., and Bittel, J. (2000). Positive expiratory pressure as a method for preventing the impairment of attentional processes by hypoxia. *Ergonomics, 43,* 474-485.

Terry, P.C. (1995). the efficacy of mood state profiling among elite competitors: a review and synthesis. *The Sport Psychologist, 9,* 309-324.

Tune, G.S. (1964). Psychological effects of hypoxia: Review of certain literature from 1950-1963. *Perceptual and Motor Skills, 19,* 551-562.

Van Liere, E.J., and Stickney, J.C. (1963). *Hypoxia.* The University of Chicago Press.

Wada, M., Sunaga, N., and Nagai, M. (2001). Anxiety affects the postural sway of the antero-posterior axis in college students. *Neuroscience Letters, 302,* 157-159.

West, J.B. (1986). Do climbs to extreme altitude cause brain damage?, *Lancet, 2,* 387-388.

West, J.B., and Lahiri, S. (1984). *High Altitude and Man*, In West, J. B. Lahiri, S. edn., American Physiological Society, 1984.

Wilken, J., Smith, B.D., Tola, K., and Mann, M. (1999). Anxiety and arousal: tests of a new six-system model. *International Journal of Psychophysiology, 33,* 197-207.

Wilmer, W.H., and Berens, C. (1918). Medical studies in aviation V. The effect of aviation on ocular functions. *Journal of American Medical Association, 71,* 1394-1398.

In: Mood and Human Performance: Conceptual, Measurement…   ISBN 1-60021-269-7
Editor: Andrew M. Lane, pp. 261-270   © 2006 Nova Science Publishers, Inc.

Chapter 14

MARATHON: A FUN RUN? MOOD STATE CHANGES AMONG RUNNERS AT THE LONDON MARATHON

Andrew M. Lane[1]*, Greg P. Whyte[2], Keith George[3], Rob Shave[4], Matthew J. Stevens[1] and Sam Barney[1]

[1] School of Sport, Performing Arts, and Leisure, University of Wolverhampton, UK,
[2] English Institute of Sport, Bisham Abbey, UK.
[3] Liverpool John Moores University, Liverpool, UK
[4] Department of Sport Sciences, Brunel University, UK.

ABSTRACT

The aim of this study was to examine mood profiles and associated coping strategies used by marathon runners. A negative mood profile was proposed to reflect an inability to cope with the demands of running a marathon. Volunteer marathon runners ($N = 28$; Age: $M = 33.58$, $SD = 8.51$ years) completed mood measures a one-day before competition one hour after finishing, and during the worst period in the race. Participants also reported their satisfaction with performance. Using pre-competition depressed mood scores, participants were dichotomised into either a no-depressive mood symptoms or depression group. Pre-competition mood results indicated that depression was associated with high tension, confusion, and low calmness scores. For mood states during the hardest point in the race, results indicated depressed mood was associated with high anger, confusion, with lower calmness and happiness scores. For post-competition mood, depression was associated with reporting high post-race anger, confusion, lower happiness and feeling that performance was poor. Individuals who reported symptoms of depressed mood one day before running the marathon experienced a negative mood profile before, during and after the race. They also perceived that they performed poorly. Interventions should involve teaching athletes to regulate symptoms of depressed mood.

---

* A.M.Lane2@wlv.ac.uk

INTRODUCTION

Over 30,000 runners compete in the annual London Marathon. Many of these are 1st time marathon runners or people returning to exercise in order to fundraise for charity. In addition, serious runners also compete with an aim to beat personal times. Research suggests that completing the marathon is a physiologically demanding task, especially for less fit and less experienced runners. For such runners, completing the marathon involves running for somewhere between 3.00-6.00 hours and with most marathons being held in spring, heat / hydration issues are important factors.

Anecdotal evidence suggests most marathon runners report satisfaction by simply finishing. In terms of scientific research, a recent study indicated that marathon runners experience intense emotional states before competition (Lane, 2001). Positive pre-competition mood was associated with perceiving form to be good, setting an attainable goal and, perceiving the course to be suitable (Lane, 2001). In endurance-based sports, research has found that athletes set difficult goals. The general trend is that goals perceived unattainable tend to be associated with negative psychological states. This relationship has been found in middle-distance running (Jones et al., 1990), duathlon (Lane, Terry, and Karageorghis, 1995a) and triathlon (Lane et al., 1995a, 1995b). The consistency of these findings suggest that a characteristic of endurance athletes is to set goals, ostensibly to direct motivation and provide ways to assess performance against self-reference standards. However, self-set goals can produce a side effect of elevating unpleasant emotional states. Lane and Terry (2000) argued that unpleasant mood states, particularly depression are linked to expectations of failure, and the collection of mood states associated with depressed mood is indexed to poor performance.

Using Lane and Terry's (2000) conceptual framework as a guide for research, Lane (2001) investigated the mood states of 100 marathon runners, of whom 40% reported indicators of depressed mood before competition. Lane, Lane, and Firth (2002) assessed the mood states of 195 runners, of who 32% reported depressed mood and dissatisfaction with performance. In both studies, mood profiles associated with depressed mood were consistent with theoretical predictions in the Lane and Terry (2000) model. A limitation of the majority of studies that tested Lane and Terry's model is that mood has been assessed at one point in time rather than taking multiple measures of mood over time. Research has not investigated temporal changes in mood states by than taking a series of measures. In terms of marathon running, it is not known whether runners had felt depressed throughout the duration of the race. If depressed mood occurs throughout a race, and can be identified using self-report measure before the race starts, then it is possible to develop interventions to reduce depression, which should make running the event more enjoyable, and / or less painful. Running 26.2 miles whilst feeling angry, confused, depressed and tense arguably makes the task feel harder. However, the development of such an intervention strategy depends on research evidence that shows that pre-race depression influence mood dynamics during the race.

In an attempt to address this limitation, recent research has investigated mood states during competition to explore mood states changes during 4 hours intense exercise (Lane, Whyte, Shave, Barney, Wilson, and Terry, 2003). A comparison of mood scores after two hours by depressed mood scores indicated marginal differences in fatigue but significantly higher unpleasant mood states such as anger and confusion among participants that reported depression (Lane et al., 2003). This finding lends support to assessing mood states such as anger, confusion, depression and fatigue independently rather than merging to form a general factor of negative mood. We suggest that fatigue experienced with anger and confusion will feel qualitatively different to fatigue being experienced independently of these constructs. In the former, fatigue is likely to lead the athlete to question his/her ability to cope. Sensations of tiredness experienced simultaneously with anger, confusion and depression would suggest that the athlete is struggling to develop an appropriate concentration plan (confusion). It would also suggest that the athlete is attributing an inability to cope to internal factors and become frustrated by these attempts, leading to experiencing anger. Therefore, it is speculated that depressed mood states before marathon performance would be associated with an overall unpleasant and negative profile as hypothesised by Lane and Terry (2000). It is also speculated that depressed mood would intensify changes in unpleasant mood states and be associated with poor coping efforts.

The aim of the present study was to explore psychological profiles associated with coping successfully with running a marathon. Specifically, the study investigated the influence of pre-race depressed mood on mood states experienced during and after the race. The present study also explored associations between depressed mood and a range of different psychological state and trait constructs. We explored relationships between depressed mood and self-esteem. Lane and Terry (2000) argued that depressed mood is a transitory construct. By exploring relationships with self-esteem, the aim is to examine the extent to which depressed mood is based on an under-current of low self-esteem (Campbell, 1990). We also explored relationships between depressed mood and dispositional coping skills. Consistent with the search for relationships with stable constructs, it is argued that depressed mood would be associated with using poor coping skills. Relationships between mood states and perceptions of performance expectation were assessed using a methodology consistent with that used by Lane (2001). In addition to this, we investigated relationships between depressed mood and concentration styles during the race. We hypothesised that depressed runners would tend to focus internally, focusing on perceptions of fatigue that would in turn exacerbate feelings of anger, confusion, fatigue, tension and vigour. Collectively, we aimed to conduct a comprehensive assessment of pre-competition mood states, selected personality traits, current form, mood states during and after the race, concentration and perceptions of performance.

METHODS

Participants

Volunteer marathon runners ($N = 28$; Age: $M = 33.58$, $SD = 8.51$ years) participated in the study. Participants has an average of 3.44 years (SD = 4.79, range 0-18 years) running experience; trained an average of 8 and half hours per week (SD = 7.5 hours), ran an average of 25.08 miles (SD = 17.20) in the previous week.

Measures

Mood

Mood was measured using a 32-item scale that used subscales from two previously validated scales (Matthews, Jones, and Chamberlain, 1990; Terry, Lane, Lane, and Keohane, 1999; Terry, Lane, and Fogarty, 2003). The Brunel Mood Scale (Terry et al., 1999, 2003) is based on the Profile of Mood States (McNair, Lorr, and Droppleman, 1971) and assesses the mood states of anger, confusion, depression, fatigue, tension, and vigour. The subscales of happiness and calmness were taken from the UWIST (Matthews et al., 1990). Recent research has questioned the use of the POMS model of mood in an exercise setting (Ekkekakis and Petruzzello, 2002). Ekkekakis and Petruzzello (2002) suggested the use of the circumplex model as a conceptual and measurement model for studying affect in the context of exercise. A limitation of the POMS model of mood is that it does not address the full range of positive mood states with recent research suggesting that positive mood dimensions, such as happiness and calmness, may also influence sports performance (Hanin, 2000). It is suggested that the eight mood dimensions assessed provide a more balanced assessment of positive mood and negative mood.

Anger items include "Bad-tempered" and "Angry", Confusion items include "Mixed-up" and "Uncertain", Depression items include "Depressed" and "Downhearted", Fatigue items include "Worn out" and "Tired", Tension items include "Anxious" and "Panicky", and Vigour items include "Alert" and "Energetic". Calmness items include "Calm" and "Relaxed" and Happiness items include "Cheerful" and "Happy". Items are rated on a 5-point scale anchored by "not at all" (0) to "extremely" (4). Terry et al. (1999, 2003) provided comprehensive evidence of factorial, concurrent and predictive validity of the BRUMS. Matthews et al. (1990) provided evidence of factorial validity.

Measurement of Performance Expectation

Constructs of performance expectation were assessed using a 7-item Pre-race Questionnaire (PRQ). Items were drawn from the PRQ (Jones, Swain, and Cale, 1990) which assessed constructs of performance expectation in middle-distance runners. Lane (2001) used a similar scale in his study on marathon runners. Items include perceptions of running form, form in the past race, confidence to attain goal, importance to achieve time goal and importance to perform well.

Coping

Crocker and Graham's (1995) modified version of the COPE (MCOPE) was used to assess coping strategies. Nine subscales were based on the original COPE measure (Carver, Scheier, and Weintraub, 1989): Seeking social support for Instrumental reasons; seeking social support for emotional reasons; behavioural disengagement; planning, suppression of competing activities; venting of emotions; humour; active coping; and denial. Based on empirical research (Madden, Summers, and Brown, 1990), self-blame, wishful thinking, and increasing effort were added. Participants responded to the 48 items of the MCOPE (4 items to each scale) on a 5-point Likert scale indicating the degree to which they utilised each coping strategy. Initial investigations of the internal consistency of the MCOPE have shown alpha coefficients exceeding 0.60 for all subscales except denial (0.42). Giacobbi and Weinberg (2000) reported internal consistency coefficients above 0.60 for all subscales.

Self-Esteem

Rosenberg's self-esteem Scale (Rosenberg, 1965) was used to assess self-esteem. Respondents completed the scale by indicating their agreement with each of the 10 items (e.g. "On the whole I am satisfied with myself", "I certainly feel useless at times") on a 4-point scale (4 = strongly agree, 1 = strongly disagree). After reversing the scoring for 5 negatively worded items, a total Self-esteem score was obtained by summing the 10 responses. The range of scores using this procedure was 10-40 with higher scores indicating higher Self-esteem. In the present study, the alpha coefficient was .82, hence indicating an internally reliable scale.

Concentration During Race

Participants were asked to describe their thoughts during the race. They completed a questionnaire that described concentration during the race as one of four types:

a) *Inward monitoring:* Attention is focused inwardly on how your body feels when running – for example breathing, muscle, soreness, thirst, fatigue, perspiration, blisters, and nausea;

b) *Outward monitoring:* Attention is focused outwardly on things important to performing the task – for example, strategy, mile markers, water stations, split times, route, and conditions.

c) *Inward distraction:* Attention is focused inwardly on anything irrelevant to the task – for example, daydreams, imagining music, math puzzles, philosophy, and religion.

d) *Outward distraction:* Attention is focused outwardly on things unimportant to task performance – for example, scenery, spectators, other runners, and environment.

Performance Satisfaction

Performance Satisfaction was assessed using the two-item measure developed by Lane et al. (2002). These items were "How do you feel about your time in the last race?" and "To what extent did your finish time relate to your pre-race expectations?' Items were rated on a nine-point scale anchored by 'Extremely dissatisfied' (1) and 'Extremely pleased' (9). The two-items correlated significantly ($r = .85$, $p < .01$), thus lending support to the decision to sum these items to produce a score for performance satisfaction.

Procedure

Participants completed mood, performance expectation, coping, and self-esteem the day before the marathon when they registered at the charity head quarters. All participants were part of a wider study that investigated cardiac screening and thus participants were in the testing centre for at least two hours. Participants completed the questionnaires whilst waiting to be assessed by the physiologists. Mood measures completed one-day before competition using the response time frame 'How do feel right now'. Within one hour after finishing the marathon participants completed a mood measure using the response time frame 'how do you feel right now?' Participants completed a mood measure retrospectively. Participants were asked to rate how they felt during the most demanding period in the race. In addition, participants rated how well they performed during the race.

Data analysis

Data were analysed by firstly dichotomizing depressed mood data into either a no-depressive mood symptoms or depression group as suggested by Lane and Terry (2000). MANOVA was used to investigate differences in mood over time, coping self-esteem, perceptions of form, concentration during the race and satisfaction with performance.

RESULTS

Descriptive statistics for mood, self-esteem, coping, perceptions during the race, post-race measures by pre-race depression groups are contained in Tables 1 to 3. MANOVA results indicated a significant mood changes over time (Wilks Lambda = .57, $p < .05$, Eta^2 = .55) and a significant effect for differences in mood states between depression and no-depression groups. The effect for depression was evidenced for pre-competition mood (Wilks Lambda = .56, $p < .05$, Eta^2 = .60); mood states during the run (Wilks Lambda = .27, $p < .05$, Eta^2 = .75) and post-run mood (Wilks Lambda = .26, $p < .05$, Eta^2 = .74, see Table 1).

A MANOVA that used all variables was also conducted. Results for Pre-race Pre-depression: (Wilks' Lambda $_{24,1}$ = .04, $p > .05$, Eta^2 = .99) indicated a large effect size but with so many variables and so few participants, significant results were not expected due to low power. MANOVA for the influence of depressed mood on measures taken during competition indicated a significant effect (Wilks' Lambda $_{12,13}$ = .25, $p < .05$, Eta^2 = .75). A significant effect was also evident for post-competition results by depressed mood (Wilks' Lambda $_{11,13}$ = .26, $p < .05$, Eta^2 = .74). It should be noted that the effect size for pre-competition differences was greater than effect sizes for differences during the race and post-race.

As Table 2 indicates, univariate results indicated that depressed mood was associated with significantly higher scores of pre race tension (Eta^2 = 0.23) and pre race confusion (Eta^2 = 0.44) and lower pre race calmness (Eta^2 = 0.37). For results of retrospective assessments of mood at the hardest point in the race, pre-competition scores of depressed mood were associated with significant higher scores for anger (Eta^2 = 0.24), depression (Eta^2 = 0.22), confusion (Eta^2 = 0.34) with lower happiness (Eta^2 = 0.22) and calmness (Eta^2 = 0.27). For post-competition measures, results pre-competition measures of depression were associated with higher scores of post race anger (Eta^2 = 0.50), depression (Eta^2 = 0.48), confusion (Eta^2 = 0.33) and lower scores of happiness (Eta^2 = 0.39). Participants who reported scores of pre-competition depression reported performing poorly in the marathon (Eta^2 = 0.20) and their time in the race (Eta^2 = 0.36, see Table 3).

Table 1. A comparison of self-esteem and coping, mood, concentration, form, satisfaction with performance by depression and no-depression groups

	No-depression		Depression				
	M	SD	M	SD	F	P	Eta2
Self-esteem	22.25	1.24	22.50	1.07	0.24	0.63	0.01
Seeking Instrumental support	12.38	2.75	13.00	2.88	0.27	0.61	0.01
Seeking emotional support	11.50	3.03	13.13	3.64	1.34	0.26	0.06
Self-blame	12.94	2.69	12.25	2.60	0.36	0.56	0.02
Planning	14.81	2.10	15.25	2.19	0.23	0.64	0.01
Suppressing negative emotions	10.50	1.67	11.25	2.82	0.68	0.42	0.03
Venting emotions	8.81	2.90	9.75	4.89	0.35	0.56	0.02
Humour	12.06	2.95	10.50	2.93	1.50	0.23	0.06
Effort	15.94	1.88	16.13	1.89	0.05	0.82	0.00
Wishful thinking	11.88	3.74	11.63	2.62	0.03	0.87	0.00
Active	14.56	2.03	14.50	2.20	0.01	0.95	0.00
Denial	9.13	3.46	7.63	1.92	1.28	0.27	0.06
Behavioural disengagement	7.75	3.09	6.75	2.31	0.65	0.43	0.03
Number of hours trained per week	9.88	9.24	6.38	2.26	1.09	0.31	0.05
Miles per week run in the last week	28.50	13.94	19.50	21.35	1.56	0.23	0.07
Running form at the moment	6.44	1.59	6.00	2.00	0.34	0.57	0.02
Perceptions about time in the last race	6.56	1.59	5.63	2.13	1.48	0.24	0.06
Extent to which finish time related to your pre-race expectations	6.19	1.76	6.00	2.33	0.05	0.83	0.00
Confidence to attain goal	6.50	1.63	5.63	1.92	1.36	0.26	0.06
How important is it for you to achieve this time goal	5.75	1.91	6.25	1.58	0.41	0.53	0.02
Importance to perform well	6.25	1.91	5.50	2.33	0.71	0.41	0.03

Table 2. A comparison of mood states before, at the hardest point of the race and post-race by depression and no-depression groups

	No-depression		Depresssion				
	M	SD	M	SD	F	P	Eta2
Pre race anger	1.19	1.97	1.63	2.26	0.24	0.63	0.01
Pre race tension	3.94	3.36	7.38	2.45	6.58	0.02	0.23
Pre race vigour	11.00	4.38	11.25	2.96	0.02	0.89	0.00
Pre race fatigue	3.06	4.17	5.75	3.20	2.55	0.13	0.10
Pre race confusion	1.00	1.46	4.13	2.23	17.13	0.00	0.44
Pre race happiness	11.19	2.23	9.00	3.59	3.41	0.08	0.13
Pre race calm	10.69	2.44	7.00	2.20	12.93	0.00	0.37
Hardest point in the race anger	1.38	2.80	4.50	2.73	6.75	0.02	0.24
Hardest point in the race tension	2.38	2.68	5.00	3.70	3.97	0.06	0.15
Hardest point in the race depression	2.00	2.80	4.88	2.36	6.18	0.02	0.22
Hardest point in the race vigour	7.06	4.42	3.75	3.45	3.42	0.08	0.14
Hardest point in the race fatigue	8.69	3.81	8.88	3.60	0.01	0.91	0.00
Hardest point in the race confusion	0.88	1.45	4.88	4.36	11.40	0.00	0.34
Hardest point in the race happiness	6.75	3.53	3.13	2.85	6.32	0.02	0.22
Hardest point in the race calmness	6.06	3.17	2.50	2.00	8.32	0.01	0.27
Post race anger	1.00	0.25	2.63	2.20	22.13	0.00	0.50
Post race tension	0.19	0.54	0.75	1.49	1.86	0.19	0.08
Post race depression	0.00	0.00	2.50	2.27	20.37	0.00	0.48
Post race vigour	8.00	3.43	6.63	2.83	0.96	0.34	0.04
Post race fatigue	9.50	4.65	8.88	3.80	0.11	0.75	0.01
Post race confusion	0.31	0.60	3.13	3.36	11.01	0.00	0.33
Post race happiness	14.06	2.05	10.63	2.33	13.75	0.00	0.39
Post race calm	10.69	2.41	9.00	1.77	3.05	0.10	0.12

Table 3. A comparison of concentration strategy and perceptions of performance by depression and no-depression groups

	No-depression		Depression				
	M	SD	M	SD	F	P	Eta2
Inward monitoring	4.44	2.31	3.50	1.41	1.10	0.31	0.05
Outward monitoring	3.44	2.25	2.75	1.83	0.56	0.46	0.03
Inward distraction	0.31	1.01	0.63	1.41	0.39	0.54	0.02
Outward distraction	2.44	2.63	2.13	2.03	0.09	0.77	0.00
How well did you run today	6.69	1.66	4.88	1.96	5.64	0.03	0.20
How do you feel about your time in today's race	6.88	1.45	4.38	2.00	12.30	0.00	0.36
How did your finish time relate to your pre-race expectations?	5.69	2.30	4.25	1.67	2.45	0.13	0.10

DISCUSSION

The present study explored mood states before, during and post marathon competition. Lane and Terry's (2000) model was used as the conceptual basis on which to explore relationships. In an attempt to examine relationships between mood states and theoretically and practically relevant constructs, an exploratory design was used. Findings indicate that pre-competition depressed mood had a significant effect on mood states experienced before, during and after competition. Further, participants that reported depressed mood a day before competition were significantly less happy with performance than participants that reported no-depression. Findings lend support for the main hypotheses in Lane and Terry's model and further, extend examination of the influence of depressed mood to psychological states experienced during competition.

Previous research has found self-set goals are associated with unpleasant emotional states before competition (Jones et al., 1990; Lane et al, 1995a, 1995b; Lane 2001). In the present study, findings show no significant relationships between mood states and the difficulty of self-set goals. However, although not significant, differences were in the hypothesized direction with the depressed mood group reporting lower confidence and poorer running form. Lane (2001) used a much larger sample of runners than the present study.

Although the research design involved using retrospective measures of mood states during competition, findings are consistent with those reported by Lane et al. (2003) where mood was assessed in real-time during performance. Fatigue scores were similar between depressed mood groups, but among depressed individuals, fatigue was experienced in combination with a range of unpleasant mood states such as confusion and anger. It is suggested that fatigue experienced independently of depressed mood feels qualitatively different to fatigue experienced with depressed mood.

Dispositional variables such as self-esteem and coping were selected based on research by Lane, Jones, and Stevens (2001) that showed they moderated changes in self-efficacy. A limitation of Lane and Terry's model is that all variables are transitory in nature, and whilst depressed mood was central, basing interventions on such variables is difficult. It was hoped that participants reporting depressed mood symptoms was show poorer coping skills and low self-esteem, thereby to provide a link with dispositional variables. However, as Table 1 indicates, depressed mood was not significantly linked to coping or self-esteem. Although individuals with low self-esteem and poor coping skills are likely to suffer depressed mood, a single assessment of depressed mood might not detect this relationship. It is suggested that multiple measures of mood states might be a better design to use to detect relationships between depressed mood and dispositional measures. This result highlights the transient nature of depressed mood experience before competition and suggests that identification of the antecedents of depressed mood could be found elsewhere.

It is suggested that future research follows two possible lines of research. Research is needed to identify the antecedents of depressed mood. The second line of research should investigate the effectiveness of self-regulatory strategies that individuals use to control feelings of depression. The present study indicated that dispositional factors did not correlate with depressed mood. It is possible that individual develop self-regulatory strategies and these override the influence of personality trait variables; that is, an individual low in self-esteem could learn to use music as a self-regulating strategy when feeling depressed. Provided the individual could recognise the onset of such feelings early enough, they could use strategies known to enhance mood.

CONCLUSION

In conclusion, findings from the present study indicate that individuals who reported symptoms of depressed mood experienced a negative mood profile before, during and after the race. Interventions should involve teaching athletes to strategies to regulate symptoms of depressive mood.

REFERENCES

Campbell, J. D. (1990). Self-esteem and clarity of the self-concept. *Journal of Personality and Social Psychology, 59*, 528-549.

Carver, C. S., Scheier, M. F., and Weintraub, J. K. (1989). Assessing coping strategies: A theoretically based approach. *Journal of Personality and Social Psychology, 56*, 267-283.

Crocker, P. R. E., and Graham, T. R. (1995). Coping by competitive athletes with performance stress: Gender differences and relationships with affect. *The Sport Psychologist, 9*, 325-338.

Ekkekakis, P., and Petruzzello, S.J. (2002). Analysis of the affect measurement conundrum in exercise psychology: IV. A conceptual case for the affect circumplex. *Psychology of Sport and Exercise, 3*, 35-63.

Giacobbi, Jr., P. R., and Weinberg, R. S. (2000). An examination of coping in sport: Individual trait anxiety differences and situational consistency. *The Sport Psychologist, 14*, 42-62.

Hanin, Y. (2000). *Emotions in sport*. Champaign, IL: Human Kinetics.

Jones, J. G., Swain, A. B. J., and Cale, A. (1990). Antecedents of multidimensional state anxiety and self-confidence in elite intercollegiate middle-distance runners. *The Sport Psychologist, 4*, 107-118.

Lane, A. M. (2001). Relationships between perceptions of performance expectations and mood among distance runners; the moderating effect of depressed mood. *Journal of Science and Medicine in Sport, 4,* 235-249.

Lane, A. M., and Terry, P. C. (2000). The nature of mood: Development of a conceptual model with a focus on depression. *Journal of Applied Sport Psychology, 12,* 16-33.

Lane, A. M., Lane, H. J., and Firth, S. (2002). Relationships between performance satisfaction and post-competition mood among runners. *Perceptual and Motor Skills, 94,* 805-813.

Lane, A. M., Terry, P. C., and Karageorghis, C. I. (1995a). The antecedents of multidimensional state anxiety and self-confidence in duathletes. *Perceptual and Motor Skills 80,* 911-919.

Lane, A. M., Terry, P. C., and Karageorghis, C. I. (1995b). Path analysis examining relationships among antecedents of anxiety, multidimensional state anxiety, and triathlon performance. *Perceptual and Motor Skills, 81,* 1255-1266.

Lane, A. M., Whyte, G. P., Shave, R., Barney, S., Wilson, M., and Terry, P. C. (2003). Mood disturbance during cycling performance at altitude. *Medicine and Science in Sports and Exercise, 35,* S162.

Madden, C. C., Summers, J. J., and Brown, D. E. (1990). The influence if perceived stress on coping with competitive basketball. *International Journal of Sport Psychology, 21,* 21-35.

Matthews, G., Jones, D. M., and Chamberlain, A. G. (1990). Refining the measurement of mood: The UWIST Mood Adjective Checklist. *British Journal of Psychology* 81, 17-42.

McNair, D. M., Lorr, M., and Droppleman, L.F. (1971). *Manual for the Profile of Mood States.* San Diego, CA: Educational and Industrial Testing Services.

Rosenberg, M. (1965). *Society and the adolescent child.* Princeton, NJ: Princeton University Press.

Terry, P. C., Lane, A. M., and Fogarty, G. (2003). Construct validity of the Profile of Mood States-A for use with adults. *Psychology of Sport and Exercise, 4,* 125-139.

Terry, P. C., Lane, A. M., Lane, H. J., and Keohane, L. (1999). Development and validation of a mood measure for adolescents: POMS-A. *Journal of Sports Sciences, 17,* 861-872.

In: Mood and Human Performance: Conceptual, Measurement...   ISBN 1-60021-269-7
Editor: Andrew M. Lane, pp. 271-295   © 2006 Nova Science Publishers, Inc.

Chapter 15

"WHEN RUNNING IS SOMETHING YOU DREAD": A COGNITIVE BEHAVIOURAL INTERVENTION WITH A CLUB RUNNER

Mark A. Uphill[1] and Marc V. Jones[2]*

[1] Department of Sport Science, Tourism and Leisure,
Canterbury Christ Church University, Canterbury, UK
[2] Centre for Sport and Exercise Research, Faculty of Health and Sciences,
Staffordshire University, Stoke-on-Trent, UK

ABSTRACT

Could an intervention designed to reduce an athlete's anxiety have unintended repercussions for a range of other positive and negative emotions? This case study reports the impact of a cognitive behavioural (C-B) intervention (designed to reduce pre-competitive anxiety) on a club-runner's emotional state and performance satisfaction. A C-B intervention comprising an awareness phase, reappraisal, imagery, and pre-competition routine was delivered over a 4-month period. The efficacy of the intervention was assessed using both visual and statistical analyses. Results suggest that the C-B intervention was effective in reducing the intensity of pre-competitive anxiety and dread. Impact of the intervention on other emotions was mixed. Results are discussed in relation to theoretical and applied issues associated with emotion regulation.

INTRODUCTION

The experience of mood and emotion constitutes an integral part of competitive sport whether one is an athlete, spectator, or sport official. Emotions experienced by athletes in particular, seem to capture the interest of those enthusiastic about sport, both lay people and

---

* Address correspondence concerning this article to Mark Uphill, Department of Sport Science, Tourism and Leisure, Canterbury Christ Church University, North Holmes Road, Canterbury, Kent, CT1 1QU. Tel 01227 767700, Ext 3184. E-mail: mu6@canterbury.ac.uk

researchers alike. Indeed, research on emotion in sport has apparently flourished in recent years. A literature search limited to English language periodicals and the term "emotion" using SportDiscus® returned 124, 307, and 1058 citations for the periods 1971-1980, 1981-1990, and 1991-2000 respectively. The escalation of interest in emotion in sport is perhaps unsurprising, particularly given that emotions may not merely be by-products of athletes' achievement strivings. Specifically, a growing body of research attests to the possible influence of emotions upon components of sport performance (for a review see Jones and Uphill, 2004a). This empirical evidence is accompanied by a widespread conviction that the ability to attain and sustain appropriate emotional conditions prior to, and during performance, is central to success (Crocker, Kowalski, and Graham, 2002; Prapavessis and Grove, 1991).

Given the premise that a certain emotional state may be associated with optimal sport performance (see Hanin, 2000), strategies to help athletes regulate their emotions would clearly be beneficial to the applied sport psychologist. Whether it is regulating feelings of anger, controlling pre-competitive nerves or coping with disappointment following perceived failure, it is widely believed that sport psychologists should employ interventions that are founded upon a theoretical and empirical base (cf. Biddle, Bull, and Seheult, 1992; Lane and Terry, 2000; Thelwell and Maynard, 2003). Therefore, it is somewhat unfortunate that to date, and with some exceptions (e.g., Brunelle, Janelle, and Tennant, 1999; Uphill and Jones, 2005), interventions directed towards emotional control in athletes have been almost exclusively directed towards coping with anxiety (cf. Cerin Szabo, Hunt, and Williams, 2000). In this chapter we broaden the focus to consider whether an intervention to assist an athlete regulate pre-competitive dread and anxiety, may inadvertently influence the frequency and intensity of a broad range of positive and negative emotions.

To provide a framework for this intervention, we begin by considering theory and research pertaining to emotions and their regulation, in particular drawing upon literature in social psychology. In the second part of this chapter we narrow the focus by using a case study to exemplify issues in the regulation of athletes' emotions. The case study describes the rationale for, implementation, and evaluation of, a cognitive behavioural intervention designed to assist an athlete attenuate feelings of pre-competitive dread and anxiety. We conclude this chapter by highlighting a number of issues in relation to the theory and practice of emotion regulation with special reference to a sport population.

THEORETICAL AND EMPIRICAL ISSUES IN RELATION TO EMOTIONS AND THEIR REGULATION

Differentiating between emotion, and other related concepts such as mood and affect, has long troubled philosophers and psychologists (Lazarus, 1994). Certainly, mood and emotion appear to share some commonalities. Both mood and emotion are experiential, that is they are felt or sensed to some degree by the person said to have the emotion or mood (Larsen, 2000). This basic sense of feeling is often termed "affect" which in essence, is the experiential aspect of all valenced (i.e., good or bad) responses (Lazarus, 1991; Russell and Feldman-Barrett, 1999). Both mood and emotion appear to be embodied, often associated with physiological and behavioural characteristics. Some emotions may be associated with distinct facial expressions (Ekman, Levenson, and Friesen, 1983) or discrete physiological patterns (Ax, 1953; Ekman, Levenson, and Friesen, 1990). Moods may be associated with changes in the hormonal and immune systems and behaviourally expressed through changes in posture, gait and tone of voice for example (Larsen, 2000). Space precludes a full analysis of these issues, but if the experiential, physiological and behavioural characteristics of mood and emotion seem to share some commonality, in what ways do mood and emotion differ?

Emotions are often considered to differ to moods on the basis of duration and intensity, although these are arguably superficial and essentially descriptive markers. For example, it is plausible that there are instances of longer-lived low intensity emotion, and short-lived high intensity mood (Davidson, 1994). There is an emerging consensus however, among cognitively oriented theorists at least, that emotions refer to those affective states which arise following an appraisal of the significance of an event for the well-being of an individual (Ekkekakis and Petruzzello, 2000). Specifically, "moods refer to the larger, pervasive, existential issues of one's life, whereas *acute emotions refer to an immediate piece of business, a specific and relatively narrow goal in an adaptational encounter with the environment*" (Lazarus, 1991, p. 48, *emphasis added*). Emotions then, are about and directed toward something, whereas moods are suggested to be related to who we are and how we are doing in life and can rarely be pinned down to anything specific (Frijda, 1994; Lazarus, 1991, 1994). The implication of these distinctions is that research directed towards emotion in sport should aim to assess athletes' *affective response to a specific event* (either real or imagined), rather than assess athletes' feelings in general. The idea that emotions are about something has implications for emotion regulation. Erber and Erber (2000) suggest that the lack of a clearly identifiable source may make it far more difficult to regulate one's moods in comparison to one's emotions. These authors further suggest that if one conceives of mood and emotion as distinct constructs, it is possible that moods and emotions possess different regulatory mechanisms (Erber and Erber, 2000) and warrant different interventions.

EMOTION REGULATION

On the one hand, the regulation of both mood and emotion is apparently subsumed under the rubric of emotional intelligence (e.g., Goleman, 2004). Specifically, emotional intelligence is considered the, "ability to monitor one's own and others' feelings and emotion, to discriminate among them and to use this information to guide one's thinking and action" (Salovey and Mayer, 1990, p. 189). On the other hand, it is also evident that distinct literatures are emerging in relation to the regulation of mood (e.g., Larsen, 2000; Thayer, Newman, and McClain, 1994) and emotion (e.g., Gross, 1999; Ochsner and Gross, 2005). In this section we draw upon literature in social psychology, particularly that of Lazarus (1991, 1999a) and Gross and colleagues (e.g., Gross, 1998a; Ochsner and Gross, 2004) to provide a framework for the regulation of emotions in sport.

As alluded to earlier, emotions can be considered multi-componential responses that may involve change in physiological, behavioural and subjective (affective) characteristics. This response is evoked when a stimulus is appraised in terms of its significance to the well being of an individual. Emotion regulation occurs when an individual attempts to modify one or more aspects of the emotional response (Gross, 1998a, 1998b). Arguably, a fundamental aspect of emotion regulation is understanding the mechanisms or processes that generate and sustain emotions.

A number of appraisal theories (e.g., Lazarus, 1991; Roseman, 1991; Smith and Ellsworth, 1985), although differing slightly in their detail, attempt to understand the role of cognition in the generation of emotion. Appraisal theories suggest that (a) the meaning of a situation or event to an individual influences that individual's emotional reaction and, (b) the meaning that an individual ascribes to a situation or event can be regarded as a composite of individual appraisal components (Bennett, Lowe, and Honey, 2003). Thus the basic premise of appraisal theories is simple; emotions by and large appear to be related to how people evaluate events in their lives (Parrott, 2001). Indeed theory and research has focussed on establishing the relationship between specific appraisals and discrete emotions (Lazarus, 1991; Levine, 1996; Roseman, Antoniou, and Jose, 1996; Smith, Haynes, Lazarus, and Pope, 1993).

One appraisal theory that has been suggested to be applicable to sport and has guided recommendations for emotional control (Jones, 2003) is Lazarus' (1991, 2000) Cognitive Motivational Relational (CMR) theory. From a CMR perspective, appraisals of events are suggested to comprise primary and secondary appraisals. Primary appraisals refer to whether an event or situation is personally relevant to the athlete and comprise three components: Goal relevance, goal congruence, and type of ego involvement (see Lazarus, 1991 for elaboration). Secondary appraisals are concerned with an athlete's perceived coping options and similarly consist of three components: an evaluation about blame, or credit for a particular occurrence, coping potential and future expectancy (Lazarus, 1991). According to Lazarus, appraisals may vary on a continuum from being rapid and occurring outside of conscious awareness, through to being slow, and deliberate cognitive processes.

The question of whether cognitive appraisals cause emotions to arise has been debated vigorously (e.g., Parkinson and Manstead, 1992; Zajonc, 1984). More recent theorising however suggests the debate has become largely superfluous. Both Lazarus (1999b) and Scherer (1999) contend that the answer to the question of whether cognitions cause emotions to arise depends on how one defines emotion and cognition and thus the issue becomes less substantive and more semantic. For example, Ellsworth (1994) suggested that if cognition is defined as including basic sensory information processing, then the elicitation of most, if not all emotions will involve some cognitive processing. On the other hand, if cognition is defined as deliberate and conscious, substantially fewer instances of emotion will be cognitively generated. Whether or not cognitive appraisals *cause* emotions to arise, the notion that cognitions are involved in the sustenance of emotions is less contentious. Recent theorising suggests that cognitive appraisals may be involved in recursive, bi-directional relations with emotion, serving on occasion to sustain or even intensify certain emotions (e,g, Lazarus, 1999a; Lewis, 2000; Ochsner and Gross, 2004). Evidence that cognitions sustain depression for example is provided by Nolen-Hoeksema (2000), who highlighted that people who engage in ruminative responses to depressive symptoms tend to have higher levels of depressive symptoms over time.

In summary, both theory and research suggest that cognitions in one form or another seem to be involved in the elicitation, maintenance, amelioration or augmentation of emotions. If cognitions are involved in the elicitation and maintenance of emotions, interventions that either indirectly (e.g., by enhancing an individual's coping repertoire) or directly influence individuals' cognitions would seem efficacious. We draw upon Gross'

(2002) consensual-process model of emotion regulation to examine this contention in more detail.

According to Gross (2002) five broad types of emotion regulation strategies which occur at different points in the emotion-generative process may be distinguished:

(1) Situation selection,
(2) Situation modification,
(3) Attentional deployment,
(4) Cognitive change, and,
(5) Response modulation.

Situation selection refers to the process of actively choosing to place oneself in a certain situation or context rather than others. A cyclist may choose to be towards the front of a peloton, rather in the centre to minimise the likelihood of being involved in a crash for instance. By choosing one situation rather than another, certain types of appraisals (and associated emotions) may be ameliorated. Situation modification involves behavioural attempts to change a situation to modify its emotional impact. For example, a soccer player angry at a malicious tackle may walk away from his protagonist to avoid further confrontation Attentional deployment involves focussing on some cues, internal or external at the expense of others. For example, focussing attention toward one's heart rate may exacerbate the experience of anxiety. Cognitive change affords the individual an opportunity to change the meaning or significance of an event or situation. For instance, a soccer player who has just missed a penalty, may reappraise the extent to which self-blame is attached for example, "I didn't deliberately miss". Finally, response modulation involves efforts to suppress or augment components of the emotional response.

Strategies implemented at different points in the emotion-generative process may have divergent implications for emotion regulation (Gross, 1998b). The first 4 types of emotion regulation strategy represent antecedent-focussed coping, designed to 'shut down' the emotion, inhibiting the emotion from developing into a 'full-blown' response. Response-focussed emotion-regulation occurs after response tendencies have been initiated effectively 'mopping-up' the emotion (Gross, 1998a, 1998b; Richards and Gross, 2000). The effectiveness of these regulatory efforts in turn has implications for our mental and physical well-being (e.g., Gross, 1998a; Ochsner and Gross, 2005), and in relation to sport, performance. As Gross and colleagues have demonstrated in experimental research, suppression of expressive behaviours increases physiological parameters (blood pressure, heart rate, skin conductance) and may exact cognitive costs such as impairing memory (Gross, 1998a, Gross and Levensen, 1993; Richards and Gross, 2000). In contrast, reappraisal has been shown to alleviate emotional experience and ameliorate behavioural responses, with little apparent physiological cost (Ochsner and Gross, 2004). Alongside Ochsner and Gross' contention that it may sometimes be difficult to change or avoid certain situations or selectively ignore certain aspects of the situation (e.g., a cacophony of noise from a crowd), and its common use in an athletic population (Uphill, Jones, and Lane, 2003), reappraisal is one strategy that both theoretically and empirically may represent an efficacious strategy to enhance athletes' emotions. In the following section, we describe a case study that is designed to assist a runner reappraise the situation which is evoking dread and anxiety in a more positive manner.

A CASE STUDY TO ASSIST A CLUB RUNNER ATTENUATE FEELINGS OF PRE-COMPETITIVE DREAD AND ANXIETY

Case History and Initial Assessment

At the start of the intervention[1], the participant was a 32-year old male club distance runner who was employed full time as a sport performance consultant providing physiological support to individuals and teams. For the preceding 2 years, he had been competing in regional cross-country and road races ranging from 10km to half marathon. Prior to being a club runner, the participant had been a competitive cyclist until a slipped disc prevented him from cycling. In his initial contact with the sport psychologist, the participant reported feelings of pre-competitive dread and anxiety prior to races and perceived that he 'shouldn't be feeling this way prior to competition'. Although he indicated that these feelings detracted from his enjoyment of competition, he was unsure whether dread and anxiety influenced his performance. Nevertheless, the participant indicated that he was very competitive and wanted to run as well as he possibly could. Although this information was informative, a more complete assessment of the participant's needs was derived from a combination of interview and self-report questionnaire. Collectively, these pre-intervention assessments helped formulate a cognitive behavioural intervention and provided baseline data to assess the efficacy of the intervention.

NEEDS ANALYSIS

Competitive Emotions and Performance

To assess the participant's competitive emotions and subjective running performance, a 'competitive feelings inventory' that comprised 2 sections, was completed. The first section consisted of a modification of the Competitive State Anxiety Inventory – 2 (CSAI-2: Martens, Burton, Vealey, Bump, and Smith, 1990), the CSAI-2 (d), in which a directional subscale is appended (Jones and Swain, 1992). The CSAI-2 (d) consists of 27 items and measures the intensity of cognitive anxiety, somatic anxiety, and self-confidence on a 4-point Likert-type scale ranging from 1 (not at all) to 4 (very much so. Intensity scores for each subscale range from 9-36, with higher scores indicative of greater anxiety or confidence. Each subscale has demonstrated adequate internal consistency with alphas between 0.79 and 0.90 (Martens et al., 1990). To assess the direction of anxiety, participants rate whether they perceive the intensity of each item to be facilitative or debilitative to performance on a 7-point scale ranging from –3 (very debilitative through 0 (neutral) to +3 (very facilitative). Direction scores for each subscale therefore range from –27 to +27. Internal consistency analyses have yielded alpha coefficients of between 0.80 and 0.89 for the cognitive anxiety direction subscale and between 0.72 and 0.86 for somatic anxiety (Jones and Hanton, 2001).

---

[1] The intervention was delivered jointly by the first author (at the time of the intervention, a British Association of Sport and Exercise Sciences – BASES – probationary sport psychologist undertaking supervised experience) and second author (British Psychological Society Chartered Psychologist and BASES accredited sport psychologist)

The CSAI-2 has been subjected to criticism in recent years by several authors who have questioned the validity of the questionnaire (e.g., Kerr, 1997; Lane, 2004, Lane, Sewell, Terry, Bartram, and Nesti, 1999). The addition of the direction scale has also created some controversy. For example, the direction of anxiety is assessed independently of the intensity of anxiety. This is particularly problematic when interpreting the effect of anxiety on groups of athletes. For example, because two participants may perceive anxiety to be facilitative yet rate the intensity of anxiety very differently; interpretations concerning the direction of anxiety may therefore be confounded. Accordingly, it has led some to advise caution when interpreting the results, including ourselves (Jones and Uphill, 2004b). Not discounting these concerns, it can be argued that one can have greater confidence that the CSAI-2 (d) is assessing anxiety if other corroborative evidence supplements the questionnaire. The advantage of the CSAI-2 (d) when used with a single participant is that it provides an established method of assessing an athlete's perception of the impact of anxiety on performance (which may be an important indicator of intervention effectiveness), and lessens the problems associated with using this scale with groups as outlined above.

Besides anxiety, the first section of the competitive feelings inventory also required the participant to report the intensity of eleven further emotions (anger, anxiety – for corroborative evidence, disappointment, dread, embarrassment, excitement, guilt, happiness, relief, regret and satisfaction. These emotions were chosen on the basis that they occupied different regions of affective space (Vallerand and Blanchard, 2000), could feasibly occur prior to and/or during running and had previously been demonstrated to be salient to athletes' competitive experience (Uphill, 2004). Opportunity was also given for the participant to report additional emotions not included on this list. The intensity of these emotions was assessed on a Likert-type scale ranging from 0 (not at all) to 4 (extremely).

The second section of the competitive feelings inventory required the participant to complete a retrospective assessment of emotions experienced during the race. The list of eleven emotions was used as in section 1, enabling a comparison to be made of the participant's pre-competitive emotions and those experienced during the race. In addition, the participant was asked to complete a single item measure of performance satisfaction on a 5-point Likert-type scale ranging from 1 (not very) to 5 (very). Although the use of single item measures is typically discouraged, they are nonetheless acceptable when situational constraints limit the use of scales (Wanous, Reichers, and Hudy, 1997). Although it may have been psychometrically more robust to ask the participant to complete scales relating to his competitive emotions and performance, this was considered unreasonable given the nature of repeated assessment and the amount of time it would have taken to do so. Retrospective assessment has also been subject to criticism (Brewer, Van Raalte, Linder, and Van Raalte, 1991), yet this was the preferred methodology given practical and ethical constraints associated with assessing emotions at the time they occur (Ntoumanis and Biddle, 2000).

Attaining a valid and reliable measure of performance was problematic given that the participant was competing in races of different types (cross-country and road races) and lengths (10km to half marathon). Objective performance indices such as time or race position were clearly inappropriate and thus a subjective measure of performance satisfaction was considered most amenable to repeated analysis. Confining analysis of the intervention to only those competitions of a similar type would have been impractical in the present study. The participant was acutely aware of his pre-competitive emotional state, and to use a baseline obtained over a more prolonged period would arguably have been unethical, particularly from a practitioner's perspective.

Interview

An interview was conducted to help clarify the antecedents of dread and anxiety. The runner reported pre-competitive feelings of dread and anxiety to be associated with an anticipation of a difficult and exhausting run ahead and a desire not to lose to his immediate peer group. He suggested that entrants to regional club races remained similar between events and entrants possessed a great range in ability. Although he felt it unrealistic to try and compete against the very best runners in the field, he described a very strong desire to beat those competitors who frequently finished in similar times to him. In addition, the runner acknowledged the importance he attached to producing maximal effort during a race, mentioning that he never wanted to feel as though he could have put in more effort at the conclusion of a race.

PROBLEM FORMULATION

The data collected from the interviews and competitive feelings inventory (see Table 1) indicate that the participant experienced moderate feelings of dread and anxiety prior to most races which detracted from his enjoyment of competition. Comparison of pre-competitive emotions to emotions experienced while running, indicate that feelings of dread and anxiety dissipated with the onset of the race. This observation parallels evidence that somatic anxiety reduces with the onset of competition (Martens, Vealey, and Burton, 1990). Although the participant perceived pre-competitive anxiety to be debilitative to performance (based on results from the CSAI-2(d) and presented in Figure 1), the participant nonetheless was broadly satisfied with his performance (see Table 1). CSAI-2(d) subscales (Table 1), together with interviews, suggest that an improvement in confidence was not an area which the participant felt he wanted to improve upon. For this reason the intensity and direction subscales for confidence contained within the CSAI-2 (d) are excluded from further analyses.

RATIONALE FOR COGNITIVE-BEHAVIOURAL INTERVENTION

Athletes' emotional reactions to competitive stress may not only influence performance, but if experienced repeatedly may have implications for long-term adherence (Gyurcik, Brawley, and Langout, 2002). Of research that has investigated the effect of interventions to assist athletes regulate anxiety (e.g., Hanton and Jones, 1999; Maynard and Cotton, 1993; Prapavessis, Grove, McNair, and Cable, 1992) much has drawn on the multidimensional model of anxiety (see Martens, Vealey, and Burton, 1990). Although interventions founded upon this model have in the main been reported to be effective in alleviating *anxiety* (e.g., Maynard and Cotton, 1993; Hanton and Jones, 1999), whether these interventions influenced other emotions experienced by the athletes remains unknown.

Table 1. Competitive emotions and performance satisfaction pre- and post-intervention (descriptive and inferential statistics)

	Mean (± SD)		Autocorrelation Coefficient	t	p	Effect Size (ES)
	Pre-Intervention	Post-Intervention				
Pre-Competition						
CAI	15.83 ± 1.05	11.40 ± 2.30	0.19	1.81	0.11	4.21
SAI	15.33 ± 2.58	11.20 ± 0.84	0.78[a]	a	a	1.60
CAD	-4.00 ± 6.26	0.00 ± 3.94	0.38	1.23	0.25	-0.64
SAD	-1.67 ± 3.88	1.80 ± 1.64	0.26	1.85	0.09	-0.89
Anger	-	-	-	-	-	-
Anxiety	1.50 ± 1.05	0.60 ± 0.89	0.19	1.51	0.16	0.86
Disappointment	-	-	-	-	-	-
Dread	1.50 ± 1.05	0.40 ± 0.56	0.00	2.11	0.06	1.05
Embarrassment	0.17 ± 0.40	-	0.01	0.91	0.39	0.43
Excitement	1.67 ± 0.82	1.60 ± 0.89	0.03	0.13	0.90	0.09
Guilt	-	-	-	-	-	-
Happiness	1.83 ± 0.75	1.40 ± 0.55	0.34	1.07	0.31	0.57
Regret	-	-	-	-	-	-
Relief	0.50 ± 1.22	-	0.11	1.00	0.36	0.41
Satisfaction	0.50 ± 0.84	0.20 ± 0.45	0.27	0.72	0.49	0.36
During Competition						
Anger	0.67 ± 1.03	0.60 ± 0.55	0.47	0.13	0.90	0.07
Anxiety	0.17 ± 0.41	-	0.11	1.00	0.36	0.41
Disappointment	0.67 ± 1.21	0.40 ± 0.55	0.11	0.45	0.66	0.22
Dread	0.17 ± 0.41	-	0.11	0.91	0.39	0.41
Embarrassment	0.83 ± 1.17	-	0.46	1.75	0.14	0.71
Excitement	1.83 ± 1.72	1.20 ± 0.84	0.10	0.80	0.45	0.36
Guilt	0.33 ± 0.52	0.20 ± 0.45	0.05	0.45	0.66	0.25
Happiness	1.83 ± 1.83	1.60 ± 1.89	0.44	0.26	0.80	0.13
Regret	0.33 ± 0.52	0.60 ± 0.55	0.16	0.83	0.43	-0.52
Relief	1.67 ± 1.37	1.80 ± 0.84	0.17	0.19	0.85	-0.09
Satisfaction	2.00 ± 1.67	1.60 ± 0.89	0.16	0.48	0.64	0.24
Performance Satisfaction	3.83 ± 0.98	3.48 ± 3.67	0.08	0.63	0.54	0.36

a = Significant autocorrelation indicative of serial dependency; - = emotion not experienced during this phase

Conclusions regarding the efficacy of an intervention might be more circumspect if a reduction in anxiety was also accompanied by a reduction in feelings of excitement or happiness associated with competition.

In addition, intensity represents only one dimension of emotion upon which the effect of an intervention can be assessed. Although studies have examined the effect of an intervention on participants' *perception* of anxiety symptoms (e.g., Hanton and Jones, 1999), research does not commonly assess the impact of interventions on the *frequency* of emotions experienced. Put another way, regardless of changes in intensity of emotions, an intervention could be considered effective if the frequency that certain emotions are experienced is reduced. In one study that did examine the effect of an intervention on different aspects of participants' subjective emotional response, Beck and Fernandez (1998) found that a self-monitoring strategy reduced the duration and frequency, but not intensity of anger.

A further consideration when evaluating the impact of cognitive-behavioural interventions is in relation to competitive performance. Because anxiety may not always debilitate performance (Hardy and Parfitt, 1991; Hardy, Parfitt, and Pates, 1994), it may not always be desirable for athletes to reduce their anxiety levels, at least in terms of performance. For example physical tension associated with anxiety has been suggested to impact muscular co-ordination and reduce running economy. Yet in an experiment to investigate this hypothesis, Martin, Craib, and Mitchell (1995) observed that anxiety was unrelated to running economy in eighteen competitive male distance runners. Similarly, Hammermeister and Burton (1995) found that there was no relationship between competitive anxiety and running performance in 293 endurance athletes, including 65 runners.

Given the issues illustrated above the aim of this intervention was threefold: to examine the impact of a cognitive-behavioural intervention on, (a) a range of athletes' competitive emotions, (b) the intensity and frequency of experienced emotions, and (c) satisfaction with performance. To accomplish this, and in keeping with the theoretical and empirical evidence illustrated in the previous section, we developed a multi-modal intervention package comprising a number of strategies, selected because of their likely impact on athletes' appraisals and concomitant emotions. These are considered briefly below.

Awareness

Enhancing athletes' awareness, although not considered a psychological skill (e.g., Hardy, Jones, and Gould, 1996), often forms a component of psychological skills training as part of an education phase (Mace, 1990). Indeed, attaining awareness of one's ideal emotional state may be considered the first step in attaining emotional control (Ravizza, 2001; Feldman-Barrett, Gross, Christenson, and Benvenuto, 2001), and perhaps through increasing the participant's cognisance of conscious and unconscious appraisal processes (Meichenbaum and Gilmore, 1984), lead to change in the participant's emotional state.

Reappraisal

Consistent with the tenets of cognitive motivational relational theory, changes in athletes' appraisals of a situation would be anticipated to elicit concomitant changes in emotions. Thus, the question of *how* to influence change in athletes' appraisal requires consideration. The didactic approach incorporated into the awareness phase may impact athletes' primary and secondary appraisals (Jones, 2003). For example, beating an opponent may diminish in relevance if the participant is educated that the goal may lie outside of his/her control. Alternatively, realising that anxiety dissipates at the onset of competition may influence the secondary appraisal component of future expectations. Specifically, because the participant realises that anxiety is short-lived and that future expectations are positive (i.e., the situation will improve).

In addition, an attempt was made to assist the athlete in re-appraising volitional exhaustion in a positive manner. Specifically, the participant was encouraged to reflect upon the benefits of pushing himself to his physical limits to recognise that physical exhaustion is not "all bad". Although there are potential dangers (e.g., injury) associated with pushing oneself to exhaustion these were undoubtedly mitigated by the participant's adherence to his training programme which (a) prepared him for intense physical effort and, (b) allowed sufficient time for recovery between exhaustive bouts of exercise.

Imagery

Martin, Moritz, and Hall (1999) indicated that at least two types of imagery may be related to attaining a more positive emotional state. Motivational general mastery (MG-M) imagery represents effective coping and mastery of challenging situations whereas motivational general arousal (MG-A) imagery involves images of stress, arousal and anxiety in relation to competition (Martin et al., 1999). Citing Lang's (1977, 1979) bioinformational theory, Martin et al. (1999) posited that when an individual images a situation he or she activates stimulus characteristics (which describe the situation) and response propositions (which represent physiological and behavioural responses to the imaged situation). Imagined response propositions may represent how an athlete reacts in real life situations, and because they are modifiable, may enable athletes to change undesirable emotional responses (Martin et al., 1999). By imaging coping and the effective mastery of stimulus events (MG-M) and the associated emotional reactions (MG-A), imagery may help athletes regulate their emotions effectively.

Support has been obtained for the use of MG-M and MG-A imagery in managing novice climbers' stress (Jones, Mace, Bray, MacRae, and Stockbridge, 2002). Participants who received an imagery script comprising MG-M and MG-A imagery reported lower levels of distress and higher levels of self-efficacy immediately prior to and during an ascent of an indoor climbing wall.

Pre-Competition Routine

Research demonstrates that elite athletes make use of mental skills, including routines in the period prior to competition (Gould, Eklund, and Jackson, 1992). Orlick and Partington (1988) highlighted that the best athletes in their study had well-established pre-performance routines that assisted their preparation for performance. Although the mechanisms through which pre-performance routines influence performance are not clearly understood, it is likely that facilitating attention onto task-relevant cues may be one way in which pre-performance routines enhance the acquisition of a desirable emotional state. By attending to task-relevant cues, positive thoughts and/or images, negative thoughts and/or feelings may be filtered out or attenuated. Re-direction of attention is an emotion-focussed coping strategy proposed by Lazarus (1991) to alter one's emotional state.

IMPLEMENTATION OF INTERVENTION

Following the needs analysis and problem formulation, the intervention was delivered over a 4-month period and comprised 5 sessions delivered on a monthly basis (with the exception of the first 2 sessions which were delivered within one month). During the first session, the participant received feedback about the results of the pre-intervention data and was educated about anxiety and its relation to sport performance. It was emphasised that pre-competitive feelings of anxiety/dread were common, and that although they did not "feel" pleasant, they may not always have a detrimental influence on sport performance. This was reinforced by considering that pre-competitive feelings of dread and anxiety appeared to dissipate with the onset of competition and that the participant was broadly satisfied with his performance despite feeling dread and anxiety. Educational material was given to the participant that, in part, described anxiety as a product of an individual's appraisal of a situation, and outlined the processes by which anxiety may impact performance. The participant was encouraged to identify the factors that contributed to how anxious he felt, and how feelings of dread influenced his performance. The participant reiterated that although he felt dread in most races he participated in, feelings of dread were exacerbated by the weather (wet and windy conditions), the course (hilly or muddy), and the competition (wanting to beat his immediate peers). Because endurance events invariably involve experiencing physical discomfort, it was explained that it may not be possible to totally alleviate pre-competitive feelings of anxiety. Specifically, it was difficult to conceive that physical discomfort and pain could be removed from the process of competition, and thus at least some feelings of anxiety may remain post-intervention.

The second session, while following up any issues arising from the previous session, was designed primarily to educate the participant about imagery and to construct a 'best performance' imagery script. The participant expressed a desire to beat one competitor in particular that he perceived to be his nearest rival. When questioned further, he could not clarify why beating this opponent assumed great significance, except that the "winner" would invariably gain pleasure from teasing and "ribbing" the "loser". In what may be described as Socratic dialogue, the sport psychologist questioned the participant about the efficacy of such a goal. Socratic dialogue describes the process of "self-discovery" whereby athletes are asked thought-provoking questions, the aim of which is to get athletes to re-evaluate self-defeating ideas or misperceptions (Jones, 2003). Because the participant recognised that he liked to pace himself during the race, let the leaders go at the start and enjoy catching them up, the sport psychologist suggested "using" other competitors as a target, reflecting intermediary goals to enhance motivation. In addition, when compared to outcome goals (e.g., beating others), a process goal (e.g., "using" other competitors) is more within the athlete's control and therefore less likely to be associated with heightened anxiety (cf. Kingston and Hardy, 1997).

The rationale for the use of motivational general mastery and best performance imagery was then described to the participant whom was receptive to the use of imagery to build confidence and cope with hard races. A best performance imagery script was then constructed, Although initially the script was expressed with few sensory recollections, with some prompting the participant was able to construct a personally meaningful script that engaged a number of senses associated with running well. These included the rhythmic pattern of feet, "breathing like a steam train" and visually "seeing" himself run past other competitors. It was advised that the participant practice the script and modify any feelings or sensations that he felt inappropriate, or to include others that better encapsulated the feeling of running well. The participant was asked to practice the imagery script for 3-4 minutes every day at a time when he was feeling relaxed, perhaps lying in bed before going to sleep.

Alongside a review of progress, the aim of session three was to help the participant develop a pre-competition routine. The benefits of having a consistent pre-competition routine was explained, and the participant remarked that he would like to feel positive going into races on a more consistent basis. The importance of developing a competition routine that was personally relevant was explained. Positive self-talk and imagery were incorporated in the pre-competition routine to assist the participant in attaining a more desirable emotional state.

Session four afforded an opportunity for the participant to explore the benefits of pushing himself hard during competition. Quotes from Lance Armstrong (2003), an American endurance cyclist were also provided to the participant. These emphasised that racing strategically was different from being "weak" and that there may be positives to the found alongside the pain of pushing oneself to the limit. When asked to consider any positives with pushing himself hard, the participant noted imagining the capillaries of his muscles growing in response to his effort.

The final session consisted of a review of progress to date. The participant mentioned using imagery before going to bed, imagining himself running a familiar training route from an external perspective. Images were associated with dodging branches, running past other competitors and having a "commentator" describing his run as if on television. In addition during training, he mentioned that he would sometimes "drift off", imagining himself running in the Himalayas. It emerged that in addition to being an imagery stimulus, competing in the Himalayan marathon was a long-term goal for the participant. The tendency of the participant to "drift off" during training is indicative of dissociation strategies described by Masters and Ogles (1998). It should be noted that the participant felt imagery to be of most benefit during training, noting that his training times improved when imagining himself running in the Himalayas. The participant found that practising imagery at home was difficult, and found it much easier to use imagery while running.

With regards to the pre-competition routine, the participant suggested that it was too long. Specifically, the behaviours took only a fraction of the time that was anticipated. In addition, he recognised that interacting with his competitors presented a barrier to completing the mental aspects of his routine effectively. For this reason, having a shorter period of time to talk positively to himself and imagine a successful performance was preferred by the participant to help attain an appropriate mental state.

The participant reported that his perceived ideal pre-competitive emotional state had changed. Specifically, completing the competitive feelings inventory, along with material discussed in previous sessions, had increased his awareness of how he would like to feel. In previous sessions, the participant outlined how he wanted to reinterpret feelings associated with anxiety more positively. In this session, the participant indicated that he preferred to feel more relaxed and unconcerned with beating opponents, to enjoy competing and not feel "bad". He also indicated a change in his perception regarding the impact of his pre-competitive emotional state upon his running performance. The participant suggested that his running performance was dictated by the amount and quality of his training, and that no matter how he felt prior to the race he would always run as hard as he could. Acknowledging that feelings of dread were exacerbated by a focus on wanting to beat opponents, he said, "You don't do all the training, the threshold runs, the speed work, in order to feel s**t going into the race." He described how he wanted to get all aspects of his fitness "right": Endurance, speed, and to put them into practice, using each competitor as a target to pull and propel himself around the race. Importantly, the participant felt that the intervention was effective in achieving a more desirable emotional state.

EVALUATION

The intervention was evaluated using visual and statistical techniques. Although all data were graphed and analysed, because of the focus upon anxiety, only the CSAI-2 (d) subscales and those competitive emotions demonstrating a large effect size (see Table 1) are illustrated (see Figures 1 and 2). Criteria provided by Martin and Pear (1996) guided visual inspection. According to Martin and Pear (1996), one can have greater confidence that a treatment effect has been observed: (a) few overlapping data points should occur between pre- and post-intervention, (b) the sooner an effect is observed after intervention, (c) the larger the size of the effect, (d) the number of times the effect is repeated within and between subjects, and (e) when baseline performance is stable or in a direction opposite predicted for the intervention. However, because the use of visual inspection alone to judge the effectiveness of an intervention is controversial (Gottman, 1981), two complementary analyses were conducted to evaluate the statistical and practical significance of the intervention respectively. The participant's competitive emotions and performance satisfaction were assessed on 11 separate occasions, 6 prior to the intervention and 5 post-intervention, and in the absence of serial-dependency[1] pre- and post-intervention data were evaluated using t-tests.

---

[1] Serial dependency is a property of single subject studies whereby successive responses by the same participant are correlated (Ottenbacher, 1986). Because t-tests assume that each data point is independent, t-tests can only be used in situations where data do not exhibit serial dependency. To determine if data were serially dependent an autocorrelation coefficient was calculated for each of the competitive emotions, CSAI-2(d) subscales, and performance satisfaction data, while Bartlett's test was used to determine if the autocorrelation coefficient was significant (Ottenbacher, 1986). A conservative approach to determining serial dependency is to compute autocorrelations pre- and post-intervention. An exception to this rule is when there are 5 or less data points in a phase, in which case the coefficient should be computed across the entire data series (Ottenbacher, 1986). Using this approach, it was calculated that serial dependency existed when the autocorrelation coefficient was above 0.60.

Finally, effect sizes (ES) were calculated[2] and evaluated using the benchmarks outlined by Cohen (1977). An effect size of less than 0.2 is designated small, 0.5 is moderate, and 0.8 or more is large. An over-emphasis on statistical significance to evaluate the effect of an intervention may be considered inappropriate as little consideration is given to the size of the effect. Small but meaningful effects, may be ignored by an over reliance on attaining the much coveted 5% significance level. In this regard visual and statistical techniques should not be viewed as competing analytical approaches (Shambrook and Bull, 1996). Rather, the complementary approaches may help to ensure that practitioners do not continue using an intervention when it is ineffective, or withdraw an intervention when it is indeed working (Shambrook and Bull, 1996).

Effect of the Intervention on the Intensity of the Participant's Competitive Emotions

Consideration of the impact of the intervention on the participant's response to the CSAI-2 (d) suggests that a practically significant reduction in the intensity of cognitive and somatic symptoms was demonstrated (see figure 1). This was accompanied by what can be described as a shift from a debilitative to neutral perception of the symptoms of cognitive anxiety and somatic anxiety on performance.

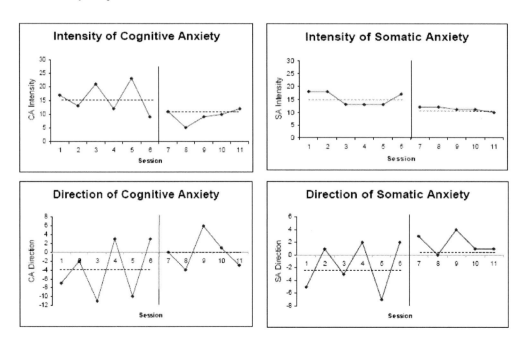

Figure 1. Effect of intervention on CSAI-2 (d) subscales

---

[2] Although several methods of calculating effect size have been proposed, we used the method suggested by Kazis, Anderson and Meenan (1989; cited in Hevey & McGee, 1998). Given the sometimes large variability in baseline data, this was considered a conservative estimate of effect size. Specifically, increases in standard deviations of baseline data decrease the estimated effect size for equivalent mean scores.

Figure 2 illustrates that although the impact was not immediate, there was a large reduction in the mean intensity of pre-competitive dread and anxiety. Besides dread and anxiety, the impact of the intervention on the intensity of other pre-competitive emotions was mixed. A moderate reduction in happiness (ES = 0.57) was also exhibited, although there was little change in other emotions pre- to post-intervention. The impact appeared to exert little influence on emotions experienced during competition, with only a moderate increase in regret (ES = 0.52) and moderate reduction in embarrassment (ES = 0.71) observed. No statistical difference in the participant's emotions pre- and post-intervention were observed, although reductions in the intensity of dread approached significance (p = .06).

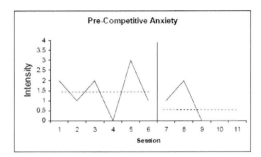 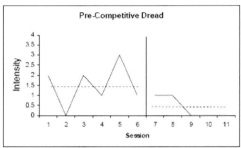

Figure 2. Effect of intervention on intensity of competitive emotions

Effect of the Intervention on the Frequency of the Participant's Emotions

Figure 3 illustrates that there is a 43% reduction in both the frequency of pre-competitive dread and anxiety following the intervention, with comparatively little change in the frequency with which other emotions were experienced (the next largest reductions were in embarrassment and relief, both 18%) pre-competition. There was little reliable impact of the intervention on the frequency of emotions experienced during competition (see figure 4). Given the small number of data points, assessment of the frequency with which emotions are experienced (i.e., whether the participant reported the emotion pre- or during competition) is quite crude. Specifically, any change between the phases represents a comparatively large percentage difference. Nevertheless, researchers and practitioners are encouraged to use multiple indices of emotion, including subjective emotion experience, to assess the efficacy of the intervention.

Effect of the Intervention on Performance Satisfaction

Data suggested that there was a marginal reduction in mean intensity of performance satisfaction post-intervention. However, given the large number of overlapping data points, there is little evidence that the intervention had a reliable effect on the participant's satisfaction with performance. This conclusion is supported by the absence of a statistical difference between performance satisfaction pre- and post-intervention and relatively small effect size (ES = 0.36).

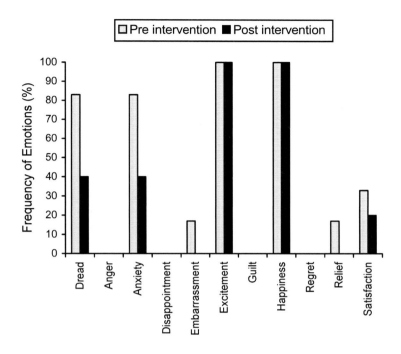

Figure 3. Effect of intervention on frequency of emotions experienced pre-competition

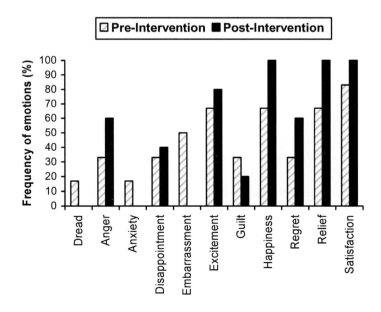

Figure 4. Effect of intervention on frequency of emotions experienced during competition

DISCUSSION AND SUMMARY

The aims of this intervention were to investigate the impact of a cognitive-behavioural intervention on; (a) a range of athletes' competitive emotions, (b) the intensity and frequency of experienced emotions, and (c) satisfaction with performance. To accomplish this, and in keeping with the theoretical and empirical evidence highlighted earlier, we developed a multi-modal intervention package comprising a number of strategies, selected because of their likely impact on athlete appraisals and concomitant emotions. Results of the intervention suggest that a cognitive-behavioural intervention designed to assist a runner reappraise the situation which is evoking dread and anxiety in a more positive manner, was at least partially effective.

Despite the lack of statistical significance, visual inspection, when considered alongside effect sizes, suggested that the intervention was effective in reducing the intensity of pre-competitive dread and anxiety, and creating a less debilitative perception of anxiety. Based on literature reviewed, it is speculated that this emotional change is associated with a concomitant change in appraisal. For example, a change in the participant's goals (wanting to enjoy competition versus wanting to beat opponents), future expectations (anxiety won't effect my performance), and an enhanced repertoire of coping skills evidenced through discussion within individual consultancy sessions (see above), provides indirect support for the possibility that cognitive behavioural interventions targeted towards athletes' appraisals may be effective in eliciting emotional change. Within Gross' (2002) formulation, this study lends support to the idea that an antecedent-focussed emotion regulation strategy (i.e., cognitive change) may assist an athlete in regulating his/her anxiety.

The impact of this comparatively brief intervention on the intensity and frequency of other emotions was mixed with.moderate effect sizes associated with comparatively small changes in emotional intensity pre- to post-intervention (e.g., regret). Effect sizes, as with statistical significance need to be treated with appropriate caution (Cohen, 1988). For example, given an equivalent standard deviation (SD = 0.8), a mean change of 0.4 pre- to post-intervention would be interpreted as a moderate effect, whereas, a mean change of 0.3 would be interpreted as a small effect based on Cohen's (1988) conventions. From an applied perspective, it would therefore be desirable to extend the duration of baseline and post-intervention phases in a multiple-baseline, between-subject design. Recognising that an intervention targeted towards a selected emotion *may* influence the intensity and/or frequency of other emotions represents an important consideration for the applied practitioner. According to Hanin (2000), there is a band of emotional intensity associated with optimal performance. From this perspective, should a reduction/increase in the intensity of one emotion extend to a range of positively and/or negatively valenced emotions, there is a possibility that performance will decline if the intensity of emotions lies above or below the band of optimal intensity. Interestingly then, the participant remained broadly satisfied with his performance despite an apparent change in his emotional state. This is not surprising however, given that the intervention was directed ostensibly toward regulating emotion, rather than enhancing performance. One can only assume that despite an apparent change in the intensity of his emotional state, the change remained either within, or outside of the optimal intensity because performance satisfaction remained largely unchanged. On this note, further understanding of the circumstances under which emotions influence sport performance is desirable (see also Jones and Uphill, 2004a). Examining the impact of emotion regulation strategies on physiological (e.g., heart rate) and cognitive (e.g., working memory) parameters thought to underlie competitive sport performance would arguably be advantageous.

The multi-modal intervention used in the present study did not permit an investigation of the contribution of individual components of the intervention to a possible change in the participant's appraisals or emotional state. However, given that not all athletes will like all psychological strategies all of the time, the use of a combination of mental skills may be considered efficacious practically, as it equips athletes with a "toolbox" of mental skills to draw upon either before or during competition (c.f. Patrick and Hrycaiko, 1998). Further research investigating relative merits of individual strategies in enhancing athletes' emotional states may yield more effective and cost-effectiveness interventions for individual athletes.

Notwithstanding the content of the intervention which was founded upon a strong theoretical and empirical base, the design of the intervention can also be defended, despite acknowledged limitations. For example, although it would have been desirable to extend the baseline over which data were collected, this would have been difficult (e.g., competitions were of different lengths and type), and arguably unethical, given that the participant was acutely aware of his emotional state which was detracting from his enjoyment of competition. Similarly, although the AB design employed in the present study may be considered a limitation, it was neither feasible nor desirable to employ an ABA or ABAB design. The main barrier to employing such a design was that the intervention effects could not be "undone", even if the intervention was withdrawn.

We began this chapter by outlining distinctions between mood and emotion, and the theoretical and empirical base for directing interventions for emotional control toward athletes' appraisals of the event. As this case study exemplifies, problematically, we only have an imperfect and indirect window into the association between athlete appraisals and concomitant emotions. If we are interested in athlete appraisals we are reliant upon either self-report (Scherer, 1999) or neuroscience (Ochsner and Gross, 2004; 2005) to provide information about the types of appraisals underlying emotional experience. Neuroscience may eventually help to shed light on what are, when closely scrutinised, somewhat crude distinctions between mood and emotion. For example, our earlier contention that moods and emotions may be differentiated on the basis of individuals' ability to recognise the stimulus giving rise to the affect has been noted as problematic (e.g., Lane and Terry, 2000). That is, individuals may have difficulty in differentiating feelings that arise in response to an event and those more generalised background feelings that underlie specific emotions (Lane, and Terry, 2000). Nevertheless, if one subscribes to the contention that a change in feeling cannot occur without an associated change in the brain, dynamically modelling subjective experiences alongside changes in neuronal networks may eventually help to underscore neuronal pathways involved in what we would commonly call mood and emotion (see also Lewis and Granic, 2000; Izard, Ackerman, Schoff, and Fine, 2000).

In summary, the theoretical and empirical premise that appraisals may be implicated in the generation, sustenance, augmentation and amelioration of emotions was reviewed. Despite acknowledged limitations, a cognitive-behavioural intervention provided tentative and indirect support for the possibility that for athletes who wish to achieve a more a desirable emotional state, this may be facilitated by influencing the way in which athletes appraise certain events and situations.

REFERENCES

Armstrong, L. (2003). *Every second counts: From recovery to victory*. London: Yellow Jersey Press.

Ax, A. F. (1953). The physiological differentiation between fear and anger in humans. *Psychosomatic Medicine, 15*, 433-442.

Beck, R., and Fernandez, E. (1998). Cognitive behavioural self-regulation of the frequency, duration, and intensity of anger. *Journal of Psychopathology and Behavioural Assessment, 20*, 217-229.

Bennett P., Lowe R., and Honey K. (2003). Appraisals and emotions: a test of the consistency of reporting and their associations. *Cognition and Emotion, 17*, 511-20.

Biddle, S. J. H., Bull, S. J., Seheult, C. L. (1992). Ethical and professional issues in contemporary British sport psychology. *The Sport Psychologist, 6*, 66-76.

Brewer, B. W., Van Raalte, J. L., Linder, D. E., and Van Raalte, N. S. (1991). Peak performance and the perils of retrospective introspection. *Journal of Sport and Exercise Psychology, 13*, 227-238.

Brunelle, J. P., Janelle, C. M., Tennant, L. K. (1999). Controlling competitive anger among male soccer players. *Journal of Applied Sport Psychology, 11*, 283-297.

Cerin, E., Szabo, A., Hunt, N., and Williams, C. (2000). Temporal patterning of competitive emotions: A critical review. *Journal of Sports Sciences, 18*, 605-626.

Cohen, J. (1988). *Statistical power analysis for behavioural sciences (2nd Ed)*. Hillsdale, NJ: Academic Press.

Crocker, P. R. E., Kowalski, K. C., and Graham, T. R. (2002). Emotion in sport. In J. M. Silva III, and D. E, Stevens (Eds.), *Psychological foundations of sport* (pp. 107-131). London: Allyn and Bacon.

Davidson, R. J. (1994). On emotion, mood, and related affective constructs. In P. Ekman and R. J. Davidson (Eds.), *The nature of emotion: Fundamental questions* (pp.51-55). Oxford: OUP.

Ekkekakis, P., and Petruzzello, S. J. (2000). Analysis of the affect measurement conundrum in exercise psychology I. Fundamental issues. *Psychology of Sport and Exercise, 1*, 71-88.

Ekman, P., Levenson, R. W., and Friesen, W. V. (1990). Autonomic nervous system activity distinguishes between emotions. *Science, 221*, 1208-1210.

Ekman, P., Levenson, R.W., and Friesen, W. V. (1983). Autonomic nervous system activity distinguishes between emotions. *Science, 221*, 1208-1210.

Ellsworth, P. C. (1994). Levels of thought and levels of emotion. In P. Ekman and R. J. Davidson (Eds.), *The nature of emotion: Fundamental questions (pp. 192-196)*. Oxford: OUP.

Erber, R., and Erber, M. W. (2000). Mysteries of mood regulation, part II: The case of the happy thermostat. *Psychological Inquiry, 11*, 210-213.

Feldman-Barrett, L., Gross, J. J., Christenson, T. C., and Benvenuto, M. (2001). Knowing what you're feeling and knowing what to do about it: Mapping the relation between emotion differentiation and emotion regulation. *Cognition and Emotion, 15*, 713-724.

Frijda, N. H. (1994). Emotions are functional, most of the time. In P. Ekman and R. J. Davidson (Eds.), *The nature of emotion: Fundamental questions* (pp.112-122). Oxford: OUP.

Goleman, D. (2004). Emotional intelligence and working with emotional intelligence (omnibus). London: Bloomsbury.

Gottman, J.M. (1981). *Time-series analysis: A comprehensive introduction for social scientists.* Cambridge: Cambridge University Press.

Gould, D., Eklund, R. C., and Jackson, S. A. (1992). 1988 U.S. Olympic wrestling excellence I: Mental preparation, precompetitive cognition and affect. *The Sport Psychologist, 6,* 358-362.

Gross, J. J. (1998a). Antecedent- and response-focussed emotion regulation: Divergent consequences for experience, expression, and physiology. *Journal of Personality and Social Psychology, 74,* 224-237.

Gross, J. J. (1998b). The emerging field of emotion regulation: An integrative review. *Review of General Psychology, 2,* 271-299.

Gross, J. J. (1999). Emotion regulation: Past, present, future. *Cognition and Emotion, 13,* 551-573.

Gross, J. J. (2002). Emotion regulation: affective, cognitive, and social consequences. *Psychophysiology, 39,* 281-291.

Gross, J. J., and Levenson, R. W. (1993). Emotional suppression: Physiology, self-report, and expressive behaviour. *Journal of Personality and Social Psychology, 64,* 970-986.

Gyurcsik, N.C., Brawley, L.R., and Langhout, N. (2002). Acute thoughts, exercise consistency, and coping self-efficacy. *Journal of Applied Social Psychology, 32,* 2134-2153.

Hammermeister, J., and Burton, D. (1995). Anxiety and the Ironman: Investigating the antecedents and consequences of endurance athletes' state anxiety. *The Sport Psychologist, 9,* 29-40.

Hanin, Y. L. (2000). Individual zones of optimal functioning (IZOF) model: Emotion-performance relationships in sport. In Y. L. Hanin (Ed.), *Emotions in sport* (pp.65-89). Champaign, IL: Human Kinetics.

Hanton, S., and Jones, G. (1999). The effects of a multimodal intervention programme on performers: II. Training the butterflies to fly in formation. *The Sport Psychologist, 13,* 22-41.

Hardy, L., and Parfitt, G. (1991). A catastrophe model of anxiety and performance. *British Journal of Psychology, 82,* 163-178.

Hardy, L., Jones, G., and Gould, D. (1996). *Understanding psychological preparation for sport: Theory and practice of elite performers.* Chichester: Wiley.

Hardy, L., Parfitt, G., and Pates, J. (1994). Performance catastrophes in sport: A test of the hysteresis hypothesis. *Journal of Sports Sciences, 12,* 327-334.

Hevey, D., and McGee, H. M. (1998). The effect size statistic. *Journal of Health Psychology, 3,* 163-170).

Izard, C. E., Ackerman, B. P., Schoff, K. M., and Fine, S. E. (2000). Self-organisation of discrete emotions, emotion patterns, and emotion-cognition relations. In M. D. Lewis and I. Granic (Eds.), *Emotion, development, and self-organisation: Dynamic systems approaches to emotional development* (pp. 15-36). Cambridge: Cambridge University Press.

Jones, G., and Hanton, S. (2001). Pre-competitive feeling states and directional anxiety interpretations. *Journal of Sports Sciences, 19*, 385-395.

Jones, J. G., and Swain, A. B. J. (1992). Intensity and direction dimensions of competitive anxiety and relationships with competitiveness. *Perceptual and Motor Skills, 74*, 467-472.

Jones, M. V. (2003.). Controlling emotions in sport. *The Sport Psychologist, 14, 471-486.*

Jones, M. V., and Uphill, M. A. (2004a). Emotion in sport: Antecedents and performance consequences. In D. Lavallee, J. Thatcher, and M. V. Jones (Ed.), Coping and emotion in sport (pp.9-28). Hauppage, NY: Nova.

Jones, M. V., and Uphill, M. (2004b). Responses to the Competitive State Anxiety Inventory –2 (d) by athletes in anxious and excited scenarios. *Psychology of Sport and Exercise.*

Jones, M. V., Mace, R. D., Bray, S. R., MacRae, A., and Stockbridge, C. (2002). The Impact of Motivational Imagery on the Emotional State and Self-efficacy levels of Novice Climbers. *Journal of Sport Behaviour, 25*, 57-73.

Kerr, J. H. (1997). *Motivation and emotion in sport: Reversal theory.* Hove, East Sussex: Psychology Press.

Kingston, K., and Hardy, L. (1997). Effects of different types of goals on processes that support performance. *The Sport Psychologist, 11*, 277-293.

Lane, A. M. (2004). Emotion, mood and coping in sport: Measurement issues. In In D. Lavallee, J. Thatcher, and M. V. Jones (Ed.), Coping and emotion in sport (pp.255-272). Hauppage, NY: Nova.

Lane, A. M., and Terry, P. C. (2000). The nature of mood: Development of a conceptual model with a focus on depression. *Journal of Applied Sport Psychology, 12*, 16-33.

Lane, A. M., Sewell, D. F., Terry, P. C., Bartram, D., and Nesti, M. S. (1999). Confirmatory factor analysis of the Competitive State Anxiety Inventory – 2. *Journal of Sports Sciences, 17*, 505-512.

Lang, P. J. (1977). Imagery in therapy: An information processing analysis of fear. *Behaviour Therapy, 8*, 862-886.

Lang, P. J. (1979). A bio-informational theory of emotional imagery. *Psychophysiology, 17*, 495-512.

Larsen, R. J. (2000). Toward a science of mood regulation. *Psychological Inquiry, 11*, 129-141.

Lazarus, R. S. (1991). *Emotion and adaptation.* Oxford: OUP.

Lazarus, R. S. (1994). Universal antecedents of the emotions. In P. Ekman and R. J Davidson (Eds.), *The nature of emotion: Fundamental questions* (pp.163-171). Oxford: OUP.

Lazarus, R. S. (1999a). *Stress and emotion: A new synthesis.* London: Free Association Books.

Lazarus, R. S. (1999b). The cognition-emotion debate: A bit of history. In T. Dalgleish and M. J. Power (Eds.).*Handbook of cognition and emotion* (pp. 3-19). Chichester: Wiley.

Lazarus, R. S. (2000). How emotions influence performance in competitive sports. *The Sport Psychologist, 14*, 229-252.

Levine, L. J. (1996). The anatomy of disappointment: A naturalistic test of appraisal models of sadness, anger, and hope. *Cognition and Emotion, 10*, 337-359.

Lewis, M. D. (2000). Emotional self-organisation at three time scales. In M. D. Lewis and I. Granic (Eds.) *Emotion, development, and self-organisation: Dynamic systems approaches to emotional development* (pp. 37-69). Cambridge: Cambridge University Press.

Lewis, M. D., and Granic, I. (2000). *Emotion, development, and self-organisation: Dynamic systems approaches to emotional development.* Cambridge: Cambridge University Press.

Mace, R. (1990). Cognitive behavioural interventions in sport. In J. G. Jones and L. Hardy (Eds.), *Stress and performance in sport* (pp. 203-230). Chichester: Wiley.

Martens, R., Burton, D., Vealey, R. S., Bump, L. A., and Smith, D. E. (1990). Development and validation of the Competitive State Anxiety Inventory – 2. In R. Martens, R. S. Vealey, and D. Burton (Eds.) *Competitive anxiety in sport* (pp.117-190). Champaign, IL: Human Kinetics.

Martens, R., Vealey, R. S., and Burton, D. (1990). *Competitive anxiety in sp*ort. Champaign, IL: Human Kinetics.

Martin, G., and Pear, J. (1996). *Behaviour modification (5th ed.).* Upper Saddle River, NJ: Prentice Hall.

Martin, J. J., Craib, M., and Mitchell, V. (1995). The relationships of anxiety and self-attention to running economy in competitive male distance runners. *Journal of Sports Sciences, 13*, 371-376.

Martin, K. A., Moritz, S. E., and Hall, C. R. (1999). Imagery use in sport: a literature review and applied model. *The Sport Psychologist, 13*, 245-268.

Masters, K.S., and Ogles, B.M. (1998). Associative and dissociative cognitive strategies in exercise and running: 20 years later, what do we know? *The Sport Psychologist, 12*, 253-270.

Maynard, I. W., and Cotton, C. J. (1993). An investigation of two stress-management techniques in a field setting. *The Sport Psychologist, 7*, 375-387.

McMullen, M. N., and Markman, K. D. (2002). Affective impact of close counterfactuals: Implications of possible futures for possible pasts. *Journal of Experimental Social Psychology, 38*, 64-70.

Meichenbaum, D., and Gilmore, J. D. (1984). The nature of unconscious processes: A cognitive-behavioural perspective. In K. S. Bowers, and D. Meichenbaum (Eds.), *The unconsciousness reconsidered* (pp.273-297). Chichester: Wiley.

Nolen-Hoeksema, S. (2000). The role of rumination in depressive disorders and mixed anxiety/depressive symptoms. *Journal of Abnormal Psychology, 109*, 504-511.

Ntoumanis, N., and Biddle, S. J. H. (2000). Relationship of intensity and direction of competitive anxiety with coping strategies. *The Sport Psychologist, 14*, 360-371.

Ochsner, K.N., and Gross, J.J. (2004). Thinking makes it so: A social cognitive neuroscience approach to emotion regulation. In R.F. Baumeister and K.D. Vohs (Eds). *Handbook of self-regulation: Research, theory, and applications* (pp. 229-255). New York: Guilford Press.

Ochsner, K.N., and Gross, J.J. (2005). The cognitive control of emotion. Trends in *Cognitive Sciences, 9*, 242-249.

Orlick, T., and Partington, J. (1988). *Mental links to excellence. The Sport Psychologist, 1*, 4-17.

Ottenbacher, K. J. (1986). *Evaluating clinical change: Strategies for occupational and physical therapists.* Baltimore: Williams and Wilkins.

Parkinson, B., and Manstead, A. S. R. (1992). Appraisal as a cause of emotion. In M.S. Clark (Ed.), *Review of personality and social psychology, Vol 13*, pp. 122-149. New York: Sage.

Parrott, W. G. (2001). *Emotions in social psychology*. Hove, East Sussex: Psychology Press.

Prapavessis, H., and Grove, J. R. (1991). Precompetitive emotions and shooting performance: The mental health and zone of optimal function models. *The Sport Psychologist, 5*, 223-234.

Prapavessis, H., Grove, J. R., McNair, P. J., and Cable, N. T. (1992). Self-regulation training, state anxiety, and sport performance: A psychophysiological case study. *The Sport Psychologist, 6*, 213-229.

Ravizza, K. (2001). Increasing awareness for sport performance. In J. M. Williams (Ed.), *Applied Sport Psychology: Personal growth to peak performance* (pp. 179-187). London: Mayfield.

Richards, J. M., and Gross, J. J. (2000). Emotion regulation and memory: The cognitive costs of keeping one's cool. *Journal of Personality and Social Psychology, 79*, 410-424.

Roese, N. J. (1997). Counterfactual thinking. *Psychological Bulletin, 121*, 133-148.

Roseman, I. J. (1991). Appraisal determinants of discrete emotions. *Cognition and Emotion, 5*, 161-200.

Roseman, I. J., Antoniou, A. A., and Jose, P. E. (1996). Appraisal determinants of emotions: Constructing a more accurate and comprehensive theory. *Cognition and Emotion, 10*, 241-277.

Russell, J. A., and Feldman Barrett, L. (1999). Core affect, prototypical emotional episodes, and other things called emotion: Dissecting the elephant. *Journal of Personality and Social Psychology*, Special Section on the Structure of Emotion, *76*, 805-819.

Salovey, P., and Mayer, J. D. (1990). Emotional intelligence. *Imagination, Cognition, and Personality, 9*, 185-211.

Scherer, K. R. (1999). Appraisal theory. In M. Lewis and J. M. Haviland-Jones (Eds.), *Handbook of emotions* (2nd Ed, pp. 637-663). Chichester: Wiley.

Shambrook, C. J., and Bull, S. J. (1996). The use of a single-case research design to investigate the efficacy of imagery training. *Journal of Applied Sport Psychology*, 27-43.

Smith, C. A. Haynes, K. N., Lazarus, R. S., and Pope, L. K. (1993). In search of the "hot" cognitions: Attributions, appraisals, and their relation to emotion. *Journal of Personality and Social Psychology, 65*, 916-929.

Smith, C. A., and Ellsworth, P. C. (1985). Patterns of cognitive appraisal in emotion. *Journal of Personality and Social Psychology, 48*, 813-838.

Thayer, R. E., Newman, J. R., and McClain, T. M. (1994). Self-regulation of mood: Strategies for changing a bad mood, raising energy, and reducing tension. *Journal of Personality and Social Psychology, 67*, 910-925.

Thelwell, R.C., and Maynard, I.W. (2003). The effects of a mental skills package on 'repeatable good performance' in cricketers. *Psychology of Sport and Exercise, 4*, 377-396.

Uphill, M. A. (2004). *Antecedents, consequences and regulation of emotions in sport*. Unpublished doctoral dissertation, Staffordshire University, England.

Uphill, M. A., and Jones, M. V. (2005). Coping with, and Reducing the Number of Careless Shots: A Case Study with a County Golfer. *Sport and Exercise Psychology Review*, 2, 14-22.

Uphill, M.A., Jones, M.V., and Lane, A.M. (2003). Emotion regulation strategies used by athletes (abstract). *Proceedings of the XIth European Congress of Sport Psychology*, 176-177.

Vallerand, R. J., and Blanchard, C. M. (2000). The study of emotion in sport and exercise: Historical, definitional, and conceptual perspectives. In Y. L. Hanin (Ed.), *Emotions in sport* (pp. 3-37). Champaign, IL: Human Kinetics.

Wanous, J., Reichers, A. E., and Hudy, M. (1997). Overall job satisfaction: How good are single-item measures? *Journal of Applied Psychology, 82*, 247-252.

Zajonc, R. B. (1984). On the primacy of affect. *American Psychologist, 39,* 117-123.

In: Mood and Human Performance: Conceptual, Measurement...   ISBN 1-60021-269-7
Editor: Andrew M. Lane, pp. 297-307   © 2006 Nova Science Publishers, Inc.

Chapter 16

MOOD-PERFORMANCE RELATIONSHIPS IN WAKEBOARDING: MEASUREMENT, PERFORMANCE, AND INTERVENTION

Richie Fazackerley, Andrew M. Lane and Craig A. Mahoney*

School of Sport, Performing Arts and Leisure
University of Wolverhampton, UK

ABSTRACT

This chapter describes three published studies that studied mood in the sport of wakeboarding. The first study (see Fazackerley, Lane, and Mahoney, 2003) focused on the factorial validity of the Brunel Mood Scale (Terry, Lane, Lane, and Keohane, 1999; Terry, Lane, and Fogarty, 2003). The second study focused on mood-performance relationships (Fazackerley, Lane, and Mahoney, 2004). The third paper focused on the effectiveness of intervention strategies designed to improve mood states and subsequently improve performance (Fazackerley, Lane, and Mahoney, 2002). The present chapter represents an attempt to integrate these studies. Data from the validity study is re-analysed to produce a 15-item six factor version of the BRUMS. Data from the third study are re-analyzed by investigating ideographic mood-performance relationships. By integrating these three studies, it is hoped that the relationship between construct measurement and using theory to interpret applied interventions will be highlighted.

INTRODUCTION

Wakeboarding is a water-skiing discipline comprising a pre-planned skill-based routine lasting approximately 3 minutes. Quality of performance is judged by complexity of tricks performed and individuals score points for their performance. In some ways, wakeboard performance contains aspects that are similar to a gymnastics routine. In both sports, performers will have rehearsed the routine on multiple occasions. The work of Terry (1995)

---

* A.M.Lane2@wlv.ac.uk

was considered relevant to help set up the research question. Terry (1995) argued that short-duration, individual sports and where performance can be self-referenced represent the ideal domain to assess relationships between mood and performance. Wakeboarding meets all three suggestions. As wakeboard performers will know the difficulty of their routine, it is possible to compare the number of points given for a performance by the judges with the number of points set as a goal.

STUDY 1: CONFIRMING THE FACTORIAL VALIDITY OF THE BRUMS

Fazackerley et al. (2003) used a well versed argument that applied researchers should use measures that are long enough to assess key constructs, but short enough to keep athletes interested. Even the most compliant athlete will see questionnaire completion somewhat of an intrusion before competition. The experience of the researchers involved in validation of the BRUMS, which involved administering over 3,000 questionnaires in the period around 1 hour before competition, found that the maximum amount of time an athlete will comfortably give is around 5 minutes. The present study sought to validate the Brunel Mood Scale for use in Wakeboarding.

Method

Participants

Participants were 345 wakeboarders (age range 16 to 39 years, men: $n = 311$, women $n = 34$). Competitors ranged in level from novice to elite water-skiers. Competitors from the disciplines of slalom, trick, jump, and wakeboarding were used for the study. It is acknowledged that the sample comprised adolescents (less 16-17 years) and adults (18 years and over)

Measures

The Brunel Mood Scale. The Brunel Mood Scale is a 24-item measure of mood. Anger items include "Bad-tempered" and "Annoyed", Confusion items include "Mixed-up" and "Muddled", Depression items include "Unhappy" and "Downhearted", Fatigue items include "Worn out" and "Sleepy", Tension items include "Anxious" and "Nervous", and Vigour items include "Lively" and "Energetic". Items are rated on a 5-point scale anchored by "not at all" (0) to "extremely" (4).

Procedure

Data were collected over two seasons from several different competitions in Europe. Before asking athletes to volunteer to participate in the study, we contacted competition organizers and the athlete's coach. As data were taken from some international competitions it was necessary to get permission from the event organizers as data collectors needed to be able to access areas dedicated to athletes, coaches and officials only. This procedure was followed also for national and regional competitions.

At the site of competition, we asked coaches if we could test the mood profiles of their athletes as a matter of courtesy. For adolescents, parental consent was also obtained. Once we had permission from the coach (and parent), we asked athletes to participate in the study. Informed consent was obtained before data were collected.

Mood was assessed approximately one hour before competition using the response timeframe, "How are you feeling right now?" Participants were given instructions from a prepared script that assured of complete confidentiality. As we collected data from several competitions, athletes who had completed the measure previously were not asked to do so again.

Confirmatory factor analysis was used to test the 15-item, five-factor model. Confusion was excluded from the data analysis strategy. Confusion assesses a cognitive state characterized by uncertainty and feeling mixed-up rather than an affective experience. For each remaining factor, one item was removed based on factor loadings from previous research (Fazackerley et al., 2003; Terry et al., 1999, 2003). The model tested specified that items were related to their hypothesized factor with the variance of the factor fixed at 1.

Results and Conclusions

Fazackerely et al. (2003) reported confirmatory factor analysis showed acceptable fit using the traditional fit criterion as laid down in previous research (Bentler, 1995). Fazackerely et al. (2003) indicated a Satorra-Bentler X^2 of 480.02, $df = 240$, $p < .001$. The X^2 : df = 2, hence at the criterion value of 2 proposed by Byrne (1989). The Comparative Fit Index (CFI) was .90, a figure that is equal to the criterion for acceptable model fit as suggested by Bentler (1995). The Root Mean Squared Error of Approximation (RMSEA: Steiger, 1990) was .07, a figure that is lower than the .08 indicated as an acceptable fit (Browne and Cudeck, 1993). However, recent research has signalled the CFI should be greater than .95 for most models, therefore, suggesting data provided marginal fit.

Data were re-analysed after the confusion construct was discarded and each factor was reduced to three items. Results of a five factor and 15-item measure of mood indicated an acceptable CFI of .951 and a RMSEA = .046, where the 90% Confidence Interval for the RMSEA were between .033 and .059. Therefore, using Hu and Bentler's (1999) .95 criterion for the CFI, results of the present study showed an acceptable fit. Fit indices for each item are contained in Table 1. Results pointed to that items showed a moderate to strong relationship with the factor.

The present study extended the validation process of the Brunel Mood Scale to a sample of wakeboarders. The inextricable link between theory and measurement means that if measures do not show evidence of validity, researchers cannot emphasize the results. Findings from the present study lend some support for the validity of the Brunel Mood Scale (Fazackerley et al., 2003; Terry et al., 1999; Terry et al., 2003). Collectively, it is suggested that the Brunel Mood Scale shows evidence of factorial validity for use in assessing water-skiers.

**Table 1. Standardised factor loadings for the 15-item
Brunel Mood Scale in Wakeboarding**

	Factor loading	R^2
Anger		
Annoyed	.742	.551
Angry	.789	.622
Bad-tempered	.730	.533
Depression		
Depression	.700	.491
Downhearted	.503	.253
Unhappy	.837	.700
Fatigue		
Worn out	.680	.463
Sleepy	.803	.645
Tired	.909	.826
Tension		
Panicky	.674	.455
Anxious	.758	.574
Nervous	.823	.677
Vigour		
Energetic	.801	.642
Active	.872	.760
Alert	.679	.462

STUDY 2: MOOD AND PERFORMANCE RELATIONSHIPS IN WAKEBOARDING

With the validity of the scale demonstrated, the next stage of the research was to investigate mood-performance relationships.

Participants and Procedure

Fifty-one international competitors with an average of 3 years ($SD = 2.35$ yr.) competing in the European tour completed the 24-item BRUMS approximately one hour before competition. To develop a self-reference measure of performance, the difference between the number of points from their previous best performance and the number of points given by the judges was calculated. Goal difficulty was assessed by asking participants to write down the number of points set as a performance goal. This was self-referenced by comparing the points set as a goal with the previous best score in competition (Points set as goal – PB). Therefore, a positive score would signal that participants set a goal that would involve beating their personal best points score. Comparing the number of points scored with their personal best (Points scored – PB) was used to develop a measure of performance. A positive score would indicate a good performance.

Given the potentially intrusive nature of collecting data on elite athletes at the site of competition it was considered good practice to contact both participants and their coaches a day before competition to discuss participation in the study. The primary goal for participants is to focus on preparation for competition and participation in the study represented a potential threat to effective preparation.

The principle researcher contacted the coach to explain the purpose of the study and then met with the wakeboarder. It should be pointed out that the principle researcher is a former international wakeboarder and was known personally to many of the competitors and coaches. It is believed that this helped the study as coaches and wakeboarders were willing to listen to what was needed rather than dismiss the study as potentially too intrusive. They were informed the purpose of the research was to study how wakeboarders feel before competition. The researcher assured participants of complete confidentiality and that data would not influence selection into their respective national teams. This explanation was spoken in English and no attempts at translation were attempted. It should be noted that the questionnaires were in English and comprehension of these was an imperative. Participants who could not speak English were identified at the initial approach. Six participants declined to participate in the study.

International wakeboarding competition typically comprises 40-50 competitors per event. In the present study, data were collected over three different wakeboading competitions. These were held in England, Austria, and Germany. As English was a second-language to some participants, an alternative word list was made available to participants could have difficulty understanding the meaning of items. It should be noted that no participants referred to the alternative word list, possibly because the BRUMS was developed for use with adolescents and so contains mood descriptors commonly understood.

The BRUMS was administered approximately 1 hr. before competition. Before completing the questionnaires, the Martens, Vealey, and Burton (1990) statement designed to reduce social desirability was read aloud using the response set "How are you feeling right now?" Participants completed the questionnaire in the waiting area away from the gaze of their coach or other competitors.

Results and Conclusions

Mood-performance relationships were guided by Lane and Terry's (2000) conceptual model that places depression as a pivotal mood state. Therefore, depression data were analysed by dividing participants into a no-depression group, that is individuals reporting zero for each depression item on the BRUMS, and a depression group. The depression group comprises participants that reported a score of 1 or more on the depression subscale. Clearly, the term depression group over emphasizes participants who reported a score of 1 on a 0-16 scale. However, as Chapter 1 indicates, a score of 1 or more on the depression subscale is typically associated with much larger scores on the subscales of anger, confusion, fatigue, and tension and lower vigour.

Table 1. A Comparison of Mood Scores between the Depressed
mood group and No depression group

	No-depression ($N = 30$)		Depression ($N = 21$)		
	M	SD	M	SD	t-value
Anger	56.62	8.40	71.13	22.21	-3.27*
Confusion	47.35	5.55	57.94	12.23	-4.18*
Fatigue	54.35	6.58	62.20	10.92	-3.20*
Tension	47.44	8.09	47.71	10.74	-.10
Vigour	50.71	8.20	49.92	9.91	.31
Goal difficulty	820.79	1712.12	852.24	1783.02	-.06
Performance	-1077.40	3446.98	-3461.43	3984.48	2.28**
			Hotellings T² = 41.00, $p < .001$		

*$p < .01$
** $p < .05$

Multivariate analysis of variance (MANOVA) of BRUMS, goal difficulty, and performance scores by depressed mood groups (see Table 1) indicates multivariate significance. Follow-up analyses signalled that higher anger, confusion, fatigue and poorer performance were associated with depression.

Multiple regression to predict performance from mood and self-set goals in the no-depression group showed that 10% (Adj. R^2 = .10, p < .05) of performance variance was explained. Tension was the only significant predictor (Beta = .37, p < .05), whereby increased tension was associated with successful performance, a finding that lends support to the notion that high tension scores, in the absence of depressed mood, are linked with successful performance.

In the depressed mood group, the same variables predicted 33% of performance variance (Adj. R^2 = .33, p < .05). Results indicated that vigour (Beta = .41, p < .05) was associated with successful performance. An accepted limitation of using multiple regression is that the participants to independent variables ratio was relatively low (4:1 in the Depressed mood group; 6:1 in the No-depression group). This low ratio suggests that regression results should be taken with caution.

Results of the present study found evidence to support the notion that depressed mood was associated with increased anger, confusion, fatigue, and poor performance. Findings also lend support to the notion that depression influences the relationships between mood, self-set goals, and performance.

STUDY 3: MOOD-PERFORMANCE RELATIONSHIPS: EFFECT OF MOOD-MANAGEMENT STRATEGIES

The purpose of the present study was to examine the influence of applied sport psychology interventions to bring about improved mood and improved performance.

Participants and Procedure

Participants were nine international standard male wakeboarders (M = 24.33 yr.; SD = 4.09 yr.) who completed the BRUMS 1 hour before competition. Measures of pre-competition mood were taken over the duration of a season, which involved competing in a number of different tournaments ranging from 11-14. The first six tournaments were used to develop a baseline score for each individual's pre-competition mood. Performance was categorised into a successful or unsuccessful tournament based on finish position. Due to the nature of wakeboard competitions being judged subjectively from 0-100 from the opinions of three judges, cross-comparison of points scores from tournament to tournament can be difficult Competitor's scores are based on complexity, execution, and intensity of tricks performed over the duration of two passes (one round). A fall leads to tricks only being subjectively judged up to this point. Two falls are allowed per round.

Developing Individual Interventions

Interventions were selected based on the largest individual discrepancy score in mood states between successful and unsuccessful tournaments. For example, if an athlete report high vigour before successful performance and low vigour before an unsuccessful performance with scores for anger, confusion, depression, fatigue and tension being similar between performance, the intervention would focus on enhancing vigour. The rationale for this decision was based on the notion that interventions should be targeted to the mood states associated with the largest discrepancy in performance. A limitation with this approach is that it assumes that mood states *cause* decrements in performance. It is of course possible that the mood-performance relationship could be causal, but it is not possible to make this claim based on a single score or from this type of research design. Further, a limitation of a great deal of mood research is that methodologies that control potentially confounding variables that would allow tests of causation are not employed. On saying this, it could be countered that research that uses a strict experimental design also involves artificial manipulation of mood. It could be argued that ensuring participants mood states are ecologically valid is more, or equally important as controlling for confounding variables. Therefore, the present study sought to develop an intervention based on a tentative relationship between mood and performance.

In the present study, four different interventions were used. The rationale for this approach was to match the intervention with the area of concern rather than to use an intervention for all problems.

(1) Relaxation training for athletes who reported that tension debilitated performance;
(2) A combination of imagery and self-talk for athletes who reported that depression debilitated performance;
(3) Activation training for individuals who reported a combination of high fatigue and low vigour;
(4) Attentional control training for athletes experiencing confusion when performing poorly.

Descriptive statistics and MANOVA results are contained in Table 2. Results indicated a significant main effect (Wilks' lambda $_{7,92}$= .83, $p < .05$, Eta ^{2} = .17). Univariate differences indicated that pre-competition Fatigue was significantly lower ($F_{1,98}$ = 10.10, $p < .01$, Eta ^{2} = .09) and Vigour was significantly higher following the intervention program ($F_{1,98}$ = 7.65, $p < .01$, Eta ^{2} = .07). Univariate results also indicated that performance improved significantly ($F_{1,98}$ = 4.29, $p < .05$, Eta ^{2} = .04).

Table 2. Multivariate analysis of variance to compare mood state and performance data before and after psychological interventions

	Pre-intervention		Post-intervention			
	M	SD	M	SD	F	P
Performance	48.03	12.93	52.10	5.08	4.29	0.04
Anger	49.19	7.87	49.04	8.78	0.01	0.93
Confusion	52.50	9.45	51.98	10.74	0.07	0.80
Depression	50.16	10.68	49.22	6.03	0.29	0.59
Fatigue	53.12	12.97	46.31	7.84	10.10	0.00
Tension	46.27	8.31	47.19	8.08	0.32	0.57
Vigour	43.57	9.52	48.12	6.81	7.56	0.01

Results of the present study lend support to the notion that mood is influenced by sport psychology interventions. Fatigue and Vigour are the moods most readily available to change. Although the present study found that mood improved significantly following psychological skills training, it is possible that psychological skills training improved performance directly, and improved mood resulted as a consequence of improved performance. An acknowledged limitation of the present study was that it was not possible to distinguish the effects of the interventions used from the effects of performance. It is suggested that there is a need for well-controlled studies designed to assess the impact of psychological skills training on mood, and the attendant impact of mood on performance.

Mood and performance relationships for each athlete are contained in Table 3. It should be noted that some participants reported the same score on each completion of the mood scale, and in these cases, the relationship between mood and performance could not be tested. Mood-performance relationships for player 1 indicated that anger, confusion, depression, fatigue and tension were inversely related to performance, with vigour showing a positive relationship. For player 2, confusion, fatigue, and tension were associated with poor performance. For player 3, tension showed a weak positive relationship with performance. For player 4, anger and depression showed an inverse relationship with performance while tension and vigour showed a positive relationship. For player 5, vigour and fatigue showed weak relationships with performance. For player 6, anger, tension and vigour were associated with good performance. Depression and confusion were associated with poor performance. For player 7, there were weak mood-performance relationships. For player 8, anger, confusion, depression, and fatigue were inversely related, whilst tension and vigour were associated with positive performance.

Table 3. Relationships between mood and performance for each wakeboarder

		Anger	Confusion	Depression	Fatigue	Tension	Vigour
Player 1	Performance	-0.28	-0.28	-0.50	-0.33	-0.37	0.44
Player 2	Performance	Not tested	-0.49	Not tested	-0.58	-0.65	0.17
Player 3	Performance	-0.09	0.15	-0.20	0.08	0.29	-0.18
Player 4	Performance	-0.27	0.00	-0.24	-0.06	0.37	0.22
Player 5	Performance	-0.13	-0.02	-0.08	-0.22	-0.04	0.28
Player 6	Performance	0.26	-0.47	-0.34	-0.11	0.33	0.31
Player 7	Performance	0.02	0.10	0.08	-0.06	-0.13	-0.11
Player 8	Performance	-0.39	-0.51	-0.64	-0.62	0.34	0.78

An analysis of mood-performance by each state indicates that anger related to poor performance among four individuals, and showed a positive associated with performance in one athlete. Confusion was associated with poor performance in 4 athletes and showed no relationship in the other four athletes. Depression was associated with poor performance in five athletes and had a weak relationship in other athletes. Fatigue was associated with poor performance in four athletes; tension was associated with poor performance in two athletes, and positive performance in four athletes. Vigour was associated with positive performance in five athletes.

When results of the analysis-by individual and by each mood state are considered together, it supports the notion that mood and performance are related (Beedie, Terry, and Lane, 2000). However, it provides stronger support for the notion that such relationships are highly individualized. Although there are certain trends such as confusion, depression and fatigue being associated with poor performance, and calmness, happiness and vigour were associated with good performance, these effects vary from person to person. In the present study, findings also support the notion that anger and tension facilitate performance among some individuals and debilitate performance among others (see Terry, 1995).

Findings of this study show support for conducting mood-performance relationships on each individual. Lane and Chappell (2001) argued that if mood and performance relationships are individualized, this presents a serious limitation for testing theoretical links using a cross-sectional design. For example, consider the following hypothetical results. A sample might comprise 33% of individuals showing tension was associated with debilitative performance (r = -.1). It also might comprise 33% of individuals in the sample showing tension was associated with facilitated performance (r = +.1), with the remaining 33% of the sample reporting zero for each tension item (r = 0). When analyzed using a cross-sectional research, the results would show that tension has no relationship (r = 0). Thus, to elucidate the influence of mood on performance, it is suggested that there is a need for idiographic research.

Findings have implications for sport psychology practitioners also. Previously, negative mood states above the 50th percentile were interpreted as potential indicators of poor performance. In the present study, results show that there was no significant difference in the intensity of mood between individuals for whom mood influences performance and individuals for whom mood has no discernible performance-relationship. Consequently, it is not possible to identify performance threatening moods from the intensity of mood alone. A high negative mood score could be threatening to performance in individuals whose mood has been found to consistently relate to performance. By contrast, a similar mood score from an individual whose mood does not consistently relate with performance would indicate that there is no need to implement an intervention strategy.

CONCLUSION

In conclusion, this series of studies demonstrated a scientific approach to using sport psychology within an applied setting. Although the validation study did not address the main point from an athletes perspective, if psychologists are to use psychometric tools in their work, these need to be valid and reliable. The second study used a cross-sectional approach to explore mood-performance links; a strategy that again does not seek to enhance performance through modifications in psychological state variables, that nonetheless, provided evidence to show mood related to performance. The second study involved minimal time commitment from the athletes who only had to complete the BRUMS. It is arguable that athletes should make some investment in the process of seeking methods to enhance performance. The time it takes to complete the BRUMS when seen against the benefits of obtaining knowledge of possible ways to enhance performance is justifiable. Importantly, if there were no relationships between mood states and performance, it would be difficult to conduct the intervention study, in which athletes had to make a greater time commitment. The findings of the third study indicate that mood-performance relationships are individualized and that enhanced mood states are associated with better performance among some individuals.

REFERENCES

Beedie, C. J., Terry P. C., and Lane A. M. (2000). The Profile of Mood States and athletic performance: Two meta-analyses. *Journal of Applied Sport Psychology, 12*, 49-68.

Bentler, P. M. (1995). *EQS Structural equation program manual.* Los Angeles CA: BMDP Statistical Software.

Browne, M.W., and Cudeck, R. (1993) Alternative ways of assessing model fit. In K. A. Bollen and J. S. Long (Eds.), *Testing structural equation models* (pp.132-162) Newbury Park CA: Sage.

Fazackerley, R., Lane, A. M., and Mahoney, C. (2003). Confirmatory factor analysis of the Brunel Mood Scale for use in water-skiing. *Perceptual and Motor Skills, 97*, 657-661.

Fazackerley, R., Lane, A. M., and Mahoney, C. (2004). Mood and performance relationships in wakeboarding. *Journal of Sport Behavior, 27,* 18-30.

Fazackerley, R., Lane, A. M., and Mahoney, C. (2002). Mood-performance relationships: effect of mood-management strategies. *Journal of Sports Sciences, 20*, 63.

Hu, L., and Bentler, P. M. (1999). Cutoff criteria for fit indexes in covariance structure analysis: Conventional criteria versus new alternatives. *Structural Equation Modelling, 6,* 1-55.

Lane, A. M., and Chappell, R. H. (2001). Mood and performance relationships at the World Student Games basketball competition. *Journal of Sport Behavior, 24*, 182-196.

Lane, A. M., and Terry P.C. (2000). The nature of mood: Development of a theoretical model with a focus on depression. *Journal of Applied Sport Psychology, 12,* 16-33.

Martens, R., Vealey, R., and Burton, D. (1990). *Competitive Sports Anxiety Inventory-2.* Champaign Ill; Human Kinetics.

Steiger, J. H. (1990) Structural model evaluation and modification: an interval estimation approach. *Multivariate Behavioral Research, 25,* 173-180.

Terry, P. C. (1995). The efficacy of mood state profiling with elite performers. A review and synthesis. *The Sport Psychologist, 9,* 309-324.

Terry, P. C., Lane, A. M., and Fogarty, G. (2003). Construct validity of the Profile of Mood States-A for use with adults. *Psychology of Sport and Exercise, 4,* 125-139.

Terry, P. C., Lane, A. M., Lane, H. J., and Keohane, L. (1999) Development and validation of a mood measure for adolescents: the POMS-A. *Journal of Sports Sciences, 17,* 861-872.

In: Mood and Human Performance: Conceptual, Measurement...   ISBN 1-60021-269-7
Editor: Andrew M. Lane, pp. 309-317   © 2006 Nova Science Publishers, Inc.

Chapter 17

EFFECT OF WATER PRESSURE ON HEART RATE AND MOOD STATE RESPONSES TO A 15-MINUTE AQUA-MASSAGE

Louise Martin[1], Andrew M. Lane[2], Alan M. Nevill[2], Claire J. Dowen[2] and Mark R. Homer[2]*

[1]School of Sport and Exercise Science, University of Worcester, UK
[2] School of Sport, Performing Arts and Leisure, University of Wolverhampton, UK

ABSTRACT

Massage therapy has been found to promote physiological and psychological well-being. An Aquamassage™ unit provides tactile and pressure stimulation via 36 water jets with adjustable water pressure through a range of 0.68 to 5.44 kg. The aims of this investigation were, to determine if aquamassage enhanced relaxation compared to an equivalent period of rest, and to evaluate the effects of different water pressures upon heart rate and mood state. Thirty-one university support staff (mean ± *s*: age = 43.4 ± 13.5 *years*; height = 165.9 ± 7.6 *cm*; weight = 74.4 ± 14.8 *kg*) undertook three experimental massages at 1.35, 2.72, and 4.08 kg water pressure and a control trial in a randomized order. Mood was assessed using a 30-item measure for balanced positive mood assessment and was completed immediately before, immediately after and 1-hour after the treatment. Heart rate was recorded throughout each trial and was similar throughout ($P>0.05$). Mood results signalled a significant interaction effect ($F_{6,24} = 4.56$, p = .003, Eta^2 = .53), in which mood enhancement was significantly greater following aquamassage than the control condition. Aquamassage could be utilized as an appropriate intervention for reducing stress in occupational environments.

* l.martin@worc.ac.uk

INTRODUCTION

The promotion of physiological and psychological well-being is important in work related settings (Shulman and Jones, 1996). Occupational stress, characterized by elevated negative mood states is linked with poor performance (Wright, Cropanzano, and Meyer, 2004). By contrast, positive mood states have been associated with productivity (Argyle, 2001) and job satisfaction (Deiner, Suh, Lucas, and Smith, 1999). A range of strategies to reduce stress has been reported including talking to someone, being alone and listening to music (Thayer, Newman, and McClain, 1994). One strategy that has received relatively limited research attention is massage.

Massage has been defined as a 'mechanical manipulation of body tissues with rhythmical pressure and strolling for the purpose of promoting health and well being' (Cafarelli and Flint, 1993; Field, 2002). Massage has been linked with reduced levels of stress, depression and anxiety in critically ill, sick or occupationally stressed populations (Field, Ironson, Scafidi, Nawrocki, Goncalves, and Burman, 1996; Field, Quintino, Henteleff, Wells-Keife, and Delvecchio-Feinberg, 1997; Hayes and Cox, 1999; Moyer, Rounds, and Hannum, 2004). Increased parasympathetic activity in response to the tactile and pressure stimulation of massage is proposed to lead to mood enhancement (Field, Morrow, Valdeon, Larson, Kuhn, and Schanberg, 1992; Hayes and Cox, 1999). Pressure stimulation provided during massage could influence the effectiveness of massage as an intervention technique. Massage as a mood-enhancing technique is not universally reported. Drews, Kreider, Drinkard and Jackson (1991) found that massage had no significant effect on mood.

A limitation of previous research is that it has struggled to adequately assess the pressure exerted by the therapist. Research has tended to use traditional massage therapist (Shulman and Jones, 1996; Field et al., 1992; 1997; Ironson, Field, Scafidi, Hashimoto, Kumar, Kumar, Price, Goncalves, Burman, Tetenman, Patarca, and Fletcher, 1996; Zeitlin, Keller, Schiflett, Scleifer, and Bartlett, 2000), with massages repeated by different therapists on different days (Field et al., 1992). It is likely, therefore, that the degree of pressure stimulation received by participants will vary due to the difficulties in quantifying and standardizing pressure. Possible pressure variation may partially explain the equivocal findings of massage research.

One method of controlling variation between therapists is to use an aquamassage unit. Aquamassage™ is a combination of massage, hydrotherapy and heat therapy in a single, convenient and user-controllable unit. Thirty-six hot water jets simultaneously stimulate three sides of the body through a canopy so the user remains dry throughout. The firing frequency of the jets can be varied to allow the replication of a range of standard massage techniques including effleurage, wringing and hacking. In addition, water pressure can be controlled through a range from 0.68 kg to 5.44kg thus enabling standardization of pressure stimulation received.

To assess the effects of massage on mood-enhancement, especially reducing negatively oriented mood states, it is important to compare reductions in stress related variables in suitable control groups. A limitation of massage research is the lack of appropriate control trials, and thus although evidence shows improvement in mood following massage, it is not known whether an individual would show improved mood following a similar period of time in which they rested or engaged in some other form of activity. Health related research frequently compares massage therapy with alternative stress reducing strategies, for example reading, listening to music, watching videos but fails to offer an equivalent period of rest in the same environment as that of the massage (Shulman and Jones, 1996; Field et al., 1996, 1997; Ironson et al., 1996). Thus the benefits of massage as opposed to rest is currently unclear.

The aims of the present investigation were twofold. Firstly, to determine if aquamassage enhances relaxation compared with an equivalent period of rest and secondly to evaluate the effects of different water pressures upon heart rate and mood states during and after a 15-minute aquamassage.

METHODS

Participants

Thirty-one university administrative and support staff (mean $\pm$ s: age = 43.4 $\pm$ 13.5 *years*; height = 165.9 $\pm$ 7.6 *cm*; weight = 74.4 $\pm$ 14.8 *kg*) volunteered to participate in the study. All participants had little experience of using massage as therapy and none of the participants had used an aquamassage previously.

Procedures

Ethical approval for the study was gained by the author at the second institution. Participants reported to the laboratory on five occasions. On the first occasion, they completed an informed consent form, a medical history questionnaire and were assessed for height and weight before undertaking a 10-minute familiarization aquamassage. The remaining four sessions were the experimental trials where a 15-minute aquamassage was undertaken at 1.35kg (low), 2.72 kg (moderate) and 4.08 kg (high) water pressure at a constant water temperature of 35°C. For the control trial, participants lay in the Aquamassage unit as normal but no massage was received. The order of the four trials was randomized, providing twenty-four possible connotations. Participants were randomly assigned to one of these sequences yet ensuring that at least one participant was allocated to each order but no more than two participants received the same order of trials. Experimental trials were separated by a minimum of 48 hours, and all trials were completed within a two-week period. Each participant completed their four trials at the same time of day, although these times ranged from 08:30 hours to 17:00 hours for the participant group.

The 15-minute aquamassage sequence was designed by a qualified masseuse and was intended to replicate a traditional massage sequence by including elements of effleurage, wringing and hacking motions (see Table 1). This was addressed by varying the pulsating speed of the water jets. The speed of the travel arm, that moves the water jets up and down the unit, was kept constant at 0.05 m.s^{-1}. During each trial (including the control) participants wore ear defenders to reduce the noise of the water jets and also to facilitate relaxation by minimizing environmental noise.

Table 1. Fifteen minute aquamassage sequence

Time(mins)	Direction[1]	Pulsator Speed (massage technique)	Body Area
0 – 2	Single	Low (effleurage)	Full
2 – 4	Double	Low	Full
4 – 5.5	Single	Moderate (wringing)	Shoulder/Back
5.5 – 7	Double	Moderate	Shoulder/Back
7 – 8	Double	High (hacking)	Shoulder/Back
8 – 9.5	Double	Moderate (wringing)	Shoulder/Back
9.5 – 11	Single	Moderate	Shoulder/Back
11 – 13	Double	Low (effleurage)	Full
13 – 15	Single	Low	Full

[1]Direction: Single = jets pulse when travel arms moves from right to left only; Double = jets pulse when travel arm moves from right to left and left to right

On arrival at the laboratory, participants were fitted with a heart rate monitor (S610 Polar, Kempele, Finland), and heart rate was continually recorded throughout the 15-minute intervention. Participants completed a 30-item mood questionnaire immediately before, immediately after and 1-hour after the massage intervention using the response timeframe 'How are you feeling right now?'. On completion of the mood questionnaire immediately after the massage, participants returned to their daily work tasks and completed their final questionnaire (1-hour post) at their desk/workplace.

Given the relatively limited usage of aquamassage in research, some explanation is warranted. Participants removed their shoes and any jackets/cardigans before lying in a prone position on the Aquamassge™ bed with their arms down by their sides. The canopy top was then lowered to cover the participant from the shoulders down i.e. head and neck were not within the range of the travel arm. Once in position, ear defenders were placed on the participant and the intervention period commenced.

Apparatus and Measures

Aquamassage

Although there was no means of calibrating the water pressure, prior to each massage checks were made to ensure that the volume and temperature of the water was standardized for each massage thus reducing the likelihood of variation in water pressure at each of the settings across the study. The water level of the Aquamassage™ was checked to ensure that it was always at the full level mark and the thermostat was set at 35°C before massages commenced. Water pressure was then set by the control unit at the start of the massage at the required setting.

Heart Rate

Participants were fitted with a heart rate monitor (S610 Polar, Kempele, Finland), and heart rate was continually recorded throughout the 15-minute intervention.

Mood

Mood was assessed using a 30-item measure with six factors (anger, confusion, depression, fatigue, tension and vigor) taken from the Brunel Mood Scale (Terry, Lane, Lane, and Keohane, 1999; Terry, Lane, and Fogarty, 2003) and two factors (calmness and happiness) from the UWIST Mood Adjective Checklist (Matthews, Jones, and Chamberlain, 1990). Both scales have been comprehensively validated. The rationale to combine two measures is based on the notion that the POMS model of mood assesses predominantly negative mood states and so adding the scale of happiness and calmness, enabled a more balanced assessment of positive mood states. A measure of mood disturbance was calculated by subtracting negative mood scores from positive scores.

Mood items were rated on a 5-point scale anchored by "not at all" (0) to "very much so" (4). Examples of negative mood items include 'bad-tempered', 'downhearted', 'uncertain', 'tired', and examples of positive mood items include 'alert', 'cheerful', 'and 'happy'.

Data Analyses

Heart rate was averaged to give heart rate at rest and at 5, 10 and 15 minutes of the massage. Mood data were analyzed separately for each subscale. Repeated measures ANOVA (time by condition) was used to determine changes in both mood over time (pre, post, 1-hour post) and heart rate over time (pre, 5, 10, 15 beats/min) by condition (control, low, moderate, high). Where significant differences were identified, effect size (Eta^2) was calculated to give an estimate of meaningfulness.

RESULTS

Descriptive statistics for mood changes over time are contained in Table 2. As Table 2 indicates, participants reported positive mood profiles in each condition and at each time point. Results indicated that there was no significant difference in participants' mood ($P > 0.05$) or heart rate ($P > 0.05$) prior to each trial. Heart rate during the four trials was similar throughout ($P > 0.05$) (Figure 1).

Table 2. Descriptive Statistics for mood scores over time by condition

Condition	Pre		Post		1 hour	
	M	SD	M	SD	M	SD
Control	8.29	3.31	7.91	3.50	8.03	3.70
Low intensity	8.19	2.99	9.04	3.09	9.76	3.00
Moderate intensity	8.10	3.42	8.55	3.18	9.01	3.05
High intensity	7.05	3.95	9.08	3.23	9.25	3.19

Repeated measures ANOVA was used to compare changes in mood over time (pre, post, 1 hour post) and by condition (control, low intensity, moderate intensity, and high intensity) (see Figure 2). Results signalled a significant interaction effect ($F_{6,24}$ = 4.56, p = .003, Eta^2 = .53), a significant main effect for mood changes over time ($F_{6,24}$ = 5.19, p = .01, Eta^2 = .27), with no significant main effect for mood changes by condition ($F_{6,24}$ = 2.03, p = .13, Eta^2 = .18). Interaction effect results indicated that mood enhancement over time was significantly greater following aquamassage than the control condition. Differences over time indicated that mood was significantly more positive immediately after an aquamassage.

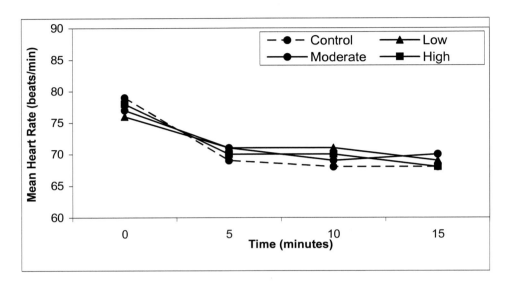

Figure 1. Heart rate response during massage conditions

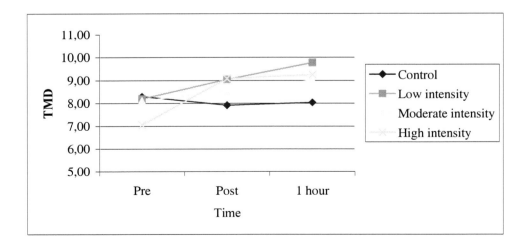

Figure 2. Mood State scores over time by massage condition

DISCUSSION

Findings of the present study indicated that in terms of relaxation as measured by heart rate, aquamassage offered no additional benefit when compared to an equivalent period of rest in the same environment (Figure 1). Resting heart rate is a relatively stable variable with inter-daily variation of ± 6 beats/min (Lambert, Mbambo, and St Clair Gibson, 1998). Therefore, significant variations in heart rate at rest were unlikely to occur particularly in the participant group, of the current investigation, who were all seemingly healthy individuals. Previous research that has reported significant decreases in heart rate with massage therapy has been undertaken using critically ill patient groups (Hayes and Cox, 1999) and children/adolescents with adjustment disorders (Field et al., 1992). Both of these researchers reported elevated heart rates prior to the massage treatment therefore significant reductions in heart rate is more likely to occur.

Despite the similar response in heart rate, results indicated that mood was significantly enhanced following the massage treatments compared to the control trial. Mood was more positive both immediately after the aquamassage and at 1-hour post massage than before the massage treatment whereas during the control trial mood was similar at all time points (Figure 2). Effect size (Eta^2) was calculated to be 0.53 suggesting that the aquamassage trials provided a large, meaningful improvement in mood. These findings are in agreement with previous research that has consistently reported reduced levels of anxiety (Shulman and Jones, 1996; Ironson et al., 1996), depression (Field et al., 1992; 1997), fatigue and confusion (Field et al., 1997; Katz et al., 1999). In contrast to the present study, participants in these earlier studies were groups of individuals specifically selected for the likelihood that they would be prone to high negative mood profiles as a result of working in stressful environments (Field et al., 1997; Katz et al., 1999) or due to medical illness (Shulman and Jones, 1996; Ironson et al., 1996). In the present study, the participant groups were considered to be both healthy and not working in an abnormally stressful environment, thus the enhancement of mood in these individuals as a result of the massage interventions is important for improving psychological well-being on a daily basis for normal populations.

The standardization and quantification of applied pressure during traditional massage is difficult and is further exacerbated in massage research by the use of more than one massage therapist (Shulman and Jones, 1996; Field et al., 1992; 1997; Ironson et al., 1996) and/or the massages taking place across a series of days (Field et al., 1992). Potential variations in the applied pressure may be a limiting factor in the overall effectiveness of massage interventions since the positive benefits of massage have been linked to increased parasympathetic activity as a result of tactile and pressure stimulation. The ability to control the pressure of the water jets in the Aquamassage™ enabled the current study to evaluate the effects of different applied pressures. Results indicated that the observed changes of mood over time occurred regardless of the water pressure applied (Figure 3). The variation in water pressure used in the present study (1.35kg to 4.08kg) is likely to be greater than the possible pressure variation that could exist either between massage therapists or within an individual massage therapist. Consequently, the finding that massage benefits are not altered by variation in the pressure applied should provide a greater degree of confidence to be given to the results of previous research where traditional massage has been provided by more than one massage therapist or by a single massage therapist across a number of days. Future research can provide massage therapy interventions via both mechanical and manual with the confidence of the treatments being equally effective.

CONCLUSION

In summary, the present investigation demonstrated that although there were no additional relaxation benefits as measured by heart rate, mood was significantly enhanced during the massage treatments compared to an equivalent period of rest. Enhanced mood in an apparently healthy participant group for a period of at least one hour following a 15-minute aquamassage has implications for increasing workplace moral, productivity and psychological well being and could be the focus of future investigations. Furthermore, results demonstrated that the enhancement of mood was not altered by changes in the level of pressure applied, thus similar findings are likely to occur using traditional massage techniques.

REFERENCES

Argyle, M. (2001). *The Psychology of happiness* (2nd). London Routledge.

Cafarelli, E., and Flint, F. (1993). The role of massage in preparation for and recovery from exercise. *Journal of Sports Sciences, 17,* 861-872.

Deiner, E., Suh, E., Lucas, R., and Smith, H. (1999). Subjective well-being: three decades of progress. *Psychological Bulletin, 125,* 273-302.

Drews, T., Kreider, R., Drinkard, B., and Jackson, C. W. (1991). Effects of post-event massage muscle recovery on psychological profiles of exertion, feeling, and mood during a ultraendurance cycling event. *Medicine and Science in Sports and Exercise. 23, (suppl),* S119.

Field, T. (2002). Massage Therapy. *Complementary and Alternative Medicine, 86,* 163-171.

Field, T., Ironson, G., Scafidi, F., Nawrocki, T., Goncalves, A., and Burman, I. (1996). Massage therapy reduces anxiety and enhances EEG pattern of alertness and math computation. *International Journal of Neuroscience, 86,* 197-205.

Field, T., Morrow, C., Valdeon, C., Larson, S., Kuhn, C., and Schanberg, S. (1992). Massage reduces anxiety in child and adolescent psychiatric patients. *Journal of American Academy Children and Adolescent Psychiatry, 31,* 125-131.

Field, T., Quintino, O., Henteleff, T., Wells-Keife, L., and Delvecchio-Feinberg, G. (1997). Job stress reduction therapies. *Alternative Therapies, 3,* 54-56.

Hayes, J., and Cox, C. (1999). Immediate effects of a five-minute foot massage on patients in critical care. *Intensive and Critical Care Nursing, 15,* 77-82.

Ironson, G., Field, T., Scafidi, F., Hashimoto, M., Kumar, M., Kumar, A., Price, A., Goncalves, A., Burman, I., Tetenman, C., Patarca, R., and Fletcher, M.A. (1996). Massage Therapy is associated with enhancement of the immune system's cytotoxic capacity. *International Journal of Neuroscience, 84,* 205-217.

Katz, J., Wowk, A., Culp, D., and Wakeling, H. (1999). Pain and tension are reduced among hospital nurses after on-site massage treatments: A pilot study. *Journal of PeriAnesthesia Nursing, 14,* 128-133.

Lambert, M. L., Mbambo, Z. H., and St Clair Gibson, A. (1998). Heart rate during training and competition for long-distance running. *Journal of Sports Sciences, 16,* S85-S90.

Matthews, G., Jones, D. M., and Chamberlain, A. G. (1990). Refining the measurement of mood: The UWIST Mood Adjective Checklist. *British Journal of Psychology, 81,* 17-42.

Moyer, C. A., Rounds, J., and Hannum, J. W. (2004). A Meta-Analysis of *Massage* Therapy Research. *Psychological Bulletin, 130,* 3-18.

Shulman, K.R., and Jones, G.E. (1996). The effectiveness of massage therapy intervention on reducing anxiety in the workplace. *Journal of Applied Behavioural Science, 32,* 160-173.

Terry, P. C., Lane, A. M., and Fogarty, G. (2003). Construct validity of the Profile of Mood States-A for use with adults. *Psychology of Sport and Exercise, 4,* 125-139.

Terry, P. C., Lane, A. M., Lane, H. J., and Keohane, L. (1999). Development and validation of a mood measure for adolescents: POMS-A. *Journal of Sports Sciences, 17,* 861-872.

Thayer, R. E., Newman, R., and McClain, T. M. (1994). Self-regulation of mood: Strategies for changing a bad mood, raising energy, and reducing tension. *Journal of Personality and Social Psychology, 67,* 910-925.

Wright, T. A., Cropanzano, R., and Meyer, D. G. (2004). State and trait correlates of job performance: A tale of two perspectives. *Journal of Business and Psychology, 18,* 365-383.

Zeitlin, D., Keller, S.E., Schiflett, S. C., Scleifer, S. J., and Bartlett, J. (2000). Immunological effects of massage therapy during academic stress. *Psychosomatic Medicine, 62,* 3-87.

INDEX

D

F

G

T